The Way to Buddhahood

The Way to Buddhahood

MASTER YIN-SHUN

Translated by Dr. Wing H. Yeung, M.D.

Foreword by Professor Robert M. Gimello

Introduction by Professor Whalen Lai

WISDOM PUBLICATIONS • BOSTON

Wisdom Publications
199 Elm Street
Somerville, Massachusetts 02144

Library of Congress Cataloging-in-Publication Data

Yin-shun.
[Ch'eng fo chih tao. English]
The way to buddhahood/ Yin-shun; translated by Wing Yeung.
p. cm.
Includes bibliographical references and index.
ISBN 0-86171-133-4 (alk. paper)
1. Buddha (The concept). 2. Buddhahood. 3. Mahayana Buddhism—Doctrines. 4. Religious life—Buddhism. I. Yeung, Wing. II. Title.
BQ4180.Y55 1998
294.3'4—dc21 97–36370

ISBN 0-86171-133-5

03 02 01 00
6 5 4 3

Designed by: L·J·SAWLit & Stephanie Shaiman
Cover painting: Jing-hua Gao Dalia

Wisdom Publications' books are printed on acid-free paper and meet the guidelines for the permanence and durability of the Committee on Production Guidelines for Book Longevity of the Council on Library Resources.

Printed in the United States of America.

Contents

Foreword

THIS FINE TRANSLATION of one of Yin-shun Daoshi's most widely read and influential works is a most welcome addition to the small English language archives of modern Chinese Buddhism.

Most western students of Buddhism have been woefully unaware of the extraordinary vitality of contemporary Chinese Buddhism, particularly as it has developed in post-war Taiwan. This has been especially lamentable in view of the fact that the foremost leader of Chinese Buddhism's intellectual resurgence, the monk Yin-shun, is both a scholar and an original thinker of the first order.

Among his many achievements is the renewal of mutually enriching connections between traditional Chinese Buddhism and the ancestral traditions of India, both the primordial Buddhism of the āgamas (the northern counterpart of the Theravāda sūtras) and the later Indian Mahāyāna traditions that had been so well preserved and advanced in Tibet.

Drawing thus upon the whole broad range of Buddhist thought—but especially upon the Madhyamaka ("Middle Way") tradition of Nāgārjuna, Candrakīrti, and Tsongkhapa—Yin-shun has emphasized the rationalism and humanism of Buddhism while also bringing traditional Buddhist scholarship into invigorating dialogue with modern critical Buddhist Studies as practiced in the West and in Japan. In the course of these ground-breaking efforts he has done more even than his own master, the early twentieth century reformer Taixu, to rescue Chinese Buddhism from the intellectual doldrums and spiritual decay into which so much of it had fallen during the late imperial period of Chinese history. He has also plotted a course for Buddhism's future development that will allow its robust engagement with the modern world without forcing the severance of its traditional roots.

The Way to Buddhahood (*Cheng fo zhi dao*) presents itself as an introductory overview of the essentials of Buddhism, rendered in the traditional rhetorical modes of Buddhist doctrinal exposition. It is that, of course, but it is also much more. In it we see, not merely a summary of cardinal Buddhist concepts but also something of the rigorous and bold revisioning of Buddhism that Yin-shun has continued to develop in his many later and more specialized works. Thanks to Mr. Wing Yeung's very effective and trustworthy translation, readers of English may now begin to have access to this extraordinary man's ample body of work and to his powerful vision of the dharma.

Robert M. Gimello
Professor of East Asian Studies and Religious Studies
University of Arizona

Preface to the Chinese Edition

BUDDHISM IS A RELIGION of reason and not just a religion of faith. In explaining principles or instructing practices, Buddhist teachings rely on reason. These teachings are both rich and correct. Because the Buddha Dharma has always adapted to people's different abilities and allowed free choice about which adaptation to follow, the teachings are diverse.

Two points will help people grasp the Buddha Dharma. First, the Buddha's teachings and the discourses of bodhisattvas and patriarchs vary according to people's different capacities and preferences at different times and places. These variations exist in order to give different people appropriate guidance. Many skillful methods are used—the easy and the profound, those pertaining to practices and those pertaining to principles. Some methods may seem to contradict one another. Viewing the different teachings is like peering into a kaleidoscope; beginners who are unable to integrate the views may feel perplexed.

Second, although the teachings are varied, all are interconnected. The different teachings start at different places, but each arrives at the others. This is like picking up a piece of clothing: whether one picks up a shirt by the collar, sleeve, or front, one gets the whole thing. Yet the adaptive characteristic of the Buddhist teachings, the different levels of difficulties, and the doctrinal interconnections are usually ignored. Instead, people tend to make generalizations and think that all teachings are similar.

These two opposing views—that the teachings are too diversified or too similar—can lead in the same direction. Some think that since the teachings are similar, one particular doctrine is equivalent to others. So they think that they do not need to practice and study extensively. Such thinking leads to the expansive development of the Dharma from a single sūtra, a single buddha, or a single mantra. Because such people are unable to grasp the Dharma completely, they "abandon the ocean and take only one drop of water," which, they think, contains the whole ocean. On the other hand, some people exceedingly praise a doctrine which they more or less understand, thinking it is the best and the ultimate. Having this doctrine, they think that they have everything and need nothing else.

In sum, the Buddhist teachings are very diverse and befitting to all. Those who are unable to integrate and organize them systematically will make the mistake of taking only parts of them. In so doing they will abandon the whole. This style of practice has brought Buddhism to its present narrowness and poverty.

It is impossible to expect all devotees to integrate and organize the Buddha Dharma in their practice. Those who propagate the Buddhist teachings should have a superior understanding of them, however. Only then will they be able to expound the Dharma and maintain its integrity without becoming confused and biased.

In this regard, the Tiantai tradition and the Xianshou tradition (also known as the Huayan School) have done good work. The masters of these traditions have integrated the Buddhist teachings and organized them into courses with graduated practices. These courses demonstrate both the differences among the various doctrines and the relationships between them. It is no wonder that in the past those who taught the Dharma followed either the four modes of teaching of the Tiantai tradition or the five modes of teaching of the Xianshou tradition. Both of these place great emphasis on the perfect teaching; directly entering the perfect teaching is their objective.

My explanation draws on what Venerable Master Taixu has said: Although the Tiantai and Xianshou traditions include all the Buddha's teachings—the lesser, beginning, final, immediate, Tripitaka, shared, distinct, and perfect teachings—these different teachings have been established for those with lesser capacities; they are not really needed by those with superior abilities. Although it is said that people who have the ability to become enlightened can use them as a teaching, they need to do so only when they are unable to attain enlightenment through other means. But who wants to admit—by following a given teaching—to being a person of lesser capacity? So the teachings of the Tiantai and Xianshou traditions are also abandoned.

Feeling the narrowness and poverty of the present decline of Chinese Buddhism, Venerable Master Taixu decided to use the "Dharma common to the Five Vehicles," the "Dharma common to the Three Vehicles," and the "distinctive Dharma of the Great Vehicle" to embrace all Buddhist teachings. These can be utilized partially or completely as the right path to perfect enlightenment. This system really corresponds to that of Tibet's Venerable Master Tsongkhapa. Tsongkhapa followed the Indian Madhyamaka and Yogācāra schools and synthesized the Buddhist teachings into the "way common to lower people," the "way common to middle people," and the "way for upper people" in order to create the sequence for attaining enlightenment and becoming a buddha.

The Venerable Master Taixu gave high praise to the complete Buddhist teachings, namely, that "having merits and virtues, people can be assured of being born as human or heavenly beings; having wisdom, they can become śrāvakas or pratyekabuddhas. All of these people must rely on all the vinayas, sūtras, and śāstras; if only a part of the teachings are utilized, one cannot attain enlightenment." These complete Buddhist teachings are worthy of being actively proclaimed.

When the Tathāgata explained the Dharma, he always began by teaching the "proper method"—giving, keeping the precepts, and abandoning desire in order to be reborn in heaven (concentration). Then, to those who might be able to renounce the world, he taught a world-transcending doctrine. Because the emphasis of the Buddhist teachings is on transcending the world, those who compiled the sūtras always skipped over the Buddha's "proper method." The ancient Abhidharma texts began with the five precepts, but the later Abhidharma texts eliminated them. Even the Venerable Master Tsongkhapa could not avoid this tendency and used the teachings of the Two Vehicles as the foundation of his own. Thus, in the Dharma common to the lower people he held that "mindfulness of death" was an important entrance to the Way. Actually, without being mindful of death, one can still practice the good deeds that will lead one to be reborn as a human or heavenly being. Although such a way for lower people follows the Two Vehicles in renunciation, it may not follow the compassionate way of the Great Vehicle.

With regard to this, Venerable Master Taixu, penetrating deeply into the Buddha Vehicle with exceptional insight, revealed the real purpose of the Tathāgata's appearing in this world—to teach people to enter the Buddha-way from human lives. Thus, the method for beginners emphasizes both practicing the ten good deeds (without abandoning the worldly affairs of daily life) and following the right deeds of the Human Vehicle to enter the Buddha Vehicle, instead of emphasizing practices of renunciation such as mindfulness of death.

Using right deeds to move from the Human Vehicle toward the Buddha-way rests on gathering the merits of the Dharma common to the Five Vehicles and the Three Vehicles. However, because some people are narrow-minded and timid, the Buddha (and some ancient masters) had to establish the Two Vehicles as a skillful way alongside the great vehicle. In the Mahāyāna teachings, there are also skillful ways of entering the Buddha Vehicle, such as practicing heavenly deeds or those of the Two Vehicles.

According to the complete Buddhist teachings as determined and revealed by Venerable Master Taixu, all these teachings are simply methods for becoming a buddha. This approach not only connects the three levels of the Dharma common to the Five Vehicles, the Dharma common to the Three Vehicles, and the distinctive Dharma of the Great Vehicle, it also connects the teachings belonging to the regular way and the skillful way. This approach reveals the entire sequence of the Buddha-way, and leads one to the supreme buddha realm.

Long ago when I was in Hong Kong, I wanted to write a concise book on the path to buddhahood. The book would draw on the discourses of Venerable Master Taixu and on Tsongkhapa's *Sequence of Attaining Enlightenment*; and, integrating partial views from the treasury of the Dharma, it would interconnect all the Buddhist teachings and return them to the One Vehicle.

Not until 1954 was I able to write a few gāthas at a time (with varying degrees of profundity) to teach the class at the Shandao Monastery in Taiwan. However, for various reasons, these verses were very brief, especially the Mahāyāna section. In the autumn of 1957, when I was preparing to teach at the Buddhist Institute for Women, I revised and expanded the gāthas, and in the winter of 1958, I revised them again and began writing short commentaries. I did not finish the whole manuscript until the end of 1959, when I was staying at the Shanguang Monastery for Chinese New Year. From start to finish, six years had elapsed.

Now that *The Way to Buddhahood* with its two hundred thousand Chinese characters is about to be published, I thought I should set out my objective: to interconnect all Buddhist teachings and turn them toward the Buddha-way.

Dharma-master Yin-shun
October 1960

Translator's Acknowledgments

MY FIRST AND GREATEST THANKS are extended to Master Yin-shun, who gave permission in 1989 for me to translate his book, *Cheng fo zhi dao*, into English. His steady interest in and support for the translation, especially an in-person consultation in 1992 to help clarify certain difficult points, have contributed immensely to the final product. I am also grateful for the Master's efforts in locating many of the quotes from the Chinese Buddhist Tripitaka in response to my queries. Master Yin-shun's steadfast dedication to the propagation of the Buddhist teachings has been a great inspiration.

I would like to also thank Dr. Evelyn Lee for initiating and organizing a class on Buddhism for me to teach in 1988 when I was working as an attending psychiatrist in Ward 7C at San Francisco General Hospital. It was in 1989 that I decided to translate this book and use it as a textbook for the class.

Without the aid of numerous other people, this work surely would never have been completed. James Wilson, professor emeritus of English, contributed greatly to the initial translation of the verse text. Many thanks also to Galina Wong, who tirelessly entered the handwritten translation into the computer and generally provided technical support throughout the translating process.

It was a pleasure working with Gray Tuttle, who provided the editing to bring my initial translation to a clear and readable format. In addition, I would like to thank John LeRoy for his further editing of the manuscript and for his suggestions that improved the clarity of the translation.

I especially want to thank my teacher, the Venerable Miu King of Fayun Monastery in Danville, California, who clarified certain difficult passages and provided me with the quiet retreat of the monastery when I was working on the early phase of the translation. I would also like to extend my gratitude for the generosity and kindness of Maisie Tsao. Lillie Or, Tammy Chen, Doreen Leung, and Marshall Kozinn, each provided essential assistance in making this translation possible as well.

Sincerest thanks are also extended to the Venerable Heng Ching, professor of philosophy at the Taiwan National University. She was the first to read the entire manuscript and gave me much valuable advice. It was her suggestion that first led me to approach Wisdom Publications, and for this she has my gratitude.

I would also like to thank Professor Whalen Lai for writing the introduction, which provides a comprehensive understanding of Master Yin-shun and his works.

Finally, I should mention the creation, in 1996, of the Yin-shun Foundation. This foundation is dedicated to propagating the Master's works in the United States and plans to sponsor further translations.

In the translation's final stages, Professor Chün-fang Yü's advice and editing of the first three chapters were an essential addition to the book. Thanks are also due to Michelle Lerner and Dr. and Mrs. David Pating for their critical reading of large sections of the text, and to Sara McClintock Jolly, Albert A. Dalia, Lisa Sawlit, Tim McNeill, and all those at Wisdom Publications who worked so hard to produce this book.

Master Yin-shun always says, "The workings of karma are inconceivable." This is exemplified in many of his life experiences. This is also well illustrated in my working relationship with Dr. Albert A. Dalia and Wisdom Publications. Fifteen years ago, when Albert was in Taiwan working on his doctorate from the University of Hawaii, he went to see Master Yin-shun. Fourteen years before that, Albert was beginning his Chinese language study at the University of Hawaii and had the same Mandarin Chinese teacher as I had, but at that time we did not know each other. Now, after returning to the United States from a long overseas stay in Taiwan, he has taken the position of Editorial Director at Wisdom Publications and his first project was *The Way to Buddhahood*, the first full-length translation of the Master's works. For the non-Buddhist, "It is a small world," but for Buddhists, "The workings of karma are inconceivable!" Albert has put in so much work and love to bring this book to final production in time for the Master's 92nd birthday, and I am very grateful.

I would like to sincerely thank my family, all my friends, acquaintances, and good people who made financial contributions to the publication of this book.

On behalf of everyone who has helped with this translation, I wish also to express appreciation to all the family members, colleagues, and friends without whose support this work would not have been possible.

May this work be of benefit to all sentient beings!

Dr. Wing H. Yeung, M.D.
San Francisco, 1997

Introduction

MASTER YIN-SHUN needs no introduction in the Chinese-speaking world. He is the foremost living Chinese Buddhist authority, and his list of works is daunting. *The Way to Buddhahood*, his most widely read work, has become part of the basic curriculum in many Chinese Buddhist schools and academies. Although presented as an introduction to the fundamentals of Buddhism, it is as much a summation of the Master's decades-long study of the Buddha Dharma. Following a classic form in Buddhist philosophical discourse, the book is built around a long poem divided in sections, each given a prose commentary. The verses aid memorization, while the commentary provides an exposition. The work begins with the basic taking of refuge in the Three Treasures and proceeds step by step through precepts, meditation, and wisdom to the highest practices and the most profound doctrines. Work is underway to complete a series of translations of the Venerable Yin-shun's works. Under preparation already is his award-winning study, *A History of Chinese Ch'an Buddhism*, which has already been translated into Japanese and for which in 1973 he was recommended (by Sekiguchi Shindai, a Tendai authority on the origin of the Ch'an [Japanese: Zen] tradition) for a doctorate of humanities from Taisho University in Japan. This distinction, along with other awards and acclaim from his countrymen, contributes to his international renown. It is only for the lack of translations that his works have not reached the English-speaking world.

Master Yin-shun's achievement is all the more extraordinary in view of his "very plain and ordinary life," as he calls it in one of his essays. What came of this life is anything but ordinary, however. Zhang Luqin (Yin-shun is his Dharma name) was born in 1906 to a farming family during the "cold meal" festival (this occurs between the extinguishing of the old hearth fire and the rekindling of a new one, when food is eaten cold). He was a sickly child, and later in life he would suffer through periods of hospitalization. The first noble truth of Buddhism—that life is suffering—

concerns more than physical illness, but much of that truth has never been very remote for Master Yin-shun, who would one day leave home for the monkhood. In his deportment as a monk and as a scholar, he would embody one of the three marks of all things: egolessness. Despite all his contributions to contemporary Chinese Buddhism, he would remain a most self-effacing, almost private scholar who always preferred to stay in the background. In the preface to his *Study of the People's Myths and Cultures of Ancient China*, he refers to his village background and speaks humbly of his lack of formal education.

Growing up in the last days of the Qing (Manchu) dynasty, Master Yin-shun went to school in the town where his father worked. As a child, he acquired his early stock of knowledge in the old-fashioned way: thumbing through old string-sewn books, pouring over primers to the Four Books and selections from the classics, and committing them to memory. I have been told that the Master's command over what he gleaned from years of avid reading is so thorough that he can locate the exact "chapter and verse" of a source in the books on his shelves. He was five when the Qing dynasty fell in 1911 and China became a republic. The young Master's formal education was caught in that time of transition: the old system in which he was born was not totally gone; the new system of primary and secondary education, not to mention modern university education, was not yet accessible. At age ten, the bright child finished the elementary levels of primary school. He then skipped two grades and by thirteen had finished the upper levels (equivalent to junior high school in the United States), having excelled in the study of literature and acquired the refined, flowing, and lucid style for which he is known. Perhaps for practical reasons—doctors were respected and secure—his father sent him to learn traditional medicine. But this training did not provide him with the intellectual stimulation he sought, so he left after three years. He then returned to his primary school to teach for the next eight years. But however precocious a young schoolteacher might be, this was not a career with great prospects. Without a university degree from the higher educational system of the new China, climbing the ladder of academic success was difficult. But in those days, it seems, Luqin had such an appetite for learning that he devoured all the books he could find. He favored books of a more spiritual nature: Taoist scriptures, stories of the supernatural, legends of the immortals, and, yes, the Old and the New Testament.

If we find it difficult to understand how the young Master Yin-shun could take the myths of Taoist immortals seriously enough to consider pursuing that spiritual path, we should be reminded that Kang Youwei, the 1898 political reformer, had lived like a wild man on a hill for a whole year, practicing Taoist circulation of the breath and manipulation of the five elements and even writing a commentary on Laozi that an older, more sedate Kang Youwei would destroy. In Sri Lanka, Dharmapala, a high-school-educated young man who would lead a revival of Pāli Buddhism, espoused Theosophist beliefs and wanted at one point to seek out some deathless master high up in the Himalayas. Far from just being pure folly, such fascination with the supernatural may have announced a neotraditional critique of encroaching modernity. With Master Yin-shun, as with the other two, the naive phase was soon over. He began reading Laozi and Zhuangzi. Philosophical Taoism was more promising than the myths of religious Taoism. The same naiveté that welcomed Taoist immortals now informed an intellectual openness to the reality of what the Buddhist tradition would call the Inconceivable. This radical openness, well disciplined by seasoned discourse, informs the works of Master Yin-shun. And his interest in gods and ghosts, the deathless and the immortal, would make an unexpected return in a book on early Chinese myths in which a world of phantasms is unlocked and comes to life with drama and realism—the product of a mind both receptive to and yet critical of the mythopoeic.

At the time he was reading Laozi and Zhuangzi, Master Yin-shun also picked up Buddhist texts, and these became his preferred reading after the sudden passing away of his parents. This painful loss led to a personal decision in 1930 at the age of twenty-five to leave the home life and enter the Saṅgha. After finding sponsors, as was the custom at Putuo Monastery, he was tonsured, received the full precepts, and was given the Dharma name Yin-shun. From that point on, he applied his innate intelligence to the study of the Buddha Dharma. Though tutored along the way, the encyclopedic knowledge and insight he infused into his treatises is fundamentally self-acquired. Over time, Master Yin-shun became the foremost modern scholar-monk in China. And it has been a long time since China has seen that opportune conjunction of monk and scholar in one person of such caliber—almost three hundred years if we count from the time of the Four Great Masters of the Late Ming.

The general English reader will appreciate *The Way to Buddhahood* for what it reveals. The reader does not really need to know how it relates to Yin-shun's work as a whole or how this body of work relates to historical currents of Chinese Buddhism. Still, this makes an interesting story. As noted above, it has been about three hundred years since the time of the Four Great Masters at the end of the Ming dynasty. By the time the Qing dynasty succeeded the Ming in 1644, the leadership of what was left of the once vibrant field of Buddhist scholarship had passed from the monk to the layman. Leading Buddhists among the gentry—an educated local elite with Buddhist sympathies—were the mainstay of the local Saṅgha if not of the major centers of Buddhist establishment. Devotion, piety, and meditative practice endured throughout the Qing period, but Buddhist scholarship as a whole remained at a low ebb until a late-Qing revival in the nineteenth century. This revival came about largely because of the dedication of the layman Yang Wenhui (1837–1911). Yang had traveled in the West, made contacts with Japan, worked with Timothy Richards, met Dharmapala during the latter's return from the Parliament of Religions in Chicago, and created a modern Buddhist curriculum in the academy he ran. Buddhist philosophy and an idealistic vision informed the utopian politics of the 1898 constitutional monarchy reform. The reform was led by Kang Youwei (1858–1927), Liang Qichao (1873–1929), and Tan Sitong (1865–98), but all three owed their exposure to Buddhism to Yang Wenhui and his Jinling publication effort.

Chinese philosophy itself was given a nudge by the reimportation from Japan, thanks to Yang Wenhui, of the Weishi (Consciousness Only [Yogācāra]) philosophy, which had died out in China after Huayan successfully displaced it. This Mahāyāna idealist philosophy became the mainstay of the Academy of Inner Learning, founded in 1922 by Ouyang Jingwu (1871–1944). It was out of that philosophy that the new Consciousness Only philosophy was developed by Xiong Shili (1885–1968), now considered by many to be a major Chinese thinker of recent times. But if we look back at that whole development, what is notable about all this modern Buddhist intellectualism is that it came from outside the ranks of the monastic Saṅgha. Some were lay Buddhists; others had Confucianism as their primary commitment. Although there is no ironclad rule that only Buddhist monks understand the subtleties of Buddha Dharma—the legendary Vimalakīrti was no monk, and Li

Tongxuan of Huayan fame was a layman—there is a certain quality rooted in the monk's lifestyle that keeps the Dharma from being diluted by lay concerns. A monk-scholar is distinct from a lay scholar. This quality distinguishes Master Yin-shun's study of the Buddha Dharma from the new crop of lay Buddhist intellectuals and academics in the twentieth century.

This distinction was made by the Master himself in his *Study of the Buddha Dharma as the Buddha Dharma*. Here he differentiated his knowledge from those who appropriated Buddhist philosophy from the outside and tailored it for ends other than the Buddha's truths. This includes much of the revived interest in the Consciousness Only philosophy, which was being detached from the larger Buddhist agenda and presented as a viably modern, universal, rational philosophy—an inner science of the mind that would outrank the sciences coming from the West. Abstracted from Buddhist precepts and meditation, this philosophy has been remade by Xiong Shili to serve the goal of a "new Confucianism" that turns aside from Buddhist truths. The Master made this clear in his critique of Xiong Shili. Confucianism is undeniably the mainstream of Chinese philosophy; its agenda is for living in this world. By the same token, Buddhism cuts across particular cultural allegiances and looks beyond this world, although in the Mahāyāna spirit it returns to the world and all its concerns after first breaking with them.

The Master's critique carries the weight of a scholar-monk. By leaving home one embraces a larger world of commitment, and then, but only then, returns to work within the world. A lay scholar studying the Buddha Dharma for non-Buddhist ends is not studying it properly. A scholar-monk, who lives what he teaches, presents us with an intimate "insider's" glimpse of the Buddha Dharma. *The Way to Buddhahood* offers just such an insider's view and is a living inducement to the Buddhist way. The Master speaks with the authority of one who has learned through a total immersion in the texts of the tradition, an immersion that has become increasingly rare in the modern educational system. Ironically, the erudition exemplified by this modern scholar-monk may be both the first and the last of its kind. The Master would probably brush aside this praise as inordinate and the prophecy as unwarranted.

To resume our story, after joining the Saṅgha at the age of twenty-five, Master Yin-shun did not take up residence in a meditative cloister or devote himself to learning the many rituals required for serving the laity.

He was soon enrolled in a new and well-staffed Buddhist study center set up by Master Taixu (1889–1947) specifically for training a new generation of monks. Master Yin-shun scored so high in the entrance examination that he was admitted to the advanced group of students and allowed to skip a grade. Here he had his first systematic exposure to the Buddha Dharma. Within a year he showed such proficiency and promise that Venerable Taixu asked him to instruct. Master Yin-shun gave lectures on the Treatise on the Twelve Gates teachings and already demonstrated an independent understanding and an expert interpretation of the philosophy of emptiness. Recognized for his talent by Venerable Taixu, he was invited to instruct or speak at a number of fledging Buddhist study centers all over China—a tireless round of spreading the new Buddhist learning that took him, after the war, to various posts in Hong Kong and then in Taiwan down to this very day.

Master Yin-shun's accomplishments rest on those of the reformer monk Venerable Taixu. It was Venerable Taixu who brought Buddhism out of the cloisters into the modern world, who revived the Mahāyāna commitment to working in the world, who directed Buddhist reflection to current social issues, and who, during the national emergency facing China at the time, encouraged Buddhists, even monks, to participate actively in national defense. Frail of body but not of mind, Master Yin-shun heeded this call during the war years but returned to his vocation after the war. Although Venerable Taixu may have been the first modern Buddhist monk to compose scholarly works, he was more an activist and a pamphleteer. Judged by the sheer weight of their scholarly work, it is not Venerable Taixu but his protégé Master Yin-shun who is truly the monk-scholar of our generation.

For all his insistence on looking at the Buddha Dharma from the inside, Master Yin-shun's Buddhist works are hardly traditional and anything but sectarian. His writings range so far and wide that even his own Buddhist colleagues are at a loss to place him within the schools or the lineages (*zong*) of transmission. His independent bent defies easy classification; his catholic sweep vitiates old divisions. His interpretation of the Buddha Dharma is guided by no better instructor than the Buddha Dharma itself. His hermeneutics listen and respond to the living voices that still speak from within the texts. It is not that he is another Nanyue Huisi (514–77), who according to tradition was "enlightened without a teacher" (meaning probably only without a teacher in attendance). This event, a first in Chinese Buddhism, elevated this Tiantai patriarch almost to pratyekabuddha status and led his school to break with the Indian authorities on the *Lotus Sūtra*. (Ch'an Buddhism had its own pratyekabuddha trade and made similar claims about a secret transmission later.) Master Yin-shun has no such hagiography attached to him, and he did not start a new lineage. But what he learned was acquired through the solitary journey that all independent minds undertake. Thus while the Consciousness Only philosophy was billed as an inner learning outranking European science and was much in vogue, the young student-turned-lecturer was striking out on his own by reviving the Sanlun, or Emptiness critique (Madhyamaka), instead. And whereas the practice of Ch'an and Pure Land had for the last few centuries all too often made a virtue out of a neglect of learning, the budding scholar-monk was seeking to integrate Buddhist teachings after the manner of the Tiantai and Huayan masters Zhiyi and Fazang.

To those who still wonder what lineage (zong) he follows, Master Yin-shun has gone back to the original Sanskrit idea behind zong and mapped out a much more comprehensive understanding of the principle, target, and end of the various teachings. He also wrote an essay whose title translates roughly as "The Teaching of the Buddha Designed for Living in This World (among Men) That Accords with Both the Universal Principle (Which Is Timeless) and the Specific Circumstances." This is a review of the philosophical agenda he has staked out in a number of his works. The practical goal is to direct Buddhist learning toward a Mahāyāna bodhisattvic recommitment to living in the here and now. This goal he sees as a rewording of Venerable Taixu's dictum "Buddhism for life in this world."

In general, the Master builds on the philosophical classification of schools that begins with the Hīnayāna Buddhists, continues into Mahāyāna, and culminates in the classic tenet-classification system of Tiantai and of Huayan. What the Master adds to all this is his diligence in retracing these steps as recorded in the Buddhist canon. What took modern Japanese Buddhologists about four generations to accomplish in a concerted effort since the Meiji Era here is telescoped into the writings of Master Yin-shun: *Compilation of the Scriptures of Primitive Buddhism*, *Abhidharmic Theses and Masters Primarily of the Sarvāstivāda School*, *Formation and Development of Early Mahāyāna*, *A Study of the Tathāgatagarbha Tradition*, and *A History of Chinese Ch'an Buddhism.* In these landmark studies, he reviews the progression of the Buddhist teachings ending in what in English may be translated as "The Final Buddha-centric and the Most Comprehensive of Teachings That Reconciles and Unifies Man and Buddha." This is a teaching about the Buddha nature hidden in all things which functions as the pure mind that produces our perceptions. Readers who follow the presentation in the present work will be initiated into the most elementary of teachings and then be drawn toward this grandest of all Mahāyāna visions. And this vision will direct him or her back to live out Buddhist truth in the midst of this human world. In this way the Master rebuilds the Buddha Dharma historically from the ground up and then concludes it philosophically with a perfect, all-encompassing unity.

Professor Whalen Lai
University of California–Davis

PART I

The Preliminaries

1

Taking Refuge in the Three Treasures

TO STUDY BUDDHISM means to learn from the Buddha. One takes the Buddha as one's ideal and one's mentor and learns from him incessantly. When one reaches the same level as the Buddha, then one has become a buddha.

The Buddha is the great Awakened One, the great Compassionate One, the one with perfect and complete virtue, the ultimate and unsurpassed great sage. For an ordinary person with little good fortune and no wisdom, reaching this supreme and unsurpassed state of buddhahood through practice and study is difficult. But by practicing and studying the necessary methods and by following the right way to buddhahood, one can reach the goal of buddhahood. Only in this way, and without skipping any steps, can one advance to this distant and profound goal. The methods necessary to become a buddha are known as "the way to buddhahood." Because beings have different abilities, the Buddha Dharma has different ways: the way of blessedness and virtue, the way of wisdom, the difficult way, the easy way, the mundane way, the supramundane way, the way of the śrāvaka, the way of the bodhisattva, and so on. But ultimately, there is only one way. All of these ways are nothing but methods to become a buddha "in order to open up and make manifest the Buddha's knowledge and insight to sentient beings, so that they can also apprehend and attain the same."[1] Thus we have the sayings "One way to one purity, one flavor for one emancipation" and "Many doors exist for tactful reasons, but only one path runs to the origin." The way to buddhahood is like a long river that has many streams, lakes, and rivers flowing into it; together they flow into the ocean. In the same manner, all doctrines are nothing but the way to buddhahood. Therefore, the Buddha Dharma is called the One Vehicle Way in the *Āgama Sūtra* and the *Lotus Sūtra.*

The Three Treasures represent the general principles of the Buddha Dharma, and taking refuge in them is the first step to entering the

Buddhist path. The merits of the Three Treasures are countless, limitless, and inconceivable. But without taking refuge in them, one cannot receive and enjoy these merits. It is like staying outside the entrance to a park: one cannot appreciate the wonderful flowers and trees inside. If one resolves to study Buddhism, the first thing one should do therefore is take refuge in the Three Treasures.

SEEKING REFUGE

1 The Sea of Existence has no boundaries,
The world is full of worry and suffering,
Flowing and turning, rising and falling,
Is there no place of refuge and support?

If one takes refuge, one must do so with sincerity. Consider the life or death situation of one who has fallen into the billowing waves of an ocean and cannot see the shore. Upon catching sight of a clump of seaweed or a patch of foam, one will reach out to grasp it; or, hearing the sound of the wind or birds, one will scream for help. With only the thought to live, one's wish to be saved is very deep, very sincere. If a ship passes by and sailors throw down ropes or life preservers, will one not instantly grab one and climb aboard the ship? The sincerity with which one seeks refuge should match this. Only then will one achieve the wonderful merits of taking refuge.

Consider the analogy of rising and falling in the sea of suffering. Sentient beings are the foundation of the world. They are living beings with emotions and consciousnesses. Every one of them has had a countless number of lives. And before being liberated from birth and death, every being will also have countless lives in the future. The continuum of sentient beings' lives thus extends endlessly like an ocean without boundaries. The current life is but another wave in the ocean of lives.

From the past to the present to the future, life goes on—this movement of time is called the world. In this world sentient beings have much more suffering than happiness, and even happiness is followed by loss and suffering. The Buddha described this state as "worry, sadness, suffering and affliction, purely the accumulation of great suffering."[2] Sentient beings are caught in the world as if in a whirlpool; sometimes their heads are above the water, sometimes submerged. At one moment they are born as divine beings, and then just as suddenly they fall into the hell realms or become animals or hungry ghosts. Sentient beings arise and descend, descend and arise, constantly turning but never escaping. Is there any condition more painful and sadder than this?

When people actually fall into the sea and, battered by the waves, fear for their lives, they call out for help. So why do sentient beings, rising and falling in the cruel sea of births and deaths, not seek help and protection to reach the other shore—liberation? When one thinks about this, the desire to seek refuge and protection will well up with sincerity and urgency. But what is the real place for refuge and support? One cannot use seaweed or foam as a life preserver.

Seeking Refuge in Things of This World

2 "Accumulations of wealth and riches can be lost,
Those with fame and high status can fall,
Those who are together may be scattered,
Those who are born must die."
The well-governed state will fall into chaos,
The world once formed faces destruction;
Of the pleasures and certainties of life,
None can be relied upon.

Some people do not know to seek refuge, while some do know but mistakenly believe in false teachers and non-Buddhists. Why do some not seek refuge? Because they are stubbornly attached to the affairs of this world, considering them meaningful and full of good fortune and happiness. When their situation becomes critical, however, they wake up from their rosy dreams in sorrow and disappointment. But by then it is too late. There are many worldly things to which people are attached, but they can be categorized into six major groups.

1. The accumulation of wealth and riches: Some people think that finances come first and that with money they can do anything. They even say, "Money makes the world go round." They do not realize that no matter how rich they become, their wealth will eventually be consumed. Do not think that this is because they are not skillful in management or that they are wasteful. Actually, no one has complete power over wealth. With regard

to this the Buddha said, "Wealth is possessed by five groups."[3] These groups are floods, fires, thieves, evil rulers, and bad children—any one of which can instantly consume one's riches. Furthermore, preserving one's accumulated wealth entails all kinds of worry and suffering. Wealth can sometimes cause disastrous suffering. At the end of the Ming dynasty in China, the conquering Li Chuang entered Beijing. He used torture devices such as clamping sticks and head hoops on rich government officials to extract gold and silver from them. Their wealth was taken, their legs were broken, their skulls were cracked, and in some cases their lives were lost. And under the tyrannical rule of the Chinese Communists, those who possessed capital and money were persecuted—not just the very wealthy but even those who had only a one-acre field and a cow. Sometimes their families, their wives and children, were also attacked. These persecutors are good examples of what the Buddha described as thieves and evil rulers. Can people really say that they can always have their way when they have money?

2. Fame and high status: People love these blindly. When they are in power and things are going smoothly, they feel that they can control everything. The high must fall, however. Hitler entered Munich triumphantly, but the night before the fall of Berlin he was at his wit's end and committed suicide. Stalin ruled the Soviet Union for thirty years and received much glory, but soon after he died he was severely criticized by his followers. In Buddhist biographical literature, there is King Mūrdhaja-rāja, who united the Four Continents and then rose to the Tuṣita Heaven to manage the heavenly palace with the sovereign Śakra. But in the end King Mūrdhaja-rāja fell down to the human realm and died in distress. Even the god Śakra, who claimed to be the lord of heaven and earth and the father of humans, was unable to escape being reborn from the wombs of donkeys and horses. High position is temporary and undependable.

3. The togetherness of beloved families: Parents and children and husbands and wives are full of domestic warmth. Deep friendships can be established at school between teachers and students or among classmates, and in society among coworkers, when people share similar aspirations and help one another. Human beings are social animals. If families can live together and good friends work cooperatively, this is most ideal and comforting. Nevertheless, loved ones become enemies, and no matter how close people become, eventually they will be separated. When the moment to separate forever arrives, people have to abandon

their parents, spouses, or children and go their separate ways. And then who takes care of whom?

4. Life itself: Experience tells us that those who are born must die. The reality of death is a definite fact, but people think of themselves as if they were immortal. Only living has meaning to them. So they seek everything, including fame and profit. Even though they may talk about death, they do not wake up to the reality of it when dealing with other people and worldly matters. "A man lives less than a century, yet he has the worry of a thousand years." This proverb illustrates people's distorted feeling of immortality, their deviant beliefs in long or eternal life. Has anyone ever really heard of someone not dying? (This concludes the commentary on the above-quoted four verses that comprise the famous "Verses of Impermanence.")

5. The prosperity of one's country: For most people, their country is like a security guard, and the strength and prosperity of their country is closely related to the comfort and freedom of its people. If the country is strong, people think they have it made. But the prosperity of one's country does not guarantee security for oneself or one's family. Political parties rise and fall and are not always faithful to the country, and the country itself fluctuates between well-governed order and chaos. Factual examples can be found everywhere. Depending solely on one's country is thus neither sensible nor safe.

6. The progress of society: Some people think that since human beings are social animals and civilization progresses, this must be the true meaning of life—so why bother to seek an empty refuge for oneself alone? This is the bias of seeing the whole but not the individual. Provisionally, the progress of society and culture might be regarded as the true meaning of life. But the social activities of humankind depend on the world we live in (the earth), and these activities cannot be separated from the kind of space we occupy (even if we could move to another world, it would be the same). However, this world is in the process of cycling from formation to destruction and from destruction to formation. Consider this for a moment: one day the earth will be destroyed, and then what will become of civilization and the true meaning of life? Those who think that the progress of society is the true meaning of life are truly dreamers! Those who cannot awaken enthusiasm to seek refuge are misled by their attachment to ephemeral circumstances or have illusions about worldly pleasures.

None of these worldly matters can be truly relied upon. All of them are impermanent and are hardly blissful. Where then is the place of refuge?

Seeking Refuge in Things beyond This World

3 Ghosts and spirits delight in violent murder,
The desirous divine beings are addicted to various cravings,
The Brahmā dwells on arrogance;
None of them are a place of refuge.

Even if one knows of the need to seek refuge, one may be misled by heterodox religions or deviant schools. One may not consciously realize it, but one can be influenced; caution is necessary. There are all kinds of religious beings in which one can take refuge. Most are not true places of refuge. Categorized according to their flaws, these fall into three groups.

The first false refuge is in ghosts and spirits. According to the Chinese there are heavenly gods, earthly deities, and human ghosts. The Chinese also believe that after people die they can become heavenly gods if they have enough merit. There are all kinds of gods: wind gods, rain gods, mountain gods, water gods, local guardian gods of the earth, the gods of the five grains, etc. In addition, there are goblins of the mountains and forests and all sorts of demons and monsters. "Essence and spirit are goblins," says the *Book of Changes*. "Wandering souls are ghosts."[4]

In Buddhist sūtras, ghosts are called hungry ghosts; the spirits governed by the gods of the four heavens include yakṣas, rakṣasas, nāgas (dragons), mahoragas (python spirits), garuḍas (golden-winged birdlike beings), the powerful ghost king, and higher-status animals. There are also demons (dragons and big snakes), ghost spirits, and angels with wings as described in Christianity. All these ghosts and spirits do have some merit and magical power. Some of them, inclined to do good, also serve the gods of the higher heavens, and under certain circumstances they can help people. Thus people often worship them, requesting their help with exorcisms, asking for their blessings, or praying for protection from harm. Ghosts and spirits are full of afflictions, however. Sometimes their characters are not as good as those of humans, particularly because their angry nature delights in violent murder. What they want from humans are sacrifices—blood and flesh; at times they even want human sacrifices. If people make offerings without respect or offend them in some way, they seek cruel revenge—violent winds, rainstorms, hail, plagues, and so forth. These spirits are equivalent to the underworld hoodlums and the evil forces in the world. When one encounters adversity, a hoodlum may help one struggle against it or assist one generously with money. But one cannot offend him; if one does, one falls into the pit of crime.

In the past in Beijing, Dharma master Da Yong wanted to go to Tibet to study the Esoteric School. According to the rules of that sect, he had to invite a Dharma-protecting spirit, a fox spirit from the Guang Ji Temple. When the fox spirit came, it objected to the Dharma master's departure for Tibet. If the master insisted on going, the fox spirit would disturb him. So it was easy to invite the spirit but hard to send it away. After much effort, people finally got rid of it. As the folk adages say, inviting a wolf into the house or allowing a ghost inside the door is asking for trouble. Often, worshippers who have done such things have ended up losing their families and lives because they offended these ghosts and spirits. So why ask for trouble? Confucius was really a great human being. His teaching—respect ghosts and spirits but stay away from them—was smart advice![5]

The second false refuge is the desirous divine beings. Desire includes the five desires of matter: the enjoyment of material form, sound, smell, taste, touch; and the sexual desires of men and women. *Deva*, the Sanskrit word for divine being, means brightness and denotes heavenly kings. In the three realms, there are six levels of divine beings. The lowest level is represented by the four kings of divine beings who govern the eight catagories of ghosts and spirits. Above them are Trayastriṃśā Heaven, Yama Heaven, Tuṣita Heaven, Nirmāṇarati Heaven, and Paranirmitavaśavartin Heaven. All six levels of divine beings have greed and sexual desire and therefore are known as desirous divine beings.

Among them, the king of Tuṣita, Śakra-devānām Indra, the sovereign Śakra, has the closest relationship with humankind. He upholds peace, loves morality, and wants progress for the human race. While ruling his heavenly kingdom, however, he sometimes has to go to war. Still, he forgives his enemies and emphasizes nonkilling. He has become the great king of the kingdom of many spirits, and he rules the world through ghosts and spirits. He also has many heavenly nymphs surrounding him, which is similar to the situation of the Jade Emperor described in Chinese legends. Compared to ghosts and spirits, such beings are naturally more lofty. The problem with them is their addiction to their cravings. In fulfilling their desires for material gain and sex, they become arrogant, wasteful, lustful, idle, and indulgent, while their spiritual life—their wisdom and morality—regresses. For example, in the past Śakra asked the Buddha to expound the Dharma, but soon afterward he went back to heaven and completely forgot what the Buddha had said. Desire is the root of suffering. Divine beings cannot protect themselves from enjoying worldly desires and degrading themselves. They too must seek refuge!

The third false refuge is the one and only Brahmā. Above the realm of desire is the realm of form, which is divided into the four Dhyāna Heavens. The first Dhyāna Heaven is again divided into three: the heavens of Brahmā's multitudes, of Brahmā's ministers, and of Great Brahmā. The multitudes of Brahmā are like the people; the ministers of Brahmā are like the government officials; and Brahmā is the one and only king. The word *brahmā* means "clean" and "pure," which is similar in meaning to "holy." Brahmā has neither sexual desire nor worldly material desire. His moral conduct is lofty, and he has a spirit of compassion and universal love. Among the gods of the common religions of the world, he is outstanding in this respect. According to the Buddhist sūtras, when Brahmā appeared, there were no people nor was there a realm of desire. Then Brahmā wanted to have heaven and earth; the realm of desire gradually formed. He wanted to have people; coincidentally people came into being. Because Brahmā's mind was filled with arrogance, he unavoidably formed the conceited and erroneous ideas that he had created the world and that the people had come from him. After he had lived for a long time—one and a half kalpas—he announced to his people that he was everlasting with no beginning and no end.

Above Brahmā are the second, third, and fourth Dhyāna Heavens and the realm of formlessness. But humankind has little contact with these realms; thus very few people believe in, accept, and obey beings of these realms. For ordinary people these heavens cannot serve as a basis for religion; therefore not much needs to be said about them. Common religions do not go beyond the scope of ghosts and spirits and the gods of polytheism and monotheism. None of these beings can save themselves; all have afflictions and are not yet liberated from birth and death. Therefore, "neither are they the place of refuge."

Real refuge: The Three Treasures

4 People seeking refuge everywhere,
Seeking refuge in all the ten directions,
Finally realize that the ultimate place of refuge
Is to be found in the most auspicious Three Treasures.

Feeling the stress of the suffering of birth and death, people want to take refuge, and they search everywhere for it. Although they seek incessantly in all the ten directions, they find only ghosts and spirits, a great god with spirits under him, or the "creator" god; but none of these is really a place for refuge. Then they realize that the only true place of refuge is in the Buddhist Three Treasures.

Praise for the Three Treasures

The Buddha, Dharma, and Saṅgha are rare, invaluable, and wonderful; thus they are called treasures. Taking refuge in them enables us to transform bad luck into good and disaster into peace, abandon evil for kindness, turn darkness into light, abandon suffering, and obtain happiness. All these auspicious things can be achieved. Claiming that the Three Treasures are the only worthy refuge is not just a way of praising one's own religion and slandering that of others. It is a conclusion derived from facts.

The facts are that soon after Śākyamuni Buddha had become a buddha, the "creator" god, Brahmā, came down from heaven and requested that the Buddha expound the Dharma because he felt that he no longer knew what to do with his children, the people on earth. Śākyamuni Buddha agreed to do this. He turned the great wheel of the Dharma (that is, he taught the Dharma) and saved many people. Brahmā became the Buddha's disciple and realized a saintly life without desire.

Once, too, the sovereign Śakra knew that he was going to die soon and that he would, unfortunately, become a pig fetus. Worried and miserable, he went to ask Great Brahmā and Maheśvara for help. Then he went all over the world, searching in mountains and waters and asking help from ghosts and spirits, non-Buddhists and immortals everywhere, but all was in vain. In the end, he met the Buddha and listened to one of his discourses. This saved him from the evil fate of becoming a pig fetus, and he was able to return to his heavenly kingdom. Thus both the great god of polytheism and the "creator" god of monotheism have had to take refuge in the Buddha. "Seeking for refuge everywhere, seeking refuge in all the ten directions" was exactly Śakra's experience.

Praise for the Virtues of the Buddha

5 The true Dharma is the body of the Buddha.
His life is pure wisdom,
Like the bright moon shining through the autumn sky;
Therefore, we should worship the Honored One of Two Perfections.

Buddha is a Sanskrit word meaning "awakened one." What the Buddha realized was the true Dharma, which can also be translated as the wonderful Dharma. The Dharma, governed by laws, is immutable. It is a truth that lies equidistant from extremes. It is unbiased, subtle, wonderful, not obvious or superficial; it is everlasting, universal, and absolute. Only after one has attained the perfect enlightenment of the true Dharma can one be called a buddha. The Buddha, who has the true Dharma as his body (the Dharmakāya), is the one who concretely reveals the absolute truth.

Why is the Buddha able to achieve perfect enlightenment? It is because the Buddha has the pure wisdom that is faultless and separate from all afflictions and defilements. Since the Buddha has the purest wisdom, the true Dharma that is realized by him is also the purest. It is called "the purest Dharmadhātu,"[6] which is the same as the Dharmakāya. The true Dharma is omnipresent and is not diminished by confusion or increased with enlightenment. Pure wisdom, which is the very life force of the Buddha, is called vital wisdom. The unification of the Dharmakāya and this vital wisdom is the Buddha. Here is an analogy: The Buddha's wisdom is like the bright moon; the true Dharma that is realized by the pure wisdom is like the autumn sky in which this bright moon shines. When there are no clouds, the clear sky looks especially pure in the bright moonlight. In the same way, with enlightened and pure wisdom the Buddha completely realizes the true Dharma, and the true Dharma is also revealed purely and exactly in the pure wisdom. The sūtra says: "Bodhisattvas are like the pure moon that travels through space."[7] If bodhisattvas are like this, what must the Buddha be!

When the Dharmakāya and the vital wisdom reach perfection, this accomplishment deserves the trust and respect of all sentient beings. Reverence is expressed in worship. Bowing and greeting are bodily worship; praising the Buddha's virtues is verbal worship; and trusting with respect is mental worship. We worship in these three ways to show our total trust in the Buddha.

In the epithet "Honored One of Two Perfections," which praises the Buddha, the two perfections are good fortune and wisdom. In addition to the Buddha, bodhisattvas also have great good fortune and great wisdom. But among sages, the Buddha is supreme. Hence he is the Honored One of Two Perfections. But the epithet can also be translated differently because the Chinese word for perfection can also mean "foot." Since humans are two-footed animals and the Buddha is the most honored among humans, he is called the Two-Footed Honored One. As it is said in a sūtra: "The truly enlightened one is the Two-Footed Honored One, while the horse is superior among the four-legged animals."[8]

TWO PERFECTIONS

6 Buddhas of the three periods are innumerable,
Buddhas of the ten directions are also countless.
Having come to this impure world because of his
compassionate vow,
Śākyamuni Buddha is deserving of our worship.

"Buddha" is a general name for a sage with great enlightenment. Whoever can completely realize the true Dharma is a buddha. Many people have resolved to study Buddhism, and many have become buddhas. From the standpoint of time, there are innumerable buddhas in each of the three periods—past, present, and future. The present buddha is Śākyamuni Buddha; among the past buddhas were Kāśyapa Buddha, Kanakamuni Buddha, Śikhin Buddha, and Vipaśyin Buddha; the future buddhas will be Maitreya Buddha, Rucika Buddha, and others. There were an uncountable number of buddhas in the past, and the same will be true in the future. Speaking from the standpoint of space, there are also countless buddhas in the worlds of the ten directions: east, south, west, north, southeast, southwest, northeast, northwest, above, and below. There are countless worlds in the ten directions, and there are buddhas for these worlds. For example, at present Akṣobhya Buddha and the

Medicine Buddha are in the east, Amitābha Buddha is in the west, and so on. Buddhists who take refuge in the Three Treasures should do so with the buddhas of the three periods and the ten directions.

From our standpoint in this world, however, the one who particularly deserves our trust and worship is the original teacher, Śākyamuni Buddha. When Śākyamuni Buddha was a bodhisattva, he had the great compassionate intention to alleviate suffering and made a great vow to endure hardship. He did not want to be born in the Pure Land. Instead, he vowed to practice and become a buddha in this impure world because sentient beings here were miserable and urgently needed help. This great resolve—"If I do not go into hell to save suffering beings, who will?"—was fully actualized by Śākyamuni Buddha. The reason he appeared in this evil world of the five impurities was to save us suffering sentient beings from abandonment.

Śākyamuni Buddha was born in India about two thousand five hundred years ago. Because he left home, practiced mental cultivation, and became a buddha, the light of his teaching came to this dark world so full of crimes and evil. This world's Buddhism came from Śākyamuni Buddha—a kindness without bounds! Not only do we respect and praise the greatness of Śākyamuni Buddha, but all the buddhas of the ten directions praise him as well. As it is said in the sūtras, "All other buddhas also praise me (Śākyamuni) for my inconceivable merits and virtues."[9] After we have reverently taken refuge with all the buddhas of the ten directions and three periods, therefore, we should pay special respects to the original teacher, Śākyamuni. This is similar to taking refuge in the Saṅgha, which is supposed to include all monks, but the person in whom we really take refuge is the one with the most kindness.

7 His wisdom is perfect, his compassion infinite.
Overcoming all obstructions, he is totally without remnants of habit.
These three virtues are equal and ultimate for all buddhas,
But for the sake of skillful means, there are differences.

In the way of the ancient sages, the three virtues serve as praise for buddhas—the virtues of wisdom, grace, and breaking free from afflictions. Not only do buddhas realize the nature of all dharmas, but they also realize each dharma's special nature, appearances, functions, and relationships; they realize the present, the past, and the future as well; they realize the various forms of all dharmas. Thus buddhas are synonymous with complete and perfect wisdom. Sentient beings, on the contrary, are unable to rid themselves of suffering because of ignorance. The Buddha, with his complete and perfect wisdom, his endless skills and tactfulness, was able not only to liberate himself but also to save sentient beings. This is the wonderful function of wisdom. Such is the praise of the Buddha's perfected virtue of wisdom.

The Buddha's great compassion, his intention to alleviate suffering, does not apply to just one person, one situation, one race, one region, or one world. It applies to all worlds, to all sentient beings, to all kinds of suffering. Penetratingly thorough, his deep compassion stops nowhere. Even in the formative stage, bodhisattvas such as Guanyin (Avalokiteśvara), Dizang (Kṣitigarbha), and others already have great compassion and great vows, to say nothing of the attainment stage—the state of buddhahood. Such is the praise for the Buddha's perfected virtue of grace.

Some beings have much wisdom but little compassion, some have much compassion but little wisdom, and some have both. But none, if they still have afflictions and defilements, are completely pure. Only the Tathāgata has eliminated all afflictions without even a trace of residual habits. Such is the praise for the Buddha's perfected virtue of breaking free from afflictions.

"Residual habit" refers to the process of becoming accustomed to afflictions from beginningless time. The Buddha's arhat disciples have overcome afflictions but often retain residual habits. That is why some arhats scold people (they are so used to scolding they do not notice it) or jump around or cling to views. Only the Buddha was able to completely break off from afflictions and residual habits. This makes him the purest and the holiest.

One does not turn to the Buddha because of superstition or identification with him. As Buddhists, we respect him because he was able to bring all virtues to completion and perfection. The only one who can actually do so is a buddha. So we should take refuge in a buddha, not in the non-Buddhist gods of heaven.

Just as all buddhas are equally and ultimately complete and perfect, so are their three virtues. It cannot be said that Buddha A has made a greater vow than Buddha B or that Buddha B has higher wisdom and more magical power than Buddha C. A difference in quality or quantity between buddhas would imply incompleteness and imperfection, and when there is incompleteness and imperfection, one cannot be called a buddha. Thus it is said, "The paths of all buddhas are the same" and "All buddhas are equal." According to the sūtras, however, it seems that buddhas have physical bodies of different sizes, lifetimes of varied lengths, lands of different degrees of purity, disciples of varied quantities, and different lengths of time for their true teachings to abide in their worlds. One must understand that in order to suit the diverse qualities of sentient beings, buddhas have to use skillful means; this is the reason for the differences. Since the true virtues of buddhas are not different, one should not discriminate erroneously.

Praise for the Virtues of the Dharma

8 The empty well is old and in ruins;
The empty village is quiet and without people;
The far shore is forested and has flowing springs.
The Dharma, honorable and beyond desires, compels our worship.

The first two lines refer to two different parables. Strolling in the wilderness, a person carelessly falls into an old, dry well. Luckily he grabs hold of a withered vine in the well so that he does not fall to the bottom. At the bottom are four poisonous snakes staring at him with their mouths open and tongues flickering. A rat is gnawing the withered vine he has grasped, and the vine may break at any moment. In desperate circumstances, he looks up and sees some honey on the vine. He sticks out his tongue to lick the honey and forgets everything. While enjoying the sweet honey, he even forgets that a swarm of bees may sting him.

This parable says that in the wilderness of births and deaths, sentient beings are endowed with a body because of karmic forces. The withered vine is like the root of life. The rat gnawing the withered vine is like the encroaching of impermanence; eventually the root of life will break. The dry well, the withered vine, and the rat all symbolize the cruel pressure exerted by the powerful force of impermanence. That is why, in the verse, the empty well is "in ruins." The four snakes represent the four elements—earth, water, fire, and air. When the four elements are not in harmony, people fall sick and die, just as they do from the bite of a poisonous snake. The honey is the enjoyment of the five desires: content with this small happiness, people forget that they are under the stress of impermanence, birth, and death. Just as they are heedless of the stinging bees, so they do not think about the bitter fruits of the five desires. How hopeless stupid people are—even the tremendous suffering of birth and death cannot wake them up!

The second parable tells of an uninhabited village. A refugee, fleeing punishment by a king, comes to a deserted village. He wants to stay there overnight, but suddenly he hears the voice of a heavenly being: "Run! This place is frequented by robbers. If they find you, you may lose your life!" So he leaves the village and proceeds to the border of the kingdom, where there is a wide river. The people who want to arrest him are close behind. But now, seeing the forest and streams on the far shore and knowing they lie outside the king's domain, the refugee feels safe and happy. He swims across the big river without regard for danger. Out of reach of death, he can finally rest.

This parable is meant to convey that some people, wanting to be free from the control of Māra, the Evil One, study and practice the Buddha's teachings but fail to guard the six sense organs. The empty village represents the six sense organs. Because the six sense organs enable people to see, hear, and feel, people usually think that there is a self, an "I," within. But actually there is no self, just as there are no people in the village. When these six sense organs without a self come into contact with the six sense objects, this gives rise to the confused six consciousnesses, which are like the robbers. Traveling through the six sense organs, these six consciousnesses generate desire and anger when they should not. With various afflictions they rob people of merits and the wealth of the Dharma. Because of this, some people fall into the evil destinies. If one wants to leave the rule of Māra and study and practice the Buddha's teachings, therefore, one should not be deceived by the six sense organs and should move toward a safer place. One who studies the Buddha's teachings, not being deceived by the senses, crosses the river of birth and death; one leaves Māra's realm and reaches Nirvāṇa's shore. Here one can enjoy the bliss of stillness beyond birth and death.

This parable illustrates the three seals of the Dharma: "All conditioned things are impermanent," "All dharmas have no self," and "In Nirvāṇa is stillness and extinction." These are the three truths of Buddhism. Furthermore, Nirvāṇa, the ultimate settling place for all sages, is achieved through realizing impermanence and the nonexistence of the self. This is the Dharma treasure in which we should take refuge and which we should respect. Although some worldly meditators succeed in discarding some afflictions such as desire, the sages of the Three Vehicles who attain Nirvāṇa through wisdom have completely discarded them. Among all the states in which one can be free from desires, Nirvāṇa is supreme and most honorable. As it is said, Nirvāṇa is "honorable and beyond desires."

9 The true Dharma is wonderful and inconceivable,
It is excellent, pure, permanent, and joyful.
If one follows the way of the ancient immortals,
One can attain Nirvāṇa.

Nirvāṇa is the place of refuge for all sages and all Buddhists. Because there are different levels of realization, there are different levels of Nirvāṇa: Nirvāṇa with residue (*sopadhiśeṣanirvāṇa*), Nirvāṇa without residue (*nirupadhiśeṣa-Nirvāṇa*), and supreme Nirvāṇa (*parinirvāṇa*). Actually, Nirvāṇa is the true Dharma, a state of self-realization that is wonderful and inconceivable. Thus it is said, "Only the one who drinks the water will know whether it is cold or warm."

Now, according to the skillful discourses of the sūtras and the treatises, the true Dharma can be briefly described as (1) excellent, an absolute perfection beyond description; (2) pure, uncontaminated by afflictions and defilements, neither causing afflictions nor defilements; (3) permanent, beyond the nature of time and beyond births or deaths, existing as it always has and always will; and (4) joyful, an absolute happiness that is free from the bondage of birth, old age, illness, death, worry, and sufferings. In short, the true Dharma is unimaginable and its virtues are inconceivable.

The state that is attainable through wisdom is called the true Dharma. Entering the true Dharma and attaining real liberation through wisdom is called Nirvāṇa. The true Dharma is thus the same as Nirvāṇa. One only needs to follow the ancients—entering the Buddhist immortals' true Way—to realize the liberation of attaining Nirvāṇa. The ancient immortals' Way is mentioned in the *Āgama Sūtra*, the *Laṅkāvatāra Sūtra*, and elsewhere. This true Way to attain Nirvāṇa, which every buddha of the past has gone through, was not created by Śākyamuni Buddha. It is the normal way of the ancient buddhas and therefore is called the Way of the Ancients.

Praise for the Virtues of the Saṅgha

10 To bring together the Saṅgha, the Buddha relied upon the Dharma,
And harmony, joy, and purity were its foundation.
With harmony in practical matters and harmony in principles,
The Saṅgha, most highly honored among assemblies, compels our worship.

After Śākyamuni Buddha became a buddha and started preaching the Dharma, many people wanted to leave home and follow him. So the Buddha organized them into the Saṅgha, a group with organization and discipline. An old Chinese translation called the Saṅgha a harmonized group.

What did the Buddha use to bring together the Saṅgha? Not his own abilities. The Buddha said, "I myself do not gather people."[10] Rather, the Buddha relied on the Dharma to form the Saṅgha. He used the Dharma to inspire people so they might solve the great matter of life and death. The Dharma also serves as the rules and regulations that accord with the discipline of a righteous life. Drawing from these perfect principles of living with one another, the Buddha formalized rules and regulations to organize the people.

The Saṅgha has the three fundamental characteristics of harmony, joy, and purity. The first, harmony, is found in both practical matters and in principles. Harmony in practical matters is subdivided into six areas called the six harmonies. (1) Harmony in understanding the doctrines refers to the unified ways of thinking, which means that all members of the Saṅgha share the same views. (2) Harmony in keeping the precepts means that all observe the same rules. (3) Harmony in the sharing of materials means there is economic equality in daily life. These three harmonies are the essence of the Buddhist Saṅgha. If the Saṅgha lives together in this way, the physical and mental activities among its members must have the three following characteristics: (4) harmony in abiding physically, that is, peaceful communal living; (5) harmony in speech without quarreling; and (6) the harmony of tranquil minds. These six harmonies, which constitute harmony in practical matters, should be practiced by all monastics.

As for harmony in principles, this is the truth that the Buddha's disciples realize: the Dharma or Nirvāṇa—the contents of both are the same. This harmony in principles is also called the "complete meeting of minds" or "exhaling through the same nostrils with all buddhas." It is possessed by sages, whether they are monastics or laypeople. A person who achieves harmony in practical matters is a monastic in an ordinary sense, whereas someone who achieves harmony in principles is a monastic person in an ultimate sense. In this evil age of the five impurities, Śākyamuni Buddha relied on the Dharma to assemble the Saṅgha as the central force for maintaining Buddhism; he thereby emphasized harmony in practical matters over harmony in principles.

The second characteristic of the Saṅgha is its peaceful joy. In this harmonious organization, monks and nuns can find physical and mental peace and joy and can practice vigorously. The third characteristic of the Saṅgha is its purity. In an organization with harmony and joy, people can encourage and keep each other alert. If an offense is committed, they can quickly repent and restore purity so that the Saṅgha remains strong and sound. The Saṅgha that was established by the Buddha was a perfect organization.

From self-cultivation to purity of body and mind, the Saṅgha—a great furnace for casting virtuous people and sages—is that extraordinary factor that enables us to attain happiness and purity. Through preaching for the benefit of others, the Saṅgha is a collective force that mobilizes the Buddha Dharma. Disciples of the Buddha should take refuge in and respect the Saṅgha, one of the Three Treasures. Religious groups resembling the Saṅgha are not limited to Buddhism. For example, the ascetic groups of the six heterodox teachers in India also have monks. Among all the monastic assemblies, however, the Saṅgha that practices the Buddha Dharma is the most honored; hence it is called the "most highly honored among assemblies."

11 One should respect the members of the Saṅgha,
And not scold them or judge them.

For they follow the Buddha as practitioners,
And maintain the true Dharma like a fortress.

This verse is especially important for lay devotees who take refuge in the Saṅgha treasure. Lay devotees should mentally respect the Saṅgha with sincerity, whether verbally (or in writing) by means of praise, or physically by means of prostrations. They should serve the monks and nuns according to the Saṅgha's instructions. According to their abilities and depending on the Saṅgha's needs, they should make offerings of clothing, food, medicine, bedding, and other daily necessities. One should not be disrespectful. In contemporary China, some people still respect the Buddha and the Dharma; but too few respect the Saṅgha. Sometimes people respect only the teacher with whom they take refuge, or only one or two members of the Saṅgha. With such incomplete respect and allegiance to the Three Treasures, no wonder that the extraordinary merits of the Buddha Dharma have difficulty growing.

Among monastics there are naturally both good and evil people. "Dragons and snakes huddle together," as the saying goes. This is to say that there are holy monastic people and worldly monastic people, those who keep the precepts completely and those who break them. When lay disciples see monastic people who are impure and not living in accord with the Dharma, they should acknowledge that this is a "Saṅgha affair" that will be handled according to the established rules and regulations. A layperson should not casually scold the whole Saṅgha or even one or a few monks or nuns. Devotees who are sincere protectors of the Dharma can make suggestions, but the responsibility and authority for handling these matters belong to the Saṅgha. According to the Buddha's system, a monastic person who has committed a crime but has not yet been expelled from the Saṅgha cannot be casually punished by secular laws. When there is a dispute, the secular ruler must follow the monastic rules for coming to a decision; he ought not decide on his own. Otherwise, secular attempts to resolve such situations could become seriously offensive, insulting the Saṅgha or increasing disputes within it.

Whoever has joined a monastery or nunnery is a member of the Saṅgha. You cannot discriminate among them on the basis of their being old or young, male or female, learned or uneducated, diligent or lazy, precept keeping or precept breaking, fellow countrymen or foreigners. All members of the Saṅgha should be honored and respected with offerings because the Saṅgha is like the ocean. The ocean does not differentiate between big dragons and fish or shrimp, between seaweed and pearls or treasure, but rather holds them all equally. In this world, there are people who prefer keeping precepts, or meditating, or reciting and chanting, or having dignified manners, or studying the meaning of the doctrines. Because of these differences some people discriminate improperly, claiming that some are right and some are wrong, some are good and some are bad, supporting some and opposing others. Devotees, treat them all equally and do not judge the Saṅgha. To the average person the virtues of the Saṅgha are not easily recognizable. For example, people in general have more faith in the aged and think little of the young. They do not realize that these elders may have much attachment but do not pursue sensuality only because their six sense organs have degenerated along with their wrinkled skin and white hair. This has nothing to do with the virtues of the Buddha Dharma at all!

Devotees should understand that all those who have left home and belong to the Saṅgha are practitioners following the Buddha's example, regardless of their different levels. As long as there are monastic people, there will be monasteries and nunneries, holy images, sūtras, and the Three Treasures to worship. Monks and nuns may be superior and inferior, good and bad, worldly and holy. But together they become the Saṅgha, a powerful force for maintaining the Tathāgata's true Dharma so effectively that even demons and non-Buddhists cannot destroy it; they are like a fortress with walls made of gold and a moat filled with boiling water. Everyone should examine their own situation; the person who awakened one's faith or interest in the Buddha Dharma was not necessarily a virtuous monk or a saint! So it is that a bhikṣu who has broken the precepts but still wears the monk's robe is still a field of good fortune for divine and human beings. Truly sincere lay devotees should especially respect, protect, and assist the Saṅgha with its harmony, joy, and purity; they should not scold and blame its members or provoke struggles among them. When the Saṅgha had disputes during the Buddha's lifetime, it did not listen even to the Buddha and split in two. The Buddha then told devotees that both groups were Saṅghas and deserved offerings. The saying "when one breaks a golden rod into two, both are gold" is a helpful insight for all lay devotees.[11]

The Virtues in Principle and in Practice

12 The real virtue of the Three Treasures,
Is faultless and pure in nature.
To transform the world, we should rely on both the real and the worldly virtues.
In this way, the Buddha Dharma can exist forever.

The Three Treasures, the objects of our absolute allegiance, are the most perfect, complete, and pure among all religious founders, doctrines, and disciples. However, images of the Buddha or saints and disciples may not necessarily meet these qualifications, of course! But one should know that at present there are the three Abiding Treasures—the Abiding Buddha, Dharma, and Saṅgha—that appeared after the Buddha passed away. The Abiding Buddha can be represented by the Buddha's image, whether of jade, stone, gold, copper, wood, clay, or paint; the Abiding Dharma can be represented by the scriptures of the Tripitaka or the discourses on the Dharma by masters of the past or present; the Abiding Saṅgha can be represented by the monastic population. These are the Three Treasures of the continued transmission of Buddhism in the world. By respecting and making offerings to them, followers can reach the real Three Treasures.

When Śākyamuni Buddha was alive in this world, he was the Buddha treasure. His teachings—the Four Noble Truths, dependent origination, Nirvāṇa, and so forth—were the Dharma treasure; those who left home to follow him, whether worldly or holy, were the Saṅgha treasure. These three are called the Three Treasures of Transforming Appearances because of the way they transformed people during the Buddha's time. When the Buddha was teaching and transforming people in this world, these three transforming appearances functioned as the Three Treasures. Through respect and offerings, one could follow them and turn toward the Buddhas of the ten directions, the true Dharma, and the virtuous and holy monks. The Three Treasures of Transforming Appearances and the Abiding Three Treasures are both concrete manifestations of Buddhism in the world. By taking refuge in them, one can reach a more profound level.

The real place of refuge is the actual virtues of the Three Treasures. These virtues have been discussed in many ways; two points of view will be introduced here.

The first sees the Buddha treasure as identical with the Buddha's faultless virtues. According to the śrāvakas, the Buddha's faultless virtues are the five attributes of the Dharmakāya, although in the Mahāyāna teaching they are embraced by perfect enlightenment (the fourfold wisdom). The Dharma treasure is the true Dharma—that is, Nirvāṇa itself. The Saṅgha treasure is identical with the faultless virtues of those who are still learners and those who are not. According to the Śrāvaka Vehicle, the faultless virtues are those of the four stages and four grades of sainthood; but according to the Mahāyāna teaching, they are the faultless virtues of the Bodhisattva Way (which includes śrāvakas and pratyekabuddhas).

The second way of talking about the real virtues of the Three Treasures draws from the Mahāyāna teachings, according to which the Buddha treasure is the purest Dharmadhātu—revealed ultimately, completely, and perfectly (embracing essence, form, action, and function). The Saṅgha treasure is the pure Dharmadhātu that is partially revealed. The Dharma treasure is the universal Dharmadhātu—without increase or decrease, neither dualistic nor discriminating (and called suchness, reality, and so on). The other standard terms for the Three Treasures—the Three Treasures in One Essence, the Three Treasures in Principle, and the Abiding Three Treasures—all refer to the same Three Treasures discussed above, but they are explained in different ways. The real virtue of the Three Treasures—the virtue of the *real* Three Treasures—is faultless. They do not respond to afflictions and defilements, nor do they arise because of them. Their nature is pure. Although the conditioned faultless virtues are also called pure, the unconditioned faultless virtues are pure by nature; they remain pure both when defilements are absent and when they are present. Pure by nature, the faultless Three Treasures are the real place of refuge.

In order to educate and transform the world for the benefit of all sentient beings by means of the Buddha Dharma, however, we should pay homage not only to the virtues of the Three Treasures but also to the worldly virtues of the Abiding Three Treasures. We should do this because if we take worldly refuge only, our worship may become a mere formality, whereas if we emphasize only the supreme meaning (reality), this will certainly be too profound for most people. People should therefore take refuge in the actual appearances of the Abiding Three Treasures (the Three Treasures of the Transforming Appearances during the Buddha's time) and follow this to proceed toward the real Three Treasures. This is the reason why Buddhism emphasizes teaching with images. The Abiding Three Treasures are the appearances through which the virtues of the real Three Treasures can be revealed. Only thus can one choose between the shallow and the profound without having any obstruction between phenomena and principles. Only thus can the Buddha Dharma exist forever for the deliverance of all sentient beings.

TAKING REFUGE

13 "All my life I vow
To take refuge in the Buddha, Dharma, and Saṅgha,
With utmost sincerity to make offerings,
And to be mindful of all the extraordinary benefits."

The Three Treasures of the Buddha, Dharma, and Saṅgha are without defilements and are perfectly virtuous; they are the real place of refuge. To take refuge, one should first repent sincerely with a respectful and pure mind. Then one should kneel upright in front of the refuge master, put one's palms together, follow the master's teaching, and take the vows by saying three times, "I, devotee so-and-so, for all my life take refuge in the Buddha, the Honored One of Two Perfections. For all my life I take refuge in the Dharma, the most honored teaching, which helps us to break free from desire. For all my life I take refuge in the Saṅgha, the most honored among assemblies." After taking these vows, the devotee should say three times, "I, being an upāsaka, wish that the master will keep me in mind and protect me with compassion. From now to the end of my life I will protect sentient beings. I have completely taken refuge in the Buddha, I have completely taken refuge in the Dharma, I have completely taken refuge in the Saṅgha." This recitation is taken from the *Da ming jing* (Great Name Sūtra) and the Vinaya texts.[12] After one has vowed and taken refuge, one must not deny or regret doing so, even in a life-or-death crisis. One cannot say even in jest, "I do not have faith in the Three Treasures" or "I am not a devotee of the Three Treasures." If one takes refuge and later gives it up, one will suffer endlessly for many lives to come. Therefore, be sure to remember the vow "For all my life I take refuge."

After taking refuge, one should make offerings with utmost sincerity. One should have a respectful mind toward all the images of buddhas (including stupas), scriptures, and monks and nuns, even though they may not seem very dignified or pure (if, perhaps, a statue of the Buddha is poorly crafted). Offerings to the Buddha include actions such as prostration, praise, and clockwise circumambulation and adornments such as incense, flowers, music, light, pennants, banners, and precious canopies. Offerings to the Dharma include activities such as copying, engraving, and printing texts or gifts of materials such as incense, flowers, and so forth for the adornment of the scriptures. Offerings to the Saṅgha include clothing, food, seats, bedding, medicines, and daily necessities. These things must be pure and things that monks and nuns can use without violating the Buddha Dharma. One should never offer things that are not in accord with the Dharma. As for the supreme offering, nothing can compare to actual practice in accord with the Tathāgata's teachings and the instructions of monks or nuns.

In China, Buddhists have practiced long recitations in the morning and in the evening, but this does not seem very suitable for busy lay devotees at home. For them it is best to follow the old Indian schedule of practice in six shorter but more frequent periods: three during the day and three at night.

The Benefits of Taking Refuge

When practicing the threefold refuge, one should be mindful of all the extraordinary benefits—the merits of taking refuge in the Three Treasures: becoming a devotee of the Buddha, having the foundation of the precepts, reducing karmic obstacles, accumulating vast blessings and merits, not falling into the evil destinies, not being disturbed by humans and nonhumans, accomplishing good deeds, and gaining the ability to attain buddhahood. If one can always be mindful of the merits of taking refuge in the Three Treasures and maintain one's practice, one can easily advance in the study of Buddhism.

14 Taking refuge in this way
Is most highly honored and supreme.
Taking refuge in other things will not
Provide bliss and security.

If one sincerely wants to take refuge, then it must be in the Three Treasures of Buddhism! One should differentiate between good and bad and not think that taking refuge in just any religion is the same. The founders, doctrines, and disciples of other religions cannot ultimately detach one from defilements. They do not have perfect virtues. Unable to save themselves, how can they be a place of refuge for others? If one takes refuge in non-Buddhists, one will receive neither the bliss of the conditioned merits nor the security of the unconditioned merits—Nirvāṇa's ultimate bliss.

The Essence of Taking Refuge

15 The aforementioned taking of refuge is,
In essence, the faithful vow;
Turning toward and following the Three Treasures,
Relying on them, people will be helped and saved.

What does taking refuge really mean? It refers to a deep faithful vow, a faith that this is the real place of refuge from which one can obtain various virtues. Knowing that the Three Treasures have such virtues, one vows to become a devotee of the Buddha, to have faith, to practice, and to earnestly request protection and acceptance from the virtuous Three Treasures. Taking refuge has this faithful vow as its foundation.

After taking refuge, one should give one's body and mind to the Three Treasures, not to demons or non-Buddhists. One should trust in the embrace of the Three Treasures at all times and in all places. A lost child who runs carelessly across busy streets full of cars and trucks is not just lost, he is in danger of being hurt. But then, seeing his mother, the child returns safely to her and falls into her arms. In taking refuge in the Three Treasures, one's frame of mind should be like this.

If one relies on the virtues of the Three Treasures with this attitude, one can be helped and saved. In Sanskrit, *sāraṇa* (taking refuge) also means to help and to save. The power of the virtues of the Three Treasures protects and embraces those who take refuge, enabling them to reach the land of permanent bliss that is without suffering. In short, for those who take refuge, taking refuge means being firmly established in faith and vows and asking the Three Treasures for their embrace and deliverance.

16 If one vows to devote one's life to them,
Through self-reliance and self-cultivation,
One can be unified with
The real meaning of taking refuge.

Generally speaking, to take refuge means to believe in and wish to receive external help so as to be saved. Although theistic religions are also dependent on an external power, the Buddha Dharma is distinct from these. In the Nirvāṇa Assembly, the Buddha gave his final teaching to his disciples: "Rely on yourself, rely on the Dharma, but do not rely on others."[13] He instructed them to rely on their own abilities and to study and practice by themselves according to the true Dharma, without being dependent on others. Similarly, in the *Śūraṅgama Sūtra*, Ānanda said, "Ever since I left home and followed the Buddha, I have thought that by relying on the Buddha's spiritual power I would not need to practice, and that the Tathāgata would endow me with enlightenment. I did not realize that one's body and mind cannot be replaced by others."[14] One has to learn and practice by oneself.

Thus, the profound meaning of taking refuge is to turn to oneself (one's mind, one's nature). One has the Buddha nature and can become a buddha; the essence of one's body and mind is the true Dharma, Nirvāṇa. If one practices by oneself according to the Dharma, then one's body becomes one with the Saṅgha. The Three Treasures of the Buddha, the Dharma, and the Saṅgha are not separate from oneself. One can attain and manifest all virtues through one's own body and mind. On the surface, taking refuge appears to mean believing in and relying on the protection of an external power; but on a more profound level, such faith and reliance are only helpful conditions that propel one's body and mind to realize one's wishes for protection and blessing.

Therefore, if one vows to devote one's life—the totality of one's body and mind—to the Three Treasures, and if one is able to practice the true Dharma through self-reliance and self-cultivation, and if one does not think (like Ānanda) that "relying on the Buddha's spiritual power, I do not need to practice," then one is in accord with the real meaning of taking refuge.

2

Attending to the Dharma to Enter the Path

AFTER TAKING REFUGE, one should hear more of the true Dharma, for only by doing so can one enter into the Buddhist way. Some people think: "The Buddha Dharma should be practiced. What is the use of hearing the Dharma? In the assembly of Śūraṅgama, the honorable Ānanda was always hearing, yet was unable to attain enlightenment,[1] and he was incapable of avoiding Mātaṅgī's enticement." They do not know that the honorable Ānanda's problem with "always hearing" was actually not a problem of hearing the Dharma. All the scriptures say that if one wants to learn and practice the Buddha Dharma, hearing the Dharma is a must. If one does not hear any of it, how can one learn about emancipation from birth and death, about the most blissful land and Amitābha Buddha, about the way to self-realization, about the true Dharma of Buddhism? If one does not listen to or hear anything, one will not even know about taking refuge in the Three Treasures!

THE BENEFITS OF HEARING

17 By hearing one knows all dharmas;
By hearing one can halt the advance of all evils;
By hearing one can end meaningless matters;
By hearing one can attain Nirvāṇa.

These are the verses in the scripture that praise the merits of hearing the Dharma.[2] It can be said that all the merits of the Buddha Dharma come from hearing the Dharma. Nāgārjuna Bodhisattva said there are three sources from which one should hear the Dharma: from the Buddha, from the Buddha's disciples, and from the scriptures.[3] To hear the Dharma from the Buddha and his disciples means hearing the spoken discourses. As the sūtra says, "The real teaching comes through listening to the sound of the teaching."[4] But since Śākyamuni Buddha has entered Nirvāṇa, we can hear the Dharma only from his disciples. Even though all the buddhas of the ten directions are expounding the Dharma, we cannot hear them speak unless we have learned and practiced to a very high level. Hearing the scriptures means to take the past as one's teacher and understanding the Buddha Dharma through reading the sūtras and discourses. Hearing the Dharma from the Buddha's disciples or from a reading of the sūtras are therefore both called attending to the Dharma. This is where the study of the Buddha Dharma begins.

The hearing of the true Dharma can be divided into four meritorious categories. (1) By hearing the Dharma one knows the dharmas. One knows the good dharmas, the bad dharmas, the faulty dharmas, the faultless dharmas, and so forth. After hearing about these, one knows them all; one knows what should be included in one's practice and what should be abandoned. (2) By hearing the true Dharma one halts all evils—evil thoughts or evil actions—both physical and verbal. When one knows about evil and its consequences, one can then put an end to it. (3) By hearing the true Dharma one puts an end to all sorts of meaningless matters. Some non-Buddhists, although they wish for emancipation, go astray and practice various ascetic deeds like fasting, refusing to sleep, going naked, and so on, thinking that with these ascetic behaviors they can attain the Way. Not only do they lead an ascetic life themselves, they teach others to do the same. The Buddha called these practices meaningless. They are foolish matters that bring suffering on oneself. Upon hearing the Buddha's true Dharma, one will naturally keep one's distance from them; one will practice the right way and not adopt non-Buddhist ways. (4) From listening to the true Dharma and practicing according to the proper way, one attains the emancipation of Nirvāṇa.

THE WAYS TO LISTEN

18 Like a vessel to hold water,
Like a seed to be planted in the ground,
One should avoid the three mistakes
By listening attentively, thoughtfully, and mindfully.

When the Buddha was teaching the true Dharma, he always exhorted his audiences by saying, "Listen attentively! Listen attentively! Think carefully and remember well!" He said this because if one listens to the Dharma improperly, one cannot receive the merit of hearing the Dharma. Two metaphors can illustrate the three mistakes to be avoided when attending to the Dharma.

First, suppose when it is raining one puts out vessels—bowls, cups or pots, etc.—to catch the rainwater. If one expects to use this water, one should avoid: (1) placing the bowl or cup upside down on the ground; (2) putting out a bowl or cup that has filthy or poisonous substances inside, so that the water obtained is harmful; (3) putting out a bowl or a cup that, although clean and poison free, is cracked and leaks. Inattention to the Dharma is similar. First, those who do not pay attention, do not concentrate, are like the upside-down bowl; even though they may listen, they do not hear. Second, people may concentrate on hearing the teachings but have prejudices, doubts, and perverted views—like the filth and poison in the bowl; then not only do they not develop merit from listening to the true Dharma, they may even commit the offense of slandering the Dharma. Third, people's minds may be without prejudices or doubts but nonetheless are scattered and busy; then, like the cracked bowl, they soon lose everything. If one attends to the Dharma like this—by making these three mistakes—one will not receive the merits of hearing the Dharma. So one should listen attentively, thoughtfully, and mindfully. RAIN

The second metaphor is of planting grain or beans: (1) Seeds scattered onto sand and rock will not germinate. (2) Seeds scattered onto soil covered with thick, coarse undergrowth may germinate but will not grow. (3) Seeds scattered onto fertilized soil clear of undesirable weeds will, if not planted deep enough, soon be eaten by birds. If seeds are sown like this, how can there be a harvest? Attending to the Dharma is similar: hearing the Dharma—being influenced through listening—is the Dharmic seed of the resolution to transcend the world. But if one is inattentive in receiving the Dharma or allows it to become contaminated after receiving it, or even if one's mind is pure but forgets the Dharma soon afterwards, then, having listened to the Dharma in this way, one will not get any results. If one wants to benefit from hearing the Dharma, therefore, one should avoid the three mistakes and be sure to hear well, consider well, and remember well. SEEDS

19 Think of oneself as being sick, in need of a doctor and medicine;
Thinking of the need to be treated intensively,
One should follow what one has learned and practice it.
The Buddha has said that the Dharma is like a mirror.

When listening to the Buddha Dharma, what attitude should one have? Śākyamuni Buddha said that he, the Tathāgata, appeared in this world for the sake of curing sentient beings' three physical illnesses—aging, sickness, and death—and their three mental illnesses—desire, anger, and ignorance.[5] In other words, the Buddha is the supreme medical doctor, the Dharma is the excellent medicine, and the Saṅgha is the nurse. The Three Treasures appear in this world for the relief of living beings' serious physical and mental illnesses. When listening to the Dharma, therefore, one should have the following thoughts.

First, one should think of oneself as sick, saying, "Since beginningless time, I have been entangled with serious physical and mental illnesses, suffering miserably and endlessly in the cycle of births and deaths." The fact that one has serious illnesses that lead to suffering must be firmly recognized. If one does not think that one is sick, or if one knows that one is sick but does not want any treatment, then there is no reason to seek the Buddha Dharma.

Second, one should think of needing a doctor. Having recognized that one's illnesses cannot be treated by ordinary people, one must seek the Buddha's disciples, those who teach the Dharma, the excellent doctors who can cure serious illnesses. Approach these good and knowledgeable people, therefore, and enlist their service with reverence and offerings, as do the sick who trust their doctors and courteously request treatment.

Third, one should think of needing medicine. A doctor administers medicine to treat illnesses; no one is cured just from reading the prescription. Those who teach the Dharma are like doctors in this way. After they have given instructions on the method of practice, one has to take this Dharma medicine. Otherwise, it is like reading the prescriptions only; this will not do any good. As the Buddha says in the sūtra, "Although I have proclaimed the excellent Dharma, if after you have heard it you do not practice, then you are like the sick man who only carries around bags of medicine; this will obviously not cure illnesses."[6]

Fourth, one should think of needing intensive treatment. The serious illnesses of birth and death are fatal. If one is fortunate, one may meet an excellent doctor with excellent medicine, which one must take for a long time before one can see therapeutic effects. However, many students of Buddhism want to see results immediately. Having practiced very little and not finding relief from the grave illness of birth and death, they are disappointed and become lazy. How can there be any hope if one does not practice diligently!

The Buddha Dharma is not just any kind of knowledge, much less is it a pastime. It is for persons who realize they are sick and in need of an excellent doctor and the medicine of the Dharma. One should follow what one has learned from the true Dharma, practicing with the utmost determination. "The Dharma is like a mirror," the Buddha said—it is for self-reflection.[7] The Buddha Dharma can be explained as that which one needs in order to see one's faults or merits. If one has a lot of faults, one should feel ashamed, repent, and stay away from them. If one has no faults, one should be happy. If one sees that one has merit, one should be happy; but if one has no merit, one should practice diligently. In short, attending to the Buddha Dharma gives one guidelines for one's practice. The most important thing is that you practice after you have heard it!

ENTERING THE PATH

THE METHOD: ASSOCIATING WITH GOOD AND KNOWLEDGEABLE PEOPLE

20 One who follows the true Dharma
Should associate with benevolent people.
Such people, knowing the true nature of the Dharma,
Have the virtues of realization and teaching,
As well as great compassion and eloquence.

Although one can understand the true Dharma by reading the sūtras, one needs to hear the Dharma primarily from those who teach it. The discourses prepared by those who teach the Dharma are understood more easily and more quickly than sūtras read by oneself. In order to follow the true Dharma to enter into buddhahood, therefore, one should associate with benevolent people—good and knowledgeable people, particularly those who are Mahāyānists. The Buddha has proclaimed that "to associate with benevolent people, to hear the true Dharma, to think properly, and to practice according to the Dharma"[8] are the four requirements for preparing oneself to enter the stream of the sages.

How does a person qualify as good and knowledgeable? Having a lot of disciples, a big temple, an appealing appearance, or a wealth of worldly knowledge does not qualify someone. Good and knowledgeable persons have five qualities. First, the virtue of realization: this includes the three studies of pure precepts, meditation, and wisdom. Second, the virtue of teaching: good and knowledgeable people must have studied widely and deeply all the sūtras so that they can teach the true Mahāyāna way. Third, knowledge of true nature—that is, the true Dharma. This is accomplished either directly by enlightened wisdom or indirectly through hearing and pondering the teachings. Fourth, compassion: to be compassionate means to be able to preach for the benefit of all sentient beings, not for the sake of fame and abundant offerings. Fifth, eloquence: with this quality one can preach skillfully and tactfully, and people will understand easily and receive benefits. If a person has attained all these virtues, then he or she is an extraordinarily good and knowledgeable person.

In this era of the decline of the Dharma, however, it is extremely difficult to encounter a such a person. Nevertheless, one needs good teachers and friends in order to practice the Buddha Dharma. So one may have to settle for the second best. A sūtra says: "One can associate with those who have one-eighth of the virtues."[9] The *Nirvāṇa Sūtra* talks about the four kinds of reliance—four kinds of people on whom one can rely as teachers. One group of people on whom others can rely are those who, although they have neither eliminated all afflictions nor realized the true nature, have understood one-sixteenth of the meaning of Buddha nature.[10] In short, because it is hard to meet a good and knowledgeable person in this period of the decline of the Buddhist teachings, you should properly associate with a person who is even just a little bit better than you in the understanding and the practice of the Buddha Dharma.

21 Observing their virtues and not their shortcomings,
One should follow their advice without resisting.
The Buddha has said this lofty conduct is complete.
Good people should be respected by those who learn from them.

Whether they are good and knowledgeable people with all the virtues or with just a few, if one does not associate with them properly, one will not receive the deserved merit. One should observe their virtues and not their shortcomings. For example, one can listen to their instructions, observe their good behavior (however moderate) and their way of getting along with people. In this way, one can receive the benefits of the Dharma even from a good and knowledgeable person with few virtues. If one observes only the shortcomings of such people and seizes upon their imperfections or inadequacies, on the other hand, then one will not receive any benefit—even if one meets a good and knowledgeable person with all the virtues. So when one associates with good and knowledgeable people, one should remind oneself: "Why am I here? I am not here to look for their faults but to learn about their good qualities." If one approaches learning in this way, one can have a teacher and one can obtain benefits, no matter where one is. Likewise, Confucius said, "When I am in the company of three people, one of them will certainly have something to teach me."[11]

In brief, to associate with good and knowledgeable people, one should follow the teacher's wishes. One should not resist the teacher's orders. If one is scolded, one should bear it without becoming angry. One should do this to please the teacher. One makes one's teacher happy by making offerings according to one's ability, by serving the teacher, and by practicing the teacher's instructions. In the Buddha Dharma, such conduct is expressed in the phrase "respect the teacher and the Way." If one's teacher wants one to do something that is not in accord with the Dharma, one should not follow the teacher's wishes, and gently explain the reason. In practicing the Buddha Dharma, it is impossible for one to attain its virtues if one cannot revere teachers properly. As it is said, "If people have persistent hatred, strong ill-will, or anger toward their teacher, there is no way they can receive merit."[12]

On one occasion when the Tathāgata praised the virtues of good and knowledgeable people, Ānanda said, "People who have half of the qualifications for pure conduct can already be called good and knowledgeable people." The Buddha replied, "Don't say that. Only people with completely pure conduct can be called good and knowledgeable people."[13] What Ānanda meant was that by associating with good and knowledgeable people, one is halfway to pure and lofty conduct. But according to the Buddha, by associating with good and knowledgeable people one may be said to have already completed pure and lofty conduct. How important the Buddha thought good and knowledgeable people were! The benefits of associating with them are explained in detail in the *Avataṃsaka Sūtra* and elsewhere.

The Requirements

Avoiding the Eight Obstacles

22 In order to listen to the Buddha Dharma, one must:
Avoid the three evil destinies,
Avoid being born in the Longevity Heavens;
Be born in a buddha age and in the central countries;
Have healthy sense organs and be without deviant views.

The ancients said, "It is difficult to encounter good and knowledgeable people, and it is rare to have the chance to hear the Buddha Dharma." If you have come across such a rare opportunity, do not think it is easy. One should know that in order to listen to the Buddha Dharma, one has to avoid eight obstructions. The first three obstructions are the three evil destinies from which one must be liberated: (1) being born in the hells, (2) being born as an animal, (3) being born as a hungry ghost. If one is born in any one of these three evil destinies, one has no opportunity to listen to the Dharma. Although the powerful king of ghosts, the king of dragons, and others attend to the Dharma, they cannot give up their worldly life to receive the precepts and follow the Buddha in practice. (4) One should also not be born in the Longevity Heavens. The Formless Realm has four heavens—infinite space, infinite consciousness, nothingness, and neither perception nor nonperception. For example, in the heaven of neither perception nor nonperception, the life span is eighty thousand great kalpas. The realm of form has the heaven of no-thought, where all beings also have extremely long lifetimes. According to the *Ba nan lun* (Treatise on the Eight Obstructions), all those who are born in these heavens are called beings of the Longevity Heavens, and they very rarely have the opportunity to listen to the Dharma and practice it. Therefore, one should avoid being born either in the heavens above or the three evil destinies below.

(5) Only as a human can one encounter this rare Buddha Dharma. Even as a human, however, one needs to be born in a buddha age, when a buddha has appeared and the Buddha Dharma still exists. If one were to be born before a buddha appears or after the Buddha Dharma has declined to the point of extinction, then even as a human, one will not have the opportunity to listen to the Buddha Dharma and to practice it.

(6) One also has to be born in the central countries. Central countries are defined relative to the borderlands. Wherever the Buddha or the Saṅgha preaches the Buddha Dharma, that is a central country; other places are borderlands. In the borderlands one cannot hear the Dharma.

(7) One has to have six healthy sense organs. If one is blind, deaf, dumb, psychotic, or retarded, then even being born in a buddha age and in a central country is still useless! (8) Even without these seven obstructions, if one is raised in a family with deviant views, or in a region of non-Buddhist religion, or in a non-Buddhist family or one with habitually distorted and deviant views, one has no opportunity to listen to the Buddha Dharma. These eight things, usually called eight obstructions, are obstacles to the study of Buddhism. In Sanskrit they are called *aṣṭākṣaṇa*, "eight that are without time," meaning eight situations that keep one from practicing the Buddha Dharma. We can see how happy we should be to have avoided them.

Attaining a Human Form

23 In the cycles of transmigration through birth and death,
It is hardest to become human.
The human abilities to recall, to have pure conduct, diligence and courage
Are superior to those of the various divine beings.

Some people think of life as very meaningless because they have low intelligence or poor living conditions. Thus they give in to self-blame, self-hate, or self-abuse and cannot set their mind on the study of the Buddha Dharma. They do not know that in the continual cycling of birth and death among the five destinies, it is most hard to become human. Being human is a rare opportunity, so one should not look down on oneself. There are two ways of looking at the difficulty of becoming human. First, in the cycles of transmigration through birth and death, those born in the evil destinies are as plentiful as the dirt on the ground, while those born in the good destinies are as scarce as the dust on one's fingernails. Those born in the good destinies, in the heavens, for example, may enjoy this state for a long time—until their stay there ends; then they usually fall back down. The rare chance of becoming human is analogous to the chance that a blind turtle swimming in the ocean will put its head through the hole of a plank of wood floating on the surface. One can see how unlikely that would be! But to be born a human in the cycles of transmigration through birth and death is just as difficult.

Second, although humans have much suffering and undesirable circumstances, it is actually very precious to be human. According to the sūtras, three human abilities—to recall, to have pure conduct, and to have diligence and courage—are not to be found among the beings of the evil destinies and are superior to the abilities of the various divine beings.[14] Humans can recall the past and preserve experiences, which gives them a particularly well-developed ability to think and to reason. This is superiority in recall. A person can, by disregarding material gain and practicing self-control, become physically and mentally pure and thus benefit other people. Some people do control themselves and devote themselves to these aims, and their moral spirit is potentially very great. This is superiority in pure conduct. In order to reach a goal, a person can endure suffering and hardship, working diligently and courageously until the goal is achieved. This is superiority in diligence and courage. These qualities are generally similar to the three virtues of wisdom, benevolence, and courage in Confucianism.

Among all the sentient beings, therefore, humans are the most precious. People who become virtuous sages, buddhas, or patriarchs all respect this potential for human greatness and strive diligently to realize their achievements. When a divine being is dying, according to the sūtras, others will say, "We hope that you are born in the path of happiness." The happy land they wish for is the human world. The human body is the happy land that the divine beings desire, so as a human how can one indulge in self-blame and self-pity and let this life pass emptily?

24 It is hard to become human, but having become human
One should vigorously practice the Dharma.
Do not waste time; this is like entering the mountain of treasure
And returning empty-handed and with regret.

Since it is hard to obtain a human form, one should be very happy to seize this precious opportunity and vigorously practice the true Dharma. Life is impermanent. "Life is just in between inhalation and exhalation," says a sūtra,[15] so one should not wait for tomorrow, next year, or the distant future to practice. One should take this great opportunity to march bravely forward through the door of the Buddha Dharma. If one spends one's time idly and wastes one's life, when the breath stops one will have attained nothing of the Buddha Dharma. This is like entering a mountain of treasure and seeing all kinds of wonderful things but not having the sense to gather some. When one's time is up, leaving the mountain empty-handed, one sighs with regret. If one does not work hard while one is alive, what good will it be to feel sorry when one is dying?

THE GOAL: THE MUTUALLY DEPENDENT THREE LEVELS OF MOTIVATION

25 So, after hearing the Dharma, one should vow to practice it.
But because of people's different capacities,
The Dharma may appear differently to each of them.

After associating with good and knowledgeable people and hearing the true Dharma, one should resolve to practice it. "To resolve" means to have a firm determination to move forward and to follow that determination as a goal. It means to decide to do something with faith and determination.

When the Tathāgata or a great bodhisattva is preaching to a single listener, in order to suit the capacity of that person the teacher chooses doctrines at the appropriate level. The Tathāgata had such inconceivable transcendent powers, however, that even when a great assembly heard him, different listeners all thought that the Buddha was preaching in the words they wanted to hear. So it is said: "The Buddha uses one language to expound the Dharma, while sentient beings understand it each in their own way."[16] It is harder for the average teacher of the Dharma to use "one language to expound the Dharma" in different ways, or to differentiate between people's capacities. Such teachers can only expound what they understand and practice, or the doctrines that most people can understand and practice. But the audience's capacities may not be compatible.

Some people learn from reading the sūtras, whether randomly, systematically, or according to others' recommendations. There is, however, no guarantee that whatever they come across will correspond to their capacities. For example, the esoteric methods are popular in Tibet, Hīnayāna Buddhism is popular in South Asia, and the Ch'an (Zen) sect was once extremely popular in China. Can it be said that all Tibetans have a propensity for the esoteric, that everyone in South Asia has a propensity for Hīnayāna Buddhism, and that all Chinese previously had a propensity for sudden enlightenment? The nature and character that one has depend primarily on the resolution one has made. Do not think that by reading, reciting, accepting, or keeping certain doctrines you automatically have a capacity that corresponds with them.

In the past, there was a lama in Tibet who practiced the esoteric methods to become a buddha, but ended up as a śrāvaka. Someone asked a good and knowledgeable person about this and he said, "If someone attains the Hīnayāna fruit by practicing the esoteric method, that is not so bad. Some who have practiced it have become devils and non-Buddhists!" Therefore, one should not become attached to or have any bias toward so-called great and wonderful methods. It is more important to examine one's own resolution.

26 People of the lower grade want to have better future lives
And happiness in the present and in the future.
People of the middle grade vow to leave the three realms
And to enjoy the bliss of liberation in Nirvāṇa.
People of the upper grade vow to attain bodhi
With great compassion, wisdom, and ultimate bliss.

Although the resolution to reach a high level through practice varies tremendously, the varieties can be grouped into three: the resolution to have better future lives, the resolution to leave the three realms, and the resolution to attain enlightenment. These are what Maitreya Bodhisattva described as the resolutions of the lower, middle, and upper people.[17]

In the Buddha Dharma, people of the lower grade—in the world at large they are superior people—vow to have better future lives. A better future life is one with greater and more plentiful rewards than in this life: a person's appearance, life span, fame, wealth, status, family, knowledge, ability, health, and harmony and friendship will all be better. From the perspective of the Buddha Dharma, this is not ultimate but is acceptable because such upward progress is obtained through means that are permitted by Buddhist ethics.

This lower grade has two subgroups: those who want to be born in the world and those who want to be born in the heavens. Both groups of people want happiness in the present and in the future. By practicing according to the Buddha Dharma, they can receive happiness in the present and rewards in the future. Under certain circumstances it is all right to suffer and sacrifice a little in the present in order to have future blessings and happiness. Having happiness in the present and in the future is the ideal, but if there is no alternative, suffering now and having happiness in the future is acceptable. Those who enjoy the present but think they will experience future suffering, or make themselves suffer needlessly now thinking that it will bring future happiness (but instead experience boundless suffering in the future), have gone wrong and are engaged in deviant practices that do not belong to the Tathāgata's true Dharma. People of the lower grade—who resolve to attain better fortune and happiness as humans and divine beings—will, even if they practice the Dharma to leave the cycle of births and deaths—only receive the reward of becoming a human or divine being. (But one who has made such a vow and then does various evil deeds that have a strong karmic force will travel the three evil destinies, and certainly will not move upward.) Despite all their progress, they will transmigrate within the three realms and not be able to reach the ultimate. For example, those born in the heavens go from the realm of desire to the realm of form, then from the realm of form to the formless realm, and eventually to the heaven of neither perception nor nonperception, where they cannot move higher. When that karmic force comes to an end, they start to fall back down.

When one profoundly understands this—when one feels that "the three realms are not safe; they are like a house on fire"—one resolves to leave the three realms' cycle of birth and death. Such is the resolve of people of the middle grade. If one can have such a resolution and practice the Dharma that transcends the world, then one can be free from birth and death and enjoy the bliss of liberation in Nirvāṇa. Obtained by leaving behind all afflictions, the bliss of liberation is completely different from the worldly happiness, which can turn into sorrow. It is completely free from the transmigratory cycles of birth and death and is thus superior to the rewards obtained by the lower people.

Within this middle stage, there are also two subgroups, the Śrāvaka Vehicle and the Pratyekabuddha Vehicle. Together they are called the "Two Vehicles." In general, the resolutions and results of these Two Vehicles are similar. As explained above, anyone who vows only to leave the three realms will at most attain the fruit of the Small Vehicle, even if he or she practices the superior Dharma of the Great Vehicle. On the other hand, if one vows to leave the three realms but does not practice the corresponding deeds or does evil deeds that do not accord with the Dharma, then one will not even get the good reward of becoming a human or heavenly being, for the force of one's karma will be stronger than the power of one's resolution.

The middle grade people's vow to leave the three realms, although it is said to be ultimate, is not lofty enough. Their situation can be compared to passengers of a sinking ship who end up in the water. One who swims fiercely to the shore and then, without concern for fellow passengers still in the water, comfortably lies down to rest—such a person, though out of danger, is certainly incomplete as far as human virtues are concerned. Some people want not only to benefit themselves by attaining liberation but also to combine their self-help with help for others, and their own benefit with benefit for others. They hope to reach the other shore along with all sentient beings. But how can one achieve this? Only the Buddha can accomplish this great vow. Only the Buddha's great wisdom, great compassion, great vow, and great power can completely save all sentient beings. However, one can have the Buddha as one's role model and have the great vow to become a buddha.

People of the highest grade make this vow. This is bodhi mind—the resolution to attain enlightenment (*bodhi* in Sanskrit). Buddhahood is the supreme universal enlightenment, which has great enlightenment as its center and includes all virtues. Developing bodhi mind means making a great determination to attain buddhahood. After one has initiated bodhi mind, practiced the bodhisattva deeds, and benefited oneself and others, then, when one attains perfection and completion, one can become a buddha. Endowed with great compassion and great wisdom, one can have the ultimate bliss of Nirvāṇa. With this goal of attaining buddhahood and transforming sentient beings as one's foundation, one vows to practice accordingly. Only in this way can a person be of the highest grade with the highest vow. May all who study Buddhism achieve this goal and practice!

27 On the lower levels, upper levels can be built;
But the higher levels include the lower ones.
Because of people's various capacities, the Five and the Three Vehicles are different.
But to return to the ultimate, there is only one Great Vehicle.

Although the Buddha Dharma is divided into lower, middle, and upper, the ultimate goal of each is becoming a buddha. Thus they are neither independent nor unrelated; in fact, the relationships among these different levels are those of mutual dependency and mutual inclusiveness, as is shown in the accompanying diagram.

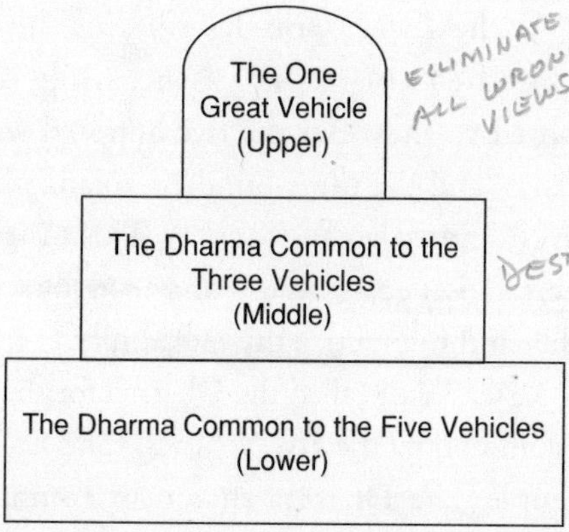

In this three-story pagoda, there is a dependent and inclusive relationship from the bottom story to the top. With the bottom level as a foundation, the middle level can be built; and only with the lower and middle levels as foundations can the top level be built. If one wants to build the top level without constructing the lower and middle levels first, one is bound to fail.

In the three categories of the Buddha Dharma, likewise, the Dharma of the middle grade is built upon the lower grade, and the Dharma of the higher grade upon the middle. This is similar to what Nāgārjuna Bodhisattva says: "After having better future lives, one can bring forth superior resolution."[18] The superior resolution is the Dharma for ultimate liberation practiced by the middle and higher grades. The sequence of these levels was originally described in the *Āgama Sūtra* as the Dharma common to all buddhas. Deva Bodhisattva also says, "First, stop all wrong deeds, then destroy the ego, and finally eliminate all wrong views. Knowing these things, one has gained good skills."[19] "Stopping all wrong deeds" is the Dharma for the lower people. They are advised to abandon evil and do good. "Destroying the ego" is the Dharma for the middle people. This emphasizes the emancipation characterized by the nonexistence of the self. "Eliminating all wrong views" is the Dharma for the higher people. This directs them to stop all elaboration. Only by knowing this proper sequence can one practice the Buddha Dharma skillfully. Therefore, Deva Bodhisattva also said, "The Buddha has spoken of this as convenience, like a set of stairs."[20]

As with the three-story pagoda, in which the top level rests on the middle and lower levels, the Dharma for the higher people includes the Dharma for the middle people, which in turn includes the Dharma for the lower people. As the *Lotus Sūtra* describes it, the path of the Two Vehicles is three hundred yojanas in extent, while that of the Great Vehicle is five hundred yojanas. But the five hundred yojanas include the three hundred yojanas, and the three-hundred-yojana mark is close to the midpoint of the five-hundred-yojana journey. This insight into the inclusiveness of the vehicles is necessary for one to embrace all the Buddha Dharmas thoroughly and to practice them skillfully.

The Venerable Master Taixu called the Dharma for the lower people "the Dharma shared in common by the Five Vehicles," and he called the Dharma for the middle people "the Dharma shared in common by the Three Vehicles." In his *Great Treatise on the Sequence of Attaining Enlightenment*, the Venerable Master Tsongkhapa called the Dharma for the lower people "the Dharma shared in common by the lower people," and the Dharma for the middle people "the Dharma shared in common by the middle people." Here the phrase "shared in common" reflects the right view that was, without discussion, agreed upon by these two wise men—one Chinese and one Tibetan; and this coincidental agreement is also the distinctive sign of these three grades' mutual dependence and mutual inclusiveness.

Therefore, in order to suit people's various capacities, the Buddha Dharma is skillfully differentiated into Five Vehicles—the Human, Divine, Śrāvaka, Pratyekabuddha, and Bodhisattva. When the Buddha spoke of the Three Vehicles—Śrāvaka, Pratyekabuddha, and Bodhisattva—he emphasized the teaching of renunciation. For people with different capacities, of course, the doctrines have to be different. The Buddha also spoke of the differences between these Three Vehicles, but all are simply ways to become a buddha. To return to the ultimate, there is only the One Vehicle, the Great Vehicle. This is not to say that all sentient beings must become buddhas, nor is it to say that having the One-Vehicle teaching is all that is needed to return to the ultimate. What it actually means is that from the standpoint of the Buddha Dharma, all Buddha Dharmas (higher, middle, and lower) lead eventually to the One Vehicle of becoming a buddha—the Great Vehicle Dharma. This can be illustrated by those of the Śrāvaka Vehicle (middle-grade people) who practice deeds for leaving the world and attaining Nirvāṇa. During the Lotus Dharma assembly, the Buddha proclaimed that the Śrāvaka Vehicle's practice was a skillful teaching because these people were actually practicing the Great Vehicle Dharma. Therefore, the Buddha said, "What you have practiced has been the bodhisattva way."[21] The *Da zhi du lun* (reconstructed Sanskrit title: Mahāprajñāpāramitopadeśa Śāstra) also says: "The two vehicles' renunciation and wisdom are the same as the Bodhisattvas' realization of no rebirth,"[22] and the *Lotus Sūtra*: "Reciting but once 'Namo Buddha,' they have attained buddhahood."[23] Even the offering of one stick of incense or one flower, the simple movement of the hands and head in prostration, and the chanting of the Buddha's name—all these practices for the human and divine vehicles—are included within the One Vehicle Dharma to become a buddha.

Some people think that the One Vehicle and the Great Vehicle are different, but they are actually the same. For example, the *Lotus Sūtra* and the *Śrīmālāsiṁhanāda Sūtra* both describe the One Vehicle Dharma, which at times they call the Great Vehicle. The terms are usually used in different contexts, however. The term "Great Vehicle" is most frequently used in contrast to the "Two Vehicles," while "One Vehicle" is usually used to explain that all Dharmas to become a buddha are included within a single vehicle. Similarly, if the emphasis is on the causal stage, then this vehicle is called the Bodhisattva Vehicle, while if the emphasis is on the merits of the resultant stage, it is called the Buddha Vehicle. These different names accord with different meanings. But in the entire course of practicing the Buddhist way, all the vehicles are included without differentiating superior and inferior.

28 So one should not become stuck at the middle or the lower levels,
Nor should one abandon them.
One should completely include them while progressing toward
the Buddha Vehicle
And not slander the true Dharma.

In practicing the Buddhist way, one should not become stuck. If one stagnates in the middle or lower levels (that is, the Hīnayāna way or the human and divine ways), this is not in accord with the Tathāgata's original purpose. This would be like someone who, heading to Fuyan temple from the town of Xinzhu, stops on the way to look at the nice scenery and gets stuck there. If one does not ascend the Guanyin Plateau and continue on to Fuyan temple, how can one get to see the panorama—the mountain, lake, ocean, and the reflection of the pagoda! Developing bodhi mind and taking as one's goal "becoming a buddha," one should not abandon the Dharma of the middle and lower people. All of the Dharma is the Bodhisattva Way and the doctrine for becoming a buddha. Some people, seeking something superior and wonderful, think that Mahāyānists do not need the Dharma for the middle or lower people. But if they do not reach the three-hundred-yojana resting point first, they will never arrive at the precious palace at five hundred yojanas! Therefore, practitioners should include the middle and lower Dharma within the Buddha Vehicle; they should not aim unrealistically high or yearn for the higher mysteries without paying attention to the fundamentals. And although there are infinite doors opening to it, the Dharma has only "one flavor"; one should not complicate it.

Two types of people needlessly twist the true Dharma out of shape. The first are those who think a certain sūtra or a certain Dharma is not the Buddha Dharma. This type of slandering can be easily recognized by others, who avoid such people. The second are who think they have such great capacities that they do not need the middle and lower Dharmas or who think that the doctrines of karma, good and evil, etc., are for lower, stupid people and have nothing to do with them. There are also people who think that within the Mahāyāna Dharma they need only a certain sūtra (or even half of it), a certain Buddha, or a certain mantra and that this obviates any need for other teachings. Some people also think that they do not need the sūtras; they only really need to practice. All of these people have something in common—they abandon the infinite sūtras and the boundless methods for practice. They take one drop of water and abandon the ocean, thinking the entire ocean is in the one drop. If the mistake is made only by these foolish and stubborn people, it is of minor significance; but for the propagation of the Buddha Dharma, it becomes an enormous obstacle. Slandering the true Dharma in this way is the result of not knowing the principles of the Buddha Dharma. As it is said in the treatises, "To have faith without wisdom enhances ignorance."[24] How horrible this ignorance is!

PART II

The Divisions of the Teachings

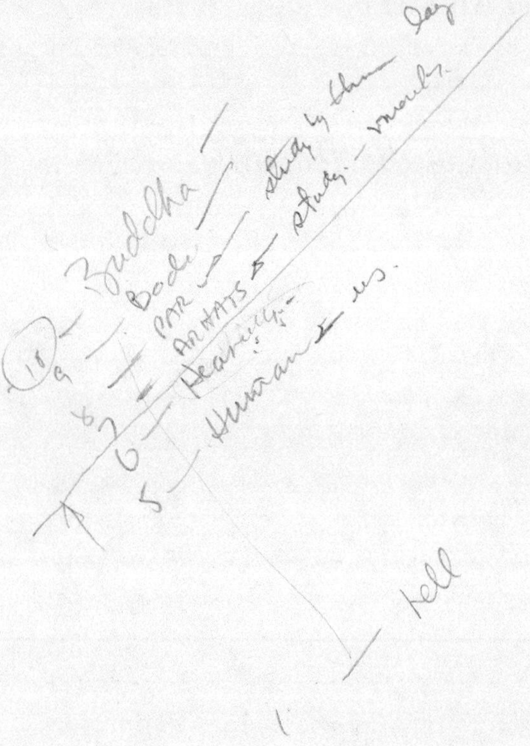
10
9
8
7
6
5
1
Buddha
ARHATS
Human
us.
Hell

3

The Dharma Common to the Five Vehicles

RESOLVING TO HAVE better future lives and practicing the various proper methods for rebirth as a human or divine being is the Buddhist way for lower people. This is also the foundation of the world-transcending Dharma and is thus called the Dharma common to the Five Vehicles. Even though one is not ultimately seeking human or divine rewards, these rewards are still required for the practice of the world-transcending Dharma of the Three Vehicles. This process is analogous to going to Taipei city from Xinzhu: although one does not get off at the town of Taoyuan, one must pass through it.

If one's goal is to be born in the human world or in heaven, one is participating in the Human Vehicle or the Divine Vehicle. These vehicles are aspects of the Buddha Dharma that are shared in common with the world's religions. Confucianism is similar to the Human Vehicle, while Taoism, Christianity, and Islam can lead to the Divine Vehicle. Since people can thus reach the goals of rebirth in the world or in heaven by following the other religions of the world, one might ask why they should take refuge in the Three Treasures and practice the Buddha Dharma common to the Five Vehicles. In fact, the Buddha Dharma does not say that whoever wants to be born as a human or divine being must take refuge in the Three Treasures and practice the Buddhist, Human, and Divine Vehicles. Taking refuge in the Three Treasures and practicing the Dharma common to the Five Vehicles is more secure than following other religions, however. When a person takes refuge and practices the Dharma, that person thereby enters the great door of the Buddha Vehicle. One then only needs to move upwards diligently in order to enter the world-transcending Dharma. Although a person can be born as a human or divine being by believing in other religions, one does not in this way accumulate good causes in relation to the Three Treasures. Such beliefs may also lead to some unnecessary stubbornness—that is, religious prejudice—that blocks the desire to enter the great way of the world-transcending Dharma, having been born in human and heaven realms.

29 One who has the right faith and has taken refuge in the Three Treasures
Should cultivate right views
And practice right livelihood;
Then it will not be difficult to make superior progress.

A person who has right faith in the Three Treasures and takes refuge in them is the Buddha's disciple, a Buddhist. Where should one start if, as a Buddhist, one wants to practice the Dharma common to the Five Vehicles? To understand Buddhism, one should first cultivate right views. To practice Buddhism, one should start with right livelihood. The Buddha has said that those with right views and right livelihood are rare. If one can practice these two things successfully, it will not be difficult to make superior progress.

Right view means correct understanding. Views are different from knowledge; they are firm opinions derived from reasoning. Right views are what one has chosen as good, and one should follow them. As an analogy, if one wants to go on a trip, one needs to knows the right route to reach the destination. Right recognition of the way things are does not necessarily become a commonly held right view. For example, it is now known that the earth revolves around the sun. This is knowledge, and Galileo, for the sake of this knowledge, was not afraid to be persecuted and imprisoned by the Christians. This is an example of a firm opinion. One should apply right knowledge, constantly practice it, and nurture firm right views.

There are worldly right views and world-transcending right views. In the Dharma common to the Five Vehicles, the right views are worldly ones. Although they are only firmly held beliefs, they are very powerful. As the sūtra says: "If someone has strong right views, that person will not fall into the evil destinies for thousands of lives."[1]

RIGHT LIVELIHOOD

What is right livelihood? Livelihood is the process of making a living. Whether one is a lay or monastic person, one has to make a living. Legally obtaining all of life's necessities such as clothing, food, lodging, and transportation is called right livelihood. Having a proper economic life is very important since the majority of crimes are caused by an improper economic livelihood. For Buddhist lay devotees, an occupation should not only be permitted by secular laws but also be in accord with the Buddha Dharma. Occupations based on killing (slaughtering, hunting), stealing, sexual misconduct (prostitution, brothel operations), lying (con-artistry), and intoxicants (making wine, operating bars) do not accord with the precepts of the Buddha Dharma. They are not upright occupations and they obstruct the practice of the Buddha Dharma. As for the monastics, as long as they live on offerings from devotees, that is the right livelihood for them. If they also, on the side, practice medicine (except when purely on a volunteer basis) or fortune telling (astrology, palmistry, and so on), or cheat devotees of their offerings, then they have a deviant means of livelihood. Right livelihood means using properly gained economic resources in a way that is neither wasteful nor miserly. Only in this way can one live in accord with the Buddha Dharma; otherwise there is no guarantee one will be a human again, let alone attain liberation from birth and death!

During the Sino-Japanese War, a Buddhist devotee living in a large and quiet villa in Hong Kong practiced chanting the Buddha's name with utmost sincerity. He wrote to Venerable Master Yin Guang and requested him to leave the war zone and come stay with him in Hong Kong. Master Yin found out from him that his family had been wine makers for generations. The master asked him to stop the wine business before he came to Hong Kong, but the old devotee was reluctant to give it up. Studying Buddhism but not practicing right livelihood may be the reason that Chinese Buddhism has declined. Even though changing one's occupation may lead to temporary suffering, one should discontinue a livelihood that is harmful to oneself and others.

RIGHT VIEWS

30 The aforementioned right views
Are the correct understanding of life.

What exactly are the aforementioned right views? In its worldly meaning, right view is a correct understanding of life, a correct outlook. Right views are those that one firmly believes in, based on a correct investigation into the meaning of life and the path to follow. For those who practice the Buddha Dharma, right views are indispensable, like the rudder of a ship. The Buddha has said that those who have right views are rare, particularly among lay devotees. For example, a person who has sincere faith in the Three Treasures, is charitable, and understands Buddhist teachings would appear to be a typical good Buddhist. But upon becoming senile such a person might, for example, listen to other people's false advice about nutrition, to the point that even after being a vegetarian for decades he begins to kill animals. Also some people who have incurable chronic illnesses seek help from spirits, from fortune tellers, from saints, or from anything else they think worth trying. Some, being poor financially, ask for help from the god of wealth or, hoping to win the lottery, go to a temple to ask an immortal to inform them in their dreams of the right lottery number. Some practice diligently but, when they get old, cultivate their life essence and energy just like non-Buddhists for the sake of their continuously aging and ever weakening body. A few years ago a learned and cultivated Buddhist in Taipei had a transplant of a monkey's pituitary gland for just this reason—and ended up dying from it. Such people are unable to firmly hold onto their beliefs. When their health and finances deteriorate, they waver.

Those who study Buddhism should not talk eagerly about ending birth and death or attaining enlightenment; they should cultivate right views first.

The Existence of Good and Evil

31 Whether one's mind is pure or defiled,
Whether one's deeds are beneficial or harmful to others,
Whether one's actions are good or evil,
Buddhists should observe these questions carefully.

The worldly right views spoken by the Buddha are found in specific sections of the sūtra. They can be roughly divided into four categories. The first category concerns good and evil in our thoughts and actions—that is, the ethical and unethical. The right views of the Buddha Dharma start with firmly seeing the presence of ethics, first in the world and then eventually beyond the world. People who strongly oppose ethics hold deviant views, as do, for example, the six Indian heterodox teachers, the skeptics, and materialistic communists.

What are good and evil? With regard to mental factors: if it is pure, it is good; if it is defiled, it is evil. There are always some defiled factors in the mind that lead to irritation and afflictions. If these defiled factors do not arise, and only pure factors do, this is good. Good factors are those that are without greed, without anger, without ignorance. They include the sense of shame that longs for what is good, the sense of integrity that resists evil, beliefs that lead to mental purity, and the vigor to practice what is right. On the other hand, greed, anger, ignorance, shamelessness, lack of integrity, lack of faith, and indolence are all defiling and evil.

As for deeds affecting others, those that benefit them are good and those that harm them are evil. Because relationships exist among people and between people and other sentient beings, everyone should cooperate, help one another, and live harmoniously. If what one does is harmful to others, then even if it benefits oneself, it is evil and should not be done. If it benefits others but may harm oneself, it is still good and should be done.

Whether a deed is good or evil depends internally on the intentions and externally on the effects. Deeds are actions. Actions in the mind are mental deeds, physical actions are bodily deeds, verbal actions are spoken deeds. There are good and bad among all of these. All Buddhists, those disciples of the Buddha who have inherited the Buddha's work, should observe these categories carefully. One not only has to have firm faith in the existence of good and evil, one also has to differentiate between the two. People should cultivate firm, unshakable right views as the standard for both thoughts and actions.

The Existence of Karma (Actions) and Consequences

32 Karma can definitely lead to retribution or reward.
Karma can change from small to large,
Can guide or complete the stages of fruition,
Is both determined and undetermined,
And can bring retribution or reward now, in the next life, or in the more distant future.
No karma will be destroyed before retribution comes.

The second right view is of the existence of karma and its results. Most people recognize that good and evil exist. In addition, it must be understood that as a consequence of good or evil actions, there are corresponding rewards or retributions. If a person does not have firm views about this, that person's belief in and understanding of the principles of good and evil will be shaken under certain circumstances. In the past, there was a loyal government official who was soon to be executed by order of the king. Before he died, this official told his son, "I want to teach you to do evil, but evil should not be done. I want to teach you to do good, but I have really not done any evil!"[2] He himself had done only good but had not received any good reward, so he became confused about the principle of good and evil. In addition to the right view of good and evil, one also needs the right view of karmic rewards and retribution.

Rewards and retribution are definitely brought about by karmic forces. Whenever there is an action (karma), there is a result. Because karma is multifaceted and complicated, so too are rewards and retributions. Karma is what one does, one's actions—mental, physical, or verbal. When some action is initiated by thinking or volition, karma comes into play. The focus of the present discussion is whether the propelling motive that causes our physical, verbal, and mental activities is good or evil; there is a value attached to actions depending on whether they are ethical or unethical. Deeds, doing good or doing evil, resemble the work of a laborer. The karmic force is like the salary earned from that work—money. The money that one gets as a result of working, representing the value of the work, can be exchanged for usable commodities.

Because of certain karmic forces, one obtains certain karmic results. Results are profoundly significant in that they mature differently. The cause differs from the effect. For example, one does good deeds and obtains the joys of the heavenly kingdoms; one does evil deeds and falls into the hells to suffer. Understanding that suffering as a retribution, and happiness as a reward, depend on the karmic force of what one has done is an important aspect of the right view.

A few aspects of the meaning of karmic result should be addressed here. First, a small karmic force can be changed into a large one. This means that a trifling good or bad action, if continuously repeated, will accumulate and become a very strong karmic force. As written in the *Dharmapada*, "Do not take minor acts of evil karma lightly, thinking they are harmless; they are like drops of water that eventually fill a big vessel."[3] Good karma is also like that. This is reminiscent of the ancient Chinese saying, "Do not perform an evil act just because it happens to be trifling; do not abandon doing good just because it is trivial." If one harms others, this evil karma may not initially be a big problem; yet if one constantly feels satisfied with one's evil, the force of small evils will equal that of a great evil. Similarly, if one constantly rejoices in even tiny good actions, they will gradually become like a great good deed. So we should neither neglect small actions nor rejoice in evil deeds, and we should rejoice in good deeds.

Second, there is a type of particularly strong karmic force that can lead us to one of the five destinies—being born in heaven, in the hells, as animals, etc. Among each of these states there are different categories; for example, among animals there are tigers, fish, and so forth. The strong karma that brings about the formation of the total resultant body of a sentient being in a certain destiny (the aggregates, sense organs, and the realms of the sense organs) is called the guiding karma.

There is another kind of karma that does not lead to the general aspects of the resultant body (which is born and dies) but rather completes many specific aspects of this resultant body. This karma is called completion karma. For example, although there are many differences among those who are born as humans, humans all have the same general form; this is the general result of guiding karma. As for the specific aspects, some have six healthy sense organs and some do not; some have dignified appearances and some are ugly; some have dark complexions and some are fair; some have bright eyes and some do not; some speak with beautiful voices and some with coarse, and so on. These differences among humans are influenced by completion karma; they are caused by the different karmic results and the different levels of effort and cultivation in people's present lives. For example, because of the karmic force, the distance of human vision has a certain fixed range (which also varies among humans). Through medication, nutrition, care, and training, however, one can expand this range or retain good vision into old age. Whether one does so depends upon one's effort and cultivation in the present life.

The third pertinent aspect of karma is that it comprises determinate karma and indeterminate karma, both of which differ in terms of timing and results. The results of some karma are determinate, but their timing—whether they occur in this life or the next—is indeterminate. For other karma, the timing is determinate but the type of result is indeterminate. In some cases, both results and timing are determinate—for example, the five actions that lead to uninterrupted hell: patricide, matricide, killing of arhats, shedding a buddha's blood, and disrupting the harmony of the Saṅgha. All these lead to the hell realms in the very next life. In other cases, both results and timing are indeterminate; this is generally true for light karma. But according to an ancient master's saying, *all* karma is indeterminate. In other words, all karma has the possibility of being improved. Therefore with strong determination, the results of all evil karma can be transformed from heavy to light or even to indeterminate results.

The *Yan yu jing* (Sūtra on the Salt Analogy) explains that if one commits an extremely evil action, it is only necessary that there be enough time to make amends. This is difficult to do if one is old or dying. According to the *Amitāyurdhyāna Sūtra* (Sūtra on the Contemplation of Amitāyus Buddha), however, reciting Amita Buddha's name helps alleviate the results of serious evil karma. If one has enough determination—if one cultivates the body, practices the precepts, and develops the mind (practices meditation) and wisdom—even extremely evil karma will bring only light or indeterminate retribution. This lessening of karmic retribution can be compared to throwing large amounts of salt into a wide river: doing so will not make the water salty. On the other hand, if one commits smaller offenses and does not know how to cultivate the body, practice the precepts, and develop wisdom, one will certainly get bitter results. This can be compared to putting a small quantity of salt into a small cup: the water will become bitterly salty.[4] That the results can change depending on one's actions is strong proof that karma is indeterminate. In the Dharma of the Great Vehicle, karma is viewed as empty, which means it can change and that one can repent serious offenses; this is what cultivating wisdom means. Therefore, one should not be discouraged by extremely evil karma; one should repent deeply and practice the Buddha Dharma.

The fourth relevant aspect of karma is that the temporality of karma and its results can be grouped into three periods: (1) the karma of present results, or karma that brings results in this life; (2) the karma of rebirth results, or karma that brings results in the next life; (3) the karma of later results, or the karma that brings results after one life, two lives, or even thousands of lives. One should therefore not just look at the present life when examining karma and its results. It is said, "One does evil but gets happiness because the evil has not matured. When it matures, one will suffer. One does good but gets suffering because the good has not matured. When it matures, one will get happiness."[5] In these three periods of karma, the present results can be the result of light karma or the "flower result" of serious karma (it is like the flower that precedes the fruit). Because the reward or retribution of the present life is the result of past good or evil karmic forces, there cannot be any fundamental or serious changes in it before one dies.

Light karma can have present results because it does not seriously change one's retributions or rewards in this life. For example, the government in power has its own fundamental policies and cannot change them significantly. However, if the opposition party has some minor suggestions, the current regime may be willing to accept them.

Why does serious karma have a "flower result," as distinct from the final reward or retribution in the future? Because this karmic force is too strong to make an impact on the present body. This is similar to situations in which the power of the opposition party is very strong. In such cases, the present regime must accept some of the opposition's suggestions and will do so to the extent that it does not endanger the existence of the current regime or party policies. Similarly, karma that brings results in future rebirths also has both light and serious results.

In short, karma is of different kinds, but all share this one quality: if one is not enlightened and emancipated, then no karma will be destroyed until it has brought about its result. When there is karma, there is reward or retribution; though it may not be in this life, in the next life, or even after thousands of lives, the karmic force still exists and will bring its result when the conditions are right. The introduction of the *San mei shui chan* (Samādhi-water Repentance) says that during the western Han dynasty (206 B.C.–A.D. 24), because of Yuanang's vilification, Chaocuo was killed. The karma that Yuanang created by instructing others to kill did not bring retribution until the late Tang dynasty (A.D. 618–907)—to Wuda, the emperor's teacher. When Wuda coveted the high status of the Aguru Seat, only then did the past evil karma manifest, in the shape of an ulcer with a humanlike face that formed on his knee. This legend illustrates the meaning of karmic forces not being destroyed.

The Existence of Past and Future Lives

> 33 According to karma, good or bad results arise
> In the constant transmigrations through the five destinies.
> Results may be caused by serious karma, one's daily habits,
> Or the thoughts of one's dying moments.
> The power of karma leads to future rebirths
> Like the flames that continue to burn the wood.

The third basic right view is that there are past lives and future lives. Most people can confidently accept that good or evil deeds have results, but some people believe only in present actions and present results, not those of the future. Whether one does good or evil, however, an immediate result is rarely obtained. Some people have the misconception that "heaven above is ignorant" because they do not get immediate results. Other people believe that the results of good or evil will happen only to their descendants. As the Chinese saying goes, "The family that accumulates good deeds will have much good fortune in future generations, while the family that accumulates evil deeds will experience many disasters." In general, these are the two types of misconceptions held by Chinese people with regard to the merits of virtuous deeds done in private. However, many people ignore that in this world some virtuous fathers have bad sons and vice versa. Had they no descendants, moreover, would their good or evil karma have come to nothing?

Some people, Christians for example, believe only in the present life and a future life but not in past lives. Although by following this line of thinking one can abandon evil and do good, without understanding past lives it is impossible to explain the myriad differences in the rewards or retributions of the present life. There is also no way that such thinking can give rise to the right belief in accord with logic and common sense. To form right views, one not only needs to have right views about good and evil and about karma and its results, one also needs to have a firm and confident understanding of the existence of past lives and future lives.

After sentient beings have generated various types of karma—good karma, evil karma, guiding karma, completion karma, the karma of present results, the karma of rebirth results, the karma of later results, and so on—these karmic forces will lead to rewards and retributions in the next life. The rewards for good karma will be in the world or in the heavens; the retributions for evil karma will be in the evil destinies of the hells and in the realms of animals and hungry ghosts.

Being reborn in hell or as an animal, hungry ghost, human, or divine being—these are the five destinies. From beginningless time, sentient beings following good or evil karmic forces have been cycling through these five destinies, life after life. A destiny is a direction in which one is inclined; following one's karma, one is born in that place. With the addition of asuras, or nondivine beings, the five destinies become six. "Path" is a different translation of the term destiny. All the Mahāyāna and Hīnayāna sūtras and treatises say there are either five or six destinies. Most asuras live in the oceans and are not very numerous; when they are grouped with the ghosts or animals, the number of destinies remains five.

Transmigration means moving through the cycles of birth and death. This does not imply a fixed movement up or down through the five destinies, whether in the past or the future; it simply means that transmigration up or down is always within the five destinies. Take the present life, for example: the karma that one creates is infinite, as are the unresolved karmic forces accumulated from past lives. Past karma has not yet been expressed, and future karma is still to come. Karma keeps accumulating. So if one dies now, which karma will lead to a result first? This cannot be determined for certain, but all karma falls into these three categories:

First, the category of serious karma. Such karma can be good karma or it can be evil, like the five actions that lead to uninterrupted hell. This karmic force is extraordinarily powerful, whether one is aware of it or not. When one is dying one may see hells or heavens, omens indicating whether one will rise or descend. After that, the serious karma will determine future rewards or retribution.

Second, the karma of one's habits. If one has neither serious evil karma nor serious good karma, one may pass away uneventfully. Although one may have no serious karma in this life, the good or evil karma that one has done previously may have developed into habits with certain good or evil karma, and this can be very powerful. When one dies, the karmic force of these habits will naturally determine one's future rewards or retributions. In the past, an elder named Da Ming said this to the Buddha: "I am usually very mindful of the Buddha. But sometimes when I am in busy streets with so many people, elephants, and horses I forget to keep the right mindfulness of the Buddha. I wonder, if I am unfortunate enough to die right there, will I fall into the evil destinies?" The Buddha told him: "No, you won't. Your usual mindfulness of the Buddha cultivates a good habit with regard to the Buddha. Even if you die without the right mindfulness at that moment, you will still move upward because the karmic force is strong and this temporary lapse does not necessarily correspond to your mind. It is like a big tree that grows leaning toward the southeast; when it is cut, it will fall toward the southeast."[6] It is therefore good if one can stop doing evil and practice good deeds, particularly very good ones. Most important, one should practice regularly and cultivate habits of good karma. When one dies one will then naturally move upward because of one's karma.

Third, the karma of one's dying moment. If a person has no serious karma, whether good or evil, and is also without habitual karma, at death a person may be puzzled and not know where to go. If one recalls one's good deeds at this time, these will lead one to move upward and gain the reward of becoming a human or divine being. If one suddenly recalls one's past evil deeds, one will be led down. For a person without serious or habitual karma, the thoughts just before death are very important. When people are dying, it is therefore best to preach the Dharma to them, recite the Buddha's name, and remind them of their past good deeds so they will bring forth the good karma for future results. The recitations practiced by the Pure Land sect to aid someone who is dying are examples of this. However, this is only helpful for those whose follow their last thoughts. For those who when dying follow their serious karma or their habits, the karmic forces are stronger. For example, if the serious karma or the habitual karma is evil, then it is very difficult to recall the Three Treasures or the virtues of giving, keeping the precepts, and so forth. Clearly, it is most important to study Buddhism and practice in ordinary times.

In the cycle of birth and death, sentient beings cannot be independent, for they are controlled by karmic forces. The present life, after an interval following death, will change into a new life—a future rebirth. The previous and future lives are neither the same nor different, neither extinct nor permanent, and the continuation from previous lives to future lives is profound, too subtle to be seen physically. The sages have no doubt that karma brings results and that death and birth continue. Those who have attained the transcendent power of the divine eye can completely understand this. Non-Buddhists can do so as well; some of them have a more or less confident understanding of the karmic result of past and future lives. For the general layperson without pure wisdom, however, what lies before birth and after death is too obscure; they know nothing about it. Although there are a few who can recall previous causes and past lives, these people are not recognized by worldly materialists. The best thing to do, therefore, is practice according to the Buddha Dharma, attain pure wisdom, and with the transcendental power of the divine eye realize this issue personally. Apart from this direct experience, one can only believe in the Tathāgata's teachings and have a confident understanding through deductive reasoning.

For beginners, these teachings are not easy to understand. To illustrate the idea of rebirth, the analogy of flames can be used. As Zhuangzi said, "The wood fire continues to burn without coming to an end."[7] The great master Huiyuan (A.D. 344–416) of Mount Lu has also used this analogy to illustrate the principle of the continuation of birth and death. A piece of wood burns brightly until the wood is consumed and the flame dies out. But while the embers are still warm, immediately another piece of wood is lit, and the flame becomes strong again. The first piece of wood is not the same as the second piece, and the later flame is not the previous flame; yet it cannot be said that the later flame did not come from the first. Similarly, when the life activities of the previous life stop, another new life begins. The previous life is not the same as the life that comes later, yet this later life comes from the karmic force of the previous life. Between death and birth, however, there may be a gap in time and space.

This gap needs to be explained. According to the profound meaning of the Buddha Dharma, physical and mental activities are manifested in life forms. When one dies, one's body and mind die instantly, and all the present overt physical and mental activities stop; but the past physical and mental activities still exist. After the extinction and passing of karma, the function of karma (as a potential for life) does not disappear. When the causes and conditions become mature, the past karmic force will bring forth new physical and mental activities to begin a new life. Hence, the analogy of the consuming wood fire is again useful: when the wood is burning with bright flames, this is like the overt activities of life. When it stops burning and the flames die out, this is like the life that ends in death. When the fire stops, the hot ashes seem to cool down, but if they come into contact with some flammable substances and a light wind is blowing, the dying ash can burn again with strong flames. Likewise, when causes and conditions are aligned, past karmic forces can bring forth a new life.

The flame from the dying ash is not the previous flame, yet it has an inseparable relationship with it. In the same way, the future life is not the same as the previous one, but it relates to the karma of that life. From the earlier fire to the later, there may be an interval, which corresponds to the gap in time and space between the previous and future lives. This is really just a metaphor, however. According to the Buddha Dharma, past karmic forces cannot really be said to be divisible into segments of time and space because the nature of things is illusory and empty. It can only be said that when causes and conditions are aligned (being born as a human requires the joining of the father's sperm and the mother's egg), they can suddenly bring forth a new life—the new beginning of physical and mental activities in a different time and space.

THE EXISTENCE OF ORDINARY PEOPLE AND SAGES

34 Although birth and death continue among sentient beings,
The sages can find emancipation.
The difference between ignorance and wisdom,
One leading to bondage, the other to emancipation,
Should be believed deeply and without doubt.

The fourth right view is that there are both ordinary people and sages. It is rare to have the right view about good and evil, about karma and its results, and about past and future lives; but if one does not believe in the blissful state of an emancipated sage, one's life is really miserable. The continuous cycling of transmigrations in the five destinies, with their endless rounds of birth and death, are the never-ending scene of human tragedy. How can they ever end? Life is definitely not as hopeless as this. If one firmly believes that sages have attained the bliss of emancipation, one can progress upward and break through the darkness and develop boundless brightness. From beginningless time, sentient beings have been continuously cycling through births and deaths in the five destinies; such is the fate of worldly people. But the sages, through practice, have attained realization and emancipation from birth and death.

How can someone be reckoned to be a sage? The sage is one who has faultless pure wisdom and realizes the nature of the Dharma—the true reality of all dharmas. (Such a one is not to be confused with those who are worldly sages by conventional designation.) Sages are of different levels of attainment, but all fundamentally differ from worldly people in having pure wisdom and realization. What does emancipation mean? It means to be untied and set free. While in the cycle of birth and death, sentient beings are not free; they are tangled as if caught in a net. Having attained pure wisdom, the sages have severed the afflictions—the roots of birth and death.

Both worldly people and sages have the same mental and physical forms. Because worldly people are foolish, due primarily to ignorance, they are chained to the cycle of birth and death and lack independence. The sages, because of their practice, have attained pure wisdom, primarily through *prajñā* or wisdom. The difference between confused worldly people and emancipated sages should be believed deeply and without any doubts. If one can believe that sages have real wisdom and great power, one can also believe in the virtues of the sages: the three insights, the six supernatural powers, the ten forces, the four kinds of fearlessness, the eighteen distinct characteristics of a buddha, and so forth. If one can believe in this way, one is practicing the doctrines of the human and divine vehicles. Even though one is not yet able to seek the Buddha Dharma that liberates one from the three realms, one can gradually cultivate the seed of the teaching to become liberated from the world.

If one does not believe in the sages and their virtues, this disbelief not only disparages the teachings, it plants a seed—a seed that leads one to be influenced by deviant teachings—and obstructs one's practice. Some people, thinking themselves smart, use their worldly knowledge to judge everything. They assume that because they themselves are not sages and have neither pure wisdom nor supernatural power, all humans must be just like them. It is pitiful that these people are so ignorant. Making such judgments can be compared to trying to use clay to make a vase without putting it through the process of firing: it will collapse when water is put in it or crack when exposed to the wind and the sun. But if it is properly fired, it becomes a porcelain vase that will neither collapse nor crack. If such a simple thing as a vase can be so different after undergoing this process, consider how much greater the change will be for humans. If one practices according to the Dharma and is refined by the fire of wisdom, or prajñā, will one still be the same as a worldly person? One has to have a profound understanding about worldly people and sages to bring forth firm right views.

HEAVEN
HUMAN
ASURAS
HUNGRY GHOST
ANIMAL
HELL

THE EXISTENCE OF THE FIVE DESTINIES

35 Circulating within the five destinies,
The body and mind sustain much suffering.

It is not really ideal for sentient beings to circulate among the five destinies, for their bodies and minds invariably sustain much suffering. If one moves from greater suffering to less suffering, of course, one will feel lighter and more comfortable. Needless to say, the suffering of the three evil destinies is great. The human world is also "nine out of ten times a case of things happening to you that are not what you wanted." Divine beings, although they have much enjoyment, also suffer, particularly when they die, because the knowledge that they will regress brings indescribable pain.

THE THREE EVIL DESTINIES

36 The great extremely hot hells,
The peripheral hells all of which one must pass through,
The eight frigid hells and the solitary hells:
These are the worst places for suffering beings.

Hell

The first topic to be addressed in this section is the suffering in the destiny of the hells. Hell, *naraka* in Sanskrit, means a place of suffering. There are four groups of hells, altogether containing eighteen hells.

The principal and fundamental group is that of the eight great hells. Beings in these hells suffer from extreme heat because of a fierce fire. According to the sūtras, these eight great hells are underneath the Earth's crust; the center of the Earth is full of raging fire—evidence of which is the volcano that erupts with molten rock and burning gases. In the Buddhist sūtras and the Old Testament as well, we find descriptions of the land being split open and people falling into hells. Some people doubt this, wondering how life can exist in such great heat. They do not understand that for sentient beings the power of karma is inconceivable! Some beings die in the water, while others can live only in water. Some beings die if covered by dirt, but others live in the soil. Sentient beings are so unimaginably varied that one should not make assumptions about other beings based on one's limited physiological circumstances and experiences. The eight great hells are named according to their characteristics. They are the hells of rebirth, black cords, squeezing, wailing, great wailing, very hot burning, extremely fierce heat, and the uninterrupted hell (*avīci* in Sanskrit).

All these hells have two characteristics: they all have raging fires, and the beings within them suffer from contact with molten copper and iron similar to magma. Those who have done evil suffer from all kinds of torture from various red-hot metals: iron floors and walls; iron troughs and hills; iron pans, plates, and knives; iron hammers, chains, and cords; iron nails, coals, tongs, and pellets. The second characteristic of the great hells is that the beings within them have large bodies and long life spans. For example, in the uninterrupted hell the life span is a medium kalpa. The most painful thing in these hells is not that these beings want to live but cannot; it is rather that they want to die but cannot. Before the karmic force comes to its end, no being in hell can die; even after they turn into ashes they are reborn. This is the place of retribution for those with the most wicked offenses.

The second group of hells is that of the peripheral hells, which are also called the hells of increasingly worse suffering. These are on the periphery of the eight great hells, each of which has four doors leading to four different hells. Since each great hell has four doors opening to four hells, there are sixteen hells adjacent to each great hell—or, adjacent to all eight great hells, a total of one hundred and twenty-eight hells. When the beings in the eight great hells have finished their suffering there, they must pass through all four of the peripheral hells behind each door. The suffering increases from one place to the next, which is why these hells are called the hells of increasingly worse suffering. The four kinds of peripheral hells are, first, the hell of hot ashes, a glowing hot pit filled with ashes; second, the hell of corpse feces, a manure pit inside of which there are worms with sharp mouths similar to maggots; third, the hell of sharp weapons, which consists of roads covered with knife blades, forests with swordlike leaves inhabited by fierce dogs, and forests of iron thorns inhabited by big birds with iron beaks—beings in these three places suffer from injuries caused by the knives, swords, and animal bites; and fourth, the hell of the boundless river, a river of boiling ash-water that fries beings like beans in hot oil.

The third category of hells is the eight frigid hells. They are said to extend from the eight great hells at the center of the earth outward to the earth's crust or to be near the encircling iron mountains that are at the periphery of the world on the earth's surface. These hells are said to be out of the reach of the sun's and moon's light so that they are incomparably frigid. Thus it may be that these frigid hells are located at the north and south poles.

The eight frigid hells are named according to their characteristics. They are called the hells of blisters, bursting blisters, atata, hahava, huhuva (these last three are named after the sounds uttered by beings exposed to the cold), blue lotus, red lotus, and great red lotus (named according to the color and the cracks in the skin that the cold has caused). Lifetimes are long in these hells as well, and they are unbearably painful. They are described as "incomparable frigidity penetrating to the bones and making the whole body shiver and curl up. Worms appear after hundreds of blisters burst, chewing and scratching on the body's fat and marrow, and causing dripping sores. The cold makes the teeth chatter and the hair stand on end, and distresses the eyes, ears, throat, and all body parts. None are spared. The union of the body and mind is extremely confused, so that living in the frigid hells is suffering to the utmost."[8]

The fourth category of the hells is the solitary hells, which are hells in the human world. They may be anywhere in remote mountains, or on islands, or in wide open spaces, or in deep forests. In each live only one or two beings whose individual karmic forces have brought them to these solitary retributions. Recently a newspaper reported that somewhere in Taiwan a father had abused his own daughter, locking her up in a dark room without any ventilation or sunshine. She had lived for fifteen years with neither enough food nor warm clothing and had the appearance of an undeveloped child. Not only was she pale and swollen, she did not even look human. The karmic forces of sentient beings are inconceivable!

In a prosperous and busy place in the middle of the city, a person can exist in isolation suffering from such heavy retribution. This situation is probably close to existence in the solitary hells.

These four groups with their eighteen hells are the worst places of suffering for sentient beings. Before being emancipated from birth and death, everyone has the possibility of falling into them. Everyone therefore should have great fear of such places and not perform evil deeds.

37 There are all different kinds of animals
But all experience similar sufferings: being preyed upon or
being enslaved.

ANIMALS

The suffering in the destiny of animals affects all the beings in the animal kingdom except human beings. Animals' appearances, colors, dwellings, living activities, and life spans are all different. According to the Buddha Dharma, animals are grouped into the footless such as earthworms, the two-footed such as birds, the quadrupeds such as beasts, and the multiple-footed such as bugs with six, eight, or more feet. As for their dwellings, all animals originally lived in the ocean and later moved from there to different places, some onto the land and some into the air. There are also animals like the amphibians that live both in the water and on the land; some animals live both in the water and on the land and in the air as well. The differences in their intelligence, life spans, and their modes of enjoyment are great. For example, some of the pleasures of the dragons, the garuḍas, and so forth are even better than those of humans. In general, however, this evil destiny is very miserable.

The sūtras say that because birds and beasts "have different minds, they have different appearances."[9] This has partially been proven by recent research. For example, it has been found that some birds' eyes activate their visual consciousness to differentiate between the colors green, red, and purple; thus the feathers on their bodies also have these colors. If they cannot differentiate between such bright colors, then their feathers are gray or dull yellow. Another example to prove this point is the protective coloration of insects. Some of them look like branches or dried leaves. This is simply because they have always inhabited such environments. The constant influence of their environments on their minds has in turn influenced their physiological systems and their colors.

The oppressing suffering in the destiny of animals is caused by their cruelly killing and preying upon one another. The big fish eats the smaller fish, a large insect eats the smaller one. A spider builds a web in the corner of the house just to catch and kill flying insects. Frogs and birds swallow insects, and their appetites are amazing. Even the small insects hidden beneath the bark of trees can be eaten by woodpeckers. Ants like to eat other insects, yet they themselves are the sole food eaten by anteaters. Even the king of the dragons has the misfortune of being preyed upon by the garuḍa.

Humans also have the evil habit of killing and eating animals. For the sake of their skins, furs, teeth and horns, people kill large numbers of animals and give it the fine-sounding name of "production." The world of animals is really a slaughterhouse: they are constantly killing each other and being killed by humans. In addition, animals like cows and horses are restrained, whipped, and enslaved by humans; they are completely without any independence. The suffering of the animals is second only to that in the hells. One day, when Śākyamuni Buddha was the crown prince, he went to the fields to observe farming. He saw the farmers working very hard at plowing, whipping their oxen to the point of bleeding. The blood dripped to the soil where worms quickly gathered. After the field was plowed, the worms were eaten by the birds. When the prince saw all the suffering, killing, and devouring among animals, he felt great compassion for sentient beings. He made his great vow to leave home and begin religious practice. Ordinary people not only have no such awareness or sympathy for sentient beings, they even eat them. How different are they from animals?

38 Hungry ghosts always feel hungry and thirsty
And they use filth as food.

In the three destinies, hungry ghosts, as is obvious from their name, are sentient beings who suffer from constant hunger and thirst. Hungry ghosts are different from the ghosts of Chinese traditions, which people become after they die. According to the Buddha Dharma, there are three main groups of hungry ghosts: those with no wealth, those with a little, and those with much. Among those with no wealth are these three: the torch mouths or flaming mouths, for whom food and drink become flames when they are brought into the mouth; the needle mouths, whose throats are so tiny that food cannot pass through; and the vile mouths, whose mouths are so decomposed and smelly that they cannot ingest anything.

The ghosts with a little wealth are able to eat small amounts. These also are of three kinds, named after specific body characteristics: needle-like hair, stinking hair, and wens. Some of them, when they are about to eat, experience their food turning into pus and blood. Some of them eat filthy sputa, saliva, urine, and feces or swallow filth as food.

The ghosts with great wealth, which have sumptuous enjoyments, are also of three subgroups: the ghosts of sacrifices, who live off the sacrifices offered by humans and are similar to spirits described in China; the ghosts of losses, who live off objects lost from the human world; and the ghosts of great powers, such as yaksas, raksasas, and so forth, who are the powerful rulers of ghosts. The ghosts of sacrifices and losses sometimes suffer from hunger and thirst, whereas the ghosts of great powers have pleasures close to those of divine beings. Among hungry ghosts, however, most have little or no wealth and are extremely hungry.

39 The evil destinies come from the three unwholesome roots
That lead to evil deeds and their retribution.

The three evil destinies discussed above all come from the three unwholesome roots of the afflictions—evil deeds such as killing, stealing, and sexual misconduct and their respective retributions. The desire realm's greed, anger, and deviant views (ignorance) are the three roots of unwholesomeness. Because of the propelling force of these afflictions, beings behave in all kinds of evil ways. Evil behavior becomes evil karma, which leads to the retribution of the sufferings of the destinies. Killing, for instance, may be caused by greed, as in murdering someone for money; or by anger, as in revenge or sudden rage; or by deviant views, as in the non-Buddhists' killing of cows and sheep as sacrifices for their gods or the killing of pigs for festivals in Taiwan. Killing, stealing, and sexual misconduct are all like this; they may be caused by any of the three unwholesome roots. The most serious evil karma will result in retribution in the hells; the less serious will result in retribution as an animal; the least serious will lead one down to the destiny of hungry ghosts. If one neither gives rise to deep afflictions nor commits serious offenses, one will not fall into these three evil destinies.

THE TWO GOOD PATHS

40 Humans, vexed with suffering and happiness,
Are the pivot of ascent and descent.
Humans are the true pivot, not ghosts;
But this traditional misconception about ghosts still lingers.

The good path of humans is the one we understand most intimately. The reward of being human is neither like the oppressive sufferings in the three evil destinies nor like the happiness in the heavens. Humans are tied to suffering and happiness, both of which fluctuate rapidly. Still, this is a good environment for practicing the Buddha Dharma. In the evil destinies, beings suffer so much that they have no time to practice. In the heavens, there is so much happiness that the beings there have enjoyment all the time. Their wisdom declines, and they make no connection with the Buddha Dharma. In the human world, religious practice can be compared to sharpening a knife on a stone; with more rubbing the knife becomes sharper. In the heavens, religious practice is like cutting sod with a knife: the more the knife cuts, the blunter it becomes.

In the five destinies, humans are the pivot of ascent and descent. For example, one is reborn in heaven because, as a human, one accumulated good karma and practiced meditation. If one is reborn very high in the heavens or is reborn in heaven straight from an evil transmigration, this can only be because of the good deeds that one has done as a human in past lives. The principal reason that one might descend to the evil destinies is that one committed bad deeds as a human. If one falls into the evil destinies from the heavens, it is not because one has done evil as a divine being, since divine beings do not do extremely evil deeds. (Above the realm of form, there are only afflictions that are neutral, without good or bad effects.) Such a fall is instead because one's good fortune in heaven has come to an end and past evil karma, unresolved until this time, has matured to the point of retribution.

Rebirth in the destiny of animals or ghosts straight from the hells is also not caused by the evil deeds of the beings in the hells. Since they are so occupied by suffering, how can they do evil? Such rebirths are all caused by the evil deeds beings have committed as humans in previous lives. Except for a few beings with higher status, the majority of ghosts and animals do not commit evil deeds. Even in the human world, an ignorant child or a psychotic lunatic cannot be held responsible for such serious crimes as killing. Animals, who are more ignorant than children, act only from their natural instincts. The phenomena of big fishes or insects eating small ones are pitiful—such beings are defiled and their behavior can have minor karma and minor retribution—but their actions definitely will not become the guiding karma that could lead them to the three evil destinies. Therefore, ascending and descending through the force of karma, except in the case of a few ghosts and animals, is primarily due to the good or bad karmic forces of humankind.

On the other hand, human beings' ability to practice meditation, with its possible consequence of being born in heaven, is good karma. Becoming a monastic person, keeping the precepts, practicing cultivation, ending birth and death, becoming a buddha—these are possible only for humans. When humans do evil, they can be extremely evil; when they do good, they can rise to the ultimate. With regard to ascent and descent in the five destinies, good or evil human conduct is the central pivot from which all movements up or down are initiated. Because of this, one should be cautious not to lose the human form and fall into the evil destinies. One should also be happy that one is a human now, because the opportunity to be free from birth and death and to become a buddha has arrived!

In general, people have much misunderstanding about the cycle of birth and death. In Hinduism, people believe that it does not matter whether people are sages, ordinary people, good people, or evil people—after they die, they will all enter King Yama's capital. After the king's judgment, the evil people are sent to various hells for punishment. The Chinese have always believed that people become ghosts after death and that being a ghost means to return to the origins. The traditional Chinese view misunderstands the Buddhist concept of transmigration in holding that all dead people become ghosts. In the Chinese view, those who have merit become spirits or gods; offenders have to go through the deserved retributions in different hells and be sentenced by the ten courts of Yama. After this punishment is over they are then sent to different places—the human world or an animal existence—for a rebirth that accords with their conduct before death.

In general, Buddhists in China do not know that transmigrations through the cycles of birth and death are based on people's lives as humans. This is to say, good or evil karma is caused by humans; after they die, they will be born as divine beings, humans, hungry ghosts, animals, or in the hells according to their karmic forces. The Chinese, assuming that all people become ghosts after death, erroneously believe that the pivot of the transmigrations is the destiny of being a ghost. Also, they do not differentiate between being a ghost and being in the hells. Thus, they think that after suffering in the hells, ghosts will then be reborn in the human world or into the destiny of being an animal. This is a serious mistake, but the traditional misconception lingers on. Some Buddhists, wishing to be born in the heavens or the pure lands, still cannot forget the traditional conception of people becoming ghosts after death. So although they constantly talk about wanting to be born in the heavens or in the pure lands, they simultaneously prepare for a family member of theirs to become a ghost: they make the paper money, paper houses, and so on that are used in Chinese mortuary rites.

Some people feel they have to do these things in order to be filial children. They do not understand that after people die, their transmigrations follow their karmic forces. Many people can be reborn as humans and divine beings, while some who are mindful of Amitābha Buddha can be born in the western Pure Land. How can these people be so sure that their parents will descend to the evil destinies of being ghosts after death? They might be insulting their parents, which is not filial at all! This Chinese belief that the ghost is pivotal has lingered on too long; people must be set straight.

41 The first of the heavens is the realm of desire
Followed by the realms of form and formlessness.
Divine beings are physically superior and have the longest lives;
Their joy and their concentration are also superior.

The destiny of the heavens is a wonderful one, superior to the human world in the cycles of transmigration through birth and death. The first of the heavens is the realm of desire, where beings have minds and bodies and live in an environment imbued with the five desires and sexual desire. The afflictions of the sentient beings that live in this heaven are bound to these states and cannot be separated from them.

The vast realm of desire includes the earth, everything underground, the waters, the sky, all the hells, animals, hungry ghosts, humans, asuras, and the heavens of the desire realm. Mount Sumeru forms its base. Two of the heavens in this realm are near the earth: the Heaven of Four Kings and Trayastriṃśā Heaven. Above them, in outer space, are Yama Heaven, Tuṣita Heaven, Nirmāṇarati Heaven, and Paranirmitavaśavartin Heaven. All are like countries in the human world with their kings, officials, and men and women, but the joy of the inhabitants is superior.

Above the realm of desire is the realm of form, where there are beings with minds, bodies, and dwelling places but without desires. The afflictions of these divine beings are bound to these forms, so this heaven is called the realm of form. The heaven of the realm of form is broadly divided into four Dhyāna Heavens and more strictly divided into eighteen heavens. The first Dhyāna Heaven actually is comprised of three heavens—the multitudes of Brahmā, the ministers of Brahmā, and Great Brahmā. Although the beings in these heavens do not have different genders, they still have the structure of countries with rulers, ministers, and populace. The second Dhyāna Heaven has three heavens—lesser light, limitless light, and light-sound. The third Dhyāna Heaven also has three heavens—lesser purity, limitless purity, and universal purity. The fourth Dhyāna Heaven has nine heavens—the heavens of no clouds, birth of good fortune, abundant fruit, no thoughts, no afflictions, no heat, good manifestations, good views, and ultimate form. All the beings above the second Dhyāna Heaven live in solitude. Each individual's palace is its own world, in contrast to the "receptacle world"—the shared world of human beings.

Above these heavens is the realm of formlessness, where bodies and their dwellings do not exist; only the mind does. The beings in this realm are bound to their mind and its attributes. Because there is no matter occupying space, the location of these realms cannot be described. The inhabitants' intensity of mental concentration achieved through meditation—concentration is the causal factor that leads to the rebirth in the heavens—is higher than that of beings in the fourth Dhyāna of the realm of form. The realm of formlessness also has four heavens: infinite space, infinite consciousness, nothingness, and neither perception nor nonperception. Thus, in total, there are twenty-eight heavens in the three realms.

The destiny of the heavens is the most joyful among the five destinies. This is so because of four attributes. First, superior bodies: the bodies of divine beings are tall and large. In the lowest Heaven of the Four Kings, the length of their bodies is one-quarter of a krośa, which is equivalent to nine hundred feet. Eight krośas are equal to one yojana. According to a

Buddhist saying, one yojana is equivalent to sixteen Chinese miles. These large-statured beings also have dignified appearances superior to those of humans. A story from Buddha's time illustrates this. Nanda, a disciple of the Buddha's, married a woman named Sundari, who was the most beautiful woman of that time. After Nanda had become a monk, he still thought of her often. Then the Buddha brought Nanda to Trayastriṃśā Heaven. After seeing the goddesses there, Nanda felt that Sundari was like a blind rhesus monkey in comparison; he never thought of her again!

Second, longer lives: in the lowest heaven, that of the Four Kings, the life span is five hundred of their years—equivalent to nine million human years. The longest life spans, which are eighty thousand great kalpas, are those in the heaven of neither perception nor nonperception. In the course of one of these lifetimes, our human world goes through eighty thousand rounds of great destruction and formation. Such longevity is beyond the dreams of those who seek longevity and eternal life.

Third, superior joy: divine beings in the realms of form, from the first Dhyāna Heaven to the third, no longer have worries or distress; they have only the wonderful joy of meditation. Above the fourth Dhyāna Heaven, the mind is peaceful and unperturbed. This state is extremely blissful compared to the noisy disturbances in the realm of desire and the excited joys in the first through the third Dhyāna Heavens.

Fourth, superior concentration: in the heavens of the realm of desire, beings have weak powers of concentration. To be reborn above the first Dhyāna Heaven is the reward for practicing the four meditations and the four formless meditations. Once one is born in the heavens, one remains in concentration for a long time—until one's power to meditate comes to an end; then that existence is over. One can see from the long life spans of these beings that the reward of being in concentration in the heavens of the realms of form and formlessness is really superior. In short, the destiny of being in heaven is the most joyful in the cycles of birth and death in the three realms.

The Origin of Suffering and Bliss

42 All suffering comes from bad karma,
And all bliss from the accumulation of good karma.
Suffering and bliss stop with the ending of karma,
So we should cultivate good karma diligently.

People dislike suffering and want to have happiness. They are also reluctant to fall into the evil destinies and want to be born as humans or in the heavens. However, one will not be born as a human or in heaven simply as a result of one's wishes; one must cease doing evil and do good. For example, the suffering of the three evil destinies, the suffering of the human world, and the worries of the divine beings in the realm of desire all come from past bad karma. All the joyful rewards—the bliss in the heavens, the joys of the human world, the pleasures of animals and hungry ghosts, even the trifling pleasures in the hells (except for the unintermittent hells)—are results of the accumulation of good karma. Since resultant joy and suffering are dependent on the commission of good or evil deeds, only by ceasing to do evil and by doing good can one become free from suffering and receive happiness.

These results are not everlasting; they stop with the ending of the karmic force. This is an important insight. If one really understands it, one will not be disappointed and pessimistic when one encounters suffering, pain, and unfavorable conditions. One will know that because these unfavorable conditions are caused by bad karma and their force is limited, this retribution of suffering will eventually pass away (even in the hells, one will eventually be set free).

The Importance of Doing Good

One should diligently do good in order to receive future happiness. If one encounters happiness and favorable conditions, one should not be carried away with arrogance, extravagance, and indolence, for they are the result of good karma. Good karmic force is also limited, and happiness will also pass away soon (even in the heaven of neither perception nor nonperception, one still unavoidably regresses); so one cannot be indolent just because of joy! The importance of doing good can be described with an analogy. When there is a famine, life is difficult. All one can do is diligently plow, sow, fertilize, irrigate, and get rid of insects. After the famine ends and the new crops can be harvested, one can experience the joy of abundance. Yet even if one has a rich harvest and full granaries, one still has to diligently plow, sow, fertilize, irrigate, and get rid of insects. If one just sits idly and eats until one's whole good fortune is used up, then when there is no food one will again be miserable.

Therefore, follow the right views with firm belief in karmic results, detest and reject suffering, seek happiness, and no matter what the situation is now, cultivate good karma diligently. One can be said to have obtained the right views of the Buddha Dharma only if one's view of life is that ,regardless of the present conditions, one will diligently do good.

43 If one has the ability to do good
But has not built up good karma,
And suddenly bitter retribution arises,
Then what good can be done?

This verse is intended to encourage people to do good in time. If, right now, one does not have the eight obstructions, if one is not a child or very old, if one is neither disabled nor psychotic, or if one has knowledge, ability, wealth, authority, and fame, one can really do good deeds. What a precious opportunity! Wasting time and not diligently cultivating good karma is a pity. Being a human with some happiness is the reward of past good karma, but this karmic force is limited and will not last forever. If one has not built up good karma and then suddenly old age and death come, bitter retribution will arrive with the maturation of evil karma. What good can be done then? People should not procrastinate!

RIGHT PRACTICE: THE THREEFOLD FORTUNATE KARMA

44 Having wished to become human and having become human,
One should cultivate the Dharma of the Divine Vehicle without wanting to be a divine being.
Also, one should cultivate the threefold fortunate karma diligently
And vow to be born when the Buddha is present.

To be rewarded with birth as a human or divine being, is it better to practice the Human Vehicle or the Divine Vehicle? What good karma has the karmic result of birth as a human or divine being? How can one avoid being bound by the karmic result of becoming a human or a divine being and avoid regressing to evil destinies because of bad karma? This verse answers these three questions.

1. Both the Human Vehicle and the Divine Vehicle are good rewards. Judged by their respective merits, the rewards of heaven are far superior to the rewards of human existence. Therefore, it is good to practice the Dharma of the Human Vehicle and better still to practice the Dharma of the Divine Vehicle. Yet one should remember that humans are superior to divine beings in three aspects, discussed above, that the Buddha came from the human world, and that the divine beings look at the human world as a happy land when they are about to die.

Thus, from the standpoint of having a suitable environment in which to practice the Buddha Dharma, the human world is better than the heavens, and the Dharma of the human vehicle is more precious than the Dharma of the divine vehicle. When studying Buddhism as humans, people should not envy the happiness in the heavenly kingdoms but should study the true Dharma of the human vehicle. If one wishes to remain human and one practices the true Dharma of the human vehicle, one will naturally obtain the precious human form in accordance with the karmic result.

One should not actually avoid practicing the Dharma of the Divine Vehicle. One can practice the Dharma of the Divine Vehicle provided one's purpose is not to be reborn in the heavens and one really does not want to be reborn there. In this way, even if one practices the Dharma of Divine Vehicle, the power of one's vow will ensure that one will not be born in the heavens as a result of the karmic force of one's practice of this vehicle. The power of a vow is inconceivable! However, it is better not to practice the profound Dharma of heaven (that is, deep meditation), because if the karmic force is stronger than the power of the vow, one will be taken upward by that karmic force and be born in the heavens. If this happens then one will have one of the eight obstructions that impede the study of Buddhism.

2. In order to obtain the joyful result of being born as a human or divine being, one has to cultivate the good karma of the Human and Divine Vehicles, which are the three blessed deeds of which the Buddha spoke. These three blessed deeds are giving, keeping the precepts, and practicing meditation. Only by cultivating this threefold fortunate karma can one receive the joyful reward of becoming a human or divine being. Some people, such as those who pray to the king of heaven with the hope that he will help them attain the goal of being born in heaven, are ignorant about cause and effect and do not cultivate the right karma because they want to be born as humans or divine beings.

The Buddha warned people that praying to be born in the heavens without cultivating good karma is like throwing a big rock into a pond and praying for the rock to float.[10] The ancient masters said, "To be born in heaven requires the appropriate karma; one will not become an immortal just by wishing it." It is a pity that many people in this world do not understand the right cause and effect or the right way to practice but instead vainly wish to be born as humans and in the heavens.

3. How can one avoid both being bound by the human and divine rewards of good fortune that come from practicing the good Dharma of human and divine beings and regressing because of evil deeds? This can be done by making vows to be born in the human world while a buddha is present, so as to be able to hear an exposition of the practice of the Dharma. If one can be born during a buddha's time and thereby see a buddha and hear the Dharma from him, one will have a causal connection with a buddha, the Dharma, and the innumerable teachers and friends who practice the Buddha Dharma. Not only will one gradually accumulate the roots of the virtues, but one will also make extensive connections with the Dharma itself. In this way, when one is born as a human in a future life, one will be guided and inspired by teachers and friends to return to the Three Treasures, to see the Buddha, to listen to the Dharma and practice it, and to again make connections with the Buddha Dharma and the innumerable people who practice it.

With increasing contacts and continuing upward progress, one's merit will increase, and one will not lose the human form through doing evil. (Regression from the human form usually happens to those who have not taken refuge in and not practiced the Buddha Dharma.) Also, having increased one's basis for good actions and matured one's potential to practice the Dharma, one will naturally enter the world-transcending Great Vehicle and make preparations for attaining buddhahood. Therefore, those who have not vowed to leave the three realms or to have the bodhi mind should diligently practice the true Dharma of the Human Vehicle and vow every day, "I wish that the Three Treasures will embrace me compassionately! I resolve to be able to see the Buddha and hear the Dharma life after life." After making such right vows to see the Buddha and hear the Dharma, one who practices the right deeds of the Human Vehicle will be guaranteed not to lose the human form and will thereby attain buddhahood.

The Fortunate Karma of Giving

> 45 Humans depend on the basic necessities of life to obtain happiness,
> But these necessities are derived from previous charities.
> Thus, for sentient beings, the Buddha
> Always praises first the good fortune of giving.

When the Tathāgata expounded the Dharma, he did not teach like we do now. He did not always begin with discourses about liberation from birth and death, birth in a Pure Land, all things being identical with emptiness, or both mind and the Buddha being identical. For all sentient beings, the Tathāgata always began by teaching "giving, keeping the precepts, and practicing meditation for the rebirth in heavens."[11] If the people were able to believe in and practice these virtues and also appeared to have the roots of virtue necessary to transcend the world, then the Tathāgata would expound the world-transcending Dharma.

Of the threefold fortunate karma, giving was what the Tathāgata always preached first. He did this for a very important reason, as was clearly expounded in the verses by Candrakīrti Bodhisattva.[12] For their happiness humans depend on the basic necessities of life such as clothing, food, lodging, transportation, and medication. Even among the lowest species of animals, the need for food is the most basic requirement; only when this need is met can they live well and happily. Our happiness (consisting of sensations at the physiological level) cannot exist without the material necessities of life; even mental joy depends on this foundation. The ancient Chinese therefore said, "After the granaries are full, people will be aware of rites and ethics; and after the country becomes prosperous, education will be thriving." The happiness derived from material life is the most basic desire of all sentient beings, including human beings. The Buddha never objected to this proper human desire for material happiness. He saw fulfilling it as a priority that was befitting for sentient beings and preached the Buddha Dharma of "cutting the root of poverty forever."

Where do the material necessities come from? People think that the only answer is through hard work and technological development. This shows that they know only about present conditions and not about the karma of previous existence. The Buddha said that all the material necessities of this life come from the good karma of being charitable with our possessions.

If we store them all up and do not use them, they will mean nothing to us when we die. If we enjoy or waste them, then they are gone. If we use some of them for charity in the field of good fortune, then they can become the basis for material happiness in future lives. The merits earned through giving are varied, as is the corresponding happiness. Giving is like sowing grains in a field, which can yield from ten to a hundred times as much in return. All of the material resources in nature come from the shared karma of all sentient beings, who in turn gather and process them in accordance with their past karmic force. Although present effort is necessary to gather, develop, and manufacture things, were it not for the past karma of giving, these material resources would not exist. For example, in some very poor areas or areas that lack certain materials, no matter how much effort is applied to change present conditions, nothing can be gained. The rise of the material happiness really does depend on the past good karma of giving.

So, material necessities are required for human happiness. Desire for them is fundamental and normal. These necessities of life are dependent on the fortunate karma of giving, so when the Buddha preached the Dharma he urged people to accumulate merit through giving; by doing so they would avoid future poverty and the hardships that affect one's economic state and one's practice of the Buddha Dharma. Praising giving first, the Tathāgata clearly saw that the enjoyment of material things is the foundation upon which to establish happiness in the human world as well as in the world-transcending holy Dharma. If people are so poor that they have nothing to live on, then happiness in the world and the practice of the world-transcending Dharma will have no basis on which to begin.

46 One should give willingly and in ways that are beneficial to others,
Having compassion or respect in different circumstances.
There are differences in attitudes, in the fields of good fortune, and in the substances given,
And accordingly there are differences in the levels of merit.

In giving, there are two main requirements: being willing and being beneficial. One should be willing to give away one's possessions, to sacrifice them. If what is given was lent and simply not returned, or is given away with reluctance and heartache, this cannot be counted as charity. What one gives to people, animals, or other sentient beings should be beneficial to them. If one gives away poisonous substances to other people with the intention of harming them, it cannot be counted as charity. The true spirit of giving is to benefit others at the expense of oneself. It is no wonder that in the Mahāyāna teachings, which emphasize benefiting others, the merits earned through giving have such an important value.

The motives for and the recipients of giving can be divided into two categories. The first is compassion: toward those without wives, husbands, parents, or children; toward the disabled and the sick; toward victims of war and of disasters such as fire, floods, and storms; and even toward an old cow begging for life before being slaughtered. Giving with sympathetic compassion is similar to present-day philanthropic undertakings. The second is respect: caring for parents, providing for elders, making reverent offerings to the Three Treasures, and the like. Giving with respect also has the meaning of returning the kindness of others. These two categories of giving are different in terms of both the motives and the recipients.

With regard to the levels of merit in giving, three differences need to be discussed: in attitudes, in fields, and in substances.

Differences in attitudes have to do with whether one does something with deep compassion and respect, with slight compassion and respect, or with no compassion and respect. With such differences in attitude, even if the giving is the same, the merits will be vastly different.

Differences in fields have to do with where one plants the good fortune of giving. For example, those who are poor or sick are considered the field of compassion, while parents and the Three Treasure are the field of respect. In the field of respect, providing for one's parents is superior to providing for elders in general. Among the Three Treasures, offerings made to a sage at the level of attaining the first fruit are not as excellent as those made to a sage at the level of attaining the second fruit, which in turn are not as excellent as those made to a sage at the level of attaining the third fruit. Offerings made to bodhisattvas are not as excellent as those offered to the buddhas. All of the merit earned through giving to other beings cannot be compared to the merit earned through giving to the buddhas because such a field of good fortune is superior to all others. In the field of compassion, differentiation is based on the degree to which the recipient deserves sympathy and help: for example, an unemployed young person without clothing and food is pitiable, but not as pitiable as the disabled, old, and weak.

Differences in the substances concern the things that are given. If the attitude and the field are the same, then the differences in the levels of merits will depend on the quantity of things given. Of the three categories, attitude is by far the most important according to the Buddha Dharma. Therefore, the merit of a poor person's gift of a penny or a piece of fruit is not necessarily unequal to the merit of a rich person's gift of ten thousand or a million dollars.

47 One should give in a proper way
And not from social pressure, from fear, or from indebtedness;
One should not expect rewards or merely follow family traditions,
Nor should one ask for divine good fortune or for fame.

The differences in the levels of merit in giving are dependent on the motives, the recipients and the substances. Therefore, one should avoid giving impurely and ignobly. What are impure, ignoble, and improper instances of giving? Briefly, there are seven categories of "don'ts":

Don't give under pressure. One may not want to give automatically, but because someone comes to the door to beg for alms, one may feel awkward about refusing and give reluctantly with heartache.

Don't give from fear. When one discovers that one's wealth, authority, or life is in danger of being lost, then one may give out of fear of losing everything. One hopes thereby to obtain merit and be rewarded with the elimination of calamities, or to prolong one's life and turn bad luck into good fortune in this present life. This type of giving is common among devotees.

Don't give from indebtedness. Because one has obtained benefits from others, one may offer to return such kindnesses. This cannot be counted as planting good fortune; it is merely paying a debt. Some people, when they encounter unfavorable conditions, make a vow to the gods and the buddhas. When their conditions improve, they give in return for the favor granted to them. This repayment does not meet the proper standards for giving.

Don't give expecting a reward. Sometimes one gives because one wants to be rewarded by others. One may want other people's help or even expect them to sacrifice their lives. In such a case, one always gives impressive gifts so that people will be glad to do what one wants.

Don't give merely to follow family traditions. Sometimes one does not have the desire to give but does so only because of family traditions, because one's parents, out of habit, give annually to the Three Treasures or charitable organizations. One may merely follow this habit routinely.

Don't give as a way to ask for divine good fortune. Such giving is done only to please the divine spirits and get their blessings in the hope of being born in the heavenly kingdoms.

Don't give for the sake of fame. Some people give because they want to be famous. For the sake of honor, these people give generously in front of a big crowd.

Of course, there is greater and lesser merit for all of these kinds of giving, but they are far from the true giving that is in accord with the Buddha Dharma! One should give properly, with deep compassion and respect.

The Fortunate Karma of Ethics

> 48 In order to control oneself for the benefit of others,
> One has to be determined and patient in keeping the pure precepts.

Giving—primarily, sacrificing one's external belongings in order to benefit sentient beings—is a valuable and virtuous conduct, but it is not the most precious. The objectives of the Buddha Dharma are to avoid evil and do good so that one may have a pure mind. Keeping the precepts is therefore superior to giving material goods. Precepts for virtuous conduct come from controlling one's selfish desires in order to enhance harmony, happiness, and the growth of good in the world—that is, from controlling oneself to benefit others. This can be explained in the following way. Keeping the precept of not stealing does not just mean for today or tomorrow, or just not from the Zhangs or the Wangs; it means that from now on, one will not steal the belongings of any person, any sentient being. Therefore, to keep the precept of not stealing means that one gives a secure guarantee that one will not violate or harm the body or belongings of any human or any sentient being. Likewise, to not engage in improper sexual conduct means that from now on one will not seduce or use force to destroy another person's chastity or family harmony for the gratification of one's selfish desires. This precept is to be applied toward all members of the opposite sex and is not just limited to certain people. For these reasons, the Buddha has praised the five precepts as "five great gifts." The kind of merit obtained from benefiting others through keeping the precepts is greater than that obtained from the common act of giving material goods, and it has greater value.

In order to accept and keep the precepts, one has to control one's selfish desires. One must have firm determination to endure various trials: hardships, sufferings, situational temptations, threats, coercion. One must endure selfish desires without being disturbed. One must even have the determination to die in order to keep the precepts, that is, one must be so determined that one will not live if one has to break them. Only with such strong endurance and the determination to control sensual desires and overcome whatever situations arise can one keep the precepts with purity and not break them. If one can live in this way, then one will not destroy with a single act the merit obtained from keeping the precepts for years. Even if only one precept is violated, then all will fail. This situation can be compared to that of a person who has been law abiding for a lifetime but who, after one criminal act, is punished by the law.

49 Use one's own feelings to measure those of others.
One should not kill or harm others,
Should not steal or engage in improper sexual conduct,
And should not make false statements.
Because drinking can destroy all virtues,
Buddhists should also keep the precept of not drinking.

There are three categories of precepts: the five precepts, the eight precepts, and the ten good precepts. These are the meritorious precepts of the Dharma that are common to the Five Vehicles. Not understanding the meaning of keeping the precepts, some people keep them because they want the merit to be obtained from so doing. Though this is good, it is not ideal. From the *Āgama Sūtra* and the *Dharmapada* to the Mahāyāna sūtras, the Buddha has clearly said that keeping precepts means "to use one's own feelings to measure those of others" for the purpose of controlling one's sensual desires toward others. In the sūtras, using one's own feelings to measure other people's (all sentient beings') feelings is called the Dharma of taking oneself as the yardstick against which to measure things. This is the same as the principle of reciprocity in Confucianism.

In the sūtra this concept is explained in the following way: "I want to live and not to die, want to have happiness and avoid suffering. Would I like it if someone were to destroy my life through the act of killing when what I want is to live and not die, to have happiness and avoid suffering? If I would not like that, then when I destroy someone else who also wants to live and not die, to have happiness and avoid suffering, that being will not like that either. In addition, that which I do not like or enjoy will not be liked or enjoyed by others either. How can I harm others with those things which I do not like or enjoy?"[13] This is like what Confucius said: "Don't do to others what you don't want to be done to you." Jesus Christ said, "Do unto others as you would have others do unto you." When one uses oneself as a measure of what others feel, the proper ethics to regulate the relations between people is not difficult to realize.

If I hate suffering and want happiness, and other people are just like me, then how can I take away others' happiness and add to their suffering? How can I not rejoice in others' happiness and not alleviate others' suffering? In Buddhism, the kindness that gives happiness and alleviates suffering is the actual putting into practice of this spirit. Therefore, controlling one's sensual desires in order to keep the precepts is nothing more than the Dharma of taking oneself as the measure. It is based on one's compassion and willingness to act in this way. This really is the practice of the Dharma that brings happiness in this life and in future lives.

The Five Precepts

The five precepts are those that should be kept by male lay devotees (upāsakas) and female lay devotees (upāsikās). These precepts are called the precepts of "attendant service," which is the literal meaning of "upa." Such is the virtue of the precepts for lay life. The foundation of the virtue of the precepts is the same for the low and the high, however; even the bodhisattva precepts are built on this foundation, although they are more complete and pure. The five precepts are all based on the principle of using one's own feelings to measure those of others.

"Do not kill." Whether one does the killing oneself or sends another to do it (conspiring with others to kill is also sinful), ending a sentient being's life is killing. An unintentional killing is not a serious offense, however. Among all the killings of sentient beings, killing humans is naturally the most serious offense. Harming others—with knives, canes, earthenware, rocks, etc.—although not counted as heavily as the offense of killing, belongs to the category of killing.

"Do not steal." This applies to all things—national, personal, or Buddhist—that have owners. One breaks the precept of not stealing if one takes, forcibly occupies, or misappropriates things without the owner's consent. According to the Buddha Dharma, one cannot use the excuse of being hungry, sick, or wanting to provide for one's parents, wife, and children to steal. All stealing is sinful.

"Do not engage in improper sexual conduct." If a man and a woman agree to be husband and wife by means of publicly recognized rites, with the approval of guardians and not in violation of secular laws, then sexual contact between husband and wife (which is an important element of family formation for the continuation of posterity) is proper and not sinful. Even in cases where the other partner consents, sexual conduct is improper for laypeople if it is not permitted by the Buddha Dharma (for example, when one has received the eight precepts), not allowed by secular law, or not agreed to by the related guardians. Buddhist lay devotees should abstain from such contact. Such contact not only harms the other person's ability to make choices free of external influences, but it is also evil conduct that ruins the harmony of families and disturbs the order of society.

"Do not make false statements." Sometimes one makes untruthful statements for the sake of one's own benefit, for the benefit of one's relatives and friends, or in order to harm one's enemy. The precept of not lying also applies to pretending to know something when one does not, and denying that one knows something when one does; to saying there is something when there is not, and saying there is not something when there is; and to calling right something that is wrong and vice versa. By making false statements that benefit oneself and one's relatives but bring harm to others, one commits the serious offense of lying. For other kinds of false statements the offense is lighter.

The four precepts discussed above are called natural precepts, because the deeds themselves are crimes. That is, to do these things is wrong whether one accept the precepts or not. Not only does the Buddha Dharma not permit these acts, but even secular laws will punish one for such conduct.

"Do not drink alcohol." Whatever substance has the ability to disturb or confuse one's mind is called alcohol, and one should never consume it. Although some people say that drinking alcohol is good for one's health, according to the Buddha Dharma it is devoid of any merit. First, drinking alcohol can disturb one's mind and lead one to lose self-control. When one is drunk, one not only makes mistakes, but one also may say things or commit evil deeds that one would ordinarily be unable to say or do. In the Vinaya there is a story about a Buddhist disciple who was very strict about keeping the precepts but who, after becoming confused and disorderly from drinking, committed the four serious offenses of killing, stealing, sexual misconduct, and lying all on the same day. Because of situations like this, drinking is said to destroy all virtues. In actuality, it is not only the virtues of the Buddha Dharma that are destroyed by drinking alcohol. The happiness of families, friendships, businesses, and wealth are often destroyed as well. Second, derangement and ignorance are the root of all crimes and can be caused by drinking. Habitual drinking is a big obstacle to the maintenance of right mindfulness and right knowledge. Some people, because they are always drunk, have children who are born insane or with serious mental retardation. Even if drinking may not seem to be evil, it really is one of the chief culprits that impedes wisdom and destroys virtues. In addition to the first four precepts, therefore, Buddhists should seriously keep the precept of not drinking in order to guard their virtues and move toward the world-transcending doctrines, which have wisdom as their foundation.

50 To one who keeps the five precepts for life,
All good fortune will come.

The five precepts discussed above are pure precepts that should be kept by the upāsakas and upāsikās. When one takes refuge, one willingly says: "All my life I take refuge in the Buddha, the Dharma, and the Saṅgha"; one should also accept and keep the five precepts for life. To take refuge means to have faith in and to vow to follow the Three Treasures; accepting the five precepts is the actual practice of following the Three Treasures. People who take refuge but do not accept and keep the five precepts can be said to be upāsakas and upāsikās in name only. When one takes refuge and says, "From today until the end of my life, I will protect living beings," this is the vow to accept the precepts.

Precepts are based on the compassionate Dharma of taking oneself as the measure. The precepts therefore have as their foundation the principle of no killing, or protecting life. Not stealing, not engaging in sexual misconduct, etc., are all specific explanations of the principle of protecting others' lives. Some people have translated "protecting lives" as "releasing life" in reference to the East Asian practice of releasing captive animals. Some people use the precept of no killing as the most explicit example when they are explaining the five precepts (not all the precepts will necessarily be explained when one is accepting precepts, even when the bhikṣu precepts are being given).

Accepting the five precepts after taking refuge is basically a way to learn more about the specific details of the precepts. Those who sincerely take refuge in the Three Treasures will not refuse to accept and keep the five precepts. Faith without a corresponding improvement in a person's conduct is clear proof of the absence of real faith. One cannot be a complete upāsaka if one does not have real faith.

The enormously compassionate Tathāgata, however, felt that lay devotees' habits are so severely contaminated that they cannot immediately accept and keep all the precepts with purity. He thought that if Buddhism were too strict, people might not dare approach the Three Treasures. To allow for their different abilities, the Tathāgata spoke of four groups of devotees: the one-precept upāsakas, who have the ability to keep one precept; the few-precepts upāsakas, who keep two precepts; the more-precepts upāsakas, who keep three to four precepts; and the complete upāsakas, who keep all five precepts. Among all the lay devotees, those of the last group are excellent.

Once one has accepted the five precepts and is able to keep them purely, one will have good fortune. This can be compared to getting a wish-fulfilling pearl; once one has it, one can get other treasures as well. By keeping the precepts, one does not break secular laws, so one gains the respect of society. This pleases both humans and divine beings, and the divine spirits will come to protect one. Evil ghosts and spirits will make all haste to retreat; everything will be auspicious. Those who have pure minds and who keep the precepts without doing any evil can be reborn as humans or divine beings; with the precepts as a foundation for meditation and wisdom, they can initiate the world-transcending merit.

The Eight-Branched Fasting Precepts

THE 5 PLUS 3 MORE

51 For additional practice, there are the one full-day precepts
That follow the lifestyle of the practitioners who have given up lay life.

The second category of pure precepts is the eight-branched fasting precepts, also called the "staying nearby" precepts. The first five of the eight precepts—not killing, not stealing, celibacy, not lying, and not drinking—are similar to the five precepts except for the precept of celibacy. While one is keeping these precepts, even normally proper sexual conduct between husband and wife is prohibited, just as it is for monastics. The sixth precept—not to wear perfumes or garlands and not to sing or dance, or watch or listen to singing or dancing—may be split into two: the first part directs one to abstain from using cosmetics, putting flowers in one's hair, and wearing extravagant jewelry. The second indicates that one should also abstain from watching and listening to dancing and singing, in addition to not doing these things oneself. The seventh precept is not to use luxurious high seats or beds, and the eighth is not to eat after regulation hours, that is, in the afternoon. The last three precepts are similar to those of monastic people. The precept of not eating after regulation hours is called the precept of fasting.

Unable to give up lay life to practice, lay disciples in the Buddha's time were very envious of the monastic life. Therefore, the Buddha established the eight precepts for the lay disciples' additional cultivation to allow them to keep these precepts for one full day. In this way, lay practitioners can follow those practitioners who have given up lay life (arhats, etc.) in order to learn and practice their disciplined and simple way of life. Those who receive these precepts temporarily live near the Saṅgha or the arhats, which is why these are called the "staying nearby" precepts. Since the five precepts are kept for life as the virtuous conduct of laypeople, to practice the monastic life for a short time laypeople take the eight precepts. If they additionally take the precept of not handling money, these nine precepts are the same as the formal monastic precepts for a śrāmaṇera.

The eight-branched fasting precepts were established by the Buddha to be kept for one full day, generally the eighth, fourteenth, fifteenth, twenty-third, twenty-ninth and thirtieth of each month of the lunar calendar, which are the days to give and perform good deeds according to Indian tradition. On those days, people generally go early in the morning to the monastery and request that the acarya transmit the full-day precepts. People then keep the precepts without breaking them until dawn of the next day.

If people then want to take the precepts for another day, they can go to the teacher again and request formal instruction. The Buddha established these precepts for one full day because it would be impossible for the laity to live like monastics; but some people think that these precepts should not be restricted to one full day. So, depending on the participant's vow, it is possible to keep the precepts for three days, five days, or a month.

The eight-branched fasting precepts are more strict than the five precepts. Because the five precepts are to be kept for life, however, they are superior to the eight-branched fasting precepts in some ways. Since the merit accrued from keeping either the five or the eight precepts depends on the way a person keeps them, it is very difficult to say which are superior. The five precepts are the regular discipline that guides the conduct of lay disciples, and it is only on occasions when they want to practice the monastic life that they keep the eight-branched fasting precepts. However, there are also some people who cannot keep the five precepts for life but instead resolve to take the eight-branched fasting precepts for a short time. Although this is contrary to the standard (which requires people to take the five precepts first), since the primary purpose of the Buddha Dharma is to lead people to do good, it is permissible.

The Ten Good Precepts

52 The ten good precepts are no killing, no stealing, no improper sexual conduct,
No lying and no backbiting,
No evil words or frivolous talk,
No greedy desires, anger, or deviant views.
The foundation of all good karma
Is these ten good deeds as explained by the Buddha.
These are the foundation for the good karma of divine and human beings,
Upon which the sacred Dharma of the Three Vehicles is established.

The third category of the pure precepts is that of the ten good deeds, which are also called the ten good precepts. The ten good deeds are not included among the rules and regulations that were established by the Tathāgata. However, the "Chapter of the Ten Stages" in the *Avataṃsaka Sūtra* (Flower Ornament Sūtra), the *Upāsakaśīla Sūtra* (Sūtra on the Moral Behavior of the Laity), the *Madhyamakāvatāra* (Treatise on Entering the Middle Way), and the *She bo luo mi duo lun* (Discourse on Embracing the Pāramitā) all say that the ten good deeds are bodhisattva precepts.

Beginning with the *Āgama Sūtra*, the ten good deeds are recognized as the principal guidelines for virtuous conduct and as equal to the five precepts. In the Buddha Dharma, the precepts and the rules and regulations are similar yet slightly different. Whether one takes the precepts by oneself or receives them from a teacher, they are considered precepts and have the ten good deeds as their foundation. Various rules are established based on a particular practitioner's environment and capacity: the eight categories of rules and regulations of the five precepts, the eight precepts, and so on. These are precepts as well as rules and regulations. The fundamental virtuous conduct of the ten good deeds is therefore discussed in this section on the fortunate karma of keeping the precepts.

The ten good deeds are divided into three groups: physical, verbal, and mental. There are three physical good deeds: not killing, not stealing, and not engaging in improper sexual conduct. These are the same as the first three of the five precepts. There are four verbal good deeds: not lying, not backbiting, not speaking evil words, and not engaging in frivolous speech. The precept of not lying is the same as that of the five precepts. Not backbiting means not destroying the harmony of others through gossiping and thereby sowing discord and dissension. Not speaking evil words means not using offensive language that causes others to be very embarrassed: scolding, mocking and ridiculing, criticizing bitterly or meanly, attacking maliciously, exposing others, and so forth. Not engaging in frivolous speech means not talking uselessly in a way that leads to stealing, sex, lustful love songs, jokes, and heedless conversation, or in a way that superficially touches on any and every subject. Not only is such frivolous speech a waste of time, it is also harmful to the body and the mind.

The fact that the ten good deeds emphasize verbal deeds clearly demonstrates that these deeds are fundamental to virtuous conduct. Human beings use language to communicate their feelings and thoughts.

If their speech is full of lies, backbiting, evil words, and frivolity, how can the peace and happiness of humankind—well-managed homes, well-governed countries, and a peaceful world—be achieved? Although it is said that "speech is as fast as the wind," it is still not easy to communicate verbally. Since the advent of written languages, it has been possible to spread information over great distances and to preserve it for a long time. With the recent inventions of the telephone, television, and so forth, people's minds are now connected as closely as each breath is to the next. Yet these close connections are full of lies, backbiting, and so forth. That is the kind of world in which we live. Trying to establish everlasting peace for humankind while going against normal virtuous conduct is like trying to find fish by climbing up a tree.

In addition to the three good physical deeds and the four good verbal deeds, there are three good mental deeds: having no greed, no anger, and no deviant views. Having no greed means having no desire to possess another person's wealth, spouse, power, or position, or plans to take possession of these. It also means being content without greed. Having no anger means being without hatred or the idea of harming others. Having no deviant views means having the right views of the existence of good and evil, of karmic results, of past and future lives, of ordinary people and sages, and so forth. Though mental deeds take place in the mind, when expressed, they become physical and verbal conduct. The opposite of the ten good deeds is the ten evil deeds. Abandoning the ten evil deeds and practicing the ten good ones is a virtuous conduct that everyone should practice.

The ways to accumulate good karma are extremely numerous, but the ten good deeds are the most obvious ways to do so. In the Mahāyāna Dharma, these ten good deeds are bodhisattva precepts and the foundation for all good conduct, whether for śrāvakas, pratyekabuddhas, divine beings, or humans. They are the foundation for the good karma upon which the sacred Dharma of the Three Vehicles is established. As is said in the *Sāgara-nāga-rāja-paripṛcchā* (Ocean Dragon King Sūtra), "The good Dharma is the fundamental basis upon which human and divine beings must rely to become complete and upon which the śrāvakas and pratyekabuddhas must rely for the attainment of enlightenment and supreme universal enlightenment. What is this basis upon which they rely? It is the ten good deeds."[14] It is also said, "The way of the ten good deeds leads to rebirth as a human or divine being, the attainment of different grades of arhatship of the śrāvakas, the enlightenment of pratyekabuddhas, and is the basis of reliance for all the wonderful deeds of all bodhisattvas and all the Buddha Dharma."[15]

The Fortunate Karma of Meditation

> 53 One should not be attached to sensual pleasures.
> One should not be scattered and confused, for this brings all kinds of suffering.
> One should be kind and persistent in keeping the pure precepts
> And have conviction that practicing meditation is most blissful.

Some people think that giving is an active good deed that benefits others whereas keeping the precepts is a passive virtuous deed that has an effect only on oneself. They wonder what good there can be in practicing meditation. These people do not know that purifying the mind is the goal of the Buddha Dharma and that within the worldly Dharma, practicing meditation is the only way that one can achieve such a goal. Whenever the foundations of the ethics of virtuous politics or virtuous religions are examined, it is impossible to avoid investigating the mind. For example, the Confucians consider managing the family, governing the country, and bringing peace to the world their responsibilities, and these can be realized only through individual cultivation. Thus the maxim "From the emperor to the ordinary people, everyone should cultivate oneself" is taken as a basic teaching. Self-cultivation must begin with "pursuing knowledge to the utmost," "acting with sincerity," and "having an upright mind."

The fundamental and ultimate obstacle to this is one's own mind. To attain a pure meditative mind without the disturbance of defilements is a very precious virtuous deed. As is said in the *Great Learning*, the sequence of practicing the fortunate karma of meditation goes from "Knowing that one can achieve the perfect state, one can then be tranquil" to "Becoming calm, one can then attain perfection."

Why should one practice meditation? There are many reasons, but the most important is that in this sinful world meditation is the only means of curing two big problems: attachment to sense pleasures and scatteredness. Humans are attached to various sensual pleasures: material goods and agreeable sights, sounds, smells, tastes, touch, and sex. They cling to present sensual pleasures; they think about past sensual pleasures; they seek blindly for future sensual pleasures. When people are without sensual pleasures, they struggle to get them; when they have them, they are afraid of losing them; after losing them, they become utterly miserable! Do not all the problems in the human world—social, economic, and political—exist because of desire for sensual pleasure? One should not be attached to the sensual pleasures, for they are like honey on a knife blade; the honey has a sweet taste, but tasting it causes pain.

The human mind is scattered, much more so than the restless movements of monkeys, and because of this people easily become emotional, unable to clearly recognize reality (those who are extremely scattered cannot even understand worldly knowledge), unable to control themselves, and continually influenced by their changing environments. Being scattered is a primary factor in the process that leads to distortion and affliction. It causes people to fall into the sea of desires, filled with worries and suffering, and it prevents them from escaping.

Only by practicing meditation can one avoid being bound by sensual pleasures or being scattered. Through meditation, one can have a clear, pure, and peaceful mind and be one's own master. In order to practice meditation, however, one must have two kinds of preparation, otherwise the meditation will cause more harm than benefit. First, one must have kindness. Do not practice meditation out of curiosity, to gratify a desire for limitless sensual pleasures, to extend one's longevity, or to activate supramundane powers in order to get revenge. Rather, one should be motivated by kind thoughts and want to practice meditation for the benefit and happiness of sentient beings. With kindness, one will have a gentle heart and can easily succeed in one's practice. After succeeding, one will not use one's meditative and transcendental powers to disturb sentient beings by doing such things as gathering people to riot and so forth. Second, one must receive and keep the pure precepts (the ten good deeds, etc.) with virtuous conduct, both physical and verbal. If one acts improperly, then practicing meditation will attract demons and evil. The meditation that one accomplishes will be deviant and cause one to become like a demon, causing harm to one's self and others.

Before practicing, one should have firm faith that practicing meditation is the most blissful of all the worldly dharmas. In terms of worldly pleasures, nothing is better than the pleasures of the five desires, and of these sexual pleasure is supreme; but these cannot be compared to the pleasure of meditation. The pleasures of meditation are complete and permeate the entire body, as if rain were filling everything, from gutters to ponds and swamps. If one can have faith and understand that practicing meditation activates an incomparable pleasure, then one will not be bound to the pleasure of external objects and will practice with diligence and without interruption.

54 Practicing meditation means to regulate and concentrate on
three things.
To have one's mind focused in one state is called concentration.
Suffering and pleasure will successively cease.

The method of practicing meditation is basically to regulate and concentrate one's body and mind. To regulate means to subdue and to refine. The human mind, like an unruly, ill-tempered horse, is hard to control. Like an untamed bull trampling through the rice plants, the mind must be controlled and disciplined; only when it is calm and gentle can it respond to one's wishes. This is why the ancient analogies compare meditation to training a horse or taming a bull. To regulate also means to harmonize. According to the *Xiao zhi guan* (the Minor Cessation-contemplation), three things have to be regulated and focused: the body, the breath, and the mind. The body has to be steady and upright, comfortable and calm, without moving unintentionally and without any feeling of stress and tension. The eyes are closed and the mouth is shut, with the tongue touching the upper palate effortlessly. One must regulate one's breathing until the inhalations and exhalations gradually become gentler and longer, without noise and in a consistent pattern, as if there were no breathing at all. This has to be done through gradual practice and should not be rushed.

To regulate the mind, one must fix it on an object, keep it from being scattered, and keep it from becoming sleepy or restless. When the mind is concentrated and in equanimity, it will naturally become secure and steady. When the mind is the master, the body is in a state of quiet stillness; the mind and breath, mutually dependent, then reach the state of concentration.

To what extent can one achieve concentration through one's practice? When one reaches the condition in which the mind is focused, this is called concentration. Concentration is *samādhi* in Sanskrit, which means "to be equal" and "to be able to hold." Being equal means having equilibrium without restlessness or stupor, and holding means maintaining single-mindedness without scatteredness. In the initial stages of practicing meditation, it is difficult to try to hold the mind in one state because it has many distracting thoughts. One's thoughts must be like lassos, continually turning the mind back and keeping it in one focused state. If one does this, then with time the distracting thoughts will gradually cease. At first, distracting thoughts will arise only occasionally. Eventually, one will be able to hold the mind in equanimity and in a state of single-mindedness. When one starts to feel mild physical and mental bliss, one will have achieved concentration.

There are different stages of concentration, ranging from the superficial to the profound. These stages are commonly described as the four dhyānas and the eight states of meditation. *Dhyāna* means calm thought in Sanskrit. Because it also has the special meaning of having both concentration and wisdom in equal proportion, dhyāna is considered especially important in the Buddha Dharma.

Two Perspectives on Achieving the Four Dhyānas

Concentration may be based on eliminating differentiation or eliminating emotions. In the first kind, the mind gradually stops differentiating. Sentient beings' minds normally differentiate: they either change the object of focus or shift mental images. Those who practice meditation—concentrating the mind, connecting all thoughts, and "abiding securely and clearly"—have minds that are calm, steady, and thoroughly clear. Only at this point can one enter the state of concentration. Some people think they have eliminated differentiation from their minds when they have but briefly put an end to confused thoughts or are simply unaware of their stupor. They do not know that after entering the first dhyāna, their minds still differentiate, even though objects and the perceptions no longer change. They still experience the coarse differentiation of reflection and the fine differentiation of investigation. This is called the samādhi of reflection and investigation. Between the first dhyāna and the second lies a middle dhyāna in which there is no coarse differentiation; this is called the samādhi without reflection and with investigation.

When one enters the second dhyāna, even the fine differentiation disappears. This is called the samādhi without reflection or investigation. At this level, although one is still aware of the state one is in (with only slight reflection), one does not differentiate conceptually. One therefore does not initiate speech, for speech is a verbalization of the reflection and the investigation of one's mind.

Entering the third dhyāna, one intuitively feels inner equanimity and purity. As it is said, "With inner equanimity, one can have right mindfulness and right knowledge." Since this state can also be achieved by non-Buddhists, one must not think that just because one has eliminated differentiation one has realized the original purity of the mind. Meditation above the second dhyāna is called the nondifferentiating concentration that overcomes reflection and investigation.

Concentration may also be based on eliminating emotions. In stages, meditation transcends all suffering and joy until one reaches the ultimate. In the realm of desire lies physical pain and mental sorrow; but when one reaches the first dhyāna, sorrow and pain from the sensual pleasures and afflictions no longer arise. Because the mind withdraws from the sensual pleasures, joy and bliss arise: joy is the happiness of the mind, while bliss is mild comfort, both physical and mental.

When one reaches the second dhyāna, the joy and bliss that one experiences arise from concentration. This joy and bliss are not like the excited state of the initial departure from desires, but happiness is still active. When one enters the third dhyāna, which is called the bliss of leaving happiness behind, there is no longer "happiness." The bliss in this concentration reaches the peak of worldly happiness. Thus, when someone wants to describe extreme happiness, they may say, "It was like entering the third dhyāna." Of course, this cannot be compared to the bliss of emancipation, which is free from afflictions. In the fourth dhyāna and above, when even bliss comes to an end, only tranquil equanimity remains. In comparison to the excited happiness, this is the supreme bliss! The first grouping of the different levels of concentration is that of the four dhyānas.

55 The four dhyānas, the four formless states,
And the four infinite states,
Methods of meditation of concentration taught by the
Buddha,
Should be practiced step by step.

The Four Formless States

Above the fourth dhyāna are the four formless states of concentration: the states of infinite space, of infinite consciousness, of nothingness, and of neither perception nor nonperception. The four formless states are worldly states of mental concentration that are relatively more profound in terms of concentration than they are in terms of wisdom. The four dhyānas and the four formless states together are called the eight concentrations. They constitute a gradation from superficial to profound according to the levels of the power of concentration. Non-Buddhists also can successfully practice and attain these concentrations.

The Four Infinite States

The four infinite states are the states of kindness, compassion, joy, and equanimity. Kindness is the vow to give others happiness; compassion is sympathy for all sentient beings who are suffering; joy is empathy with others' happiness; and equanimity is a mental equilibrium toward all beings, without a biased love for one's relatives or a discriminatory hatred of one's enemies. After one has practiced and attained the four dhyānas, one can practice the four infinite states (the state of joy is limited to the first two dhyānas, however).

These states are called infinite because when one practices them, one contemplates one's relatives first but then one's enemies; one moves from one person to a few people to many, from one country to a region to the whole world, and finally to all the sentient beings of the realm of desire in all the worlds of the ten directions. One's mind becomes full of kindness, compassion, joy, and equanimity, and one wishes that all sentient beings might have happiness and be without suffering. Since these thoughts are focused on infinite sentient beings, and since one who practices can receive the infinite reward of good fortune, these states are called infinite.

When the Buddha spoke of the fortunate karma of practicing meditation for laypeople, the emphasis was mostly on practicing these four infinite states. The maintenance of these states of mind and the constant mindful recollection of them is similar to the benevolence of Confucianism and the universal love of Christianity. Such teachings were originally the same the world over; they are the world's most virtuous teachings and entryways for rebirth in the heavenly kingdoms.

These methods of meditation that the Buddha taught should be practiced step by step, from the first dhyāna to the second, to the third, all the way up to the state of neither perception nor nonperception. When learning, these steps cannot be skipped, but once one is proficient in the practices then one can skip steps or go in the reverse order.

Ranking the Three Fortunate Karmas in Order of Importance

56 Acts of charity are often impure.
Practicing meditation may lead only to self-benefit.
To aim for buddhahood while still a human being,
Keeping the precepts is therefore the most important element.

In a previous section it was said, "Having wished to become human and having become human, / One should cultivate the Dharma of the divine vehicle without wanting to be a divine being." If one is aiming for the attainment of buddhahood as a human while cultivating the deeds of the Human and Divine Vehicles, which should one emphasize more, the keeping of the precepts or the practice of concentration? The emphasis should be on keeping the precepts, because most people improperly cultivate the fortunate karma of giving; they are often defiled by afflictions. No matter how vast one's good fortune that comes from giving, if one does not keep the precepts, one cannot even become human. Instead one can enjoy these good fortunes only as an animal, a hungry ghost, or an asura, and one's future is very dangerous.

Practicing meditation is, of course, outstanding. But when one practices meditation—whether one renounces the five desires or becomes a forest recluse—the emphasis may be on one's own blissful meditation, which may lead to the path of self-benefit only. When one is rewarded by being born above the second dhyāna, one lives an independent existence.

This does not really correspond with the bodhisattva practice, which is directed to the realization of peace and happiness and the deliverance of all sentient beings. If one hopes not to lose the human form in future lives and aims toward attaining buddhahood as a human, therefore, one must keep the five precepts and the ten good deeds in constant focus. Novice bodhisattvas, called "the bodhisattvas of the tenth stage" (ten stages of faith), also emphasize the ten good deeds.

Through keeping the precepts, one can continue to be born in the human world. Even if one is poor, one is not prevented from studying Buddhism. If one keeps the precepts and also practices the acts of giving, one can have vast fortunate karma while living among people; this is even better. If one keeps the precepts without practicing meditation, one will not lose the human form. But if one keeps the precepts and practices profound meditation, one will be born in the longevity heavens, and this creates a big obstacle to the study of Buddhism. So, in order to steer oneself toward the Buddhist way as a human, one should primarily keep the precepts with their emphasis on human ethics and sound character. With the keeping of precepts as one's foundation, one should give according to one's ability. If one wants to practice meditation, one should practice the four infinite states, because they are closely connected with the world-transcending One-Vehicle Dharma of benefiting sentient beings.

THE PRACTICE OF RECOLLECTION

57 For those whose minds are timid and fearful
The Buddha taught the practice of the six recollections:
Being mindful of the Buddha, the Dharma, the Saṅgha,
The merits gained both by giving and by keeping the precepts,
And the possibility of being reborn in heaven,
Is like entering the convergence of light;
Darkness will instantly disappear.

Some people, timid by nature, have all kinds of fear. For example, they are afraid of spirits and ghosts when they walk alone at night or stay in a quiet room alone. Some people are afraid of illness, death, or regression to the three evil destinies after death. Full of worry and regret, they are extremely miserable. The Buddha said that people whose minds are timid and fearful should practice the doctrine of the six recollections. "Recollection," which means being mindful and remembering, is a convenient method for practicing meditation. Those whose meditation practice is profound attain a state of recollection without scattering, while those whose practice is more superficial are able to reach a state of each recollection being connected one to the next.

The Six Recollections

What are the six recollections? The first recollection is of the excellent and solemn appearance of the Buddha, as well as the Buddha's virtues: wisdom, grace, and freedom from defilements. The second is of the Buddha's true Dharma, which is comforting and can lead to emancipation. If one can accept it and follow it appropriately, one can thoroughly understand and realize the Truth at any time.

The third is of the four stages and four grades of arhatship of the śrāvaka Saṅgha. These are beings who virtuously keep the precepts, practice meditation, and have wisdom, liberation, and perfect knowledge of liberation; they are the field of good fortune in this world. Also included in this division is the recollection of the bodhisattva Saṅgha: those who have great compassion and great wisdom and are a benefit to themselves and others. This describes the mindfulness of the virtues of the Three Treasures and the act of turning toward the Three Treasures to be embraced and protected by them.

When one's mind is focused securely on the pure and awesome virtues of the Buddha, one can leave behind deviant thoughts, defiled desires, worries, regrets, and fears. According to a parable in the sūtras, the sovereign Śakra's troops (nagas, yaksas, etc.) battling with the asuras became a hundred times more courageous when they saw the sovereign Śakra's banner. If sentient beings have right recollection of the virtues of the Three Treasures and have firm faith that they are being embraced and protected by them, their minds will be calm and stable. What then can they have to fear?

The fourth recollection is that one has kept the perfect and pure precepts. The fifth is that one has properly practiced pure giving in the field of good fortune. The sixth is that one has practiced the virtues of giving and precept keeping, so one can have the rewards of being adorned with the Seven Treasures and being born as a divine being with superior, wonderful happiness.

According to the sūtras, those who are fearful of illness, death, and regression after death should practice these recollections. People cannot avoid illness or death. If they have practiced and gained merit, they will have a better future life than at present. This is comparable to leaving darkness and entering into bright light, leaving a hut and going into a mansion, or being promoted from a low position to a high one. If one can remember these recollections, one should be able to rejoice and celebrate—how can one be fearful? What actually needs to be feared is not the arrival of old age and death but rather a life lived emptily without giving and precept keeping.

Mindfulness of the virtues of the Three Treasures is derived from taking refuge in the Three Treasures with faith. For example, even in Amitābha's most blissful Pure Land, everyone must still recollect the Buddha, the Dharma, and the Saṅgha. If one can completely take refuge in the Three Treasures, then one can recollect the three. Whether one is mindful of the virtues of the Three Treasures (their external power) or remembers the merit of giving, keeping the precepts, and the reward of becoming a divine being (the power that comes from oneself), firm faith and understanding come from recollection. When one firmly and profoundly has faith in being embraced and protected by the Three Treasures and also has great faith in the inevitability of good causes, it is like entering a great illumination where the darkness of fear and worry instantly disappear.

Right Recollection of Maitreya Buddha

58 To have right recollection of Maitreya Buddha
And vow to be born in his Pure Land—
This method is most precious and rare.
It is very close, easily attainable, and open to all.
If one sees a buddha and always hears the Dharma,
Why should one worry about future regression?

Since Śākyamuni Buddha has passed away and Maitreya Buddha has not yet arrived, one might think that one needs to have a specific buddha as one's place of refuge when one practices the seven branches or the six recollections, or worships and prostrates to the Buddha, or recites the Buddha's name. One might feel that only in that situation could one have firm faith, thinking: "Since this buddha has a special connection with me, only in this way can I be protected without fear of regression." Although these conceptions lack a profound and thorough understanding of the virtues of the Three Treasures and the principle of cause and effect, this is the way the sentient beings usually feel.

In response to this concern, the great and compassionate Śākyamuni Buddha taught the doctrines of being truly mindful of the honored Maitreya and of seeking to be born in the Maitreya's Pure Land. In one assembly, Śākyamuni Buddha personally designated Maitreya Bodhisattva as the next buddha of this world. At present, Maitreya Bodhisattva is living in the Tuṣita Heaven in a special region called the inner court of Tuṣita. Whoever will be the next to descend here as a buddha must first live there; Śākyamuni Buddha did so in the past. The inner court of Tuṣita is an adorned Pure Land where Maitreya Bodhisattva frequently preaches the Dharma to infinite numbers of beings. After some time, Maitreya Bodhisattva will come to Jambudvīpa to become a buddha. By then, this world will have already been transformed into a Pure Land. In this world, Maitreya's human Pure Land, Maitreya Buddha will transform and save infinite sentient beings in the three Dragon-flower tree assemblies.

Therefore, if one vows to be born in the Pure Land of Tuṣita, one will see Maitreya Bodhisattva and will follow him in his descent to the human world of the future. Seeing a buddha and hearing the Dharma, one will progress upward naturally. How could one worry about regression? This compassionate discourse by Śākyamuni Buddha is contained in the sūtras such as the *Mi le xia sheng cheng fo jing* (Maitreya Descending as Buddha Sūtra) and the *Mi le pu sa shang sheng jing* (Ascension of Maitreya Bodhisattva Sūtra).

In comparison to rebirth in other pure lands of the worlds of the ten directions, the doctrine of rebirth in Maitreya's Pure Land is most precious and secure. This can be explained with reference to its three aspects.

1. Closeness: Maitreya, now in the Tuṣita Heaven, will come to our human world in the future—to this very world, in this same realm of desire. These two locations, Maitreya's Pure Land and this world, are very close. Maitreya's Pure Land is not like the other pure lands of the ten directions. In order to reach these other pure lands, one must pass through many Buddha-lands. As for the length of time involved in this process, after one is reborn in the inner court of Tuṣita in the next life, it

will not be too long before one will return to the human world. This is not like being reborn in other pure lands, where the length of time required to return to this world is unknown.

2. Easy attainability: The Pure Land of Tuṣita and the Pure Land of this world, as it will exist in the future, are both lands in the realm of desire. One therefore needs only to take refuge in the Three Treasures, keep the precepts purely, give properly, and in addition vow to be born in Maitreya's Pure Land, reciting, "Praise the future descending Maitreya Buddha." Then one can be born in the Pure Land of Tuṣita. This is different from being born in other pure lands, in which one has to be single-minded without scatteredness. To be single-minded without scatteredness in meditation is certainly not easy.

3. Universal accessibility: To be reborn in Maitreya's Pure Land, one need not necessarily vow to attain the bodhi mind or the mind of renunciation. This is because those people with good roots for human and divine rebirth who want to have better future lives can be reborn there with their vows. In the Pure Land of Tuṣita and the future Pure Land of this world, the honored Maitreya, in accord with the various capacities of all beings, expounds the human and divine Dharma, the Two-Vehicle Dharma, and the Bodhisattva Dharma, so that everyone will receive benefits accordingly. Through seeing a buddha and hearing the Dharma, beings are gradually transformed with steady upward progress—from having human and divine capacities to having the capacity to transcend the world, from having the capacities of the Two Vehicles to having those of the Great Vehicle—and finally return to the way of the Buddha. The beings of the Two Vehicles cannot be reborn in those other pure lands, so of course they cannot receive human and divine beings. Therefore, the doctrine for the Pure Land of Maitreya is the one that is really open to all those who would attain the deliverance of the Five Vehicles.

Some people say, "If we are to be reborn in Maitreya's Pure Land now, what will we do after Maitreya Buddha enters Nirvāṇa if we have not been liberated from birth and death by that time?" These people are fearful of not seeing a buddha or hearing the Dharma and thereby regressing. They do not know that Śākyamuni Buddha is so compassionate that he has given us the future descending Maitreya Buddha. The paths of all the buddhas are the same, so will not Maitreya Buddha tell us how to associate with the future Buddha too?

Some people say, "Previously it was said that one should cultivate the divine Dharma without wanting to be a divine being, so why talk about seeking to be reborn in Tuṣita Heaven?" The primary reason that one wants to avoid being born in the heavens is that one does not want to be born in the longevity heavens through one's profound meditation. In the heavens of the realm of desire, and in Maitreya Bodhisattva's inner court of Tuṣita in particular, one frequently sees the future buddha, listens to the Dharma, and practices, so it is all right to be reborn there. Some people say, "Why not advocate being reborn in Amitābha's Pure Land?" They should know that Amitābha Buddha's most blissful Pure Land is a Pure Land particular to the Great Vehicle—in which the śrāvaka Buddhists generally do not believe or of which they are ignorant. This will be explained in the Dharma of the Great Vehicle in chapter 5. For now, the discussion concerns the Dharma that thoroughly connects and is shared in common by the Five Vehicles.

Some people say, "In the past, Buddhasiṃha practiced the doctrines of Maitreya, vowing to be born in the inner court of Tuṣita, but instead he ended up in the outer court enjoying sensual pleasures. So it may not be reliable to be reborn in the pure land of Tuṣita." These people do not know that the story of Buddhasiṃha being born in the outer court was purposely spread by other people with ulterior motives but was never mentioned in the biographies of those who transmitted the doctrines of Maitreya, such as Paramārtha, the Tripitaka master Xuanzang, Asaṅga, and Vasubandhu.

In brief, regardless of the kind of capacity one has for studying Buddhism, one needs only to take refuge in the Three Treasures, give properly, keep the precepts purely, and vow to return to Maitreya's Pure Land. One is guaranteed to progress upward in the course of practice through seeing the future buddha and hearing the Dharma frequently, so one should not worry about the possibility of future regression. Therefore, please sincerely vow to be reborn in the inner court of Tuṣita and recite, "Praise the future descending Maitreya Buddha!"

4

The Dharma Common to the Three Vehicles

THE DHARMA COMMON to the Three Vehicles, the world-transcending Dharma, is established on the foundation of the Five Vehicles. If one does not have human and divine virtues but is instead immersed in the three evil destinies, obviously one cannot vow to be emancipated from birth and death. One may be born as a human, but if one does all kinds of evil without shame or remorse, harming people and the world, one will lose one's human nature and cease to be an ordinary person. How then could one vow to end birth and death? Only those who have first accomplished the human and divine virtues can practice the Dharma common to the Three Vehicles.

RESOLVING TO RENOUNCE

59 All conditioned things are impermanent;
So, says the Buddha, all sensations lead to suffering.
Because of this, one may grow weary, renounce the world,
And go toward the way of liberation.

Since the foundation of the world-transcending Dharma of the Three Vehicles is the resolution to renounce, the first thing one needs to learn is to develop this resolve. All things in the world are impermanent; they are neither ultimate nor independent. Such is this world in which sentient beings are miserable. Only by recognizing this can one develop the resolution to renounce. As for the general experience of sensations and feelings in the world, there are states of suffering, states of happiness, and states of neither suffering nor happiness. Thus, the human world cannot be described as consisting completely of suffering. But one should know that the proposition "the world is suffering" is profound. In the sūtras, the Buddha says, "Because all conditioned things are impermanent, all sensations lead to suffering."[1] From a superficial perspective, there are different sensations of suffering, happiness, and neither suffering nor happiness;

when one looks deeper, however, one cannot avoid saying that all sensations are suffering. This is because all things in the world are changing and created: "changing" in that they are in the process of creation and extinction, birth and death, formation and destruction, and "created" in that they are formed by causes and conditions. That which is changing and created is called a conditioned thing, that is, a phenomenon. All these conditioned things are impermanent, not everlasting.

Since all conditioned things are impermanent, all one's present worries and afflictions are suffering. The Buddha called such worries and afflictions "ordinary suffering." Even if one has satisfactory wealth, respect, health, and intelligence, when changes come, suffering follows. The Buddha called this "the suffering of change." Even if one experiences neither suffering nor happiness but instead feels contented and serene, sooner or later this situation will become one of suffering. We are like a sailor on the ocean who, dead drunk, steers toward the beach through a treacherous reef. Is it not sad that a drunkard is not even cognizant of suffering or happiness? The Buddha called this "the suffering of conditioned states." Thus, because all conditioned things are impermanent, not lasting, not ultimate, and not secure, it must be said that all sensations lead to suffering, that the world is like a burning house, and that the three realms are like prisons.

If those studying the Buddha Dharma have profound understanding, then regardless of how happy they are, they will not be reluctant to leave the world. They will not be interested in rising to the divine kingdoms of wholehearted enjoyment. Because of their profound understanding, they are determined to renounce birth and death.

Miserable! Miserable! Such is this world for those possessing this determination. The world is a place where they cannot stand to stay even for a moment. Living in it, for them, is like being in a house on fire: they need to escape quickly. When their aspiration becomes firm, such people enter the great way of liberation and will bring birth and death to an end. Without the resolution to renounce, all practices and virtues belong only to the worldly Dharma. But if it is present, it will embrace and guide all virtues so that they become factors for liberation from birth and death, factors that move one toward emancipation. The resolution to renounce is the foundation of the world-transcending Dharma. Our fellow Buddhists who constantly talk about putting an end to birth and death should examine themselves to see whether they have such a frame of mind.

PRACTITIONERS OF THE DHARMA COMMON TO THE THREE VEHICLES

60 Because such people have different capacities, the Buddha established Three Vehicles.
The main group for instruction and guidance, however, was the śrāvakas.

Those who have the resolution to renounce and practice the world-transcending Dharma can be differentiated according to their capacities. Basically, the Buddha established three different vehicles in accord with the different capacities of his followers.

The Three Vehicles are the Śrāvaka Vehicle, the Pratyekabuddha Vehicle, and the Bodhisattva Vehicle. The *Lotus Sūtra* and other sūtras say that the Buddha preached the Four Truths to the śrāvakas, the twelvefold dependent origination to the pratyekabuddhas, and the six pāramitās to the bodhisattvas. Actually, all the world-transcending Dharmas contain the profound meanings of the Four Truths and the twelvefold dependent origination; the bodhisattva way, however, emphasizes the great accomplishments of the six pāramitās.

The main group of practitioners to be instructed and guided were those of the Śrāvaka Vehicle; the bodhisattva and the pratyekabuddha groups can be said to have been marginal in the historical Buddha's time. In the sūtras of the Dharma common to the Three Vehicles—the *Āgama Sūtra* and others—only two bodhisattvas are mentioned: Śākyamuni Bodhisattva before he became the Buddha (when he preached the Dharma, he had already become the Buddha, the founder of the religion, and was no longer a person in training) and Maitreya Bodhisattva, who was in the assembly of Śākyamuni Buddha and was designated as the next buddha. Thus, even though the Buddha had spoken of the Three Vehicles, during his lifetime there was only one practicing bodhisattva, Maitreya. According to these sūtras, the six and ten pāramitās of the bodhisattva way originate in the jātaka stories told by the ancient monks, and it is not known to whom they were preached. As for the pratyekabuddhas, there were not too many people endowed with this nature. Originally, the pratyekabuddhas were enlightened without teachers; they did not need to be taught the Dharma. People like Mahākāśyapa possessed the fundamental nature of the pratyekabuddha, but they became the Buddha's disciples when Śākyamuni Buddha began to preach the Dharma. In fact, among the śrāvaka disciples of the Buddha there were some with the fundamental nature of the pratyekabuddha. Therefore, according to these sūtras, which speak solely of the Śākyamuni Buddha's Dharma in this world during his lifetime, the main group of practitioners, then, consisted of the śrāvakas.

In the past, "śrāvaka" was a general name for all the Buddha's disciples, and this name indicated that these disciples had become enlightened after hearing the Buddha's teachings. The Tiantai school called it the "Tripitaka teaching" because it includes not just the Hīnayānists but also bodhisattvas. But the Xianshou school called it the "small teaching" because it is primarily based on the Śrāvaka Dharma of the Small Vehicle. In fact, Śākyamuni's Buddha Dharma, such as he taught it during his lifetime, revealed both the partial and whole truth.

The Diversity of Śrāvaka Practitioners

61 The way of liberation should be far away from
The two extremes of asceticism and pleasure seeking.
The Buddha, to accommodate those who wanted to have pleasure,
Allowed laypeople to remain at home to practice the Dharma;
And, to accommodate ascetics,
He allowed them to leave home to be śramaṇas.

The Buddha's śrāvaka disciples had different fundamental natures. First, there were the two categories of laypeople and monastics. During Śākyamuni Buddha's time, the social customs in India were moving toward extremes. The majority of people were pleasure seekers and hedonists who pursued endless desires and became enslaved by them. The most extreme were the materialistic Lokāyatas and the Saktas, who worshipped sexual desires and regarded sexual intercourse between men and women as the greatest happiness and the most wonderful method of liberation from birth and death. At the opposite extreme were ascetics who believed in suppressing their desires. Such people were present in all the groups of śramaṇas and were found among the non-Buddhists who gave up lay life during that time. Most extreme were the Jains, some of whom did not wear clothes, slept on thorns, ate no cooked food but lived solely on wild vegetables and fruits, drank nothing but water, or practiced special modes of breathing. All these injurious activities of the body and mind were regarded as holy practices. When Śākyamuni Buddha turned the Dharma-wheel, he began by revealing the Middle Way—the practice of neither asceticism nor pleasure seeking. He considered both extremes incapable of leading the body and mind to a normal state, and hence not conducive to liberation. The Middle Way means to live in a way in which the desires have been transformed by wisdom. One controls but does not injure oneself; one enjoys things that are necessary for living but does not indulge. This alone is the true way of liberation.

The Buddha offered the Middle Way as the proper target, but the capacities of the people he taught were inclined toward either asceticism or pleasure. To guide these two different types of persons, two categories of śrāvaka disciples arose: lay and monastic. The primary difference between those who remained at home and those who left home and gave up lay life was their lifestyle.

During his lifetime, the Buddha preached the Dharma to people. After listening to the Dharma or realizing the truth, some volunteered to take refuge in the Three Treasures to become the Buddha's lay disciples. Others volunteered to give up lay life to become the Buddha's monastic disciples. Between the lay and monastic disciples there were no differences in their beliefs, practices, and realizations. Why then did some volunteer to remain at home and others to give up lay life? They did so because of different personalities and lifestyle preferences.

In order to accommodate those who wanted to continue life's pleasures, the Buddha allowed disciples to remain laypersons. They remained husbands, wives, and children; they continued to live as householders and to work as politicians, servicemen, farmers, laborers, and businessmen. These disciples included such people as King Bimbisara, Queen Mallika, Elder Sudatta, Elder Citta, and General Isidatta. Although they lived as laity, they practiced the Buddha's true Dharma, taking refuge in the Three Treasures, keeping the five precepts, practicing meditation, and attaining wisdom. As long as they kept the resolution to renounce and as long as living a full lay life did not hinder their practice, they were still able to become liberated from birth and death.

At the same time, in order to accommodate the ascetic nature the Buddha provided the opportunity for disciples to renounce lay life.

People of this category were mostly those from among the monastic non-Buddhists who were transformed by the Buddha's teaching. These included the first five bhikṣus, Mahākāśyapa, the three Kāśyapas, Śāriputra, and Maudgalyāyana. Such people were accustomed to being renunciates and living solemn lives. Since they were content, had few desires, did not want to save up money, and kept away from sexual desire, they volunteered to give up lay life in order to be śramaṇas. "Śramaṇa" is a Sanskrit word that means "diligent stopping" and is the general name for various kinds of people who have renounced lay life. This is a broad categorization. Obviously, if people have impure motives or give up home life regretfully, their basic nature may remain that of one who seeks pleasure. For example, when the Buddha returned to his native land, a large number of young people from the Śākya clan followed his example in giving up lay life. Yet these young people, such as Ānanda, did so with a spirit that was different from that of Mahākāśyapa and others. On the other hand, there were also lay disciples who led solemn lives.

In short, whether people stay at home and pursue pleasure or give up lay life and pursue asceticism, they are the Buddha's śrāvaka disciples as long as they have the resolution to renounce and live according to the Middle Way—without too much indulgence or too much asceticism. It is possible for those who practice according to the Dharma to realize the fruit of the śrāvaka way and be liberated from birth and death.

62 They may prefer to live by themselves alone
Or to live among people.

Those who gave up home life in the Buddha's time were also of different fundamental natures. Some of them, the forest-dwelling bhikṣus (*araṇya bhikṣus*), preferred to live alone. They lived in the mountains, wildernesses, or graveyards and slept under the trees or in simple and crude grass huts. Everything they ate and wore was simple and poor. In order to avoid the afflictions of human affairs, they did not want to live with people. They did not even want to beg for alms or to preach the Dharma. These hermit bhikṣus' minds were strongly oriented toward benefiting themselves, and they eagerly wanted to practice meditation.

Others preferred to live among people, so they were called village-dwelling bhikṣus. They lived harmoniously with people and did not leave the Saṅgha. Most of them lived in the outskirts of villages. They frequently traveled among people and preached as might be appropriate. Although they also practiced diligently, they lived in a community and kept in close contact with society. The development of Buddhism was primarily the work of these village-dwelling bhikṣus.

For example, Śākyamuni Buddha frequently lived with his disciples, traveled to various countries, and taught and transformed sentient beings; this was the model for the bhikṣus who live among people. The Buddha also lived alone for three months practicing *ānāpānasati* (meditation on the breath), which served as a model for living alone. According to the true meaning of the Buddha Dharma, to live alone means to live without afflictions in the mind; otherwise, regardless of how quiet the environment is, one will still have confused and scattered thoughts. On the other hand, if one's mind is tranquil and liberated, one can live alone or live among people, and travel and teach among them. Thus are the differences in the fundamental natures and preferences of these two categories of learners, which are similar to the different styles of the śrāvakas and the pratyekabuddhas.

63 Their behavior may follow their belief
Or their behavior may follow their understanding.

During the Buddha's time, another broad distinction was made, one that is still applicable to both lay and monastic people. Among the śrāvaka disciples, those who were dull based their practice on beliefs and faith; those who were intelligent based their practice on understanding. A capacity for both belief and wisdom is essential for the study of Buddhism; it distinguishes the Buddha Dharma from some non-Buddhist teachings. Belief is emotional while wisdom is rational, so Buddhists should have these two equally developed and in harmony. "Having belief but not wisdom, one becomes more ignorant; while if one has wisdom but not belief, one's deviant views multiply."[2] The Buddha Dharma says that belief and wisdom are just one. But when one looks at the fundamental nature of actual Buddhist practice, one will see that some Buddhists emphasize belief and faith, while others emphasize wisdom. Although the ultimate goal is the same, they start with an inclination toward either belief or wisdom.

"Behavior" means the specific characteristics formed from one's usual and consistent habits: greedy behavior, angry behavior, etc. Those whose behavior follows their beliefs tend to trust others easily, and everything they do revolves around their beliefs. If people with such characteristics encounter the Buddha Dharma, they will do whatever their teacher tells them. They are not interested in finding out the reasons; they believe what they hear and behave accordingly. Those with this type of character should not be given detailed discourses, for not only do they not feel the need for much instruction, but extensive instructions may even confuse them. Such people can be told to follow but cannot be told the reason. People like this learn primarily by associating with good and knowledgeable people and by following the instructions of teachers. They just believe and behave accordingly, and from their practice their wisdom gradually grows.

Those who practice according to their understanding are different. They are always rational and want to find out the reasons first; they insist on getting to the bottom of the matter. After listening to the teacher's instruction, they want to add their own observations, analyses, and references to the sūtras and discourses. Reaching a profound understanding, they believe firmly and practice diligently. Their minds are sharp, and they have the ability to guide others in their practice. Neither type of person is without some belief or wisdom, but people inevitably have an inclination one way or the other. Not only beginners but even those who have attained enlightenment have different characters.

64 Although they have different characters,
They can cultivate the renunciation of the world in similar ways.

Among those who had the resolution to renounce there were śrāvakas, pratyekabuddhas, bodhisattvas; laypeople and monastics; those living alone and those living among people; those whose behavior followed their beliefs and those whose behavior followed their understanding. Despite their different characters and styles, all could equally cultivate the behavior associated with renunciation and achieve the goal of liberation from birth and death, provided they really had the resolution to renounce.

Ordinary people always judge everything in terms of their own characters and preferences, unaware that the study of Buddhism (that is, the Dharma common to the Three Vehicles) accommodates different types of persons. Those who value belief more than understanding look upon those who study the meaning of the Dharma as people who do not practice; they believe that they themselves are better endowed to practice. Those who emphasize wisdom and understanding more than faith look upon the behavior of those who value belief as blind practitioners (for practice can indeed be blind, depending on the teacher's instruction). As well, those who are inclined toward living in the mountains and forests praise the simple and austere life. They even say, "Whatever we do is asceticism (*dhūta*), wherever we dwell is a hermitage (*araṇya*)," and they look down on the bhikṣus who live among people. Those who travel among people usually deprecate the hermit bhikṣus, saying that they are selfish. Finally, the lay and the monastic people frequently disdain each other because of their different viewpoints.

In the past, Buddhism emphasized the monastic life. Followers left home whether or not they were suitable for the monastic life, could content themselves with little, and detach themselves from thoughts of wealth and family. For the most part, however, their characters were not suitable for leaving home, so the standards of the Saṅgha fell. They competed for fame, profit, and enjoyment. Under the guise of transmitting the Dharma and benefiting others, they competed for influence and territory. Or they gathered disciples and competed for devotees, creating a factionalism that was irrelevant to the Buddha Dharma. Maybe they were better suited to be lay disciples; they might have practiced and reached greater virtue that way! In short, since there are different characters and different styles in the study of Buddhism, one should respect others and know oneself.

THE FOUR NOBLE TRUTHS AND DEPENDENT ORIGINATION

65 The way of liberation as taught by the Buddha
Is the Four Truths and dependent origination.
All the profound Buddha Dharmas
Are evidenced by these.

Although the doctrines that the Buddha taught to people of different capacities are infinite and boundless, the way of liberation is, in brief, contained within the doctrines of the Four Truths and dependent origination. Apart from these, there is no world-transcending Buddha Dharma.

"Truth" means nondistortion; truth is that which is real. The Buddha's world-transcending doctrine has four aspects: suffering, accumulation, extinction, and the Way—that is, it correctly reveals the specific character of the human world (suffering) and its cause (accumulation), and it explains the state of overcoming the world and being rid of suffering (extinction) and the methods for doing so (the Way). One has to recognize the suffering in life and its causes; then, in the process of extinguishing these causes, one can realize the truth and be liberated from suffering's limitless births and deaths.

Dependent origination is not particularly different from the Four Truths. It is concerned with the discovery of the origin of suffering and with the inexorable law of the mutual conditioning of the causes of suffering and its effects. The origin of suffering and the law of cause and effect are found by thoroughly investigating the reality of suffering. The way this law operates is that ignorance conditions volitional action, volitional action conditions consciousness, consciousness conditions mental and physical phenomena, mental and physical phenomena condition the six faculties, the six faculties conditions contact, contact conditions sensation, sensation conditions desire, desire conditions clinging, clinging conditions existence, existence conditions birth, birth conditions aging, illness, and death. These are the classic twelve links of dependent origination. Actually, this is the explanation of the first and second truths—suffering and accumulation—in the form of a series. Dependent origination holds that suffering and accumulation are dependent on conditions (relationships, factors, and causes) for their genesis and existence. So, if the conditions are changed, they can be extinguished. Their being extinguished will lead to emancipation—the third and fourth truths of extinction and the Way. The main outline of the following explanation, therefore, follows the Four Truths, but the doctrine of dependent origination will be explained as well.

In general it is thought that the Four Truths and dependent origination are the Small-Vehicle Dharmas. People who think this do not know that these teachings are also evidenced in all the profound Buddha Dharmas of the Great Vehicle. As for their respective inclinations, it can be said that the Small-Vehicle Dharma emphasizes the explanation of suffering and accumulation, while the Great-Vehicle Dharma emphasizes the extinction and the Way, especially the explanation of extinction. For example, in the two sects—Madhyamaka and Yogācāra—of the Great Vehicle, the Mādhyamikans (on emptiness) and the Yogacarins (on dependent origination) never departed from the scope of the Four Truths and dependent origination. It is clearly stated in the sūtras (*Śrīmālādevīsiṃhanāda Sūtra*) that the Four Truths of the Small Vehicle are limited and require effort to become complete, whereas the Four Truths of the Great Vehicle are unlimited and require no more effort to be considered complete.[3] It is also said in the *Nirvāṇa Sūtra* that people with less wisdom contemplate dependent origination and attain the enlightenment of a śrāvaka, while people with superior wisdom contemplate dependent origination and attain the enlightenment of a buddha.[4] The Buddha Dharma never departs from the doctrines of the Four Truths and dependent origination; the only differences are in the partial or complete realization and the different levels of teaching.

66 Suffering, accumulation, extinction, and the Way
Are called the Four Noble Truths.

The Four Truths are those of suffering, accumulation, extinction, and the Way. These four are called the Four Noble Truths in the sūtras. Since everyone has suffering and everyone has afflictions (accumulation), why specifically talk about the Four Noble Truths? In reality, suffering is the actual misery of the human world; accumulation means the afflictions and the karmic force that the afflictions generate; extinction means to extinguish afflictions in order to put an end to the recurrence of suffering; the Way is the precepts, meditation, and wisdom, which are the methods practiced to counteract the afflictions and to reach Nirvāṇa. But these truths can be recognized only from knowledge of reality and can be truly realized only by the sages. Therefore, it is said in the *Nirvāṇa Sūtra* that the ordinary people suffer but do not know the truth of suffering, while the sages suffer and know this truth.[5] Also it is said in the *Yi jiao jing* (Sūtra of the Teachings and Regulations…), "The Buddha spoke of the truth of suffering: that reality is suffering, and that suffering cannot be changed to happiness. Accumulation is the real cause of suffering; there is no other cause. If suffering is extinguished, it is the same as the cause being extinguished; when the cause is extinguished, so is the effect. The way to extinguish suffering is the real way, and there is no other way."[6]

The suffering nature of the human world, the causal nature of afflictions, the nature of Nirvāṇa as extinction, the therapeutic and Nirvāṇa-attaining nature of the precepts, meditation, and wisdom—these are all real, inevitable, and absolute. Only the sages can realize them profoundly and firmly without lingering doubt, so they are called the Four Noble Truths.

THE TRUTH OF SUFFERING

67 Suffering arises from not getting what one desires,
From associating with those who one dislikes and parting with those one loves,
From being born, becoming old, getting sick, and dying,
Which all come from the union of the five aggregates.

In the Four Truths, suffering is described first. This means that the first thing to recognize is that suffering constitutes the real world, our bodies and minds. Suffering is an oppressive annoyance, an oppression of the body and mind that makes one feel trapped and distraught.

THE EIGHT SUFFERINGS

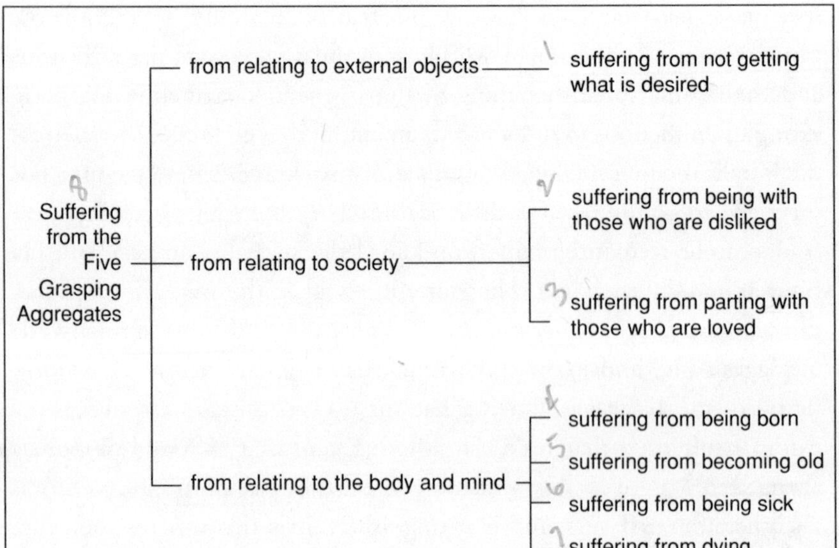

The Buddha has described the various categories of suffering, but from the human standpoint, the most important are the eight sufferings. (1) Suffering arises when one does not get what one desires. Fame, power, position, family, wealth, etc., are all desired by people, but frequently they are unobtainable. To seek but not to get something is suffering. After getting the desired object, one wishes not to lose it; or, if one has trouble with it, one hopes to get rid of it but cannot. The sūtra says, "If what one seeks is not obtained, one will suffer as if being shot by an arrow."[7] This is the suffering from not getting what is desired, which is triggered by dealing with external things. (2) The suffering that comes when one associates with those whom one dislikes and (3) the suffering that comes when one is separated from those one loves are sufferings arising from social relationships (encountered in all the realms of rebirth). Some people have disagreements or blame and hate one another. It is best for them not to associate, but sometimes they have to live together, work together, or talk to one another. Unable to forgive one another yet unable to part, they experience extreme misery. Loved ones, on the contrary—parents, siblings, spouses, children, friends, and lovers—have to part, sometimes forever; they miss one another and live with unhappy thoughts that this miserable separation will last indefinitely. (4) The suffering of being born, (5) the suffering of growing old, (6) the suffering of becoming sick, and (7) the suffering of dying all stem from our experiences with our own bodies and minds. Ordinary people always think that birth brings happiness while old age, sickness, and death bring sadness. They do not realize that after being born one cannot avoid becoming old, getting sick, and dying. Aging, sickness, and death come from being born, so what is so happy about being born? Birth is the root of suffering; old age, sickness, and death are like the branches, leaves, flowers, and fruit of birth. From the roots to the fruit, all is bitter.

From our relationship with external things, with society, and with our body and mind come seven different sufferings. With further investigation, one can realize that these sufferings all come from (8) the union of the five aggregates. The five aggregates are the five categories of elements that make up our body and mind. They are the crux of all suffering. With respect to external things, society, and our body and mind, the above-mentioned seven sufferings cannot be avoided. We have all our problems and afflictions because we have these five aggregates. The five (grasping) aggregates—the total body of suffering—together with the previous seven different sufferings, are called the eight sufferings.

The Five Aggregates

68 These five aggregates are
Forms, sensations, perceptions, mental formations, and
consciousness.
Grasping consciousness, which exists everywhere,
Is contaminated and cannot be disentangled.

The five aggregates are five different categories of elements. Similar categories assemble together, and each category includes many elements; hence their name, "aggregates," meaning "collecting together." When the Buddha spoke of the truth of suffering, he often referred to the five aggregates. They are, he said, like armed robbers, confining sentient beings, their victims, within their evil territory of suffering. They are forms, sensations, perceptions, mental formations, and consciousness.

Form is defined as "changing resistance," which can obstruct and can also be divided. Form, having substance and being resistant, has volume and occupies space; it can be analyzed and destroyed. In modern terms it would be called "matter," but in the Buddha Dharma the forces that arise from matter are called "form." Although these forms, or forces, refer to the hidden forces of good or evil conduct, they are somewhat similar to the modern view of "energy." *Sensation* is defined as reception. When the mind is in contact with an external object and "receives" it, this reception triggers internal feelings—sorrow or happiness. These sensations are the emotional functions of the mind. *Perception* is defined as "making an image," which is the function of cognition. In recognizing the external object, the mind makes an image of that object and then reveals it; through the formation of conceptions and associations, various acts of speech and writing are established. *Mental formation* is defined as "creation." When an object triggers the mind, the mind will, after mental consideration and decision making, initiate a physical or verbal action. Mental actions are basically the attributes of the mind known as thoughts. These mental formations mobilize the mind to create, which is a function of volition. All actions that center on thinking—all volitions and all associated mental functions with the exception of sensations and perceptions—are included in this aggregate. *Consciousness* is defined as "clear differentiation"—clear understanding and discrimination. The mind is actually very complicated: it consists of attributes such as sensations, perceptions, thinking, etc., and it is an encompassing awareness. This encompassing awareness that can differentiate in the recognition of objects is called consciousness.

Form is material; sensations, perceptions, formations, and consciousness are mental. Sentient beings in the cycle of birth and death are synonymous with these five aggregates. Things that we think of as "I and mine" are actually not separate from the five aggregates; they are nothing more than the physical and mental activities, nothing more than matter and spirit.

The five aggregates of sentient beings are called the five grasping aggregates because they are formed from past grasping afflictions. Because they arise from grasping, their intrinsic qualities are inevitably miserable. And now, because of the confused attachments of the grasping afflictions, these five grasping aggregates become even more miserable. The Buddha spoke of the doctrine of the fourfold abiding consciousness: our grasping consciousness, a consciousness associated with afflictions, cannot be without objects. These objects are material forms, feelings or sensations, discriminating perceptions, and creative formations. The grasping consciousness constantly dwells on these four material or mental objects, acting as if they could be grasped, dwelled on, attached to, and obtained. It is like the glue affixed to lacquer; it cannot be disentangled. When consciousness is attached to—concerned about—an object, any change in that object will cause one's mind to be involuntarily either sad or happy. Of course, this is unavoidably miserable. You may not have any reaction when the leaves of the tree fall because you do not see that as something relating to yourself. But if a loved one—or the power, position, or wealth that you cherish, or some other object that especially concerns you—is endangered or on the verge of death, you will then feel incomparable pain and suffering. This is because you are so attached that it is as if this object were yourself or part of yourself. Attaching to objects is like falling into an ensnaring net or a thorn bush. In other words, consciousness forms attachments; form, sensations, perceptions, and formations are objects of attachment; together they are the five aggregates—the conglomeration of all suffering.

The Six Sense Organs and the Six Consciousnesses

69 This also can be illustrated by the six sense organs,
Which, grasping external conditions, produce consciousness.

The body and mind of sentient beings is the confluence of all suffering. Besides the discourses on the five aggregates, the Buddha also spoke of the six sense organs (or the twelve places) and the six objects (or the eighteen objects). So this conglomeration of suffering can be illustrated by the six sense organs. The six sense organs are the eye, ear, nose, tongue, body, and mind. The six sense organs are also called the six roots, a word that carries the sense of growth. The six sense organs constitute a further classification of the twofold entity of body and mind. Grasping after objects proceeds through the six sense organs, and this produces the differentiating consciousness. The six sense organs are the entrances through which the activities of cognition must pass; only by passing through them can cognition be produced. Five of these organs—the eye, ear, nose, tongue, and body—are material and have physiological functions: to see visible forms, hear sounds, smell odors, sense tastes, and feel tangible objects. The Buddha said that these organs are of extremely subtle form, which most likely means that they are the nerves. The sixth sense organ—the mind—recognizes all objects of cognition; it is the mental faculty and the source of the consciousness. Sentient beings' cognition cannot happen without the six sense organs. The six sense organs grasp six objects—visible forms, sounds, odors, tastes, tangible objects, and objects of cognition—and this grasping generates the six consciousnesses: eye, ear, nose, tongue, body, and mind consciousness.

The six consciousnesses arise in dependence upon the six sense organs, so these organs are described as contributing factors. The six consciousnesses are also dependent on their six objects, so these objects are called influencing factors. Because both the sense organs and their objects produce the differentiating consciousness, they are called the twelve places. Most sūtras, however, emphasize the six sense organs rather than these twelve. When the six consciousnesses arise, not only do they differentiate between sense objects, they also become associated with afflictions and attachments. Attaching to objects, the entity of body and mind falls into the abyss of suffering.

The Six Elements

70 Or by the union of the six elements.
The suffering of the world derives from all these.

The Buddha also emphasized the classification of matter and spoke of the union of the six elements, also called the six great elements. "The four great elements enclose a space with consciousness inside, this is called a human being."[8] The six elements—six categories or factors that form sentient beings—are earth, water, fire, wind, space, and consciousness. The four great elements of earth, water, fire, and wind are classifications of the characteristics of matter. These characteristics have different levels of meaning, but a simple explanation is that the solidity of the bones and flesh is the earth element; the fluidity of the blood, sweat, and the like is the water element; warmth and heat is the fire element; and the motility of breathing and movement is the wind element. These four are material elements, the foundation for all physiological functions. The space element refers to empty space—for the material body is full of space: spaces among the internal organs, eyes, ears, nose, mouth, and so forth, and the pores of the body. The consciousness element refers to the six consciousnesses that differentiate objects and become attached.

The entity of body and mind that constitutes sentient beings is usually described in the sūtras as "the aggregates that have been obtained, the elements that have been obtained, and the senses that have been obtained";[9] these are all the accumulated sufferings of sentient beings. According to a popular saying, accompanying these three groups of things, there is life and also suffering. This is like the saying of Laozi, "I have great trouble because I have a body." But according to some non-Buddhist thinking, besides the body and mind there is also an everlasting "soul" or "self," which is the principal entity that transmigrates among the hells, the human world, and the divine kingdoms. Actually, such conceptions are the ignorant products of sentient beings' fantasies. Sentient beings in the world suffer from the cycle of birth and death in the six ways of rebirth; suffering's causes and effects, continuing endlessly, are nothing more than the aggregates, the elements, and the sense organs.

In his discourses on the conglomeration of suffering, the Buddha pointed out its two aspects: it is thoroughly miserable and it is real. "Reality is suffering, and it cannot be changed into happiness." Unless thoroughly remedied, this situation is completely hopeless. Through understanding this, sentient beings can be liberated from confused religious teachings about a supposedly free and independent "soul" or "true self." To practice the holy world-transcending Dharma, one has to understand these teachings profoundly.

The Truth of Accumulation

> 71 Suffering comes from the accumulation of karma.
> Accumulation of karma comes from confusion,
> Which can be triggered or nurtured by afflictions.
> Encountering the right conditions will bring about the fruit of suffering.

Accumulation refers to that which arises due to causes and conditions. Why do the fruits of suffering in the world of sentient beings continue to arise? Because of the accumulation of karma.

Karma

Karma is good or evil conduct (karma that is expressed) and the hidden force that is triggered by the good or evil conduct (karma that is not expressed). Due to the accumulation of karmic forces, the fruits of suffering accumulate. But why does the accumulation of karma occur? Because of confusion. Confusion is the common name for afflictions. Precisely because of these factors in sentient beings' minds, karma accumulates.

It is important to understand that the afflictions are the primary power through which karmic force brings about the fruit of suffering. Afflictions have two types of karmic power. First, the power of triggering. Whether karma is good or bad, so long as actions reach fruition in birth and death, they are all triggered by afflictions directly or indirectly. If the afflictions are eliminated, therefore, no conduct can become the karmic force bringing about birth and death. Second, the power of nurturing. When an action (karma) is performed, it becomes a karmic force, but this force must be further triggered by afflictions before it can produce suffering as its fruit. This can be compared to the sprouting of seeds: without water, they will not sprout. If the afflictions are eliminated, all the karma seeds will wither and lose their power to produce fruit. Otherwise, when causes encounter the right conditions—when karma seeds are nurtured by afflictions—they will produce the fruit of suffering. So, the common saying that karma is the cause of rewards or retributions is not clear enough. Rather than saying that karma is the cause of birth and death, we should say that the afflictions are.

72 Karma consists of the physical, verbal, and mental,
As well as the good, the bad, and the neutral.
The extinction of karma can be compared to seeds or perfuming;
No karma will be lost in hundreds and thousands of kalpas.
Sentient beings, experiencing birth and death in accordance with their karma,
Cannot escape from the three realms.

Karma, which means action, is threefold. Its threefold nature can be explained in two different ways. First, when classified according to the basis upon which karma is manifested, karma is either physical, verbal, or mental. Physical actions may be either evil, such as killing and stealing, or good, such as not killing and not stealing. These actions, which are by nature ethical or unethical, are called "expressed physical karma." These physical actions trigger latent energy, which also has effects; this energy is called "unexpressed physical karma." Although no expression of this karma is visible, the transformation of matter into energy has the function of bringing about rewards or retributions. In the same way, the expression through speech (or through writing, which can be described as the transformation of verbal karma into physical karma) of lies, back-biting, etc.—all of which is evil—and of honest words and harmonious talk—which is good—is called "expressed verbal karma." Through these verbal expressions arises the latent energy called "unexpressed verbal karma." Physical and verbal karma, which are physiological activities, and the potential energy they trigger are categorized as belonging to matter.

Likewise, mental karma is categorized as belonging to the mind. That phenomena of the mind and those attributes that are associated with the formation of mental actions are mental karma. Some people say that mental actions are the essence of karma because they are the source from which the physical and verbal expressions arise. They assert that such thoughts, which cause physical and verbal actions, *are* physical and verbal karma. This type of explanation tends toward the "mere mind" theories. However, the Buddha said that good and evil physical and verbal karma have forms that are visible to the divine eye. Therefore, to say that "unexpressed karma" is the specific energy that is triggered by matter is more accurate.

Second, karma is threefold because it is either good, bad, or neutral. Leaving aside good and evil karma, one might ask what neutral karma is. It is the karma associated with meditation. The karma associated with the meditations of the realms of forms and formlessness is, of course, good. But there is a special characteristic of meditation that is designated "neither moving nor chaotic," and the corresponding karma is called neutral karma. This neutral karma can bring about birth and death in the realms of forms and formlessness, whereas the so-called good and evil karma specifically describe the karmic force that causes birth and death in the realm of desire.

According to the Buddha Dharma, both expressed and unexpressed karma—both physical and verbal actions and the energy triggered by them—are impermanent and pass away instantly. If karma is extinguished instantly and passes away, how can it bring about future effects? To answer this question, the sūtras use the analogy of seeds. For example, the plant that flowers and bears fruit may wither, but its seeds can germinate, sprout, and produce new branches and leaves. Another analogy is that of perfuming: a box in which special incense has been stored still retains the fragrance even after the incense has been taken out. Later scholars worked out the theories of seeds and perfuming to illustrate the possibility of karmic force bringing about effects; these are, however, merely popular analogies.

According to the profound meaning of the Buddha Dharma, to say that karma has passed away or has been instantly extinguished does not mean that it has become nothing, but rather that it was transformed from actual existence into another phenomenon. It can be said that becoming extinct or having passed away is not synonymous with nonexistence, for karma still exists. Of course, the karma that has passed away is different from that which exists now. When matter is transformed from substance into energy, for example, it is definitely not the case that it is nonexistent; it can no longer be confined to the material concepts of volume, substance, and resistance, however. Likewise, after the instantaneous disappearance of karmic force, it still exists. Of course it does not exist right now, but when it encounters the union of certain causes and conditions, it will bring about rewards or retribution—which is just how energy transforms back to matter. If certain causes and conditions do not unite, the karmic force will remain forever. It will not be lost in hundreds, thousands, or innumerable kalpas; it will still be able to bring about effects.

Sentient beings, experiencing the retribution of birth and death in accordance with their particular karma, transmigrate within the five destinies for life after life. Because this movement is triggered and nurtured by afflictions, no matter how good or lofty the karma of sentient beings may be, they cannot escape from the three realms—that is, the three worlds for the activities of sentient beings: the realms of desire, form, and formlessness. In these three realms birth and death continue forever. The goal of the world-transcending Dharma of the Three Vehicles is to extinguish the fundamental causes of birth and death so as to avoid being bound by them in the three realms ever again. Only through this can one achieve the Buddha Dharma's goal of great emancipation.

3 REALMS

THE THREE EVIL ROOTS

73 The afflictions: desire, anger, and ignorance
Are the roots of all evils.
Ignorance is like being drunk and confused,
The fault of anger is serious and that of greed is deep.

Bad factors and evil portions of the mind—whether they are intellectual, emotional, or volitional—are all incorrect and inappropriate; they cause us to be agitated and annoyed. That which causes instability, disharmony, and uneasiness is called an affliction; afflictions create all kinds of karma leading to future suffering. Afflictions are very complex, but three of them—desire, anger, and ignorance—are the sources of all evil. They are called the three evil roots.

Calling them "roots" means that all afflictions can be divided into the three broad categories of desire, anger, and ignorance. All other afflictions are simply the branches and divisions of these three. For example, craving, defilement, covetousness, attachment, stinginess, fraudulence, arrogance, restlessness, etc., are forms of desire. Fury, hatred, annoyance, jealousy, etc., are forms of anger. False views, doubt, unbelief, stupor, forgetfulness, nondiscernment, etc., are forms of ignorance. All sentient beings have afflictions, but each has different inclinations. People who have a certain category of afflictions will have a corresponding personality; for instance, there are people with desirous, angry, or ignorant personalities. People who do not have a particular inclination toward any one of the three categories have personalities that are equally made up of all three. As a more detailed classification there are also nineteen types of personalities.[10]

Since the afflictions are too numerous to explain here in detail, the three evil roots will suffice as an illustration. *Ignorance* is stupidity; it is also a state of being unenlightened, of not knowing anything about the practical aspects or the principles of reality. This is not to say that one does not know anything. On the contrary, one has a certain kind of knowledge, but it is wrong, distorted—it seems to be correct but is really incorrect. It is like being drunk and confused. Thus one takes the affirmative as the negative and the negative as the affirmative, and the existent to be nonexistent and the nonexistent to be existent. One says what one should not, laughs at what one should not, cries when one should not, and does what one should not. Confusion, distortion, and suspicion—such are the forms of ignorance; these afflictions are the most difficult to treat completely. As for what is not known, this includes not knowing about good and evil, not knowing about cause and effect, not knowing about karma and result, not knowing about ordinary people and sages, not knowing about practical aspects and principles. As for what *is* known, one knows the impermanent as the permanent, unhappiness as happiness, the impure as the pure, the nonexistence of the self as the self. One either has doubts about the practical aspects or the principles of reality or has erroneous views about them.

Anger is aversion that comes from being dissatisfied with conditions. If expressed, it is described as fury, disputation, harmfulness, and anger. If stored in the mind, it is described as resentment, hatred, and jealousy. These faults are very serious. Not only are bad things done because of them, but also good deeds may be destroyed because of one's lack of tolerance, perhaps by a single angry thought.

From the past to the present, each of us has been in a close relationship with all other sentient beings. One should therefore have compassion (without anger and harmfulness) in order to be of benefit to oneself and not harm others; being harmonious with others benefits both oneself and others. The affliction of anger is just the opposite of this harmony. It is the source of all extremely violent and wicked crimes. As a sūtra says, "The rise of an angry thought can open eighty thousand doors to obstacles." It also says that anger is like a fire that burns up all good roots.

Greed is the attachment to oneself and to all that is related to oneself. One broods over the past, is attached to the present, and is desirous of the future. Although greed is not as serious as the fire of anger, it penetrates thoroughly like water; this fault is very deep. Greedy desire is primarily self-love that is concerned with the present and the future. With regard to others, for example, this is love for one's parents, children, siblings, and friends. With regard to things, it is love for one's wealth, business, scholarships, and fame. Although one can do many good deeds through greed, they are only partially good because they are based on the defiling love of the self.

Sometimes, such love can turn into anger toward others, for anger is the other side of love. Loving to an extreme can become the utmost hatred sometimes. According to the Buddha Dharma, this is also the way people are. It is also characteristic of this selfish love, which is attached to everything, that it is affected by change and therefore causes suffering. So the Buddha says, "When love arises, suffering arises."

74 The Buddha, to include all the afflictions, points to
Self-centered views, self-love, ignorance, and arrogance.
Because of the attachment to "I and mine,"
Birth and death will always continue.

The three types of afflictions describe the realm of desire, particularly the experience of human beings. For example, in the realms of form and formlessness, anger will not arise. To include all the afflictions of sentient beings, the Buddha had a separate fourfold classification of afflictions into self-centered views, love, arrogance, and ignorance. These four can be explained in different ways.

In ancient times, the virtuous ones called these the "four unregistered roots."[11] They are not seriously evil, but they are still afflictions; and they are called hidden and unregistered. When minute afflictions were investigated, these four were discovered. These four afflictions are considered to be associated with the seventh consciousness, particularly in the Mahāyāna teaching of "mere consciousness." Sages who have not realized the truth or cut off the afflictions always have these four afflictions, which are also special characteristics of sentient beings' afflictions. The four are (1) ignorance with regard to the self: thinking there is a self when actually there is no such permanent, unchanging, and independent self; (2) self-centered view: the illusion of the self and the firmly held belief in it; (3) arrogance of the self: insistence upon such a self and the erroneous feeling of self-importance; and (4) self-love: arrogance of the self joined with love of this self. All the self-centered activities of sentient beings develop from these internal special characteristics of afflictions.

In the *Āgama Sūtra* another classification is frequently seen. Faults from afflictions are divided into two groups: faulty views, or faults in human cognition, which can be corrected with true and firm understanding; and love, or faults in human action, which can be corrected only with a firm and true understanding, frequent awareness, and continuous training in the behavior of daily living. Therefore, some people say, "Knowing is not difficult; doing is very difficult." The process of an ordinary person becoming a sage, in which only part of the afflictions are cut off, is described as a situation in which residual arrogance has not been completely extinguished. Arrogance is a minute sense of self-importance through which the self-centered activities are triggered. If all the afflictions are cut off, then one is liberated. In the case of arhats, residual habits—most minute bits of ignorance—are not completely purified. If one can eliminate these, then one truly is completely pure.

Ignorance, or nonillumination, is the universal characteristic of all afflictions. When classified according to this meaning, faults in knowledge are faulty views; faults in emotion are love; and faults in volition are arrogance. All the afflictions fall within these three.

Every affliction has the function of triggering and nurturing karma, so it has the power of causing births and deaths. But what are the most fundamental afflictions? The explanation of the Four Truths deals primarily with love, because it is the root of attachment which leads to suffering. Other sūtras and discourses always say that ignorance is the root, or that the view of "I and mine" is. As an analogy, a blindfolded person trapped in thick thorn bushes cannot get out even with much struggle. The blindfold is like ignorance; the barrier of thorn bushes is like love. Thus the sūtras say that the parents (i.e., causes) of birth and death are ignorance and love. But if one wants to get out of the trap of the thorn bushes, taking away the blindfold is most important.

From this one sees that ignorance is the root of birth and death and that the emancipation that comes from birth and death is primarily from the power of wisdom. The primary ignorance is not understanding both the nonexistence of the self and the attachment to "I and mine." The self, the "I," carries the sense of having mastery and control, of making decisions for oneself and controlling others. The view of "I and mine" takes the "I" as the center and makes all others belong to it. All I own, all I know, and all I control are to be decided by my wishes. Intentionally or not, sentient beings actually go about all their activities in just this way, embracing all and holding the self as the center (although, of course, not even the most powerful dictator can succeed in this) and also firmly attaching to all. This self-centeredness is a very strong and cohesive centripetal force. The power (karma) generated from these activities is the force that brings about birth and death and forms the individual entities of sentient beings.

Actually, there is no unchanging and independent entity, no self such as the "atman" or the "soul" described by non-Buddhists. There is only the sum total of the activities of the body and mind (the five aggregates, the six sense organs, the six elements). Because of the attachment to the view of "I and mine," the illusion of a permanent and independent self arises. Because one grasps onto "I and mine," a centripetal force is formed and condenses into individual entities. But this is brought about by karmic force which is, by nature, limited. So after some time (one life span) the karma comes to an end and the individual dies. There are also those who die because the blessings come to an end; they die suddenly. However, the afflictions based on the view of "I and mine" still exert their embracing and condensing power, leading to a new life and another series of karma processes. Thus sentient beings continue in endless cycles of death and birth, birth and death.

Dependent Origination

75 Suffering and accumulation become entangled with one another.
Death and birth arise from dependent origination
Which has twelve links, as taught by the Buddha.
They are like a castle or a fruit tree.

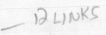

Dependent origination is a "vertical" explanation of the mutual production of accumulation and suffering, complementing the horizontal explanation of the first and second Noble Truths. One should know that not only does accumulation cause suffering, suffering also causes accumulation. For example, sentient beings, after suffering the retribution of birth, resume the activities associated with afflictions and karma arising from the karmically caused miserable fruit that is the body and mind. Suffering and accumulation thus attract and become entangled with one another, alternating as cause and effect. If one understands this, one comprehends the arising of death and birth from conditions.

The Buddha said that there was no beginning to birth and death. Just as in the case of accumulation and suffering—suffering comes from accumulation and accumulation also arises from suffering—birth and death occur in a circular fashion. In an hour the minute hand of a clock moves from one to twelve and then from twelve to one, but it is hard to say where an hour starts. A true understanding of dependent origination discloses the beginningless continuation of birth and death.

The main meaning of the doctrine of dependent origination is that all that exists has arisen from causes and conditions. These causes and conditions have also arisen from causes and conditions. Therefore, everything that exists has arisen from past causes and conditions; it is their fruit. This thing that exists right now has power to influence the future, so it is also a cause. From this perspective, a creation such as theists proclaim is impossible. A creator who causes what exists without being caused is unreal, a product of fantasy.

The Buddha gave different discourses about dependent origination because people had different capacities. The version with twelve links happens to be more complete and has become the classic exposition. Alternatively, the Buddha taught a version with three links: afflictions, karma, and suffering. From afflictions comes karma, karma causes the fruit of suffering, which in turn leads to the arising of afflictions. He also taught a version with five links: desire, clinging, existence, birth, and aging, sickness, and death; this is frequently seen in the *Āgama Sūtra.* He also taught dependent origination in ten links: consciousness, name and form (mental and physical phenomena), the six faculties, contact, sensation, desire, clinging, existence, birth, and aging, sickness, and death. But the twelve-link version is taught: ignorance causes volitional actions, volitional actions cause consciousness, and so forth, ending with birth as the cause of aging, sickness, and death. All twelve links are parts of the process of the continual birth and death of sentient beings. The sequence of past and future mutual production of causes and effects is divided into twelve, which the ancient masters very reasonably called the "separate stages of dependent origination." Only by such an examination can one fully comprehend the process of the round of birth and death. Although the explanations do vary somewhat, there is only one principle of dependent origination. Further research has suggested that these twelve links are probably a summary of different explanations, so they may not necessarily be exactly the same as the ancient masters' "separate stages of dependent origination."

The Buddha used different parables to explain the twelvefold dependent origination. First, he said it is like a castle. Sentient beings are like people enclosed in a castle unable to get to the door. The only exit is blocked by guards, so if they approach a door they are unable to get out. Sentient beings, even though they have the possibility of liberation from this situation, are confused by afflictions; they are unable to break through this continuous chain of dependent origination and find liberation.

The Buddha also said dependent origination is like a fruit tree. Seeds germinate and sprout to form branches and leaves; flowers bloom and bear fruit; fruits contain seeds that in turn germinate, sprout, and bear leaves. Although the previous growths are not same as the future ones, they have a close relationship of cause and effect. In the mutual production of seeds and fruits, the seeds and fruits continue to exist. This is the most appropriate analogy to illustrate the continual dependent origination of birth and death.

76 Cloaked in ignorance,
Bound by the knots of desire,
The body with consciousness continues,
Ceaselessly continues.

Many of the descriptions of the links of dependent origination start with consciousness. So the sūtra says, "Returning to the link of consciousness, one cannot go further."[12] However, some versions add the two links of ignorance and volition before the link of consciousness, so the ten links become twelve. The *Āgama Sūtra* also says, "Being cloaked in ignorance and bound by the knots of desire, one obtains this body with consciousness."[13] The three links of ignorance, desire (volitional actions), and consciousness can be regarded as a complete and independent doctrine of dependent origination. When they are united with the links following consciousness, they become the twelve parts.

The meaning of this independent system of the three links will be explained here. The analogies of being cloaked in ignorance and bound by the knots of desire have already been described. The transmigrations of birth and death are like falling blindfolded into a trap of thorn bushes, from which one cannot escape. Ignorance means knowing confusedly and erroneously; it is like having one's eyes covered by a cloth. The sūtra says, "The mind that realizes truth should arise, but it is always obstructed by common ignorance, which is active all the time."[14] Ignorance really has the effect of concealing and obstructing the wisdom that can realize truth. Desire has the effect of attachment, causing people to be bound to birth and death, so it is metaphorically described as knots. With regard to afflictions, ignorance afflicts knowledge and is the confusion of cognition; desire afflicts emotion and is the attachment of volitional action.

With these two causes, ignorance and desire, sentient beings obtain a body with consciousness, the essence of sentient being, and continue in the cycle of birth and death. This is also the meaning of ignorance being the father and desire being the mother; together they produce sentient beings tied to birth and death. This also generally accords with the saying in the sūtras, "All karma, desire, and ignorance are the causes for the aggregates of future life."[15] These three things are the primary causes of the cycles of birth and death. Having a body with consciousness represents the continuation of the grasping consciousness united with existence and is the beginning of a new life. Such a body, along with ignorance, desire, and consciousness, has arisen in an endless continuation since beginningless time, from past to present to future.

In the twelvefold dependent origination, the second link is volitional action, which is another name for karma. Such action is simply the conduct associated with desire and initiated by the attributes of the mind. Ignorance, desire, and consciousness in the three-link teaching are therefore interchangeable with ignorance, volitional action, and consciousness in the twelve-link teaching. From the perspective of the twelve links, consciousness is the beginning of this life. In the case of humans, when the father's sperm unites with the mother's egg, consciousness instantly arises and becomes a new life with the function of mental consciousness.

Where did this new life come from? It was initiated by the karmic seed of the previous life; karma is the link of volitional action. When the previous life finally ended, although the body and mind broke down, the karmic energy created from the past was not extinguished. When and where the causes and conditions were in harmony, a suffering or happy resultant body took form according to the different evil or good karmic forces—becoming a new individual entity, a new life.

Karma's engendering of results is not separable from the triggering and nurturing of karma by afflictions. Ignorance is synonymous with affliction; it is the general name for the affliction of the "I and mine" view. In this way, because of the afflictions (ignorance), and the karma (actions) of a past life, the beginning of the present life (consciousness) arises. The sequence leading from ignorance to actions to consciousness explains the journey of birth and death from the past to the present.

77 Originating in consciousness there is name and form.
From these come the six sense organs.
The meeting of faculties and objects forms contact.
From contact comes sensation.
Through sensation arises desire.
Increasing desire becomes clinging.
Therefore they accumulate to form existence in the future,
And birth, aging, and death all follow.

In the twelvefold dependent origination, consciousness is the beginning of the life span. Some sūtras start dependent origination with consciousness. This is because they trace the activities of body and mind back to the stage of the continuing mutual production of entanglement and rebirth, which comes from consciousness. In this way they reach the nucleus: the consciousness that brings about the retribution of birth and death. It would seem that scholars of the Yogācāra school who take *ālaya* consciousness as the nucleus explaining all the defilements in birth and death are in accord with the Buddha's original teaching.

Through this consciousness bound to rebirth, name and form arise. Name is mental, and form is physical. Because consciousness is bound to rebirth, the body and mind begin to develop. According to the sūtras, not only do name and form arise because of consciousness, but also consciousness arises because of name and form. This means that, on the one hand, the existence of all the activities of our body and mind are dependent on the embracing of the grasping consciousness (Yogācārins call it the *ādāna* consciousness), and, on the other hand, the grasping consciousness is dependent on the activities of body and mind. This is similar to the situation in which without a leader there cannot be an organization and the activities of people; yet if there are no people, there is no point in there being a leader. Nevertheless, in the twelvefold dependent origination, the emphasis is on consciousness causing name and form. This can be explained by observing that at the outset, after the union of the sperm and egg, name and form are still at an embryonic stage.

With further development, the eyes, ears, nose, and tongue arise from this name and form; with the addition of the body and the mind, the differentiated six sense organs come into existence. Having reached this point, the fetus has a human form. Although it has such faculties as eyes, ears, and so forth, the fetus cannot yet see forms or hear sounds. After birth, the activity of these six sense organs relating to the six objects begins; the cognition arising from the meeting of the sense organs and objects is called contact. These three things—sense organs, objects, and consciousness—unite because of contact; or, alternatively, the union of these three things brings about contact.

Once cognition has begun, the developing person has reached a crucial point. When making contact with objects, the developing person first has the reactions of liking, disliking, or neither liking nor disliking. These can be called agreeable contact, disagreeable contact, or neither agreeable nor disagreeable contact. The cognition of sentient beings is, unfortunately, cloaked in ignorance—this is described as "contact that is associated with the darkness of ignorance." Therefore, after making contact with objects, and based on the self-centered attachment that immediately follows, various complicated mental processes arise. All kinds of good and evil conduct are created, and the cycle of birth and death cannot be avoided. So the Buddha taught his disciples to "guard the doors of sense organs." If there is contemplation of wisdom when the sense organs contact objects, it is called "contact that is associated with the illumination of enlightenment." In this case, one can get out from under the cloak of ignorance and break through the chain of the twelvefold dependent origination.

Contact that is agreeable or disagreeable immediately produces sensation. That which is agreeable engenders joyful or happy sensations; that which is disagreeable engenders suffering or sorrow; that which is neither agreeable nor disagreeable engenders indifferent sensations. If there is wisdom and the presence of right mindfulness, desire will not arise, and one will not be confused by the emotions of sorrow or happiness; otherwise, this contact is dangerous.

In persons without right mindfulness, sensations of sorrow or happiness engender deep desire for the self and objects. Lacking self-control, they play an active part in increasing desire for this life and the world. They sink deeper and deeper and cannot free themselves. The above explains the process of the development of the body and mind starting from a rebirth that is bound to consciousness and from mental activities that arise from contact with objects. Contact is cognition, sensation is emotion, and those links that follow desire are volitional activities.

The existing and increasing desire in the mind develops to become clinging. There are four types of clinging: Attachment to the self is called "clinging to the conventional designation of the self." The general pursuit of the five desires is "clinging to desire." Religious practitioners and philosophers either cling to various erroneous views, which is "clinging to views," or to all kinds of meaningless or ascetic precepts, which is "clinging to inappropriate precepts." This behavior comes from a strong desire for life and the world, which develops into clinging in thoughts or actions and leads to all worldly suffering.

At this stage, desire and clinging are the only afflictive activities. The accumulation of the activities of these afflictions becomes the karmic seed of future existence. In the twelve links, this link is called existence, which has three aspects: desirous, material, and formless existence. They are the essence of life in the three realms. The existence described in dependent origination, however, is not the existence of the present life but rather the karmic force that brings about future life, and it can be described as the potential for future life. Once this element exists, after the present life ends, consciousness is bound to be reborn again in the future. Having been born, one cannot avoid aging and death. Birth, aging, and death come in succession. This is the brief explanation of the continuation of future birth and death.

The twelve links can be divided into three periods and two sets of cause and effect. Past causes (ignorance and actions) engender present effects (consciousness, name and form, the six sense organs, contact, and sensation); present causes (desire, clinging, and existence) will engender future effects (birth, aging, and death). Also, there were lives before the previous life, and there will be lives after the next one (unless one is liberated from birth and death). The continuity of causes and effects—through the past, present, and future—forms the whole picture of the continuing journey of endless births and deaths.

The Truth of Extinction

78 To stop birth and death, confusion should be eliminated.
When it is extinguished, suffering ceases.
Being liberated from ignorance and desire,
One immediately realizes the bliss of stillness and extinction.

Extinction has two meanings: elimination and stillness. Only after the root of suffering is eliminated can one be liberated from the suffering of birth and death and realize the bliss of stillness and extinction.

The object to be eliminated is the endless suffering of sentient beings in the cycle of birth and death. To alleviate the suffering from birth and death, the Buddha Dharma does not emphasize improving the external world, because the improvement of external things does not ultimately solve the problem. The Buddha Dharma also does not concentrate effort on the physical body, the way some non-Buddhists cultivate an essence and pursue longevity, because when there is birth there will be death; longevity (e.g., Taoism) and eternal life are just delusions of sentient beings.

Although the retribution of suffering is caused by karmic force, the real problem is the afflictions. As long as afflictions exist, they will trigger and nurture karma; if the afflictions are eliminated, though there may be infinite karmic seeds, they will wither and lose their effectiveness. Therefore, the Buddha firmly pointed out that to stop the great suffering of birth and death, confusion—the afflictions—should be eliminated. If confusion is eliminated, one will not create more karma, and all past karma will wither. Thus the suffering resulting from birth and death will be thoroughly removed.

To eliminate afflictions, one has to start with the fundamental ones. This is like chopping down a big tree; cutting only the branches and leaves will not achieve the goal. If the roots of a tree are cut, even though it may still grow leaves temporarily, it will ultimately die.

The root of afflictions is of course ignorance, which is primarily the lack of comprehension of the nonexistence of the self and also the desire to attach to objects. On the one hand, ignorance hinders the development of one's wisdom; on the other, it prevents one from practicing properly. By studying the Buddha Dharma one should first completely understand the nonexistence of the self and realize true wisdom, and then one must continuously eliminate desires in daily activities. In the end, they will be all eliminated. The sūtras say: "Those who depart from greedy desires will have their mind liberated, while those who depart from ignorance will have their wisdom liberated."[16] Neither one's knowledge nor one's conduct will be bound by the afflictions; they will be completely eliminated. One can then directly realize the bliss of stillness and extinction in Nirvāṇa.

Direct realization is intimate and immediate; it is a faultless and direct experience. What is experienced is stillness and extinction, the peace and happiness of being liberated. The stillness of Nirvāṇa is actually realized in the present; it is not delayed until after one is dead. When the afflictions in the mind are destroyed, one directly experiences the nonexistence of obstruction, the state of equality, motionlessness, and comfort. This is like escaping from a house on fire; one experiences security and coolness. It is also like leaving behind a situation of noise and struggle to enjoy the state of harmony and quietness. The sūtras and discourses often use stillness, quietude, wonderfulness, or the act of leaving to describe Nirvāṇa. The bliss is not a happy, impulsive sensation but the comfort from abandoning the burden of afflictions—the bliss of being free from bondage.

The Truth of the Way

79 That which can eliminate suffering and accumulation
Is only the way of the One Vehicle.
The three studies and the eightfold right path
Can lead to Nirvāṇa.

When the causes of suffering (accumulation) are eliminated, thereafter the great suffering of birth and death ends. One attains the great liberation of Nirvāṇa. Because suffering and accumulation have continued incessantly from beginningless time, however, it will not automatically stop. One must practice the Way to counteract it. The Way is the essence of Buddhist practice. Practicing it can be compared to seeing a doctor and obtaining medicine to cure oneself.

What is the Way that eliminates suffering and accumulation? The capacities of sentient beings are different, some being sharp and others dull; the śrāvakas, pratyekabuddhas, and bodhisattvas, to whom the Buddha taught somewhat different doctrines, also had different capacities. For all these, however, only the way of the One Vehicle truly liberates, and there is only this One Vehicle. A vehicle is a form of transportation that can carry people from here to there. The doctrines taught by the Buddha are vehicles that bring sentient beings out of birth and death and lead them to the state of ultimate liberation.

Similarly, a "way" is a course along which one has to travel to reach a destination; so the method of practice is called the Way. We know that all sentient beings have the same birth and death, and the root of birth and death is the same confusion. The substance and nature of suffering and accumulation are everywhere the same, so how can the doctrine of liberation from birth and death be different? This is why in the *Āgama Sūtra* the Buddha clearly spoke of the One-Vehicle Dharma,[17]—that is, "the one way to leave birth and death"—and of "ascending to the same seat of liberation."

THE PRACTICE OF THE WAY: THE THREE STUDIES AND THE EIGHTFOLD RIGHT PATH INTERWOVEN

From the perspective of the realization of the truth, the One-Vehicle Dharma that transcends birth and death—the Dharma of nonduality—is neither plural nor diverse ("a realization of the singular nature of things"). This is also true from the perspective of the methods of practice. It is true that the Buddha taught different methods in order to suit the different capacities of sentient beings, but otherwise the Way is the same and always lies within the scope of the three studies.

The three studies, more properly called "the three superior studies," are the superior study of the precepts, the superior study of the mind (meditation), and the superior study of wisdom. "Study" means learning and practice, not just gaining knowledge; and "superior" has the meaning of being strong, dependable, and enhancing. The relationship between the three studies is one of mutual enhancement and mutual causality. They are the indispensable curriculum for those who want to be liberated. Without practicing the precepts, one cannot succeed in meditation; without practicing meditation, one cannot attain wisdom; and without cultivating wisdom, one cannot be liberated.

When the Buddha expounded the truth of the Way, however, the most commonly used classification was the eightfold right path. The eightfold right path should be called the "eightfold noble path" or "the eight branches of the noble path." This path, the right one to follow to become a sage, has eight indispensable ingredients: right understanding, right thought, right speech, right action, right livelihood, right effort, right mindfulness, and right concentration. The eightfold right path is the same as the three studies: right speech, right action, and right livelihood are the study of the precepts; right mindfulness and right concentration are the study of meditation; right understanding and right thought are the study of wisdom; right effort is common to all three studies. The eight branches of the noble path are also the same as the One Vehicle. The Buddha told Subhadra that because non-Buddhist religions do not have the eightfold right path, they do not lead to holy fruition or liberation, but his Dharma does lead there.[18] We thus see that the eightfold right path is the only doctrine that can lead to Nirvāṇa. The Mahāyāna *Laṅkāvatāra Sūtra* also says: "Only the One Great Vehicle has the soothing eight branches of the path."[19]

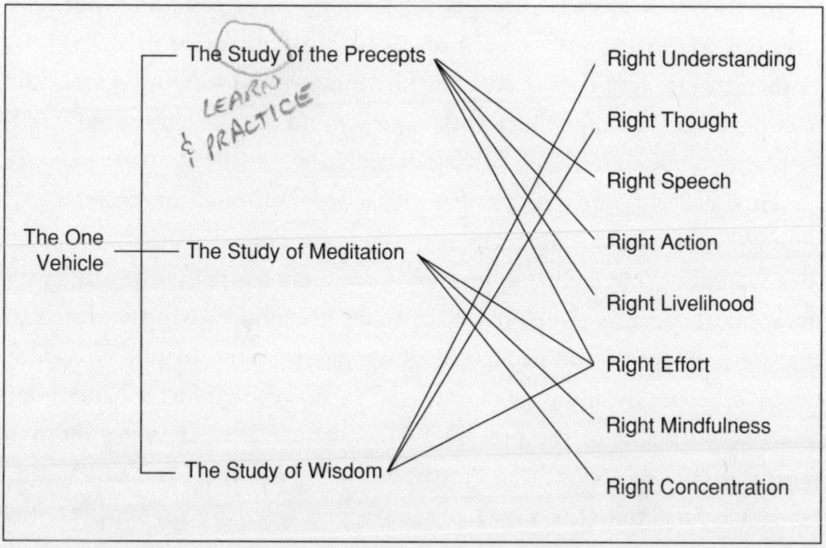

The Three Studies

80 First, the superior śīla,
With the power of a pure mind
Can protect the mind from committing offenses
And each precept, by itself, is liberating.

The system of the eightfold right path is the most complete explanation of the truth of the Way. This truth will be explained according to the three studies, and the eightfold right path will be described when we reach the study of wisdom.

The Study of the Precepts

First, *śīla*, a Sanskrit word translated as "precept," means calming, soothing. Generally, when people hear the word precept, they associate it with rules—with the written disciplines that vary according to period, place, and circumstances; the most important thing, however, is the actual substance of the precepts. The function of the precepts is to stop evil and encourage the doing of good. The Buddha's original intention was not to restrain people by rules and regulations alone; he encouraged the restraint of a purified mind. When the mind is restless and annoyed, it engages in all kinds of evil, which leads to nothing but torment and regret. If one keeps the precepts with a pure mind, one does not have regrets, and without regrets one can have peace and happiness. Afflictions are like thorns covering the ground and keeping good grain from growing. Precepts kept with a pure mind are like cultivated weedless land in which seedlings of virtues can grow.

How can the mind be purified? Through faith and taking refuge. If one believes in the Three Treasures and the Four Truths with a deep understanding and sincere vows, and if one truly has faith, one can have a pure mind. Faith is therefore described as "the mind having purity as its nature,...just like the water-purifying pearls that can purify muddy water."[20] From this pure belief arises the power of stopping evil and doing good, the essence of the precepts. When one actually receives the precepts, therefore, regardless of whether they are the lay upāsaka and upāsikā precepts (the eight precepts practiced by laypeople), the śrāmaṇera and śrāmaṇerikā precepts (those bhikṣuṇī precepts practiced by śrāmaṇerikās), or the bhikṣu and bhikṣuṇī precepts, one has to begin with the threefold taking of refuge. When one takes refuge, one proclaims that one is an upāsaka or so on; this is called actually receiving the precepts.

Later, to formalize the event, the taking of precepts by bhikṣus and bhikṣuṇīs was revised, becoming the Jñapticaturtha-karman ceremony. Without purity of belief one cannot attain the precepts, even with the Jñapticaturtha-karman ceremony. So the precepts are the pure mind that comes from a profound faith accompanied by vows; this pure mind leads to a strong power that protects the mind from committing offenses.

The precepts are also called the rules and regulations. The equivalent Sanskrit word is *saṃvara*, which literally means "equally protecting," referring to the way rules and regulations protect one from doing evil.

There are three types of rules and regulations: (1) If true wisdom arises, one is then free from afflictions and attains the rules and regulations of the Way. (2) If the meditative mind arises, then with concentration one is free from afflictions and attains all the rules and regulations of meditation. (3) If pure belief (belief in the Three Treasures and Four Truths) arises and one vows to practice the Buddha Dharma as a lay disciple or a disciple who has given up lay life, then one attains the specific rules and regulations of liberation. Since these are healing, pure, and soothing, they are all precepts; they are the essence of the rules and regulations and exist prior to the individual precepts.

The specific rules and regulations of liberation pertain to human beings; they are attained through belief and taking refuge—whether by men, women, laypeople, monastic people, adults, or children. Because of differences in social relationships, lifestyles, physical strength, and so forth, the Buddha established different specific precepts—the five, the ten—to provide practitioners with a guide to put an end to evil and to encourage good in their physical and verbal conduct. They are therefore called *prātimokṣa*, meaning the specific precepts for liberation. Each of these precepts should each be kept, for they can liberate one from specific faults.

In general, people who regard the precepts as important probably emphasize the rules and regulations but neglect the essence of the precepts, which is the mental purification taught by the Buddha. The ancient meditation teachers always spoke of the "natural precepts," emphasizing the pure mind with inner virtues. But the inclination toward purity of realization is not attainable by ordinary people. Actually, in the Buddha Dharma, "faith enables one to enter the Way"; "faith is the origin of the Way." The truly pure faith and the vow to practice are the real foundation of the study of the precepts.

81 The five and eight precepts for the laity
Are as described before.

Among the precepts taken by lay disciples are the "attendant service" rules and regulations, which are the five precepts for upāsakas and upāsikās; there are also the "staying nearby" rules and regulations, which are the eight precepts of monastic disciplines practiced by the laity for a whole day or a short period of time. These have been previously described in the Dharma common to the Five Vehicles. Originally, the five precepts and the eight precepts were for the lay disciples of the Śrāvaka Vehicle. The world-transcending precepts are taken for the purpose of liberation from birth and death and are practiced with the resolution to renounce. If the precepts are taken with the resolution to have better future lives, however, they then become part of the Dharma of the Human and Divine Vehicles—but it is wrong to assume that the five precepts are *only* the Dharma of the Human and Divine Vehicles.

82 The precepts for monastics are grouped into five:
Śrāmaṇera, śrāmaṇerikā,
Bhikṣu, bhikṣuṇī,
And śikṣamāṇā.

For the disciples of the Śrāvaka Vehicle there are five groups of monastic precepts. The first two, the śrāmaṇera and śrāmaṇerikā precepts, are a preparatory course for monastic people who have recently left the home life and do not yet have the full monastic qualifications. *Śrāmaṇera* is translated as "diligently going forward," meaning diligently seeking liberation from birth and death (*śrāmaṇera* is the male form, *śrāmaṇerikā* the female). The precepts for śrāmaṇera and śrāmaṇerikā are the same—the ten precepts. These are: (1) no killing, (2) no stealing, (3) no sexual relations, (4) no lying, (5) no drinking, (6) no use of perfumes, garlands, or personal adornments, (7) no partaking in singing, dancing, or play and no watching or listening to them, (8) no use of luxurious high seats or beds, (9) no eating at improper times, (10) no accepting of treasures or of coins or objects of gold and silver. The first nine are similar to the "staying nearby" precepts.

After leaving home and having received these ten precepts, one can then be a śrāmaṇera or śrāmaṇerikā. These are monastic precepts, so one has to completely refrain from sex. The sixth, seventh, and eighth precepts are for maintaining a simple life with contentment and minimal desire. The monastic life established by the Buddha rests on the principle of being content with only the basic needs. The monastic community's clothing, food, lodging, and medicine—the four requisites—should all come from begging. To avoid giving rise to desire, no clothing or food should be saved, and certainly gold, silver, and treasures cannot be accepted! Because monks beg for alms, they keep the precept of not eating after noon. The last two precepts along with the precept of no sexual relations reveal a special characteristic of monastics in the Buddhist system: the abandonment of the marital relationship and of the economy of private ownership.

In China, although the monks live by collecting alms, they actually have adopted methods of economic self-management: they cook their own food (little wonder that few keep the precept of not eating at improper times), manage their own wealth, and build their own houses. By collecting rent on their properties, negotiating prices for performing ceremonies, and so forth they depart even further from the original meaning of monastic life. Even the good monks in China usually keep only the fundamental precepts rigorously. Strictly speaking, Chinese bhikṣus may not be on par with the śrāmaṇeras!

The third and fourth groups, the bhikṣu and bhikṣuṇī precepts, are for those who live completely away from evil and sensuous conduct: monks and nuns, who form the principal body of the Saṅgha. A bhikṣu—the word means "mendicant"—is a practitioner who lives by begging for alms. The female is called a bhikṣuṇī. As regards their content, the bhikṣu and bhikṣuṇī precepts are equally complete. But because of social relationships and different emotional strengths, the Buddha established separate bhikṣu and bhikṣuṇī precepts. In all, there are two hundred and fifty precepts for bhikṣus and five hundred precepts for bhikṣuṇīs. This number is only approximate. In fact the bhikṣuṇī precepts, which are much stricter than bhikṣu precepts, number about three hundred and forty.

In the fully developed system of the Saṅgha, after leaving home, one has to receive the śrāmaṇera (or śrāmaṇerikā) precepts first and then receive the bhikṣu (or bhikṣuṇī) precepts. The original system established by the Buddha was intended to admit those adults who of their own free will took refuge in the Three Treasures and voluntarily vowed to leave home. The Buddha said to such persons, "Welcome, bhikṣu! Quickly practice pure conduct in my Dharma."[21] Thereby they could be considered to have received the bhikṣu precepts and become bhikṣus. Originally, they were not required to have the rank of śrāmaṇera, let alone have received the śrāmaṇera precepts.

Later, for the sake of the orphaned children of his deceased disciples, the Buddha compassionately allowed those older than seven to become śrāmaṇeras (śrāmaṇerikās) and receive śrāmaṇera precepts. When these children reached the age of twenty, they could receive the bhikṣu precepts. Ever since the Buddha permitted this, there has been a preparatory rank prior to that of the bhikṣu (bhikṣuṇī). Those who gave up lay life when older than twenty or who gave up lay life without the complete causes and conditions, and therefore did not receive the bhikṣu precepts, were also called (old) śrāmaṇeras. Nevertheless, in the Saṅgha's system, if one gives up lay life at the age twenty or later, although one directly receives the bhikṣu precepts without having received the śrāmaṇera precepts, one still attains the precepts that accord with the Buddha's original intention. From the perspective of a completely developed system of the Saṅgha, however, this is not ideal.

The fifth category, the śikṣamāṇā precepts, were for women in the rank above the śrāmaṇerikā and below the bhikṣuṇī. The śikṣamāṇās—the term means "women studying the Dharma"—were to receive and keep the six Dharma precepts for two years. Initially when the Buddha allowed women to join the Saṅgha, there was only the rank of bhikṣuṇī; later the śrāmaṇerikā rank was added, and still later the śikṣamāṇā. These became the three ranks for monastic women. The reason for these additions was that there were some women who had been married before leaving home and were already pregnant. After they received the bhikṣuṇī precepts, their pregnancy became visible and they gave birth. This led to ridicule and suspicion among ordinary people, who defamed the Saṅgha. So the Buddha established the śikṣamāṇā rank for all married women above the age of ten (in India women were married as young girls) and for unmarried women over eighteen. After taking the śrāmaṇerikā precepts, they received the six Dharma precepts for two years. Although at the beginning the purpose was to eliminate the possibility of pregnancy, later it became a very rigorous stage of testing. If these women broke the six Dharma precepts within the two years, they could not take the bhikṣuṇī precepts; instead they could take the six precepts for another two years and then, if they kept the precepts strictly, advance to the bhikṣuṇī precepts. These rules were much more strict than the śrāmaṇerikā precepts.

Some persons are of unstable temperament and give up easily. So before women were allowed to become bhikṣuṇīs they had to pass these rigorous tests. Among Catholics, nuns are questioned three times before leaving home; this is much stricter than for men. Such a system probably was never propagated in China and possibly was not respected in India either. This is because the śrāmaṇera and śrāmaṇerikā precepts, as well as the bhikṣu and bhikṣuṇī precepts, are generally similar, although there are some differences among different schools. The main exception is the two years of the six Dharma precepts, which different schools handled differently.

The ten recitation precepts of the old Sarvāstivādin school[22] and the four divisions of precepts of the Dharmagupta school,[23] both of which are described as the six precepts, are not entirely the same. The bhikṣuṇī Vinaya of the new Sarvāstivādin school describes "two years of the six precepts and the six associated behaviors"[24]—two sets of six precepts. The Sāṃghika Vinaya of the Mahāsāṃghika school describes "two years of the associated behaviors and the eighteen events"[25]—three sets. The ancient descriptions of the requirements for the two years of the six precepts were the same, but the contents of the precepts differed. Such different customs existed, one can imagine, because the ancient śikṣamāṇā system had not been strictly carried out for a very long time.

Although among Buddhists there are two groups of laypeople and five groups of monastics, and among precepts there are eight categories (if the "staying nearby" eight precepts are included), the essence of the pure precepts—guarding against wrongdoing and stopping evil as well as engendering concentration and wisdom—is still the same. So whether they are laypeople or monastics, men or women, children or adults, only those who have sincere faith and have developed the essence of the pure precepts will be able to rely on them to be liberated from birth and death.

83 Among these, the full precepts
Are the truly superior.
Receive these solemnly,
Guard them carefully, and do not lose or spoil them.

Among these eight categories of precepts, those that are received by the bhikṣus and bhikṣuṇīs are called full precepts. "Full" is the old translation; the new translation is "near completion," which means close to Nirvāṇa. Receiving the bhikṣu and bhikṣuṇī precepts brings one close to Nirvāṇa. If kept purely, every category of precept established by the Buddha can engender concentration and wisdom and liberate one from birth and death. In comparison to the other categories of precepts, the bhikṣu and bhikṣuṇī precepts enable one to transcend the world, to live a life apart from desire. In a world full of materialistic wants, only the most rigorous and pure precepts have the ability to overcome desire. Such precepts are truly superior. After receiving the full precepts, these people become the Saṅgha treasure and the principal body of the Saṅgha, and are able to receive offerings from people and divine beings.

Receiving the full precepts is therefore difficult. With regard to age, one has to be at least twenty. With regard to the teachers transmitting the precepts, one has to have three preceptors—a master monk, a karmācārya, and an instructor (ācārya). There must also be seven monks as witnesses. In the outlying regions where the Buddha Dharma is not flourishing, at least three preceptors and two witnesses are required. Compared to the lay precepts received from one preceptor and the śrāmaṇera and śrāmaṇerikā precepts received from two preceptors, these are obviously more difficult to receive. To receive the bhikṣuṇī precepts, people have to receive two years of the six precepts first, and then receive the precepts from the two sections. This is a solemn event indeed.

Those who want to receive the full precepts must obtain the three regulation garments, the preceptors, and the approval of the Saṅgha. Then, with a solemn and sincere mind and so many favorable factors, one can receive the full precepts. Since it is so difficult to receive them, one should treasure them and guard them carefully, the way one would a life preserver when crossing the ocean, or the way people protect their eyes. Do not become careless and idle or spoil such an invaluable treasure under the temptation of the environment or the impulses of afflictions. If one cannot follow these superior precepts in order to be born as human or divine being, or to be liberated from birth and death, but instead loses the human body while wearing the kāṣāya (monk's robe), this is a very sad thing.

84 Violation of the four most serious precepts—
Killing people, taking what is not given,
Having sex, and telling serious lies—
Will destroy the nature of the śramaṇa.

Of the two hundred and fifty bhikṣu precepts, four (eight of the bhikṣuṇī precepts) are the most serious. If they are violated, it is like a tree being uprooted, or a person being beheaded or defeated in a battle in which the other side triumphs completely. If one violates the most serious precepts, one can be described as being dead to the Saṅgha.

The first of the four is the precept not to kill. As one of the most serious precepts, this means not killing people, whether one does it oneself or sends others to do the work; and it also includes abortion and similar acts. Killing is also prohibited in the five precepts and the ten precepts.

The second precept is not to take what is not given, which is stealing. This is primarily the stealing of money, but it includes taking anything without consent and with the intent to steal, regardless of the methods utilized. The Buddha established that only a theft of more than five coins constitutes a violation, however. What does "five coins" mean? Since currency systems are vary, why did the Buddha set up such a criterion? He did so because according to the secular law of Magadha at that time, anyone who stole more than five coins would be sentenced to death. If taking what is not given subjects one to the death penalty according to the law of a particular time and place, then this constitutes the violation of one of the most serious precepts. This was probably the Buddha's original meaning.

Third, having sex is absolutely forbidden. No matter what form it takes—conjugal relations or sexual relations between people and animals—anyone who has sex for even a very short time violates this serious precept. The Buddha Dharma differs from the Neo-Confucian scholars who emphasize physical chastity, however; for this precept to be broken, the mind must have both sexual desire and sensual gratification. So if one is forced to have sex but one's mind is devoid of sensual pleasure, then one has not violated this precept.

The fourth serious precepts forbids telling the most serious lies: claiming to be enlightened when one is not, claiming to have transcendental powers without them, or falsely proclaiming to see spirits and ghosts in order to attract devotees. Also prohibited is glorifying oneself or someone else as a highly virtuous person or a sage, or purposely appearing to be mystical so as to delude people. These most serious evil acts destroy the true Dharma of Buddhism and are opposed to sincere practice.

Those who violate these four serious precepts destroy the essential nature of the śramaṇa. They also lose the śramaṇa qualifications—the qualifications of a monastic person. *Śramaṇa*, as noted earlier, means "diligent stopping," that is, diligently practicing the Way and stopping all evil conduct. By violating these four serious precepts, one thereby loses monastic qualifications. One will be expelled from the Saṅgha with one's monastic qualifications annulled. Not only is one no longer a bhikṣu, one is not a śrāmaṇera either. However, if one commits a sexual violation and immediately realizes it and is remorseful, one can request not to expelled from the Saṅgha, thereby remaining a śrāmaṇera and receiving and keeping the bhikṣu precepts. No matter what, however, one will not accomplish the Way and become a sage in this life!

85 The remaining precepts range from light to serious.
One should not conceal it if one violates a precept.
After repentance, one can resume purity
With joy and without regret.

Except for the most serious precepts that do not allow for repentance (those who have violated them can remain in the Saṅgha without being allowed to repent), those who violate the remaining precepts, either light or serious, should repent properly. For the lightest, one needs only to feel ashamed, and reprimanding oneself once is enough. For some violations, one has to face a bhikṣu and tell him about one's fault before one can be regarded as pure. For the serious violations, one has to repent in front of twenty bhikṣus before one can be rid of the offense. In short, one should repent those offenses that allow for repentance.

It is important that one who violates a precept should not conceal it. To repent means to beg for tolerance and then to disclose one's fault. Someone who violates a precept and fears being discovered by others and purposely hides it will never become pure again. Who does not have faults according to the Buddha Dharma? We unavoidably violate the precepts, both light and serious. As long as one feels ashamed and is willing to repent, this is good enough. This is similar to the Confucian saying, "Don't be afraid to change if you are wrong." If one violates a precept and conceals it, the fault becomes more serious. Ordinary people usually make small mistakes at the beginning. If they do not repent and continue to in this manner, in time they will shamelessly violate the most serious precepts.

For example, if a jar has dirt and poison inside, when it is emptied and exposed to the sun, the jar will quickly become clean. If it is kept tightly closed for fear of letting out the foul odor, not only will it not become clean, it will become increasingly noxious. So for those who commit serious offenses and conceal them, the Buddha established precepts and regulations to give them heavier punishments. At the same time, when bhikṣus see their fellow students, teachers, and disciples committing offenses, they should, out of a sense of shame and compassion, persuade them to confess. If the offenders do not listen, then the observers should disclose them openly (but this should be done at a suitable time). This helps others to act well and maintains the purity of the Saṅgha. One should not conceal wrongdoings and mistakenly think that one does so for the sake of Saṅgha unity.

In the Buddhist system, repentance follows specified methods. If one repents properly, it is called "coming out of an offense," as if one had served a complete sentence. After coming out of offense, one resumes the purity of the precepts and the pure standard of a monastic person. For all who have completely come out of offense, their fellow cultivators cannot reopen the matter, nor ridicule or attack them; to do so would be to violate the precepts. With regard to attaining purity from repentance, there can be two meanings. For all those who violate the general regulations of the Saṅgha, usually the light precepts, they need only honestly confess their faults and everything will be fine. But if their wrongdoing belongs to the categories of killing, stealing, having sex, or lying, they will not be free from sinful karma just through repentance. They should know that committing serious offenses not only affects the future and causes future effects, it also has the power to influence the present life, impeding the power of doing good. It is like getting involved with criminal society and becoming controlled by it; it becomes difficult to free oneself.

Confession and repentance can eliminate sinful karma. Their influence on the present life can be likened to one's having died to the past and been newly born into the present. Henceforth, the past no longer obstructs one from doing good and does not impede one's practice of concentration and wisdom; one can still be enlightened and liberated. This is like being born again, so it is called pure, that is, resuming the pure standard of a monastic person. If one does not repent, the sinful karma will harm one's mind. Awake at night, when one's conscience is moved, one will inevitably feel ashamed, annoyed, and remorseful. Such annoyance and regret only add to the pain inside, which becomes an obstruction to practicing the Way and doing good. But after repenting, one feels that "there is nothing one cannot tell others." Naturally one's mind is honest; one does not have to regret the offenses anymore and feels peaceful and joyful. The Confucians say, "When a man of virtue is at fault, everyone can see it." They also say, "A man of virtue has an open and honest mind." These are the situations in which there are no accumulated offenses and one has achieved a peaceful mind. Only in this way can one have the power of courageously doing good.

The precepts for monastic people are profound and refined. Practitioners have to study the broad precepts before they can understand what is permitted or prohibited, how precepts are kept and violated, and how repentance restores the precepts' purity.

86 One who can keep the pure precepts
Will purify the threefold karma.

The meaning of these verses and those that follow should be studied by lay devotees, although, from the perspective of practice, the Buddha specifically taught them to monastic disciples. These are the necessary provisions for going toward both the worldly and the world-transcending Way. Emphasizing the practice of the precepts is the skillful means to practice meditation.

In practicing the worldly and world-transcending Way, the seven groups of lay and monastic disciples should first abide calmly in the pure precepts, having these as their foundation. All who can keep the pure precepts will be able to purify the threefold karma of body, speech, and mind and then produce and realize all the virtues in and beyond the world. As the *Yi jiao jing* says, "If people can keep pure precepts, they can have the Dharma; if they have no pure precepts, no virtues will be produced."[26]

Following the full precepts entails the following for bhikṣus and bhikṣuṇīs: (1) They should keep the individual precepts they have received; if they violate them, they should instantly feel ashamed and repent properly. (2) With regard to the rules and regulations established by the Buddha—the dignified manners of walking, standing, sitting, sleeping, and so on; the regulations on clothing, food, etc.; all the good deeds of respecting teachers, caring for sick people, listening to the Dharma, practicing meditation, etc.—they should properly study and practice them according to the regulations of precepts while adapting to the world. In this way, they will not be scolded by upright people of society, high monks, and virtuous people within the religion. (3) They should not go to places where there is singing and dancing, or visit brothels, red-light districts, bars, and political organizations, because doing so can easily arouse defiled thoughts and deeds. (4) They should not take trivial offenses lightly but should guard against them with seriousness. If one can study and remain like this, one can stay calmly in the pure precepts, initiating all the good virtues.

87 Closely guard the gates of the senses;
Control the consumption of food and drink;
Diligently practice wakeful yoga,
And live with right knowledge.

This instruction includes four items of practice. "Closely guard the gates of the senses" means controlling the five faculties and the mind as is taught in the *Yi jiao jing*. The six faculties—eye, ear, nose, tongue, body, and mind—are the gateways for cognition and also the entrances for the thieves of virtues, namely, the six consciousnesses. The first five faculties see visible forms, hear sounds, smell odors, taste flavors, and feel tangible things; the sixth, the mind, knows objects of cognition, and is therefore the principal faculty. In our daily lives, our activities are simply the seeing of visible forms, the hearing of sounds, and so forth. We have to guard these gates closely like a watchful doorman. When chickens and dogs rush into a house or thieves try to break in, we try to stop them or chase them out. When ordinary people see visible forms, hear sounds, etc., they always cling to what they experience. When something is agreeable, they cling to it, and greed arises; when something is disagreeable, again they cling, and anger or hatred arises. When one cannot control one's mind and is caught in the cycle of the afflictions, one will create karma and regress, like a confused cow that wanders into a field and destroys new crops.

Guarding the gates of senses does not mean that one does not see visible forms or hear sounds, but rather that after seeing and hearing, one is able to "control and not follow" the cycle of the afflictions. For example, one sees beauty but does not feel lust; one sees money but does not have improper desire. This requires one to have right knowledge and right mindfulness. Right knowledge is this ability, with regard to the external or internal states, to distinguish correctly between the good and the bad. Right mindfulness is the capacity to remain always alert and aware with regard to right knowledge. If one does not have right knowledge, then when an external object appears, one's mind is caught in the cycle of afflictions. One "treats a thief as one's father," offering him a tremendous welcome. But how then can one subdue the thieves of virtues? If one does not have right mindfulness and is always forgetful, it is like allowing a thief to come in and steal things while you are sound asleep.

How then does one subdue the thief? Only by closely guarding the gates of the senses can one stop evil. As evils are subdued, virtues increase. As for these practices, efforts should be put into these areas of one's ordinary daily activities.

"Control the consumption of food and drink," the verse says. For monastics who rely on almsgivers, this is particularly important. Being born in the human world with biological requirements, people have to have food and drink. As the Buddha said, "All sentient beings depend on food to live."[27] But those who rely on almsgivers to live should consider food and drink as mere necessities to maintain life; they should not pay attention to good flavors. Once it has been swallowed, how good can it be? In order to obtain and store up material things, monastic people encounter all kinds of difficulties (the majority of the reasons for wars are similar to this). Now, since almsgivers give for the sake of virtue, should not recipients diligently practice to repay their generosity?

Thus one should eat and drink neither out of lustful desire nor for the sake of stoutness, strength, good health, or longevity; one should consume food not to become attractive or have a pleasing complexion but only to survive, to maintain this brief human existence. Only when one is physically and mentally strong can one practice in order to leave behind birth and death. If one lacks self-control and has insatiable desires, not only does one specifically pay attention to the body and to the flavors of food, one may also become upset and hateful toward the almsgivers—engendering more afflictions and creating more evil karma. For laypeople have to regulate their economic lives, quite apart from the monastics who depend on their giving of alms!

"Diligently practice wakeful yoga." This pertains to the methods of practice concerned with sleep. Sleep is necessary for the recuperation and the maintenance of mental and physical health. According to the Buddhist system the initial period of the night (dusk begins at 6 P.M. and the night is divided into twelve hours) is from 6 to 10 P.M., and the last part of the night is from 2 to 6 A.M. During these two periods, the monastic disciples should participate in walking and sitting meditation. In the middle of the night (from 10 P.M. to 2 A.M.), they should sleep but should also diligently practice wakeful yoga. In other words, one practices well even while asleep.

When it is time to sleep, one should first wash one's feet and then lie down properly. One should lie on the right side of the body with the left leg on top of the right leg, which is called the lion posture and is the most beneficial position for the body and mind. When one is about to fall asleep, one should cultivate the thought of brightness; with skillful practice, even one's sleep and dreams will become bright. This way one will not be overly somnolent. Not only will one wake up easily, one will not dream; or if one dreams, the dreams will be free from afflictions and be about the Buddha, the Dharma, and the Saṅgha. When one is sleeping soundly, one has to maintain an alertness; one has to practice good deeds diligently even in one's sleep. Such a habit of sleeping is most useful for the recuperation of the body and mind. One's dreams will not become distorted, and one will not become lazy or desirous of sleep.

According to the Buddha one should sleep in the middle period of the night and rest one's body and mind. People who engage in ascetic practices always sleep without lying down, which is commonly called the "no lying down" position. Although they do not lie down, it is not the case that they do not sleep; rather, they maintain full alertness. The *Yi jiao jing* says, "In the middle period of the night, one should recite the sūtras in order to rest, and should not waste one's whole life for the sake of sleep."[28] According to all the teachings in the sūtras and treatises, however, one should sleep and rest in the middle period of the night. During meditation in the initial period of the night, if one becomes sleepy one should get up and walk; if one is still sleepy, one can wash the face with cold water and then recite or read sūtras.

One should not mistakenly believe, therefore, that one has to recite sūtras even in the middle period of the night without sleeping at all. Perhaps the translation was too brief, or there was a misunderstanding in which the recitation of sūtras in the initial and later periods of the night was translated as recitation in the middle period. Or perhaps "to recite the sūtras to rest oneself" actually means to retain right mindfulness of the Dharma even when sleeping.

"Live with right knowledge" means that in ordinary life, monastics should maintain the right knowledge regardless of whether they are coming or going, unintentionally seeing or purposefully looking, bending or extending an arm; whether they are receiving, keeping, or protecting their robes and bowl; whether they are eating, walking, standing, sitting, lying down, waking up, talking, keeping silence, sleeping, or whatever. In every action of daily life, one should know what one is doing, what one should or should not do, whether the time is right, and whether it is done well. In short, if one has the right knowledge in all matters, one will not be at fault.

88 Be content and detached
So as to follow the vehicle of liberation.

Those who practice the world-transcending way have to be able to feel at ease under all circumstances and not desire too much. As the common saying goes, "When one has no desire, one's moral character is superior." One should be content with regard to clothes, food, medicine, and daily articles obtained according to conditions. One should be content not only if one gets much but also if one gets little, or if one does not get what one likes. If one can be like this, one's mind will be peaceful; one will have fewer afflictions and greater ease in practice. If one likes to talk about the affairs of the world and enjoys being among people, this will obstruct detachment. Some persons are always busily caught up in worldly affairs. Some gossip frivolously all day long, "discussing kings, thieves, food, drink, wonderful clothing, red-light districts, various countries, legends about great people, legends about the world, and legends about the ocean."[29] Such talk increases desire and attachment; it prevents one from becoming physically and mentally detached enough to practice in quiet places.

If one wants to be detached and concentrate on the Buddha Dharma, one must cease to enjoy worldly discussions and worldly deeds. Detachment generally means leaving the crowd far behind and living alone in a pure place. But it is primarily the mind that should be detached; if it is not, even living in a secluded hut is useless. In mainland China in the past, some of those living in seclusion became mentally deranged, and others withdrew from seclusion with the excuse of illness. This is because their minds could not become detached. How can living with attachments liberate one from birth and death? Only by becoming content with one's material state and detached from human affairs can one follow the doctrine of the Three Vehicles of liberation and undertake the way of world-transcending liberation.

89 All these can purify śīla
And be skillful means for achieving concentration.

All these practices—closely guarding the gates of senses, controlling the consumption of food and drink, practicing wakeful yoga, living with right knowledge, being content and detached—can purify śīla. Although the foundation of the precepts is not killing, stealing, having improper sexual relations, and lying, if in one's daily life one is desirous of food, drink, and sleep, is unable to guard the sense gates, is heedless of what one is doing, is not content with one's material state, and is attached to human affairs, then one will certainly have many afflictions, violate the precepts, and do evil.

The Buddha did not just establish the precepts for the sake of strictly maintaining the natural moral law; the precepts also involve daily life, group regulations, manners, and dignity of demeanor. Having all daily activities included within rules and regulations will naturally reduce the occasions for violating the precepts; when such occasions arise, one will instantly be aware and on one's guard. In this way, one can keep the precepts naturally. So in studying the precepts, do not slight the rules dealing with daily activities such as drinking and eating, believing that they are unimportant.

The Study of Meditation

The pure study of the precepts is also the skillful means for meditation. It is the foundation for the practice of meditation and a necessary preparatory work. The sūtra says, "When the precepts are kept purely, one has no annoyance and regret; without regret one is joyful; being joyful one is happy; with a happy mind, one's body attains mild tranquillity; because the body is tranquil, one receives superior bliss; because of bliss, one's mind is concentrated."[30] Those who keep the precepts purely have an easy conscience and naturally tend toward the study of meditation. As for proper daily life: not being desirous of flavorful food, overeating, or drinking; not being desirous of sleep or drowsy; closely guarding the gates of senses; acting with right knowledge—these will eliminate the obstacles of meditation. Those who keep the precepts purely will therefore "sleep calmly, awake calmly, and leave far behind all physical and mental afflictions." Moreover, "there is nothing frightening; thus the mind is without fear";[31] and the body and mind are always in stillness. The study of meditation will come naturally, and one will succeed easily.

Ordinary people only envy the virtues of meditation but do not know they have to start by keeping the precepts. Not knowing that one's body and mind are constantly afflicted and restless like a violent storm, one hopes to suppress it instantly by bending the legs, closing the eyes, and counting the breaths; no wonder it is difficult to attain concentration. Even in the case of persons who have some meditative power, if their precepts are impure and their volition and motives are improper, whatever concentration they achieve becomes deviant, and they end up being disturbed by devils and nonhumans, harming themselves and others.

90 To further the study of meditation
One should stay away from the five desires and the five
hindrances.

To keep the precepts for the sake of practicing meditation is called the superior study of the precepts. Through the pure study of the precepts one further practices meditation. One has to recognize firmly that if one wants to meditate successfully, one has to "keep away from desires and evil things." This is because superior concentration is included among the good dharmas of the realms of form and formlessness. If the mind is caught up in the cycle of desirous affairs that do not keep away from the evil things of the realms of desire, then one cannot enter the good dharmas of the realm of form. Some people neglect this point. Those who want to attain concentration and transcendent power but constantly think of food and sex are attached to the five desires; they do evil and live in extreme confusion. The most extreme confusion, which exists in Taoism and Hinduism but has sometimes become mixed with the Buddha Dharma, involves holding that meditation can be practiced through sexual pleasure between a man and a woman and that such practices are the practice of both sex and life and of both body and mind! This not only deceives ignorant people but specifically lures those with money and power and, as well, those who are growing older and weaker physically or mentally and who want to indulge yet can no longer do so (this was common in the past in the royalty and among the government officials).

There are in fact Taoists who cannot stand such deviant practices and who solemnly criticize them. Even among shallow Taoists, there are people who know the difference between deviance and righteousness, so how can those with right knowledge and understanding go so wrong? In its origins, the Sanskrit word *samāpatti* means "attaining equilibrium" with regard to the state of the meditative mind. But the Indians also call sexual intercourse between man and woman *samāpatti*—in this case, the attaining of equilibrium between the female and the male—because in this situation the couple's minds are concentrated and pleasure is experienced throughout the body, which is similar to the phenomena of meditation.

This is like those non-Buddhists who consider present enjoyment to be Nirvāṇa, who pat their bellies after a full meal and say, "This is Nirvāṇa." They want to attain concentration but are reluctant to give up sensual pleasures. They intentionally or unintentionally mix the meanings of *samāpatti* together; then they cultivate their life essence and energy, expending great effort on their body and lustful desires without realizing that they are on the wrong path. This is really a pity!

Among the desires and unwholesomenesses that one should stay away from are the five desires and the five hindrances. The five desires are the desires for appealing visible forms, sounds, odors, tastes, and tangible things. Those who practice meditation have to collect the mind inwardly, so they have to stay away from these desires. They should not be confused by the momentary satisfaction that pleasures afford but should realize their faulty appearance and use various theories and facts to degrade them. Look upon the five desires as deceivers, as violent people who want to appear good but are bad, or as a sugar-coated poison, or as honey on the blade of a knife. Only in this way will one not take their appearances as pure and wonderful and as things to which one should not become attached. When mental attachment does not arise, this is called "leaving the desires."

Among the five desires, sexual desire is the most serious; this is primarily a desire for tangible things along with visible forms, sounds, odors, and tastes. It is extremely difficult to stay away from intimate sexual entanglement. How many people commit boundless evil with boundless suffering because of love between the sexes? The sūtra describes sexual desire as a rope that binds one extremely tightly; it wounds the skin, severs the tendons, and breaks the bones, but one is still reluctant to be free of it. Such a state is opposite of meditation. So even lay disciples, if they want to practice meditation, have to control their sexual desires.

The five hindrances are desire, anger, stupor and sleep, restlessness and worry, and doubt. These all hinder the development of wholesomeness and the practice of meditation and wisdom. Desire arises from appealing sense objects. Anger arises from disagreeable objects. Stupor occurs when the mind sinks and becomes dull, as if asleep, and comes from lack of clarity. Its opposite, restlessness, is the excitability of the mind. Worry, a feeling of regret about the past, arises from thinking about one's relatives or home, from desiring immortality, or from thinking in a confused way about the three periods of time—past, present, and future. Doubt or uncertainty also arises from thinking about the three periods of time. When one does not have the right understanding of how all conditioned things transmigrate through the three periods, one will become attached to "I and mine" and imagine who one was in the past.

One must practice the contemplation of impurity to subdue desire, the contemplation of compassion to counteract anger, the contemplation of dependent origination to treat doubt, the contemplation of brightness (the investigation of the meaning of the Dharma) to counteract stupor and sleep; the contemplation of cessation to subdue restlessness and regret. When these five hindrances are eliminated, meditation will be achieved.

91 Contemplation of impurity and controlled breathing
Are called the two ambrosias.

The practice of meditation for the sake of cultivating true wisdom is called the superior study of the mind (meditation). The Buddha usually taught the contemplation of human impurity and controlled breathing to his disciples who were starting to practicing meditation and cultivate true wisdom. Practicing these two great doctrines can liberate one from birth and death, so they are called the doctrines of ambrosia. The Indian word for ambrosia, like the pill of life in Chinese legend, means an elixir of immortality. It is used as an analogy for Nirvāṇa—the state of having neither production nor extinction. Later, the Abhidharma philosophers added the contemplation of the differentiation of realms and called them the "three doctrines of deliverance."

The ancient teachers grouped the meditative contemplations taught by the Buddha into the "five contemplations to calm the mind" (Master Xuanzang called them the five pure deeds). They are the contemplation of human impurity to counteract desire, the contemplation of compassion to subdue anger, the contemplation of dependent origination to treat ignorance, the contemplation of different realms to counteract arrogance, and the mindfulness of controlled breathing to counteract deep thinking and scatteredness. They are intended to counteract a specific type of strong affliction with an opposite force. But in general, the Buddha mostly taught the two doctrines. Not only do these counteract desire and scatteredness (which are the most serious hindrances for meditation), but if one follows them to achieve concentration, one can also cultivate true wisdom and be liberated from birth and death.

The practice of the contemplation of human impurity is based on how corpses appear. They are the nine contemplations: the contemplation of bruises on the corpse, of the appearance of pus, of the further decay of the corpse, of the bloated corpse, of the corpse being eaten by vermin, of blood stains, of the corpse falling into pieces, of the skeleton that remains, and of the broken and decayed bones. These contemplations are most powerful in subduing greed—sexual desire and the love of the body.

In the mindfulness of controlled breathing, commonly known as the contemplation of counting breaths, one practices meditation by being mindful of the inhaling and exhaling of breaths. These are the six wonderful steps: counting, following, stopping, contemplating, returning, and purifying. There are also the sixteen superior deeds that are superior in the mindfulness of controlled breathing.

92 Following these to collect the mind,
One can attain right concentration.
The development of true wisdom
Comes from the seven dependable concentrations taught by
the Buddha.

Practicing meditation means following the previously mentioned doctrine of the contemplations of human impurity and controlled breathing to collect the mind and keep it from being scattered. When beginning to practice meditation or cultivating the wisdom that comes from contemplation, one needs an object of focus such as the bruises on a corpse and so forth or the inhaling and exhaling of breathing.

If one investigates and ponders an object that one perceives, one is practicing contemplation; if one focuses on the object and collects the mind, concentrating and staying on the object, then one is practicing meditation. There are many methods to practice meditation and many perceptible objects on which to focus the mind. To overcome the two primary obstacles of meditation—desire and scatteredness—and to build right concentration, however, the two methods described above are definitely effective and safe. If, in the process of collecting one's mind, one can stay far away from the five desires and eliminate the five hindrances, then one will quickly engender virtue and succeed. In general, if concentration is not deviant or attached, it is right concentration. But according to the world-transcending Dharma, only faultless concentration is the right concentration.

The virtuous and holy disciples of the Three Vehicles practice meditation for the sake of cultivating true wisdom. The meditative states range from the superficial to the profound in different stages. So what type of meditation can be followed to cultivate true wisdom? The methods of meditation include the four dhyānas and the eight concentrations. (The concentration characterized by the extinction of sensation and thought, as practiced and realized by sages, will not be discussed here.)

The four dhyānas are the first, second, third, and fourth dhyāna. The eight concentrations are these four plus the states of infinite space, of infinite consciousness, of nothingness, and of neither perception nor non-perception. If beginning with an ordinary scattered mind one gradually practices and enters a meditative state, the first state one attains is a peripheral concentration that precedes the fundamental concentration of the first dhyāna. This is the state of "approaching concentration." Entering it is like reaching the suburbs before getting to the city. Advancing further, one attains the first dhyāna.

Between the first dhyāna and the second dhyāna is something called the intermediate dhyāna, the "approaching concentration" prior to the second dhyāna. From here on, every level of concentration is divided into three groups: the intermediate concentration, the "approaching concentration," and the fundamental concentration. But the broad grouping is of the four dhyānas and eight concentrations.

In the eighth concentration, the state of neither perception nor non-perception, the concentrated mind is so refined that the power of the mind cannot be relied on to cultivate true wisdom. To develop the true wisdom one must rely on the seven dependable concentrations: the four dhyānas and infinite space, infinite consciousness, and nothingness. The initial peripheral concentration, the state of "approaching concentration" of the first dhyāna, can also develop wisdom, so it is included in the first dhyāna.

The Study of Wisdom

93 The study of superior wisdom is
Right understanding that transcends this world.

The truth of the Way comprises the three studies and the eightfold right path. The study of the precepts and the study of meditation have been explained; now the study of wisdom will be discussed. This is the right understanding about the eightfold right path. Superior wisdom, a right understanding that transcends this world, is the cultivation of wisdom as the basis for liberation. Of course, this is not worldly knowledge or worldly understanding. It is world transcending; it surpasses the ordinary world. It is the knowledge that there is good and evil, that there are karmic results, that there are past and future lives, that there are ordinary people and sages. All this is the Buddhist right understanding of the world.

The Sanskrit word for wisdom is prajñā. Among all the virtues cultivated in the Buddha Dharma, prajñā is the ultimate virtue. Having prajñā can be described as having reached home, because the realization of the truth and the great event of being liberated from birth and death have been accomplished; the great door of the city of Nirvāṇa has been opened. Without prajñā, none of the doctrines can liberate one from birth and death. Prajñā is also the most fundamental virtue. Being the leader, prajñā guides all the meritorious practices and is in accordance with all virtues. As a basis for liberation, wisdom is the third of the three studies, but in the eightfold right path it is listed first. This is why the involvement of prajñā extends throughout the Buddha Dharma, from beginning to end; it both leads and finishes!

In the sūtras of the Dharma common to the Three Vehicles, wisdom is given many other names: view, understanding, contemplation, patience, knowledge, enlightenment; right contemplation, right understanding, right knowledge, right thought; true contemplation, true knowledge, true understanding, true knowledge and understanding, true thought, that which discerns the Dharma, and so forth.

94 The Buddha told Ānanda that
The meaning of dependent origination is profound:
When this exists, that exists;
When this arises, that arises.
Everything is impermanent and has no self,
Having only worldly conventional existence.

The world-transcending doctrine of liberation comprises the Four Truths and dependent origination. The wisdom that transcends this world thoroughly understands both. What follows is a discussion of the right understanding of dependent origination.

The Eightfold Right Path

Right Understanding of Dependent Origination

To an ordinary person, the doctrine of dependent origination is simply an explanation of the afflictions that bring about karma and its fruition, suffering, and it explains only the continuity of birth and death. Even some discerning Buddhist scholars have similar ideas. But this is a worldly understanding of dependent origination. How can that liberate one from birth and death?

Ānanda once represented dependent origination as easy to understand. The Buddha said to Ānanda, "The true meaning of 'All things arise interdependently' is very profound."[32] Indeed, dependent origination is profound like the ocean; it is not easy to fathom its depths. After the Buddha realized dependent origination under the Bodhi tree, no divine beings (such as the Jade Emperor) or devils or brahmās could understand it, let alone humans. Dependent origination is the fundamental root of the Buddha Dharma's transcendence and superiority; naturally it is "profound, extremely profound; difficult to understand, extremely difficult to understand!"

Consider, for example, the mutual production of the cause and effect of the twelve links, which explains the limitless continuation of birth and death. Upon examination it is clear that sentient beings always undergo births and deaths and transmigrate because of the twelve links. As long as they are sentient beings attached to birth and death, they cannot escape. The twelve links are both certain and universal. With firm belief and an grasp of cause and effect and of the natural law common to all sentient beings, one can attain an initial understanding of dependent origination. But one has to go further and realize its more profound meaning.

According to the Buddha's teaching of dependent origination, "When this exists, that exists; when this arises, that arises" and "ignorance causes action, action causes consciousness" and so on up to "birth causes aging and death."[33] One should know that the mutual production of cause and effect in the twelve links—ignorance, action, and all the others up to aging and death—is the sequence of dependent origination and that "when this exists, that exists; when this arises, that arises" is the rule of dependent origination. Cause and effect and birth and death are what they are because "when this exists, that exists; when this arises, that arises." Once one understands this, one can delve further into the general nature of the dependent origination of things.

Let us pose this question: What is the real meaning of cause and effect? According to the Buddha's discourse on dependent origination, existence does not imply an inherent or permanent existence but rather one that arises and passes; therefore the Buddha's discourse speaks of the arising or appearance of phenomena. (Ultimately, what exists is what appears, and what appears is what exists.) How can things exist and why do they appear? They do so only due to causes and conditions.

These causes and conditions also exist and appear. If they did not, they could not become the causes and conditions for the existence and appearance of the effects! Since those causes and conditions are existent and have arisen, they naturally depend on other causes and conditions. If one investigates deeply, one finds that all the events and things in the world, all the cycles of birth and death of sentient beings, are formed only through such principles. Where there is a cause, there is an effect; where a cause appears, an effect appears. Everything depends on causes and conditions and cannot depart from them; apart from causes and conditions, nothing can exist.

From the law "when this exists, that exists; when this arises, that arises" one will see that nothing exists by itself or forever; everything in the world—all births and deaths, whether in the past, present, or future—exist through indirectly relating to one another in mutual dependence. Only by existing through indirect relationships and mutual dependence can they become cause and effect. Such is the profound meaning of cause and effect.

Following upon this profound view, one correctly understands that everything is impermanent and has no self. All things that exist and arise are impermanent. Look! The formed world is decaying, prosperous countries are declining and falling, sentient beings are aging and dying. Roughly speaking, things last for at least a limited amount of time: the formation and decay of the world, the birth and death of sentient beings—apparently everything goes through a period of stability and then becomes extinct. But actually, things last for a *kṣaṇa* (an instant): everything is being born and becoming extinct from moment to moment; as soon as it is born it perishes.

Why do all come into being and become extinct? This is the nature of dependent origination! That which exists from causes and conditions has to rely on causes and conditions; when the conditions disappear, it becomes extinct. All things engendered by causes and conditions (such as the bodies of sentient beings) are impermanent, unreliable, and in the end lead to extinction. When describing impermanence, the sūtras use terms such as "not everlasting," "not reliable," "not guaranteed," "insecure," as well as "impermanent."

There are many different explanations concerning emptiness and the nonexistence of the self. The self in this context has the meaning of mastery, being in control. Mastery means making one's own decisions, while being in control means being able to manipulate others. In short, the self is free, at ease, and independent. All people think there is such a self, and religions in general also say that sentient beings (or, more specifically, human beings) have a self, which some call the soul. But where is this self? What is it? Ordinary people have not thought about this. When these questions are put to religious scholars and philosophers, problems arise and opinions differ. They feel there has to be something that is permanently unchanging, free, and independent, something that is the principal substance of the life of sentient beings and of humans in particular. They also feel that such a permanent and independent entity is peaceful and at ease and that it can return to the divine kingdom or can become liberated to enjoy permanent freedom in the future.

But in the Buddha's right contemplation, such a self does not exist. Sentient beings are nothing more than the five aggregates, the six sense organs, the six elements, and the phenomena of cause and effect in body and mind—arising and having existence. In all these constant transmigrations, where is the permanently unchanging self? How can that which exists interdependently have an independent self? Without a permanent and independent nature, can there be an independent and free (that is, happy) self? In the Buddha's right contemplation of impermanence and the nonexistence of the self, "All conditioned things such as visible forms are impermanent; impermanence is suffering (not secure and not free); this suffering is not the self; there is no 'me,' so there is no 'mine.' Contemplation like this is called real right contemplation."[34]

In this way, the world as a receptacle, sentient beings, and every single thing are all part of worldly conventional existence. Other than worldly conventional existence, there is nothing else. "Worldly" means being insubstantial and unreal. We (all sentient beings) erroneously differentiate; we discover things that we take to be this or that; and, based on our thinking of what they are, we name them accordingly. All those things that are commonly recognized—substance, appearance, and function—are of the world.

Worldly things are part of conventional existence. "Conventional" means that a thing has an established existence (also called a conventional designation) that arises and exists dependent upon causes and conditions.

Although the law of cause and effect is never disorderly, this existence is conventionally established. The Buddha said in the *Extraordinary Emptiness Sūtra*, which is part of the *Āgama Sūtra*, that such an existence is impermanent, empty, without a self—"beyond worldly dharma. The worldly dharma is: 'when this exists, that exists; when this appears, that appears.'"[35] The Buddha therefore called all the impermanent and the selfless things that come from cause and effect "worldly conventional existence."

For example, a person consists of the collective activities of the six faculties clinging to the objects that initiate the six consciousnesses. The eye faculty sees visible forms, so it is determined that there is an eye faculty. But in reality what is the eye faculty? Actually, "the rise of the eye is not real and is subject to complete extinction"; also "when the eye arises, it comes from nowhere, and when it becomes extinct it goes to nowhere."[36] Because the eye faculty exists interdependently and arises interdependently, you should not imagine there is a real eye faculty appearing by itself from somewhere. With regard to seeing visible forms, not a single existing entity can alone carry out the function of seeing visible forms completely; seeing visible forms requires different factors for its success. Similarly, the eye faculty, after arising, immediately becomes extinct. You should also not imagine that there is a truly self-existent entity of the eye faculty that, when it becomes extinct here, goes somewhere else.

The discourse in the *Extraordinary Emptiness Sūtra* is clear enough. All things—the world as a receptacle, sentient beings, forms and minds—are part of worldly conventional existence and dependently originated existence. That is, they are impermanent and without self, having instead indirect relationships and mutual dependence; sentient beings are united, exist continuously, and turn endlessly in the ocean of birth and death. This is the endless continuation of birth and death, death and birth, endless transmigration and endless suffering.

95 When this does not exist, that does not exist;
When this ceases, that ceases.
The empty and calm nature of dependent origination
Has an even more profound meaning.

Birth and death—impermanent and without self—come from affliction, which causes karma; from karma, which causes suffering; and from this resultant suffering, which gives rise to the karma of confusion. Is this birth and death of dependent origination going to continue forever? No, it is possible to escape because the cause of birth and death also lies within dependent origination.

After the Buddha expounded on the dependently originated transmigrations of birth and death, he addressed their extinction: "When this does not exist, that does not exist; when this ceases, that ceases. This means that the extinction of ignorance leads to the extinction of action, the extinction of action leads to the extinction of consciousness, and so forth down to the extinction of the conglomerate of pure great suffering."[37] Because of causes and conditions, dependently originated things exist; all that relies through conditions will not remain permanently unchanged; what exists will become nonexistent; that which has arisen will eventually become completely extinct.

Although things that arise and become extinct do so instantly, because of the endless continuation of the afflictions and karma, after extinction they are born again, so the suffering effects also continue endlessly. If one can counteract the afflictions, that is, ignorance, desire and so forth, so that they will not arise, then the karmic force will disappear and birth and death will also cease. For example, when a wind rises and continues to blow, the ocean is stirred into great waves; but once the wind stops, the ocean becomes calm again. The reason that birth and death can be escaped is that birth and death have a dependently originated conventional existence. As the Buddha said in the *Āgama Sūtra*, "There is not a single thing to which one can become attached without making a serious mistake."[38] Thus, if one becomes attached to some actual thing and also maintains that it does not exist, one is mistaken. That which actually exists cannot be nonexistent; if one says that something that actually exists is nonexistent, one has made a big mistake in one's thinking. The Buddha said no such thing. Rather, that which arises and becomes extinct is dependently originated and is conventionally existent, so it is impossible to become attached to it. Since there is no real arising to begin with, there is no actual thing to become extinct.

Because the law of dependent origination is illusory, one discovers the possibility of liberation from birth and death, and from there one reaches the state of being completely liberated from birth and death. How can one reach that state? All things are conventionally designated based on dependent origination. Conventional things and the conventional self are illusory, impermanent, and empty—without a self. As for ignorance—all the afflictions of self-infatuation, self-perception, arrogance, self-love—this conceals the truth; it views all things, particularly sentient beings, as real, imagining that these have permanent and independent selves. Being self-centered in all one's activities, one becomes attached to everything, creating good and evil karma and transmigrating.

If one truly contemplates dependent origination and understands that everything is impermanent and without a self, then one's confused, self-centered attachment will lose its object, afflictions will not arise (afflictions are also engendered and become extinct in accordance with the law of dependent origination), and birth and death will cease. That is why the Buddha said, "Those who think of impermanence can establish the thought of the nonexistence of the self. Holy disciples who hold the thought of the nonexistence of the self and who keep the mind far from arrogance smoothly attain Nirvāṇa."[39]

If one truly contemplates impermanence and the nonexistence of the self, leaves afflictions behind, and becomes liberated from birth and death, one attains Nirvāṇa. What actually is Nirvāṇa? This is a very profound question. For Ānanda's benefit, the Buddha expounded both the conditioned dharmas, which rely on dependent origination, and the unconditioned dharmas, which rely on the extinction of dependent origination; the latter are said to have an even more profound meaning. "What is profound," the Buddha said, "is the so-called (conditioned) dependent origination. Even more profound and difficult to understand is the so-called staying away from all clinging, the eliminating of all desires, that is, the extinct and quiet Nirvāṇa."[40]

This is why in the Mahāyāna sūtras the ocean is an analogy for the profundity of the dependent origination of birth and death, and the deepest bottom of this ocean is the most profound nature of things. Relatively speaking, dependent origination is a convention designation. Sentient beings, cloaked in ignorance, are unable to see that the fundamental nature of dependent origination is actually extinct, and they also do not know that it is only the continuity of karmic effects that are impermanent and without a self. If one can truly contemplate dependent origination without attachment, eliminating all afflictions and stopping birth and death forever, one will realize the extinct nature of things in dependent origination. Then, as when the wind stops, one can experience the peacefulness of the ocean.

Generally speaking, śrāvakas are enlightened gradually. From impermanence, they understand the nonexistence of the self; from understanding the nonexistence of the self, they stay away from the views of "I and mine" and from self-love, and they enter Nirvāṇa. They do so, however, after truly contemplating dependent origination. Dependent origination is in accordance with and aligned with extinction, as is said in the *Āgama Sūtra*: "The sūtra as taught by the Tathāgata is profound, illuminating, difficult to understand and to realize, and inconceivable; only with refined, determined, and illuminating wisdom can one know that emptiness corresponds with dependent origination."[41] This is an "everlasting extinction that is very profound and broad, immeasurable and infinite," which can be known only through realization.

In other words, Nirvāṇa cannot be said to have any boundary, for it surpasses the relative world of conventional designation and cannot be described as having an extent or a quantity. Also, it cannot be imagined as being here or being there, for it is said, "It will never arise in a future life, whether in the east, south, west, or north. It is really not like this. It is very profound and broad, immeasurable and infinite, forever extinct."[42] Then is it not nonexistent? It cannot be said to be existent and cannot be said to be nonexistent. "Once one has completed the process of leaving desire and becoming extinct, this state should not be described as existent, should not be described as nonexistent, should not be described as both existent and nonexistent, and should not be described as neither existent nor nonexistent.... Staying away from all the conventions, one attains Parinirvāṇa, as Buddha taught."[43] In short, as for surpassing the relative world of conventional designation (dependent origination) and entering the absolute world, nothing can be said; anything that is said is wrong. Rather, this is realized by truly contemplating dependently originated extinction, which is also the realization of the nature of dependent origination.

96 Such was taught by the Buddha:
Dependent origination from the perspective of the Middle Way
Is not attached to the view of either existence or nonexistence.
One can be liberated with such right understanding.

The teaching discussed above was taught by the Buddha in the *Āgama Sūtra* and elsewhere and is called dependent origination from the perspective of the Middle Way. The Middle Way is true, just, without deviation, and detached from the two extremes of deviant views. The contemplation of the Middle Way in the Buddha Dharma, which comes from the true contemplation of dependent origination, is the Buddha's fundamental stance in teaching the Dharma. Therefore, true contemplation is also called the contemplation of the Mean, and the true Dharma is also called the Dharma of the Mean.

In order not to fall into the two extremes, all the sūtras rely on the description of sentient beings themselves, which are born and die in accordance with dependent origination. Dependent origination does not fall into the two extremes, unlike the imagination of sentient beings who are attached to the extremes. This is in accord with the Buddha's teachings: "That life is identical to the body is not what a person who practices holy deeds would say; that life is entirely different from the body is also not what a person who practices holy deeds would say. One's mind should not follow these two extremes, but should go truly toward the Middle Way. Dependent origination causes birth, aging, and death…causes ignorance, and in turn causes action."[44] This is the Middle Way of dependent origination which is neither the same nor different.

It is also said, "Thinking there is self-creation and self-reception, one falls into eternalism; thinking there is creation by another and reception by another, one falls into nihilism. Departing from the two extremes of subject and object, one should stay on the Middle Way and preach the Dharma, which is to say, 'When this exists, that exists.'"[45] Again it is said, "If one thinks there was a self first, that is eternalism; if one thinks that at present the self is annihilated, that is nihilism. The Tathāgata preached the Dharma which stays away from the two extremes: the so-called 'when this event exists, that event exists.'"[46] All these are the Middle Way with neither eternalism nor nihilism. This view of the Middle Way based on dependent origination is a most important teaching of the Buddha's.

The Buddha expounded this teaching to Ṣaṇḍha Kātyāyana, a great master who profoundly practiced "extraordinary meditation" and was not attached to any form. The *Mūlamadhyamaka-kārikā* by Nāgārjuna and the *Yogācāra-bhūmi Śāstra* by Maitreya cited this teaching of the *Āgama Sūtra* to explain the true characteristics of all dharmas. The Buddha said to Kātyāyana, "People who cling to either existence or nonexistence are confused." Speaking of his own holy disciples, he said, "Those who truly contemplate worldly accumulation will not have the worldly view of nonexistence. Those who truly contemplate worldly extinction will not have the worldly view of existence. Kātyāyana! The Tathāgata leaves behind the two extremes and speaks from the Middle Way. This is what is called 'When this exists, that exists; when this appears, that appears...when this does not exist, that does not exist; when this ceases, that ceases.'"[47] So people who do not understand dependent origination will remain confused, erroneously attached, and unable to free themselves from the two extremes of existence and nonexistence.

When Buddhists truly contemplate according to dependent origination, the views of existence and nonexistence should not arise. But when ordinary people see the birth of a human being, they insist that this is a real existence, and when a person dies, they insist this is a real nonexistence. So they have the views of existence and nonexistence. With regard to the transmigrations of birth and death, most ordinary people insist that this also is a real existence. Hearing about the ending of birth and death and the entrance to Nirvāṇa, people mistakenly insist that this is nonexistence.

Buddhists, who rely on the Middle Way of dependent origination when they observe things, see worldly extinction as liberation from birth and death and should not have the view of existence. This is because the nature of dependent origination is relative and illusory and cannot be established in the quiet extinction of Nirvāṇa. Moreover, because things can become extinct, when a thing is produced this is not a case of real existence. If it were real existence, the thing would not become extinct according to conditions. When one sees the rise of accumulation in the world of birth and death, one does not have the view of nonexistence. This is because it is not the case that the illusory and conventional existence of dependent origination does not exist at all.

Also, since a thing can be produced, it is definitely not the case that there is real nonexistence when the thing becomes extinct. Besides, if one understands that "when this exists, that exists; when this appears, that appears," then when something appears to arise, one will be aware of the continuous transmigrations of dependent origination. Then one will not hold that death is the end of everything and have the view of nonexistence.

And if one is liberated from birth and death, one will not cling to a "real self" being liberated.

In sum, everything originates dependently. There is no real self or real thing, so the view of existence does not arise. Without real selves and real things, the view of nonexistence also does not arise. Truly contemplating dependent origination, free of attachment to the views of existence and nonexistence, one attains liberation. Both the superior study of wisdom—the profound prajñā—and the right understanding of the eightfold right path are the contemplation of the dependently originated Middle Way. Therefore, Buddhists can be detached from a permanent, eternal self without falling into the biased views of nihilism and eternalism, identity and difference, existence and nonexistence, thereby breaking through ignorance and becoming liberated from birth and death.

Right Understanding of the Four Noble Truths

97 Right understanding also means
Insight into the Four Truths.
Knowing the Four Noble Truths as they are,
One should sever accumulation and practice the Way,
And should realize the extinction of the pain of confusion,
For from extinction one realizes Nirvāṇa.

The essentials of the world-transcending way of liberation are dependent origination and the doctrine of the Four Truths. In addition to the right understanding of dependently originated accumulation and extinction, the sūtras emphasize the right understanding of the Four Truths. A true understanding of the Dharma of dependent origination of transmigrations and extinction relies upon causes that arise and become extinct. But this is not a hollow contemplation of cause and effect or of existence and emptiness; it is, rather, an understanding of conditioned existence—"ignorance causes action" and so forth—and of conditioned nonexistence—"the extinction of ignorance leads to the extinction of action" and so on. From the standpoint of the Middle Way and the contemplation of the illusory and conventional nature of dependent origination, one should truly realize the certainty of the mutual dependence of cause and effect and enter the holy state of leaving confusion behind and realizing the truth.

The Four Truths are also concerned with cause and effect: suffering comes from accumulation; the realization of extinction relies on the Way. These are the two sets of the worldly and the world-transcending causes and effects. The object for investigation is still the real human life of suffering. From contemplating suffering (such as that of old age and death) and accumulation (desire, clinging, and so forth) as its cause, one realizes the truth of extinction: when accumulation is extinct, so is suffering. For example, one sees that when ignorance is extinct, and so forth, age and death are also extinct.

But how can one eliminate accumulation and realize extinction? By practicing the Way. The Way is the condition for realizing extinction and also a means to eliminate the accumulation of suffering. Knowing the Four Truths and knowing dependent origination are interrelated. The twelve links of dependent origination can be used to contemplate the Four Truths, for example: ignorance, the accumulation of ignorance, the extinction of ignorance, and the way to the extinction of ignorance. These contemplations are described in the sūtras as the forty-four wisdoms.[48]

The right understanding of dependent origination is therefore also the wisdom that comes from knowing the Four Truths. They differ in that dependent origination emphasizes vertical connections and the Four Truths emphasize horizontal classifications.

When the Buddha first turned the wheel of the Dharma in Deer Park for the five bhikṣus, he taught the doctrine of the Four Truths, also called the Dharma wheel of "three turnings and twelve processes," which clearly illustrated in depth the sequence of the Four Truths. At that time, the Buddha first pointed out the nature of suffering, accumulation, extinction, and the Way. These should be clearly differentiated with detailed instructions. It is not only necessary to know what suffering is and what the causes for the accumulation of suffering are; one must also know that suffering necessarily comes from accumulation, that with accumulation there must be suffering. It is also necessary to know that suffering is real and it is certain that there will be suffering. This first turning of the Dharma wheel (with its four processes that are the disciplinary applications of the "turning") enabled these five bhikṣus to understand and firmly believe.

The Buddha further said that suffering should be known—it should be profoundly understood and recognized, because only if one profoundly understands that the world is, by nature, oppressive will one wish to renounce the world and seek liberation. Accumulation should be severed; if it is not, it will engender suffering, and one will be unable to leave birth and death. Extinction should be realized; this alone is liberation. The Way should be practiced, for without such practice one cannot put a stop to accumulation and realize the truth of extinction. This was the second turning of the wheel, which urged people to "know suffering, sever accumulation, realize extinction, and practice the Way," thereby moving from knowledge to action and from action to realization.

After that, the Buddha explained to his disciples his own experience: "I have completely understood suffering, severed accumulation, realized extinction, and accomplished the Way." In other words, "From knowing, severing, realizing, and practicing the Four Truths, I have accomplished the great event of becoming liberated from birth and death and realized Nirvāṇa. Why do you not follow me and practice to accomplish this too?" This was the third turning, in which the Buddha used his own personal experience as proof to strengthen his disciples' determination to believe, understand, and practice.

The doctrine of the Four Truths as taught by the Buddha does not exceed this Dharma-wheel of the three turnings and twelve processes.[49] When disciples practice the doctrine of the Four Truths, they should first really know what the Truths are. From them—from their causal interrelationship, from their certainty (the reality of suffering), and from contemplating the dependently originating accumulation and extinction—one will know the impermanent transmigration and extinction that are without self, and from this knowledge one will realize the profound truth. If one can understand them in this way, as they really are, one will know that accumulation must be severed, that the Way must be practiced, and that the extinction of suffering born of confusion must be realized. Following right knowledge and understanding with right action, one will eventually reach the stage of being beyond learning, which means one has already understood, already severed accumulation, already extinguished confusion and suffering, and already practiced the Way. Due to the extinction of suffering and accumulation one attains Nirvāṇa.

As for knowing and understanding the Four Truths as they really are, this raises questions about attaining the Way and seeing the truth. What does a person need to see in the Four Truths to attain realization? Because of the differences in fundamental natures and in methods of practice, students of Buddhism are divided into two schools: the school of gradual understanding and that of sudden understanding. The practice of the school of gradual understanding entails contemplating the Four Truths and the sixteen processes, and relying on the sixteen (sometimes described as five) minds to see the Way. Such was the view held by the northwest Indian school of thought. The south-central Indian school of thought held the view of sudden understanding; that is, they understood the truth of extinction in order to attain the Way.

This is, of course, an ancient argument, which has lasted for hundreds and thousands of years; it is therefore difficult to make a definite judgment about which is better. If one relies on the present teachings and views the origin of the Buddha Dharma as being one, it would seem that reaching an understanding of the Four Truths should happen gradually and sequentially. But this view is not at odds with the realization of the extinct nature of dependent origination—that is, attaining the Way by understanding the truth of extinction. The sūtras say that without the intuitive experience of the first three truths, one cannot have the insight of the truth of the Way, and that the Four Truths are to be entered gradually, just as one would climb a stairway. All these points convincingly favor gradual understanding and gradual realization.

However, the profound understanding of and belief in the direct realization of the Four Truths, also called the belief that has been realized, is not about the realization of four real substances. Truth means investigation without distortion; therefore, is someone can firmly identify the values of these four, that person has realized belief. For example, for the truth of suffering: birth and death are impermanent, insecure, without a self, and uncomfortable. The ability to understand profoundly and believe, without doubts, that the nature of the facts of birth and death is distressful—this is seeing the truth of suffering.

Afflictions and the good and evil karma that are triggered by them can lead to birth and death; the real reason for the continuation of birth and death is the causal nature of confusion and karma. If one profoundly understands and believes without doubt, one sees the truth of accumulation. Once the afflictions are eliminated, birth and death will no longer arise. If one profoundly understands and believes, without ever doubting, in the quiet, wonderful, renouncing, and transcendent nature, which is also the independent nature without any binding or attachment, then one sees the truth of extinction. With the eightfold right path there is renunciation; without there is definitely no renunciation. The ability to understand profoundly and believe, without ever doubting, that the inevitable nature of the eightfold right path goes towards Nirvāṇa—this is called seeing the truth of the Way.

This doubtless firm belief in the affirmation of suffering, accumulation, extinction, and the Way is the profound understanding and belief in the four types of value, which of course come in sequence. But this belief is not in conflict with the extinct nature of dependent origination—the realization of the truth of extinction. The extinct nature of dependent origination is "very profound and broad, immeasurable and infinite, forever extinct"; this is the "true Dharma" that surpasses the relative nature of dependent origination. The extinct nature is fundamentally like this, inevitably like this, and is called "the nature of the Dharma, the dwelling of the Dharma, or the realm of the Dharma." Seeing the truth of extinction is not like the aforementioned firm belief in the values; it is the actual realization of the extinct nature itself, which surpasses relativity and is equal, nondual, and without any sequence.

In the process of truly contemplating the dependently originated accumulation and extinction, practitioners attain a distancing from love, a desirelessness, and a realization of the nature of extinction; thus, in attaining the Way, they have also realized the Four Truths. However, with regard to the wisdom to see the Way, there should be some sort of sequence to how it arises. This is like suddenly discovering a collection of treasures but checking them and taking each item one by one—this is one of the ancient masters' explanations. Both instant understanding or gradual understanding should be like this. Seeing extinction and attaining the Way—this is what innumerable students of Buddhism have practiced and realized in the past. This fact should not be doubted. This realization of the truth of extinction is the realization of the extinct nature itself, and is not the same as seeing the Four Truths (firmly recognizing the four types of value).

Using the Worldly to Enter the World-Transcending

98 First attain the wisdom that abides in the Dharma,
Then attain the wisdom that comes from Nirvāṇa.

Following conventional truth to align oneself with reality
Is the way of right contemplation.

In the right understanding of the Middle Way, there is a fixed sequence. First one attains the wisdom that abides in the Dharma, and then one attains the wisdom that comes from Nirvāṇa. The Buddha told Susīma, "Whether you know it or not, you should first attain the wisdom that abides in the Dharma and then the wisdom that comes from Nirvāṇa."[50] How unambiguous this is!

What is the wisdom that abides in the Dharma and that which comes from Nirvāṇa? According to *The Sūtra on the Seventy-seven Types of Wisdom*, the dependent origination of all sentient beings' births and deaths is the same in the present, the past, and the future. Realizing that origination cannot happen without a definite relationship of cause (ignorance) and effect (action) is the wisdom that abides in the Dharma.

The wisdom that abides in the Dharma is thus decisive in understanding the dependent origination of cause and effect. Even though this is an understanding of the illusory, worldly dependent origination—if one cannot understand that dependent origination is relative and conventionally designated, but believes instead that good and evil, karmic retribution, the three periods, and so forth really exist, one only has a worldly right understanding that cannot be called wisdom—knowing and understanding it is nevertheless required for the attainment of the Way with right understanding.

Sūtras say that following this method to contemplate the law of dependent origination—in which there is birth and extinction (ending, decaying, departing)—is wisdom that comes from Nirvāṇa. From contemplating the impermanence of dependent origination, one sees that all things are like sparks or flashes of lightning that vanish instantly, that they come from nowhere and go nowhere, which corresponds to the Dharma's nature: calmness and extinction. As it is said, "'All conditioned things are impermanent' is the law of birth and death; after birth and death come to an end, extinction is bliss."[51] The practices that realize impermanence (and then the nonexistence of the self) and thereby align one with extinction are the principal doctrines of emancipation in the Dharma common to the Three Vehicles. (There is also the doctrine of aligning oneself with extinction through the contemplation of emptiness and formlessness.)

Through the wisdom that abides in the Dharma, therefore, one knows that there is transmigration and knows the certainty of cause and effect; and through the wisdom that comes from Nirvāṇa one knows the return to extinction and the extinct and empty nature of cause and effect. With the wisdom that abides in the Dharma one knows that there is birth and extinction; with the wisdom that comes from Nirvāṇa one knows that there is neither birth nor extinction. With the wisdom that abides in the Dharma one knows the conditioned and the worldly; with the wisdom that comes from Nirvāṇa one knows the unconditioned and the world transcending. Realizing the conventional truth of cause and effect in dependent origination and subsequently aligning with the reality of dependent origination's extinction—this is the inevitable course of the way of right contemplation.

In Buddhism there seems to be a mistaken tendency on the part of some—especially those who are older and have considerable worldly knowledge but now want to seek the Buddha Dharma—to want only the wisdom that comes from Nirvāṇa, not the wisdom that abides in the Dharma. They usually do not seek to understand dependent origination's certainty of cause and effect or to determine the values of the Four Truths. Some think they already know these, but in fact they have not even a vague notion of them. They think that what they need is enlightenment and an understanding of the mind and its real nature. They do not know that without attaining the wisdom that abides in the Dharma, the wisdom that comes from Nirvāṇa will not arise. Because of their inclination toward enlightenment, whatever they say or do seems to always revolve around the mind, its nature, practice, and realization. Thus they miss out on the required process of enlightenment. Talking emptily about the nature of the mind, emptiness and existence, principle and practice, they become unable to differentiate between the internal and the external.

In the past there were masters who missed the point, thinking that the "happy state" of Confucius and his student Yan—the manifestation of highest virtues in the *Great Learning*—and the extending of one's conscience as taught by Mencius were identical with the main ideas of Buddhism that came from the West. So some people said glibly that "the sages of the East are of the same mind as the sages of the West," as if Confucianism and Buddhism were integrated. Yet, among those Confucian masters who have studied the recorded lectures of Ch'an masters and practiced internal discipline, have any firmly recognized the cause and effect of the three periods of time? Have any sought right understanding from dependent origination's transmigration and extinction? Have any realized that all sentient beings are equal? Fundamentally, they did not have the decisive wisdom that abides in the Dharma: the knowledge of the cause and effect of the three periods; inevitably they drifted beyond the gate of the Buddha Dharma. Those Neo-Confucian masters could not agree with the Buddha Dharma. Moreover, why did they reject Yang and Mo in order to exclude Buddhism and Taoism? They did so because they did not have the right understanding of the Buddha Dharma; they did not know that the wisdom that comes from Nirvāṇa depends upon cultivating an understanding of the Dharma of dependent origination's cause and effect.

Thus, if people think that the highest Buddha Dharma is concerned only with the mind, nature, or absolute spirit, they are going astray and abandoning themselves to degeneration.

Right Thought

99 Right thought leads to renunciation,
To the abandonment of desire, and to extinction.

The different aspects of the faultless eightfold right path are to be accomplished simultaneously. But in the course of practice they arise in sequence. After right understanding has arisen, right thought arises, which further ponders right understanding's views. Right understanding can be said to be wisdom that comes from hearing (the Buddha, a disciple of the Buddha's, or the sūtras), whereas right thought is wisdom that comes from thinking carefully and differentiating clearly.

Those who have right understanding will definitely achieve right belief; those with such belief will have the intent of attaining realization. Thus, right thought arising from right understanding triggers the motivation toward liberation. Because of this, the old translation of right thought was "right intent" or "right desire." Right understanding of impermanence leads to right thought and toward renunciation. Sentient beings are deeply attached to the self and the world. Within the framework of right thought, seeing that everything is impermanent and involves suffering allows one to let go of fame, wealth, power, resentment, and so forth. This letting go, which leads toward renunciation, comes from a deep belief in cause and effect. One renounces the world, yet one courageously does good and seeks the truth, which differs from the ordinary pessimistic outlook on life that leads to doing nothing.

Right thought, which is without self, leads to the abandonment of desire. One can stay unattached to the five desires and sexual desire. For example, when hearing exquisite singing, it becomes like the sound of the wind; one does not necessarily find it unpleasant, for it stirs up no emotion. After the singing stops, there is also no attachment to the memory. This is like moving one's limbs in the air; there is no obstruction. The right thought of Nirvāṇa's stillness leads to extinction. With the mind focused on Nirvāṇa, practice the Way with everything aiming at this goal.

Renunciation, abandonment of desire, and extinction are evidence of a mind moving from the world toward liberation. The resolution to renounce remains consistent from the start to the end of the way of liberation, that is, the eightfold right path; it is just that right understanding emphasizes the knowledge of renunciation, the knowledge of the abandonment of desire, and the knowledge of extinction. The following six branches of the right path are practices directed toward these knowledges.

Right Speech, Right Action, and Right Livelihood

100 Right speech, action, and livelihood
Have pure precepts as their basic nature.

Right understanding and right thought are the study of wisdom. The right thought to seek realization will inevitably lead to the three branches of right speech, right action, and right livelihood. Right speech, or proper speech (and writing), means not lying, not back biting, not engaging in evil or flirtatious speech. Right action, or proper physical action, means not killing, not stealing, and not having sex. Right livelihood means having a proper economic life. Having the correct view to seek liberation from birth and death, one will definitely manifest proper conduct. All three have pure precepts as their basic nature.

For lay devotees, right livelihood means having a legal occupation and a reasonable means of getting money. They should neither be too wasteful nor too stingy in spending, but should follow the life of the Middle Way as taught by the Buddha. All along, monastic disciples have relied on the offerings of almsgivers, as the Buddha had especially advised them to do.

I like to quote a section of the *Yi jiao jing* to explain the right livelihood of monastics. "Those who keep the pure precepts should not sell and trade, set up farms and houses, support people and keep servants, or raise animals; they should stay away from planting and from all treasures as if they were avoiding a deep flaming ditch. They should not cut grass and trees, reclaim land, mix medicines, tell fortunes, use astrology to make predictions, or calculate the almanac. They should be frugal and live a pure life. They should not participate in worldly affairs or be treated as government officials. They should not practice magic, make 'immortality medicine' remedies, befriend high-ranking people, or be indecent and arrogant. They should have proper minds and right mindfulness which seeks liberation. They should not cover their flaws, or display special abilities for the purpose of deceiving people. They should be content with the four offerings and should not store up alms. This is the brief explanation of the characteristics of keeping the precepts."[52]

101 Start with upright views,
Follow through with pure conduct.
These in cooperation, like the eyes and the legs,
Can bring one to the other shore.

Those who practice the way of liberation should begin with upright views—right understanding and right thoughts—and follow up with pure conduct—right speech, right action, and right livelihood. Right speech, right action, and right livelihood are like two legs: not only does one need to have both legs to walk, but they have to be healthy. Right understanding and right thought are like eyes that can see the road clearly. Eyes, too, have to be healthy and able to see accurately. Regardless of where one wants to go, one has to recognize one's destination, know the way, and be able to move on step by step. With legs and eyes cooperating, one can reach one's destination. This cooperation is of course necessary to bring one to the Nirvāṇa of the other shore.

As explained above, within the world-transcending doctrine of liberation one must first have correct understanding and pure conduct (it is the same for worldly good ways). Otherwise, all your talk about practice directed toward realization will never come true. It is like a blind man and a cripple in a house on fire: if the blind man, who has legs, and the cripple, who has eyes, refuse to cooperate, or if only one of the two is in the house, how can they escape from the fire?

Right Diligence

102 Right diligence can generally propel
One from mindfulness to right concentration.
Relying on concentration, the realization of wisdom arises;
Having attained wisdom, one becomes emancipated.

With correct understanding and pure conduct, one naturally feels physically and mentally calm, and one is able to practice for the purpose of attaining realization. This requires right diligence, diligence directed toward renunciation, the abandonment of desires, and extinction, which is also called right vigor. Right diligence was described by the Buddha as fourfold: it prevents evil from arising, puts an end to existing evil, brings good into existence, and increases and broadens the good that exists. Of all the efforts one can make, right diligence has the power to abandon evil and do good.

In the study of the precepts, for example, right diligence is the effort to abstain from violations and to keep the precepts pure. For the study of meditation, right diligence is the effort to practice and to avoid the hindrances of meditation, such as the five hindrances. For the study of wisdom, it is the effort to stay away from deviant knowledge and views and from confused attachments, and also the effort to attain right understanding and right thought. All these can be achieved only by diligent practice. Even worldly good deeds require effort, to say nothing of the great deed of transcending the world! Thus, when the Buddha was resting during his travels and heard Ānanda talk about diligence, he immediately sat up to express his boundless respect for diligence.

Right Mindfulness and Right Concentration

With right understanding and pure precepts, one can practice meditation, which develops from the practice of mindfulness. Mindfulness, attentive focus, is the principal method of collecting the mind and not letting it be scattered. But at this point, mindfulness still requires the resolution to renounce as a guide. The mindfulness to be practiced is not mindfulness of others but the right mindfulness that comes from right understanding and right thought. This right mindfulness is in accord with wisdom and aimed toward Nirvāṇa. When right mindfulness is accomplished, one can attain right concentration.

The states of concentration can be briefly summarized as the aforementioned seven dependable concentrations. Of these the Buddha particularly emphasized the four dhyānas (these are the ones that can most easily initiate concentration). This is not ordinary concentration, but the extraordinary concentration oriented toward Nirvāṇa; it corresponds with mindfulness and wisdom, and thus is called right concentration. Practicing meditation and wisdom together by relying on right concentration will, in the end, give rise to the faultless wisdom that comes from realizing the extinct nature of dependent origination, which is the wisdom that comes from Nirvāṇa.

With the attainment of faultless wisdom that transcends this world, one will eliminate afflictions, realize the truth, put an end to birth and death, and be emancipated. At this point, one will have completed the goal of practicing the way of liberation that transcends this world. Emancipation and Nirvāṇa come from the practice of the eightfold right path. That is why the Buddha, when expounding the truth of the Way, always taught the eightfold right path and praised it as "the eightfold right path leading to Nirvāṇa."[52]

In this description of the three studies and eightfold right path, the two seem to have different sequences. The three studies move from precepts to concentration and from concentration to wisdom, while the eightfold right path moves from wisdom to precepts and from precepts to concentration. Actually, the sequence of the Way is always the same. The study of wisdom is both its beginning and the final outcome. So the sequence of the eightfold right path is this: right understanding is the wisdom that comes from hearing; right thought is the wisdom that comes from thinking; and the thoughts leading to right speech, right action, and right livelihood are the study of the precepts. Right effort is common to all, particularly the practice of right mindfulness and right concentration, which is the study of meditation. When meditation and wisdom are in accord, this is wisdom in practice. When, through concentration, faultless wisdom comes into existence, this wisdom comes from realization and the true study of wisdom. From this point on, one is emancipated.

The ways of liberation that the Buddha taught—the three studies and the eightfold right path—are therefore the same. The sequence of wisdom that comes from hearing, thinking, practicing, and realizing is the same as the sequence from precepts to concentration, from concentration to wisdom, and from wisdom to emancipation. The identical nature of the three studies and the eightfold right path are illustrated in the accompanying chart.

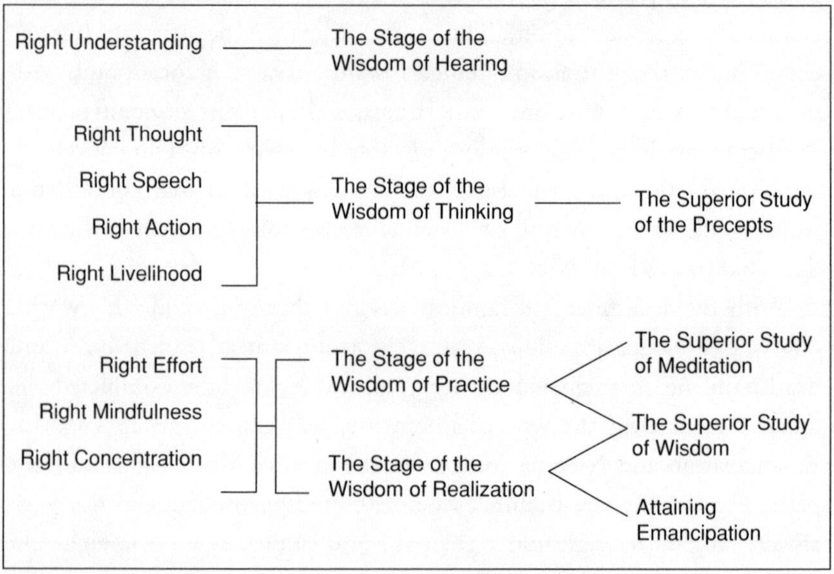

103 All the grades of the Way as taught by the Buddha
Are grouped into thirty-seven.
The Way is the same, but the presentations vary according to people's capacities,
Or they differ in the level of difficulty.

When the Buddha expounded on the truth of the Way, he always taught about the parts of the eightfold right path. But dispersed among various sūtras are teachings about the various grades of the Way.

The grades of the Way, which total thirty-seven, are grouped into seven major categories: (1) the four stages of mindfulness, (2) the fourfold diligence, (3) the fourfold basis of supernatural power, (4) the five roots,

(5) the five powers, (6) the seven branches of enlightenment, and (7) the eight parts of the right path. Why are these thirty-seven categories called grades of the Way? "The Way" is the free translation of *bodhi*. These are the different items that are practiced to attain *saṃbodhi*—perfect enlightenment; thus they are called the grades of the Way. The fourfold diligence and the eightfold right path have already been explained. The four stages of mindfulness are mindfulness of the body, mindfulness of sensations, mindfulness of the mind, and mindfulness of phenomena.

The stages of mindfulness refer to the mindfulness that corresponds with wisdom; they emphasize the wisdom that comes from contemplation —such as contemplating the body as loathsome, contemplating how sensations result in suffering, contemplating the mind as impermanent, and contemplating the selflessness of things. The fourfold basis of supernatural power concerns concentration, for concentration is the basis of such power. Although the basis is concentration—but because the primary cultivating force of samādhi can also involve aspiration, diligence, cessation, or contemplation, which are not the same—it is divided into four supernatural powers.

The five spiritual roots are faith, diligence, mindfulness, concentration, and wisdom. These five virtues, if practiced with determination, are called roots because they give rise to virtues. The five powers are derived from these roots; they have the capacity to subdue afflictions and so are called powers. The seven branches of enlightenment are mindfulness, investigation of the Dharma, diligence, joy, easefulness, concentration, and equanimity. Of the grades of the Way, which are all factors for bringing forth perfect enlightenment, this last is an important group.

Why are the grades of the Way of liberation from birth and death divided into these seven categories and thirty-seven grades? The ancients thought that the essence of the Way was the same. Originally, the virtues of practice were numerous; the Buddha selected only the principal ones to teach. The birth and death of all sentient beings are the same, so the way of liberating from birth and death cannot be different. But since people have differing capacities, the Buddha spoke of different grades of the Way. From the perspective of the sūtras, any grade (although any one of the grades includes all virtues, only the important ones have been selected for explanation) can liberate one from birth and death and said to be "the way of the One Vehicle." If we group the grades together, the principal items of the Way can be reduced to ten: (1) faith—the root of faith, the power of faith; (2) diligence—fourfold diligence, the root of diligence, the power of diligence, the diligence branch of enlightenment, right diligence; (3) mindfulness—the root of mindfulness, the power of mindfulness, the mindfulness branch of enlightenment, right mindfulness; (4) concentration—the fourfold basis of supernatural power, the root of concentration, the power of concentration, the concentration branch of enlightenment, right concentration; (5) wisdom—the four stages of mindfulness, the root of wisdom, the power of wisdom, the investigation of the dharma branch of enlightenment, right understanding; (6) reflective thinking—right thought; (7) precepts—right speech, right action, right livelihood; (8) joy—the joy branch of enlightenment; (9) equanimity—the equanimity branch of enlightenment; (10) easefulness—the easefulness branch of enlightenment.

Although the principal items of the Way have these ten categories, if one achieves right understanding one can then attain the achievement of faith. And joy, equanimity, and easefulness are simply virtues of concentration. Therefore, the description of the eightfold right path is the most complete and the three studies are the most concise.

Alternatively, it can be said that in the course of personal practice, one needs these seven categories; though they differ in their levels of difficulty, one can practice them category by category. That is, in the beginning one practices the fourfold stage of mindfulness; upon reaching the stage of warmth, one practices the fourfold diligence; at the crown stage, one practices the fourfold basis of supernatural power; at the stage of tolerance, one practices the five roots; at the stage of being on top of the world, one practices the five powers; at the stage of beholding the truth, one practices the seven branches of enlightenment; and at the stage of cultivating the truth, one practices the eightfold right path.

THE RESULTS OF PRACTICING THE WAY OF THE TWO VEHICLES

104 These are practiced by the sages
And are realized by them.
The sages of the Three Vehicles
Experience the same emancipation and enter the city of
Nirvāṇa.

The doctrine of liberation that transcends this world—that is, the doctrines of the Four Truths, dependent origination, the three studies, and the eightfold right path of the truth of the Way—is as explained above. These doctrines are practiced by the sages and are realized by them. Neither practice nor realization depart from them, for they are the true Dharma as expounded by Śākyamuni Buddha himself. In no other doctrine can one take refuge; there is no other path for liberation and no other everlasting home to which to return. This is what Buddhists should firmly believe, accept, and practice without doubt! All the sages of the Three Vehicles—śrāvakas, pratyekabuddhas, bodhisattvas, and buddhas—follow this single true Dharma and experience the same emancipation; just as many different rivers and streams enter the sea, which always has the same salty taste, all sages enter the city of Nirvāṇa and attain ultimate rest. The treatise says: "Three animals cross the river,"[54] "Three birds flee the net."[55] Although they differ in the width of water that they cross or in the distance that they fly, they still cannot separate themselves from the wide river or the sky. Therefore, it is said, "The Three Vehicles enter the same nature of things," and "The Three Vehicles occupy the same seat of emancipation."

105 Generally, along the way to emancipation,
One has to go through the planting, maturing, and liberating stages.
Realization from one's practice may be attained quickly or slowly,
But this does not depend on one's level of intelligence.

This section will briefly describe those sages who realize the Four Truths and dependent origination. First, regardless of whether they are śrāvakas, pratyekabuddhas, or bodhisattvas, every sage has to go through the three stages of planting, maturing, and being liberated in the practice of the way for emancipation. (1) The initial hearing of the Buddha Dharma gives rise to the resolution to renounce. This is the root for liberation, just as if a seed were being planted. If one does not have the mental seed of renunciation, no matter how much one hears the Dharma and practices, one will not be liberated. (2) Later, seeing the Buddha, listening to the Dharma, and maintaining a practice, the mental seed of liberation gradually matures just as a seed germinates, grows leaves, and blooms. (3)

Finally, when everything matures, one can then attain the fruit of realization, just as a tree bears fruit after blossoming.

Some Buddhists immediately attain the fruit of realization after listening to the Buddha Dharma; some cannot accomplish the Way even after diligently practicing for their whole life. In this lifetime, whether one can with practice attain realization or not and whether this realization comes quickly or slowly depends on one's practice in past lives. If one has not planted the mental seed for liberation in the past, but instead has only just begun to renounce and practice in this life, then hoping to attain the fruit of realization quickly is similar to expecting a recently planted seed to immediately bear fruit. But if one has practiced and reached the stage of maturation in past lives and then is born into this life, seeing the Buddha and hearing the Dharma, one can be enlightened (some can even have complete realization without much effort).

Whether this life's course of practice is fast or slow will therefore vary. It will depend on one's preparation in past lives and not on one's level of intelligence. Of course, there are people with sharp capacities and people with dull capacities; as discussed above, there are those who follow their beliefs and those who follow their understanding. Emphasis on the need for a teacher and for faith indicates a dull capacity, while emphasis on independent studying and wisdom indicates a sharp capacity. People of both capacities must go through the three stages of planting, maturing, and being liberated, however.

In the modern Buddhist world, there are many people who have concepts that contradict the sūtras and treatises. They differentiate between sharp or dull capacities merely by looking either at the effort in practice that people apply toward realization in this life or at the time needed for their realization, not knowing they have it completely reversed. Besides being differentiated in terms of emphasis on faith or on wisdom, those who are eager to succeed quickly are of dull capacity, while those who succeed later are of sharp capacity. As far as the Three Vehicles are concerned, the fundamental nature of śrāvakas is dull, that of pratyekabuddhas is medium, and that of bodhisattvas is sharp. Śrāvakas are of dull capacity in that the time between resolving to practice and attaining liberation spans at least three lives and possibly as many as sixty kalpas. The fundamental nature of pratyekabuddhas is sharper in that they require at least four lives and up to one hundred kalpas. Bodhisattvas, with the sharpest capacity, have to practice for three great countless kalpas before they can be ultimately emancipated! Sharp and dull capacities will be further explained according to the sūtras in the following chapter.

The Fruition of the Śrāvaka's Practice

The First Fruition: Śrotāpanna

106 One who truly understands the true Dharma,
Is initially called śrotāpanna.
The three bonds are completely cut,
And endless births and deaths are ended.

When the cultivators of the Śrāvaka Vehicle attain the holy fruit, they pass through four levels. Here is an explanation of the initial fruit.

Contemplating the impermanence and selflessness of dharmas within dependent origination in accord with the extinction of dependent origination, which is itself a realization of the true Dharma, is called "entrance into the Dharma realm." A sage who initially realizes the true Dharma is called a *śrotāpanna*, a Sanskrit term meaning "belonging to the stream" or "entering the stream." A person who has practiced to this level is in accord with the stream of the nature of things and belongs among the sages of the stream level. The sūtra describes the realization of the fruit of śrotāpanna as "understanding the Dharma, attaining the Dharma, realizing the Dharma, entering the Dharma, leaving behind all doubts but not through reliance upon others, entering the true Dharma having attained fearlessness."[56] Thus, this fruit is concerned with clear understanding, self-enlightenment, and absolute faith in the true Dharma.

The sage of the initial fruit has already cut the root of birth and death and the primary afflictions. According to the analysis of the later philosophers, there are many afflictions. Generally, they can be divided into two categories. The first comprises afflictions that are cut off by understanding the Way; these "confusions of understanding" are overcome by the wisdom that comes from realizing the nature of things. The second category comprises afflictions that are cut off by practicing the Way. These "confusions of practice" have to be cut away bit by bit through continuous practice. Those afflictions that are overcome by the initial fruition belong to the confusions of understanding, which are extremely numerous. The philosophers call them the eighty-eight confusions. But in the sūtras the Buddha always emphasized "cutting away the three bonds." The three bonds—the bond of self-perception, the bond of keeping inappropriate precepts, and the bond of doubt—are completely cut, without any residue, by the initial fruition. The bond here is that of birth and death. So when the three bonds are cut, this means that the knots of birth and death are untied.

The bond of the perception of a permanent self, the illusory attachment to the self, is the root of birth and death. Arising from the perception of a permanent self are the views of "I and mine," nihilism, eternalism, monism, pluralism, existence, nonexistence, and so on. When self-perception is cut through, all these are cut through as well.

Inappropriate precepts are meaningless non-Buddhist precepts. After understanding the truth, one will no longer mistakenly think that non-Buddhist religious conduct can lead to liberation. One will no longer cling to such things or study with heretics. There are many inappropriate non-Buddhist precepts. The simpler ones include, for example, not eating cooked food, not cutting one's hair, assembling on certain days of the month to make offerings to spirits, imitating cows and dogs, not eating pork, not eating blood, and so forth. The stranger ones involve eating feces, urine, semen, and menses and exposing oneself to the sun in the summer and sleeping on ice in the winter. There are also all kinds of taboos and prayers. One no longer clings to all these diverse inappropriate precepts as pure.

The bond of doubt is having doubt with respect to the Buddha, the Dharma (the Four Truths and dependent origination), and the Saṅgha. Understanding the true Dharma means to see things completely clearly; there will no longer be any question of belief or doubt. In the course of practice, this affliction becomes subdued; only when one realizes the nature of things is the root cut through completely, such that it will never arise again.

By understanding the true Dharma and overcoming the afflictions one ends the cycle of birth and death. Because the bitter fruit of birth and death comes from the afflictions, when the cause is cut, so is the effect. After attaining the initial fruit, it can be said that one has stopped endless births and deaths. The sūtra describes this as analogous to a big pond that is drying up with only one or two drops of water left.

This analogy can be explained in more detail. Before one realizes the nature of things, future births and deaths are endless. After entering the stream and cutting the three bonds, one never falls into the evil destinies again. Since the karma that leads to the three evil destinies has ceased to be effective, the bitter fruit of the three evil destinies never arises. What is left behind is the karmic reward of being born as a divine being or a human. This is known as "the maximum of seven existences": one may be born in the heavens or in the human world seven times at most, after which birth and death will cease forever and one will enter Nirvāṇa. Thus, at the stage of the initial fruition, birth and death are almost completely cut off. Although there is a body that is born and dies and although there is still the possibility of seven births and deaths as a divine being or as a human, the end of birth and death is near.

Of the holy stages, the initial fruition is the most precious and most difficult to attain! After one attains the first fruit, it can be said that birth and death will definitely come to an end. It is like splitting bamboo: after cutting through the first node, cutting through the second and the remaining ones up to the end is effortless. Attaining this fruition should be the only current goal for those who study the Buddha Dharma.

The Second and Third Fruitions: Sakṛdāgāmin and Anāgāmin

107 The second is called sakṛdāgāmin.
Confusion is reduced through further practice.

In order to explain the transition from the first fruit to the second, third, and fourth fruits, the cutting through of confusion needs to be explained. This has some special meanings that differentiate it from the cutting through of confusion to attain the initial fruit. If a big tree has been uprooted, it will definitely die. However, within three days, five days, a fortnight, or a month, it may continue to sprout leaves and bloom. Only after quite some time will it completely wither and die. This should be understood as follows: the big tree continues to live because the roots absorb water and nutrients. Although the tree itself has the ability to live (like karma), it must have the nourishment of water and fertilizer. Although the bark and the leaves can sustain the tree's life for a short while, once the roots have been exposed the tree will eventually die. If it is exposed to the fierce sun, it will wither even more quickly.

Sentient beings' liberation from birth and death is the same. The real source of birth and death is the perception of a permanent self; the śrotāpanna has cut through false self-perception and so is liberated from birth and death, just as a big tree that has been uprooted will undoubtedly die. The remaining uncut afflictions, that is, those that are cut off by practicing the Way, nourish the existing karmic force that causes one to be born in the heavens or the human realm. The residual afflictions—whether one does (a little) evil or practices the precepts or meditation—will not become general resultant karma or guiding karma. Instead they will become what is called specific resultant karma and completion karma. Were this not the case, birth and death would continue in the heavens and the human world; but this does not happen, for the residual afflictions nourish only the old karma that enables one to be born in the heavens and in the human world. In this way, because the view of the false self is cut through, the confusions of practice also cannot continue to nourish rebirth forever. This is like the bark and leaves that, although they can absorb nutrients, cannot maintain the long-term survival of the big tree.

If those who have realized the initial fruit continue to practice, they may even realize Nirvāṇa in this life. This is like the big uprooted tree withering quickly under the hot sun. Even if they stop practicing—perhaps they are lay devotees with the burdens of family, work, and livelihood—nevertheless the afflictions will still shrink and be completely eliminated; at most they will only last for seven rounds of birth and death. Although those who have realized the initial fruit may remain confused from having been reborn, they are definitely unlike ordinary people. For them, birth and death will come to an end no matter what.

The second fruit is called *sakṛdāgāmin*, which means "coming back once." When—through the realization of the first fruition, through further practice, or after six rounds of birth and death in the world and the heavens—the afflictions are further reduced in strength, the nurturing power of the remaining confusions of practice yields only one life in the heavens or one return to the human world. Because these confusions of practice have the power for only one more birth and death, this stage is called the fruition of sakṛdāgāmin.

108 The third is called anāgāmin.
The realm of desire has been left behind; there is no returning.

One step further is the third fruit, *anāgāmin*, which in Sanskrit means "not coming back" or "never returning." After an anāgāmin dies, he or she leaves the realm of desire and is born in the realm of form or the formless realm, from which he or she will definitely enter Nirvāṇa, and there is no returning to be reborn in the realm of desire. This stage may come from further practice after the second fruition (resulting in the realization of the "never returning" fruition in this life) or from returning to the human world with only one more birth in the heavens after death. With regard to cutting off afflictions, confusion in the realm of desire is now completely eliminated, so it can no longer give rise to birth and death in this realm.

In the sūtras the Buddha always says: "When the five lower bonds are eliminated, one is called an anāgāmin." The five lower bonds are self-perception, clinging to inappropriate precepts, doubt, greedy desire, and anger. These five groups can bring about birth and death in the realm of desire, so they are called lower (relative to the two realms above). But perception of a permanent self, clinging to inappropriate precepts, and doubt have already been completely eliminated at the time of seeing the Way and attaining the initial fruition. Now, advancing further, greedy desire and anger are completely overcome—that is, the confusions of practice in the realm of desire are completely eliminated. Anger is the affliction that belongs specifically to the realm of desire. Greedy desire is common to the three realms, but here it refers to desire in the realm of desire. When one completely eliminates greedy desire and attains the third fruition, although one may live physically in the human world, one does not become attached to the five desires and sexual desire. If one attains the third fruition, then, one extinguishes sexual desire, even though one may be a lay disciple.

The Fourth Fruit: Arhatship

109 One who completely cuts off all confusion
Is called an arhat.
Previous karma is ended, and new karma is not created;
Nor is any condition for rebirth and death provided.

The sage who realizes the true Dharma and cuts off the confusions of understanding—this person has knowledge and understanding that are absolutely correct. But the power of attachment toward circumstances is still strong. Such a person may therefore stop practicing or be reborn as a human or divine being and forget the past. But the confusions of practice will naturally shrink (just as a tree, once uprooted, will wither); the potential power of the noble Way will certainly grow, and one will advance again. In this process of further practice, whether one is walking, standing, sitting, lying down, dressing, eating, talking, remaining silent, being slandered or praised, gaining or losing, growing old, getting sick, or dealing with people and affairs, in all these circumstances one can summon right mindfulness, be constantly attentive, and practice continually. In this way, one can gradually and completely eliminate the confusions of practice that are based on desire and attachment. This is the case from the second fruit onwards.

When all confusion is ultimately cut off, one realizes the fourth fruit, arhatship. This is accomplished either through continuous practice after one has attained the first, second, or third fruit in the present life or through being reborn in the higher realms with the rise of the noble Way when one dies after being an anāgāmin. The Sanskrit term *arhat* means "to receive." This means that this sage truly receives offerings from humans and divine beings. It also means that one is "without rebirth" and a "slayer of the enemy," which means that having reached this stage, one has killed all the thieves of the afflictions and will not have any more births or deaths. In short, this is the highest fruition in the eradication of afflictions and birth and death.

The philosophers described these afflictions as eliminated in the two realms of form and formlessness. In the sūtras, the Buddha said that when the "five upward moving bonds"[57] are cut, one becomes an arhat. The five upward moving bonds are greed for forms, greed for formlessness, restlessness, arrogance, and ignorance. The first two are greedy attachments to the realms of form and formlessness. The remaining three—restlessness, arrogance, and ignorance—might also be differentiated according to these two realms; but since the confusions of practice arise only from defiled desires, only the first two are divided according to the two realms. These five bonds cause sentient beings to be born in the upper realms; once these bonds are cut, all the afflictions binding one to the three realms are ultimately severed.

When the afflictions are completely eliminated, all previous karma—which depended on being nurtured by afflictions to bring about its fruit, or whose karmic force previously depended on taking self-perception as central—is completely ended and becomes ineffective. As well, because no new karma is created, the bitter fruit of future rebirth and death will not be provided with any causal condition. So when this life ends, the arhat's present body (which is born and dies) will become thus: "the previous aggregates are extinct, and the later aggregates arise no more," and the arhat will enter Nirvāṇa without residue, where there is no further birth or extinction. The practice of the Śrāvaka Vehicle has this as its ultimate resultant stage.

110 They may be liberated by their wisdom
Or be liberated completely.
Having the six supernatural powers and three insights,
The arhats are the superb fields of good fortune in the world.

In the sūtras, the arhats are said to be of six or nine types. Here they will be described according to two broad categories: as emancipated by wisdom or as completely liberated, that is, emancipated by both concentration and wisdom. One should know that both concentration and wisdom are hindered by the afflictions; thus, if emancipation arises, it is because one has been liberated from these obstructions. As the sūtras often say: "Those without desires are liberated by their mind (concentration); those without ignorance are liberated through wisdom."[58] This means that if one has the power of wisdom to realize the nature of things, obstructions such as ignorance are eliminated; and if one has the quieting power of concentration, obstructions such as desire are eliminated.

For example, worldly non-Buddhists are able to leave behind the afflictions of the desire realm and attain the first dhyāna; they are able to leave behind the afflictions of the first dhyāna and attain the second, third, and fourth dhyānas (when the afflictions of the realm of form become completely extinct); they are able to attain the state of infinite space of the formless realm and eventually leave behind the afflictions of the state of nothingness; and they are able to attain the state of neither perception nor nonperception. But they are unable to leave the afflictions of the state of neither perception nor nonperception, and thus they are unable to be free from birth and death.

In Buddhist disciples' practice, which is directed toward realization, there is liberation through both concentration and wisdom: one both awakens faultless wisdom and cuts through the confusions of understanding by relying upon the peripheral concentration or the seven dependable concentrations.

All things considered, there are great differences, however. Those who have practiced and become arhats by relying on the power of wisdom that completely severs the foundational root of ignorance—eradicating all the afflictions arising from the false perception of self—are all the same. But those who attain emancipation by relying on the power of concentration differ. If one follows the peripheral concentration or the first dhyāna to attain arhatship, then one will not be liberated from the obstructions beyond the first and second dhyānas. Even if one attains the four dhyānas and the eight concentrations, one still cannot completely be liberated from the obstructions to concentration.

Arhats who can attain the state of complete extinction of sensation and thought, regardless of whether they do so through wisdom or concentration, have ultimate emancipation. When one attains concentration and wisdom completely free from obstructions, one is called a completely liberated arhat. If one realizes the truth with wisdom but does not attain the state of complete extinction of sensation and thought, one is called an arhat liberated by wisdom. One can escape the bitter fruits of birth and death through relying on the wisdom that realizes the nature of things; it does not even matter that one's power of concentration is incomplete. Since the powers of concentration of all arhats are not of the same level, they can be divided into several groups.

Completely liberated arhats, needless to say, can attain the virtues of the six supernatural powers and the three insights. All arhats liberated by wisdom who have achieved the four fundamental dhyānas can also develop these insights and powers. The six supernatural powers are magical transformation, divine eye, divine ear, knowledge of the minds of others, knowledge about previous existences, and the power to end faults.

With the power of magical transformation, one can change many into different shapes, become invisible or visible as one pleases, and penetrate mountains, rivers, and stone walls. One can also travel underwater and underground, fly into the air, reach the moon and the sun, and so forth. With the power of the divine eye, one can see things that are coarse or refined, near or far, in light or darkness, external or internal. In particular, one can see the form of the karma of sentient beings, whether they will be reborn in the heavens or on the evil destinies, and the like. With the power of the divine ear, one can hear all kinds of sounds near or far, understand different human languages, and even comprehend the sounds of the heavens, birds, and animals. With the knowledge of other minds one knows the thoughts of other sentient beings. With the knowledge about previous existences one knows the previous lives of sentient beings, what kind of karma they have created, and the places from which they have come. With the power to end faults, one can know the circumstances that liberate beings from afflictions and recognize whether one's own afflictions are completely overcome.

Of the six supernatural powers, the power to end faults is universally possessed by all arhats, while the remaining five depend on the arhat's meditative practices. These five powers can be developed not only by Buddhists but also by non-Buddhists. Although it is said that in all arhats the six supernatural powers are completely unobstructed, arhats with these powers vary in the scope of what they can know or see; only for buddhas are these powers ultimate.

Although the first five of the six supernatural powers are common to non-Buddhists, the three insights are specifically possessed by arhats. The three insights are the insight of the power of the divine eye, the insight into previous existences, and the insight into the ending of faults. These resemble the three powers so named, but when the three are possessed by arhats, they are so thorough and ultimate that they are also called insights. These three insights yield clear knowledge of the karmic results of the past, present, and future. Because arhats have such special virtues, they are the superb fields of good fortune in the world, and are worthy of the respect and offerings of human and divine beings.

111 Clear, pure, and always unmoving,
They are like the sun in the clear sky.
All their actions on earth
Are undefiled, like lotus flowers.

Sages who have attained arhatship, who have completely cut off all afflictions through wisdom, are clear and pure. When in contact with circumstances, they are always unmoved. Among the virtues of arhats are the six constant abidings. Whether seeing forms, hearing sounds, or contacting some other object of the six senses, they are constantly "neither suffering nor happy, but are indifferent and abide in right mindfulness and right wisdom."[59] Although the six objects may be agreeable or disagreeable, greed and anger will not arise. In the mind of these sages, all the external circumstances of wealth, fame, gain, and loss have no effect on them and "do not hinder the liberation of their mind and wisdom."[60] The popular phrase "not being moved by the eight winds" (gain and loss, defamation and eulogy, praise and ridicule, sorrow and joy) describes the state of arhats. As is said in the sūtra: "The six faculties and the six objects are always in contact, but they are unable to move the minds of the arhats; their minds invariably abide firmly and truly contemplate the law of birth and extinction."[61]

In the sūtras two metaphors are invoked to praise the virtues of arhats: the sun in a cloudless sky and the lotus flower. When clouds dissipate the sun becomes visible. Ordinary people are like thick dark clouds which completely cover the sun. When they attain the initial fruit, it is as if the dark clouds suddenly disperse and the sun appears. But the clouds are still thick, so the sun fluctuates from being hidden to being suddenly revealed. The clouds gradually become thinner and disperse, and finally they all disappear. The arhats' extreme clarity and extreme purity are like the sun shining brilliantly in the cloudless clear sky.

Sages who have attained arhatship, regardless of the level of their powers of concentration, always live in the world before they pass away. They still eat, wear clothes, travel, go about preaching, and deal with people and things. Their bodies and environment are still the imperfect things of the world, and as such are impermanent, suffering, and impure. But although they live in this world, arhats are not influenced by their defiled environment. Therefore, all their actions on earth are clean and undefiled, like lotus flowers. Lotus flowers grow in the mud but are wonderfully fragrant and clean. Zhou Maoshu used lotus flowers as a simile for virtuous people, but how can the virtuous among ordinary people be compared to lotus flowers? Actually only arhats are like lotus flowers!

Pratyeka Buddhahood

112 Those who are enlightened without teachers
And who live far away

Are called pratyekabuddhas.
Together with the śrāvakas, they are called the Two Vehicles.

The primary group to be taught the Dharma common to the Three Vehicles is the śrāvakas. The next group is the Pratyekabuddha Vehicle. With regard to the position of cutting off confusion and realizing the truth, both the śrāvakas and pratyekabuddhas are the same. Their main differences are, first, that pratyekabuddhas are not enlightened by others, that is, they became enlightened without teachers. A legend says that there was a king who roamed in the imperial garden and upon seeing that the flowers were in full bloom was very happy. Soon afterwards, a group of imperial maids came to pick flowers, and those splendid blooming trees quickly became disfigured. When the king saw this, he was deeply influenced by the sense of impermanence. As he meditated and pondered on impermanence, he realized the extinction of dependent origination and attained the holy fruit. Such people cannot turn the wheel of Dharma like the Buddha because they become enlightened without a teacher. But they are superior to the śrāvaka disciples, who depend on a teacher's instruction; their fundamental nature is somewhat sharper.

The second difference is that the wisdom derived from being enlightened without teachers comes from living far away. "Living far away" means living far from noise and disturbances, from people and their affairs. They live alone in accord with the twelve disciplines of dhūta, without teachers, fellow students, or disciples. It is said such persons are found during the periods that are without the Buddha Dharma; they appear as monastic people and beg for alms, but they are unable to preach the Dharma and manifest supernatural powers only. The legends say that there are also pratyekabuddhas who live together with people; however, their basic nature is actually that of śrāvakas. When the conditions are right, they will naturally realize arhatship.

Nontheless, because they appear in a time without a buddha they are also called pratyekabuddhas—the term means "self-enlightened" or "enlightened by conditions"—because they accomplish the Way by contemplating dependent origination. The position of those who attain pratyekabuddhahood is equal to that arhats in the Śrāvaka Vehicle. Therefore, the vehicles of pratyekabuddhas and śrāvakas are usually grouped together and called the Two Vehicles. When the two are discussed in terms of the Great Vehicle, which is characterized by the resolution to attain bodhi, they are called the Small Vehicle.

5

The Distinctive Dharma of the Great Vehicle

THE DISTINCTIVE DHARMA of the Great Vehicle is based on the virtues common to the Human, Heaven, Śrāvaka, and Pratyekabuddha Vehicles and explains the causal deeds and resulting virtues of buddhas and bodhisattvas. The Human Vehicle and the Divine Vehicle are ultimately imperfect and cannot enable one to escape birth and death. The Śrāvaka Vehicle and the Pratyekabuddha Vehicle, though faultless and liberating, are biased in that they benefit only their own individual practitioners. These vehicles are all good, but they are imperfect.

According to the *Lotus Sūtra*, the only important reason for the Tathāgata to appear in this world was to enable sentient beings to realize the Buddha's knowledge and views, that is, to enable them to realize the Buddha's great bodhi (enlightenment). Therefore, only the Great Vehicle doctrine—resolving to attain bodhi mind, practicing the bodhisattva deeds, and accomplishing Buddhahood—is the real meaning of the Buddha Dharma and the real purpose of the Tathāgata's teaching.

The doctrine of becoming a buddha is called the Great Vehicle in comparison to the Small Vehicle. It is superior to the Small Vehicle, broader than and therefore inclusive of it. "Great" in this sense refers to relative superiority or inclusiveness. But the superiority of the Great Vehicle Dharma is such that nothing can be compared to it; its inclusiveness is so vast that it includes everything. So the meaning of the Great Vehicle cannot really be expressed in terms of the relativity of great and small: it is absolute.

In the phrase "distinctive Dharma of the Great Vehicle," the word "distinctive" also has two meanings. It refers to this Dharma's absence from the Human, Heaven, Śrāvaka, and Pratyekabuddha Vehicles; it indicates that the minds and deeds of buddhas and bodhisattvas constitute it. As is said in the "Mahāyāna Chapter" of the *Prajñāpāramitā Sūtra*, "because this vehicle includes all virtues, it is called the Great Vehicle."[1] This is like birds flying as high as "Mount Sumeru and having a gold color like that of the mountain."

This vehicle was the real purpose of the Tathāgata's appearing in this world to teach the Dharma. Having now explained the Dharma common to the Five Vehicles and the Three Vehicles, it is now necessary to explain the distinctive doctrine of becoming a buddha.

RESOLVING TO ATTAIN BODHI

113 Ashamed for not knowing,
Ashamed for not being able,
Ashamed for not being totally pure,
The arhats should turn to and enter the Great Vehicle.

Needless to say, practicing the Great Vehicle Buddha Dharma primarily means resolving to attain bodhi. But the capacities of sentient beings vary, so the causes and conditions for resolving to attain bodhi also vary. The ways in which bodhisattvas express themselves are also somewhat different in the beginning of their practice. One has to have considerable understanding of this concept in order to avoid the tendency to judge everything based on one's own preferences, thereby praising oneself and defaming others and unintentionally damaging the Buddha Dharma.

From the Śrāvaka Vehicle to the Bodhisattva Vehicle

The aforementioned Dharma common to the Three Vehicles is primarily that of the Śrāvaka and Pratyekabuddha Vehicles. The practitioners of these two vehicles can also resolve to attain bodhi and enter the way of the Great Vehicle. Some start by studying the deeds of the śrāvakas and, unsettled, switch to the study of the Great Vehicle; some are already settled (at the stage of patience) as śrāvakas or have already realized the nature of things and attained the first fruit (śrotāpanna) or beyond; some have already realized the fourth fruit of arhatship; and some have already entered the Nirvāṇa with residue and have resolved to attain bodhi. Since the Buddha Dharma is the way of the One Vehicle, the Small Vehicle is actually the skillful way to the Great Vehicle, and naturally sooner or later leads there. But from the standpoint of the Small Vehicle practitioners, initially, there are some unavoidable barriers.

For example, all the arhats say, "My life is ended. I have established pure conduct; what I set out to do is accomplished. I know I will not have future rebirths."[2] They feel that they have reached the stage at which no further learning or advancement is possible. The Buddha was an arhat and his enlightened disciples were also arhats; the Buddha was emancipated, and they, too, were emancipated. Thinking they had reached the ultimate, for the moment they naturally did not want to practice the way of the Great Vehicle. But did not the Buddha become a buddha by practicing the bodhisattva deeds and saving innumerable sentient beings? Why then did the Buddha not teach his śrāvaka practitioners to practice bodhisattva deeds to become buddhas? Why did he instead advise them to practice deeds to benefit themselves in order to end birth and death?

These are important questions. Having realized the nature of things and become liberated from birth and death, were the śrāvaka arhats really equal to the Buddha in everything? In comparison, they were poles apart! Through their actual experiences and under the Buddha's skillful teaching, the arhats inevitably felt ashamed and blamed themselves. Eventually they rid themselves of the mental block of thinking of themselves as the ultimate, resolved to attain bodhi, and progressed along the Buddha Way!

Some of them felt ashamed upon understanding that there were things they did not know and that they were unable to match the Buddha, who knew everything. The *Mahāvibhāṣā Śāstra* says that when the Buddha expounded the Dharma to Maitreya Bodhisattva and others, the arhats were unable to understand. For example, in the past, there was a person who went to Jetavana, an ancient Indian monastery, wanting to be a monk there. The arhats investigated his fundamental capacity and found that he did not even have a little bit of a good root and so was unsuitable to give up lay life; even if he gave up lay life, he would not be able to attain enlightenment. They refused to help him to become a monk, but the Buddha did so, and soon he attained arhatship. The arhats were surprised, so the Buddha told them, "Infinite kalpas ago, while being chased by a tiger, this person uttered 'Namo Buddha.' This virtuous act and his earlier good root of having turned toward the Buddha have now matured and delivered him."

This illustrates that compared to the Buddha's profound and vast wisdom, the arhats' wisdom is like the dim light of a lightning bug in broad daylight. They felt ashamed of not being as able as the Buddha and bodhisattvas. As Śāriputra said, "Alas, I blame myself deeply. How could I have been so deceived? Realizing the faultless Dharma, we are the

Buddha's disciples, but in the future we will not be able to expound on the supreme way."[3] Actually, there are many things that arhats cannot do, such as the bodhisattva deeds that "with magical supernatural power purify the Buddha's land and transform sentient beings."[4] They were also ashamed to see that they had not cut off their afflictions completely; they still had certain impurities.

For example, when King Druma-Kiṃnara played music, even the elderly and virtuous Mahākāśyapa could not refrain from dancing for joy. Mahākāśyapa said, "Although I can stay far away from worldly desires and happiness, I am still attached to the wonderful joy of the bodhisattva deeds!" And when a goddess scattered flowers, the flowers fell off the bodhisattvas' skin but stayed on śrāvaka arhats, proving that they still had attachment in their minds. Another example: When a bird passed through Śāriputra's shadow, it had some lingering fear, but when it passed through the Buddha's shadow, it did not have any fear at all. Arhats have not eliminated all their old habits, afflictions that bodhisattvas have cut off. After the Buddha skillfully taught them, the arhats turned their minds from benefiting themselves to resolving to attain bodhi and entering the Great Vehicle way of benefiting both themselves and others.

Ways to Enter the Great Vehicle

114 Not tolerating the decline of the noble teachings,
Not tolerating the suffering of sentient beings,
Through the arising of great compassion,
Enter into the Great Vehicle.

The resolution directed toward the way of the Great Vehicle does not necessarily require the realizations of the Small Vehicle sages; on the contrary, the primary group practicing the Great Vehicle Dharma comprises ordinary people who have resolved to practice. The causes and conditions leading to such a resolution vary. In the Buddha's time, some made a resolution after seeing the physical appearance of the Buddha and bodhisattvas; some did so after witnessing the transcendental power of the Tathāgata, and some after hearing the perfect sound of the Tathāgata's voice when he was teaching. Those born after the Buddha's time have made their resolutions after listening to the teachings of Buddhist disciples or after delving into the profound meaning of the sūtras. Some have done so entirely on their own, while others have been persuaded.

To resolve to attain bodhi means primarily to have the Buddha's enlightenment as an ideal and to vow to attain it. Of course, the main substance of the resolution to attain bodhi is an emphasis on the lofty, profound virtues of the Buddha and on the vow to seek Buddhahood. If another important factor—the vow of compassion—is missing, however, then the resolution is incomplete or easily lost. As the sūtras say, "Bodhisattvas arise from great compassion,"[5] so to resolve to attain bodhi is "to resolve to benefit others and seek perfect enlightenment."[6] Without such an emphasis on the compassionate vow, it is easy to retreat from one's resolution.

Entering through Compassion

The resolution that emphasizes the compassionate vow has two categories: (1) "Not tolerating the decline of the noble teachings (that is the Buddha Dharma)," one resolves to protect the Dharma, knowing that the wonderfully superior virtues of the Three Treasures have the power to save people and the world, and to awaken the good worldly Dharma and the world-transcending Dharma. In the periods of the imitative Dharma and the latter days of the Dharma, however, when the Buddha Dharma is degenerate, one is disturbed by evils both within religion and outside it and is unable to save people and the world. One knows that resolving to attain bodhi, seeking enlightenment, and saving all sentient beings are the only methods to rejuvenate Buddhism and to benefit all. Intolerant of the decline of the noble teachings, one has great compassion, which leads one to make the great vow of enlightenment. (2) "Not tolerating the suffering of sentient beings," one resolves to benefit living beings. One may be born in chaotic times when people's lives are difficult; one wants to help but does not have much power to provide relief. Investigating this in depth, one knows that only by studying Buddhism and becoming a buddha can one really save sentient beings from suffering. One thus has great compassion that leads one to seek enlightenment and to save all.

These two categories of resolution arise on their own from profound wisdom and compassion, so they are firm, powerful, and can easily succeed. If one can follow this compassionate vow and resolution, one can enter into the Great Vehicle from the level of an ordinary person. These days, the Buddha Dharma is in decline and people are suffering, so now is the time to resolve to attain bodhi!

Entering through the Three Virtues

115 Some enter with the faithful vow;
Some enter with wisdom, some with compassion.

In order to enter the complete bodhi mind of the Buddha Way, one should have the three virtues of the faithful vow, compassion, and wisdom. The beginners' resolve to enter will inevitably differ depending on their natures. Beginners will have different inclinations with regard to practicing these three virtues. If one gives more emphasis to one area without neglecting the others, this will not hinder one from entering the Great Vehicle way. Nāgārjuna explained the *Prajñāpāramitā Sūtra* by saying, "Bodhisattvas enter the Buddha Way through various gates: some from the gate of compassion and some from the gate of wisdom and diligence."[7] He also said that "prajñā has all kinds of gates through which to enter: if one hears and holds to the teachings and remains mindful of them, one enters through the gate of wisdom and diligence; if one copies the sūtras and pays homage, one enters through the gate of faith and diligence."[8]

Beginners who are entering the Buddha Way are either those with wisdom, those with compassion, or those with the faithful vow. Those who emphasize wisdom and enter through the gate of wisdom are described as "bodhisattvas who differentiate between various sūtras, recite and read, recall, ponder, and differentiate between various Dharmas in seeking the Buddha Way, and who have the light of wisdom to benefit themselves and other sentient beings."[9] These are the bodhisattvas of superior wisdom who are similar to śrāvakas; they act according to their understanding of the Dharma, and when they practice or teach others, they emphasize the wisdom that comes from hearing, thinking, and practicing.

Those emphasizing compassion and entering through the gate of compassion are described as bodhisattvas that "have a lot of kindness and compassion for sentient beings."[10] These bodhisattvas are the same as those who enter through the gate of compassion. They have a fundamental capacity for kindness and compassion; this capacity differentiates them from the two vehicles and can also be said to be the special characteristic of the Great Vehicle bodhisattvas. They are called the bodhisattvas of superior compassion.

The third type of bodhisattva emphasizes entering through the gate of the faithful vow. The faithful vow to practice the easy way of Pure Land is of this type. Such people are described as bodhisattvas who "gather the virtues of all buddhas and, doing so with joy, they reach the pure, One Vehicle world with infinite life."[11] These are the bodhisattvas of superior faith who are similar to the śrāvakas.

In the initial stage of studying there are these three different groups. Their different habits develop into characteristics until they become bodhisattvas above the initial stage; although they practice the three virtues simultaneously, they each exhibit a distinctive style. For example, Guanyin (Avalokiteśvara Bodhisattva) is associated with compassion, Wenshu (Mañjuśrī Bodhisattva) is associated with wisdom, Puxian (Samantabhadra Bodhisattva) is associated with faithful vows, and so forth. When people are differentiated according to their basic natures, those whose conduct is desirous need superior compassion, those whose conduct is angry need superior wisdom, and those whose conduct is ignorant need superior faithful vows.

Entering through the Other Vehicles

116 Some enter as śrāvakas;
Some enter as divine beings, some as humans.

There are three different sets of deeds through which one can enter the Buddha Way. There are those who enter through the deeds of the śrāvakas, those who enter through the deeds of divine beings, and those who enter through the deeds of humans. This was originally described in the Great Vehicle sūtras. The Venerable Master Taixu's has a more illuminating analysis and grouping, however: during the time of the true Dharma most people relied on Śrāvaka Vehicle deeds to enter the Great Vehicle, during the time of imitative Dharma most followed Divine Vehicle deeds, while during these latter days of the Dharma most follow Human Vehicle deeds.

Entering through the Śrāvaka Vehicle

According to a description in the sūtras, those who follow the Śrāvaka Vehicle to enter the Buddha Way first practice the Dharma of the śrāvakas (and pratyekabuddhas); some who have not attained enlightenment as well as some who have already attained enlightenment then turn their minds to the Buddha Way. Some of those who practice only the deeds of the śrāvakas think that they are accomplishing the ultimate, but other cultivators, with sharp capacity and profound wisdom, already have "the bodhisattva deeds hidden inside but appear to be śrāvakas."[12] Before the Buddha exposed the partial teaching and revealed the whole truth, their minds were already dwelling peacefully on the Great Vehicle way.

Entering through the Divine Vehicle

Those who follow the deeds of the Divine Vehicle to enter the Buddha Way fall into two groups. The first consists of cultivators of the Pure Land who single-mindedly want to be reborn in the divine Pure Land and then gradually practice the Buddha Way there. Among these, according to the *Guan wu liang shou jing* (The Sūtra on the Contemplation of Amitāyus Buddha), some with a superior grade and sharp capacity have already resolved to attain bodhi, have read and recited the Great Vehicle sūtras, and have understood the empty nature of things. Soon after they reach the Pure Land, therefore, they are able to completely realize birthlessness and return to this world to practice the bodhisattva-way. The second group comprises esoteric practitioners, who emphasize cultivating the divine body of the realm of desire, have the vajrayaksa as their object of worship, practice to become immortals with magical words, and then stay in the world for a long time to practice the Buddha Way. Although they are of "very poor wisdom, the teaching that form exists is also included in order to accommodate their desire."[13] There are some who specifically cultivate the essence and energy of the physical body as their main work. Those who do so with sharp capacity are in accord with bodhi mind, using great compassion as their foundation and having skillful means to reach the ultimate.

Both groups that rely on the Divine Vehicle emphasize yoga or samādhi. Meditation is the special characteristic of the deeds of this vehicle. To include all, however, beginners can do verbal recitations—just reciting the mantras and invoking the names.

Entering through the Human Vehicle

Those relying on the deeds of the human vehicle to enter the Buddha Way do so by resolving to attain bodhi, practicing the ten good deeds, not abandoning righteous worldly conduct, and extensively practicing right action by stabilizing their countries and benefiting people. Beginners who follow this practice and reach the level of just being a "commoner" of the Great Vehicle are actually equivalent to the virtuous and good people of the world.

The original purpose of the Tathāgata appearing in the world to teach humankind was to enable them to realize the Buddha's knowledge and understanding. Relying on the human or bodhisattva deeds to follow the Buddha Way is therefore not only befitting to the capacities of the people of the present time, it is also the fundamental and unobstructed way to attain Buddhahood.

Entering through the Teachings

117 Those who enter into the Great Vehicle
Do so either directly or indirectly.
The corresponding teachings
Are the real teaching and the skillful teaching.

Practitioners who enter into the Great Vehicle have always been grouped into either bodhisattvas who enter directly and bodhisattvas who enter indirectly. Directly entering means going directly toward the bodhisattva-way; indirectly entering means practicing other teachings first and then turning to enter the Great Vehicle way. Those of the Two Vehicles who turn toward the Great Vehicle, "exposing the partial teaching and revealing the whole truth" as described in the *Lotus Sūtra*, are examples of indirect entrance.

The teachings that correspond with the direct and indirect entrances are the real teaching and skillful teaching respectively. Why did not the Buddha teach the Great Vehicle way directly and explain the Buddha

Vehicle to all sentient beings instead of imparting the skillful teaching? The Buddha's skillful teaching is extraordinarily significant. Without it, many sentient beings would be unable to enter the Buddha Way. For example, in their practice directed toward realization, practitioners of the Small Vehicle discovered that there were things they did not know and were unable to do and also that they were impure. Through this understanding they could then accept the Buddha's teaching and be transformed by the Buddha. As well, when one attains the enlightenment of the Small Vehicle, birth and death are ended, and there is no longer any need to worry about the transmigrations of birth and death. So the skillful teaching is a most worthy one.

There are also skillful teachings in the Great Vehicle teachings called "special skillful means" or "superior skillful means."[14] Some people differ from those of the Two Vehicles by having a fundamental weariness of birth and death, but they still experience hindrances upon entering the Great Vehicle. Thus the Buddha spoke with superior skillful means of the doctrine of the pure and happy land and the pure and happy physical body in order to transform them. This is the doctrine of "using desire to hook them first and then enabling them to enter the Buddha-wisdom"[15] and "using happiness to attain happiness." If people can really be reborn in the happy Pure Land, they do not need to worry about regression. Through the teachings of buddhas and bodhisattvas they can resolve to attain bodhi and enter the Buddha Way. If they can really cultivate a pure and happy physical body—a divine physical body—they can also profoundly practice superior wisdom.

Therefore, although the Buddha's original intention for appearing in the world was to teach human beings to go from the Human Vehicle toward the Buddha Way (that is, for humans to become buddhas), he had to use skillful methods. For those who were fundamentally disgusted with suffering, he taught the deeds of the śrāvaka and the indirect entrance into the Great Vehicle. Such people for the most part had superior wisdom and were inclined toward self-reliance. For those who fundamentally desired pleasure, he taught the divine deeds as the entrance to the Great Vehicle. Such people had superior faithful vows and were inclined to rely on external help. The Tathāgata opened the gates of both the skillful teaching and the real teaching so as to enable all sentient beings to turn toward the Buddha Way.

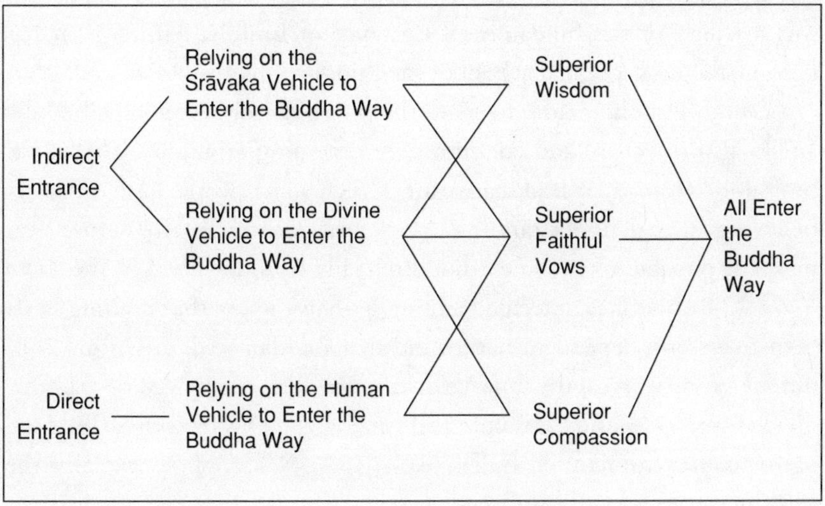

BUDDHA NATURE

118 Sentient beings have Buddha nature,
Which encompasses absolute nature (the fundamental principle)
And functional nature (the phenomenal developments).
Initially, relying on practice, they develop this nature.
Then, relying on this nature, they become more practiced.
Only through practice can all become buddhas.

That all sentient beings have Buddha nature is the major teaching of the Great Vehicle Buddhism, and this is where the principle that all sentient beings can accomplish the Buddha Way is found.

Buddha nature can have two meanings. First, it is the essential nature of the buddhas, just as "gold ore has a gold-nature, and white ore has a silver-nature."[16] Although sentient beings are in a state of confusion about birth and death, they are not without a component of the buddhas. If ore has a component of gold, it can be processed into gold; otherwise it cannot. Of course substances that are not gold can be transformed to look like gold. The teachings regarding Buddha nature are the same. Sentient beings fundamentally have the essential nature of the buddhas; or they are said to have fundamentally the Tathāgata's superior virtues and solemn appearance, or are said to fundamentally be buddhas, and so can become buddhas with practice. In general, people readily understand and accept this teaching of the fundamental existence of Buddha nature, so it has become the most popular school of the Buddha Dharma.

Second, Buddha nature refers to the possibility of becoming a buddha and is also the cause and condition for becoming a buddha. This is the profound meaning of Buddha nature, which some people have difficulty believing in and understanding. Now, what exactly is the nature that makes it possible to become a buddha? This is as described in the *Lotus Sūtra*: "The buddhas, esteemed among humans, know that nothing has a permanent or independent nature and that Buddha-seeds arise from conditions, so they reveal the One Vehicle."[17] Buddha nature can be skillfully divided into two kinds: absolute and functional. This division of Buddha nature comes from an old Indian explanation. What follows explains the teachings from a Mādhyamika perspective.

Absolute Buddha nature means that all things are fundamentally without an independent nature of their own; that is, their fundamental nature is empty and still. All things are without a permanent or independent nature (the ancients spoke separately of permanence and the nonexistence of independent nature, which were part of the explanation of the three truths), and all things are ultimately empty. The nonexistence of independent nature is emptiness; emptiness is the nature of things that neither arises nor perishes, and this can be called Buddha nature. These statements are true because otherwise—if all things were not empty and had independent natures of their own—the existence of ordinary people would be real and they would forever be ordinary people. Likewise, the existence of defilements would be real, and they would forever be defilements; what already exists could not become extinct, and what does not yet exist could not come into existence; there would be nothing for anyone to sever and nothing for anyone to practice, so no one could become a buddha (as is explained in the *Mūlamadhyamaka-kārikā*).

Fortunately, all things are empty and without an independent nature, so defilements can become pure, confusion can become enlightenment, and the common can become holy. The nature of things being empty is the principle of having the possibility to be common or holy, defiled or pure, and is also the principle of having the possibility to become a buddha. Therefore, it is said, "Because existence is empty, all things can be formed." This is the profound meaning of calling Buddha nature empty.

Although the nature of things being empty is the universal principle through which all things are formed, emptiness is nevertheless extraordinary. It is the nature of things that one realizes when one becomes a sage and upon which one relies to give rise to purity. Realizing emptiness is the important cause for becoming a buddha. Because emptiness is universal in all things and does not correspond to confusion, it is in accordance with the faultless and pure virtues. The nature of things being empty is described as Tathāgatagarbha, or Buddha nature, and people are said to fundamentally have the Tathāgata's wisdom, virtues, and so on. The nature of things being empty is universal and of one flavor, being the same for all sentient beings. So all sentient beings are said to be able to become buddhas.

Functional Buddha nature is the causal nature for becoming a buddha from practice and resolution. Scholars of the Mere Consciousness system say that relying on "the hearing and practicing of the universal outflow of the Dharma realm (the Buddha's teaching)," one has the potential to become a buddha. The *Lotus Sūtra*'s passage "Buddha-seeds arise from conditions" is based on the teaching of the developmental nature. The empty nature of all things serves as the principle for the possibility of sentient beings becoming buddhas. Reliance on the buddhas' and bodhisattvas' teachings and the resolution to learn and practice serves as the nature through which beings develop into buddhas.

The phenomena and the principle are consistent: if a thing does not arise from conditions, it is not empty; if it is not empty without an inherent nature, it does not arise from conditions. Because a thing is empty without an independent nature, it arises from conditions; because it arises from conditions, it is empty without an independent nature. Due to the nonexistence of independent nature there is dependent origination and due to dependent origination there is nonexistence of independent nature—this is the enlightenment the Buddha attained. "Contemplating ignorance (and so forth) like empty space without limit…is called the distinctive and wonderful contemplation of all bodhisattvas."[18] Having used these practices to become a buddha, the Buddha also relied on this approach to teach the One Vehicle, affirming that all sentient beings have Buddha nature. According to the teaching of absolute Buddha nature, all sentient beings have Buddha nature. According to the teaching of developmental nature, things happen in dependence upon conditions, so sentient beings may or may not have Buddha nature.

The Dharma-seed of the Great Vehicle is the bodhi mind. To resolve to attain bodhi and all related virtues is the developmental nature of the Buddha nature. A passage in the *Lotus Sūtra*, "Buddha-seeds arise from conditions," teaches about the bodhi-mind seed. In the past, among those who had resolved to attain bodhi in the Dharma assembly of the Buddha of supreme penetration and wisdom, some people regressed to practicing the Small Vehicle. They were like a drunk man whose friends have tied an invaluable pearl on him; unaware of this, he remains extremely poor. Actually, "all vows of wisdom (vows to attain enlightenment) remain and are not lost."[19] The situation of being drunk and given an invaluable pearl is like being in the ignorant cycle of birth and death when one encounters the guidance of the Buddha and bodhisattvas and resolves to attain bodhi. (Some people explain the pearl that is tied on as absolute Buddha nature, but this contradicts the meaning of the sūtra.) Resolving to attain bodhi, one can become a vessel of the Great Vehicle Dharma and can in turn engender boundless virtues.

The *Shi di jing* (Daśabhūmika Sūtra), the *Da ji jing* (Mahāsaṃnipāta Sūtra), and other sūtras all use the analogy of bodhi mind as a precious pearl, which with practice and perfecting becomes the virtuous fruit of buddhahood. According to these sūtras, the development of Buddha nature has approximately two stages: the primary seed nature stage and the functioning seed nature stage. In the first, which depends on the causes and conditions of seeing the Buddha and hearing the Dharma, one resolves to attain great bodhi and to have the Buddha nature of the Great Vehicle. This is the same as planting a seed, so it is called the primary seed nature.

Once the resolve to attain bodhi has arisen, it will always be the cause and condition for one to become a buddha and will not be lost—this is described in the *Lotus Sūtra*'s analogy of the pearl that has been tied on. But this resolve cannot be said to be originally possessed; it is formed from making the resolution and from being influenced by the universal teaching of the Buddha. When one has the bodhi-mind seed, one relies on this Buddha nature to practice gradually. Gradual practice causes the pure function of the Buddha-seed to grow from the bottom grade to the middle and then to the top. The virtue and pure function of the Great Vehicle (the Mahāyāna) that are incessantly practiced with increasing superiority are called the functioning seed nature. After much practicing, one brings forth faultless and pure virtues. Then not only is this nature the causal factor for one to become a buddha, it has also become part of the essential nature of the buddha.

The empty nature of things (absolute Buddha nature) is the same for ordinary people and sages; it is the same for all realms of sentient beings, bodhisattvas, and buddhas. Whether all these beings become buddhas or not depends on practice. Have they resolved to achieve bodhi mind? Have they practiced incessantly and grown in accord with the seed of bodhi mind? If they do not practice, ordinary people remain ordinary; if they can rely upon the Great Vehicle to practice, all sentient beings can attain buddhahood.

THE BODHISATTVA

119 Having made the resolution, one can be called a bodhisattva
Who presides over all sentient beings.
The worldly and world-transcending virtues
All come from the bodhisattvas.

Although all things are empty by nature and all sentient beings have Buddha nature, this does not imply that all sentient beings are bodhisattvas. One has to make the resolution to attain bodhi before one can be called a bodhisattva. Bodhisattva, abbreviated as "*pusa*" in Chinese, is Sanskrit for "enlightened sentient being." This name comes from "seeking bodhi" (enlightenment) and "transforming all living things" (sentient beings). A bodhisattva can also be explained as a sentient being who seeks great bodhi. After one has resolved to attain bodhi, one is a bodhisattva. Bodhisattva is the common name for all those practicing the Great Vehicle way, from beginners and experienced practitioners up to the final rebirth of a bodhisattva, encompassing myriad types of different levels.

Generally people associate the term bodhisattva with the great bodhisattvas such as Guanyin, so they do not dare to call themselves bodhisattvas. Although bodhisattvas with the initial resolution do not yet have great virtue, they preside over all sentient beings. Not only are they respected by ordinary people, they are also respected by the sages of the Two Vehicles. In the sūtras several analogies are used to describe the bodhisattvas. For example, they are like the newborn prince who is respected by the elderly ministers or the newborn lion who is feared by all animals. They can also be compared to the voice of the Kalavinka bird, which even in its shell is superior to all birds, or to the gentle brightness of the new moon. Any bodhisattva who has made the resolution is honorable and respectable like these examples, to say nothing of the great bodhisattvas.

Why is this? Because the worldly and world-transcending virtues all come from the bodhisattvas. This is to say, all good dharmas of the world—of śrāvakas, of pratyekabuddhas, and so forth—come from buddhas and bodhisattvas. The virtues of the buddhas also come from bodhisattvas, so bodhisattvas are the root of all good dharmas. "Bodhisattvas receive various bodies," it is said; "sometimes they receive the body that comes from causes and conditions of karma, and sometimes they receive the transformed body—in order to teach the various good dharmas and worldly dharmas, national laws, and secular affairs in the world."[20] Some who have practiced bodhisattva deeds but have temporarily failed are called "defeated bodhisattvas who still have a mind of compassion. They govern countries with national laws that are free from greed; although there are some disturbances, most people are peaceful, since even for the sake of individual families, an evil person will be punished."[21]

The initial resolution to attain bodhi emphasizes the firm establishment of the great vow to seek the Buddha Way and transform sentient beings, the bodhi-mind vow: "I vow to save boundless sentient beings. I vow to eliminate endless afflictions. I vow to learn innumerable doctrines. I vow to accomplish the unsurpassed Buddha Way."[22] Resolving to attain bodhi mind means more than just occasionally thinking about becoming a buddha in order to benefit sentient beings; it requires practicing with firm effort. Cultivation of bodhi mind is the first important step to practicing and entering the Great Vehicle. Bodhi mind comes from the mind of compassion: from respect for elders and a wish to save one's loving mother, bodhi mind expands to a vow to save all sentient beings and seek the Buddha Way. It arises from the thought that others and oneself are the same, and that benefiting other sentient beings and cherishing oneself are also the same, which requires one to practice until one is willing to sacrifice oneself to benefit others. The motive for and method of cultivating bodhi mind is similar to Confucianism's benevolence and forgiveness. But in its depth and extent, bodhi mind practiced to the point of complete success is enormously different from the worldly dharmas. Bodhi mind, the cornerstone of the Great Vehicle way, should be practiced first and then more and more.

THE BASIS FOR THE PRACTICE OF THE BODHISATTVA WAY

120 The vehicle of the bodhisattvas
Corresponds with bodhi mind,
Is guided by kindness and compassion,
And has the wisdom that comes from emptiness as its skillful means.
Enter by these three important gates,
And cultivate all practices skillfully,
For they all lead to the One Vehicle to become a buddha.

After resolving to attain bodhi mind, one should put the Great Vehicle into practice. This requires some discussion of the key elements of bodhisattva deeds. The Śrāvaka Vehicle and the Pratyekabuddha Vehicle share the same cause and the same result. But within the Great Vehicle, the aspect that emphasizes causal deeds is called the Bodhisattva Vehicle, whereas the aspect that emphasizes the resultant virtues is called the Buddha Vehicle. The completed cause and the perfected result constitute the entire body of the Great Vehicle Dharma. What follows explains the way to perfect enlightenment, the causal deeds. This is the Great Vehicle, which serves as the bodhisattvas' vehicle of doctrine. Relying on this doctrine, bodhisattvas enter great bodhi, also called the sea of wisdom.

The Three Gates of the Great Vehicle

As for the bodhisattva deeds, in all practices three important principles are present. First, one's giving must correspond with bodhi mind; that is, it must be for the sake of seeking enlightenment and transforming sentient beings. Second, when one gives, one's actions must be guided by kindness and compassion. Third, the wisdom that sees the emptiness of things is a skillful means, which means it is tactful. If one is not attached to the giver, the receiver, and things given, this is called possessing skillful means. If one lacks the wisdom that sees the emptiness of things and attaches to the act of giving, one is unskillful and tactless and cannot leave birth and death behind to enter the sea of wisdom.

It can be said that bodhi mind is the aspiration, the compassionate mind is the motive, and the wisdom that sees the emptiness of things is the skill to perform deeds. If one relies on these three important gates as the foundation and skillfully cultivates all practices—whether they are the worldly good dharmas of the five precepts, the ten good deeds, and the threefold fortunate karma; or the world-transcending good dharmas of the Four Truths, dependent origination, the three studies, the eightfold right path, and the thirty-seven grades of the Way; or the six pāramitās, the four all-embracing virtues, the one hundred and eight samādhis, and the forty-two siddham letters of the Great Vehicle—all these practices can lead to the One-Vehicle doctrine of the way to perfect enlightenment. Simply speaking, with these three minds, all good deeds are doctrines of the Great Vehicle; if one lacks or is deficient in any of these three minds, then there is no way to become a buddha.

When describing the practices of bodhisattvas the *Mahāprajñāpāramitā Sūtra* says, "All the thoughts that correspond to the wisdom that comes from all wisdom should be guided by great compassion and take nonattainability as a skillful means."[23] This passage refers to the three minds explained in the verses and commentary above. Nāgārjuna's *Bao man lun* (Treatise of the Precious Garland) explains that "the bodhi mind, which is strong like the king of all mountains, is fundamental; compassion extends to the ten directions; wisdom does not rely on the two extremes."[24] The *Vairocana Sūtra* also describes bodhi mind in a similar way: "Great bodhi is the cause; kindness and compassion are the foundation; and skillful means is relied on to reach the ultimate."[25] (The Chinese version of this passage was mistakenly translated as "taking skillful means as the ultimate.") "All the thoughts that correspond to the wisdom that comes from all wisdom" is the same as "all the vows of wisdom" in the *Lotus Sūtra* and is another name for bodhi mind. Great compassion comes from all sentient beings of the ten directions, so it is said to extend to the ten directions. Nonattainment is prajñā, the wisdom that comes from emptiness that does not rely on the two extremes of existence and nonexistence. The *Vairocana Sūtra* also has the teaching of the phenomenal being real, so, according to this sūtra, to have various kinds of skillful means is to reach the ultimate.

It must be said, however, that the main skillful means to become a buddha is the nonattaining wisdom that comes from emptiness. If one is attached to phenomena, no matter what, one will not reach the ultimate. In the Great Vehicle Dharma, all three gates are equally important, and one of them cannot be lacking. But the Great Vehicle sūtras do have different emphases. They may emphasize bodhi mind, or the great compassionate mind, or the nonattaining prajñā; each takes its own teaching as the most important; each relies on its own particular emphasis to teach skillfully. Although beginners may emphasize a particular one, they should not neglect the others.

These three minds, present throughout all the practices of the Great Vehicle, are similar to the three virtues of Confucianism—wisdom, benevolence, and courage. The three are superior qualities of humankind: superior ability to recall, superior pure conduct, and superior tolerance. Confucians emphasizing the right deeds of the Human Vehicle reveal the virtues that permeate the Human Vehicle: wisdom, benevolence, and courage. The Great Vehicle Dharma fundamentally emphasizes relying on the Human Vehicle to enter the Buddha Way directly; thus, like the Confucians, it reveals three virtues: (1) the unsurpassed and ultimate vow—bodhi mind; (2) universally impartial sympathy—kindness and compassion; and (3) the utterly thorough wisdom that comes from the Dharma—emptiness wisdom. These are all requisite virtues common to all the Great Vehicle deeds.

The practice of the Great Vehicle Dharma enables human nature to be purified or distilled, allowing the virtues to develop harmoniously and reach completion. When one becomes a buddha, the bodhi mind becomes the virtue of the Dharmakāya, the compassionate mind becomes the virtue of liberation, and the wisdom that comes from the emptiness of things becomes the virtue of prajñā.

The Tathāgata's hidden treasury of the three virtues is the highest completion of the virtuous conduct of human life. The true meaning of the Great Vehicle is not at all similar to the Small Vehicle practices, which are inclined toward reclusiveness, or to the Divine Vehicle practices, which have an esotericism about them. The true meaning of the Great Vehicle is actually this: human life heading toward the ultimate, human beings becoming buddhas.

The Three Cumulative Precepts

121 The bodhisattvas' "places of learning,"
Having the ten good deeds as their foundation,
Are included in the three cumulative precepts,
Which all the seven classes of disciples can keep.

Only the Great Vehicle way is the course of practice for the bodhi mind. The resolution to attain bodhi has the Great Vehicle's faithful vow as its essence; it is the same as taking refuge in the Great Vehicle. When making the resolution to attain bodhi, one has to take refuge in the Great Vehicle first. This does not just mean taking refuge for a single lifetime; rather, it means taking refuge "from this day until the attainment of enlightenment"[26] in the Buddha Dharma and the Saṅgha of bodhisattvas who never regress. Vowing to attain bodhi, one vows to use all one's good roots to attain the unsurpassed great bodhi just like the Buddha and bodhisattvas, "saving those who have not been saved, liberating those who have not been liberated, consoling those who are disturbed, and enabling those who have not attained Nirvāṇa to do so."[27] This is also the ultimate meaning of the common form of taking refuge: "From today and until my death I will protect living beings." Theoretically speaking, taking refuge is the expression of the vow of faith; one attains the precepts in reliance upon taking refuge. Further transmissions of the five precepts, etc., serve only to deepen one's understanding of the specifics of the precepts. Under the Tathāgata's skillful and gradual teaching, however, there were some disciples who took refuge but did not accept the precepts.

Similarly, by taking refuge in the Great Vehicle and resolving to attain bodhi, one receives the bodhisattva precepts by relying on bodhi mind and is then called a bodhisattva. Later, when one receives the bodhisattva precepts again, this additional transmission of the precepts serves only to deepen one's understanding of the specifics of the precepts. But through the skillful teaching and guidance of the Tathāgata, in the Great Vehicle Dharma, there are those who made the resolution to attain bodhi mind without receiving the bodhisattva precepts. The scriptures say, however, that "bodhi is strengthened by righteous deeds" and that "without righteous deeds one cannot attain bodhi."[28] One cannot become a buddha only by having faithful vows. So after making the vow to attain bodhi, one should go further and practice the righteous bodhi deeds (the actions of the bodhi mind), which means one should receive and maintain the "places of learning" of the Great Vehicle bodhisattvas. (Bhikṣu precepts are called bhikṣu places of learning, and bodhisattva precepts are bodhisattva places of learning.)

The bodhisattva precepts have the ten good deeds as their foundation. Not only does the learning of the beginning bodhisattvas start with the ten good deeds (which is why they are called bodhisattvas of the ten good deeds), even bodhisattvas of the ten grounds practice the righteous ten good deeds in great depth and extent. "Making great resolutions," it is said, "bodhisattvas of the ten good deeds depart from the sea of suffering of the three realms forever."[29] Besides being physically and verbally pure in righteous deeds, they have profound right wisdom because they do not have deviant views; they have vast kindness and compassion because they are not angry; and they accomplish infinite samādhi because they are not desirous. These ten deeds that are the basis of bodhisattva precepts can be grouped into the three cumulative pure precepts: (1) With regard to abandoning evil and preventing mistakes, they are called the rules and regulations precepts. (2) With regard to including all the good deeds, they are called the precepts that embrace the good Dharma. (3) With regard to benefiting and saving all sentient beings, they are called the precepts that benefit sentient beings. In sum, the precepts of bodhisattvas leave no evil uneliminated, no good thing undone, and no sentient being unbenefited.

In the śrāvaka Dharma, there are differences in the rules and regulations precepts for men and women, as well as for the Saṅgha and the lay community. The precepts are grouped into upāsaka precepts, upāsikā precepts, śrāmaṇera precepts, śrāmaṇerikā precepts, bhikṣu precepts, bhikṣuṇī precepts, and śikṣamāṇā precepts. Buddhist disciples are thus divided into seven classes. In the bodhisattva precepts, however, no differentiation is made between men and women or between the Saṅgha and the lay community (or rather there are only minor differences); so these precepts can be kept by all seven classes of disciples. If one wants to receive the bodhisattva precepts, one has to receive the corresponding precepts of one of the seven classes first. For example, an upāsaka (a man who has received the five precepts) who receives the bodhisattva precepts is called an upāsaka bodhisattva; a śrāmaṇerikā who receives the bodhisattva precepts is called a śrāmaṇerikā bodhisattva; and a bhikṣu receiving bodhisattva precepts is called a bhikṣu bodhisattva.

With regard to the precepts, the śrāvaka canon has the most extensive precepts. Although the bodhisattva canon is said to have had a separate section for the bodhisattva precepts, the bodhisattva precepts that were transmitted to China (as well as Tibet) are merely appended to the sūtras. The existing ones include the text of the *Fan wang jing* (Brahmā Net Sūtra), said to have been translated by Kumārajīva, which lists the ten serious and forty-eight minor precepts; the *Upāsakaśīla Sūtra*, translated by Dharmarakṣa, which lists six serious and twenty-eight minor precepts; and the *Yogācārin Bodhisattva Precepts*, translated by Master Xuanzang, which lists four serious and forty-three minor precepts. The minor precepts are somewhat different in the different versions, but the serious precepts are generally the same. This is also true for those precepts mentioned in the *Xukongzang jing* (Kṣitigarbha Sūtra), the *Pu sa ying luo ben ye jing* (Sūtra of the Original Karma of Bodhisattvas as a Necklace of Precious Stones), the *Śrīmālādevīsiṃhanāda Sūtra* (Sūtra on the Lion's Roar of Queen Śrīmālā), and so forth. In China, the *Fan wang jing* has always been the primary source for the precepts. The *Yogācārin Bodhisattva Precepts*, however, gives much more specific and extensive explanations of the behaviors that are permitted and prohibited, how the precepts are maintained and violated, and whether violations are light or serious matters.

122 Withdrawal and loss of bodhi mind,
Jealousy, stinginess, anger, and arrogance
Obstruct the acts of benevolence
And violate the precepts of the Great Vehicle.

Of the prohibitive precepts for bodhisattvas, some are more important. Numerous Great Vehicle sūtras equate reliance on bodhi mind with a single, fundamental bodhisattva precept. For example, with regard to benefiting sentient beings, if one has thoughts of being weary and abandoning one's purpose, or of not wanting to realize the unsurpassed bodhi but instead wanting to attain self-benefiting arhatship, or of seeking the sensual pleasures of the world and not wanting to seek enlightenment and transform sentient beings, a single such thought leads to the withdrawal and loss of bodhi mind and violates the pure bodhisattva precepts. Bodhi mind can be described as the fundamental, all-inclusive precept for bodhisattvas; it should be protected and kept by students of the Great Vehicle.

As for particular bodhisattva precepts, these share with the śrāvakas the prohibition of killing, stealing, sexual misconduct, and lying. As for the serious bodhisattva precepts not shared in common with the śrāvakas, these occur in slightly different form in the various sūtras and texts, but all sources mention four serious precepts regarding jealousy, stinginess, anger, and arrogance, which will be explained drawing on the *Yogācārin Bodhisattva*

Precepts. (1) Jealousy: due to greed for personal gain, offerings, and respect, one becomes jealous of others, and because of this one purposely praises oneself and slanders others. (2) Stinginess: although one may have wealth and the Buddha's teaching, when people come and ask, one gives neither. (3) Anger: one hurts others by scolding, and when others come to apologize and ask for forgiveness, one continues to hate them. (4) Arrogance: considering oneself extraordinary, one preaches some seemingly correct but really incorrect Buddha Dharma and slanders the true Dharma that others preach.

All four serious precepts deal with obstructions of the bodhisattvas' acts of benevolence. If one violates even one of them, one violates the pure bodhisattva precepts of the Great Vehicle and cannot become a bodhisattva. This is just like bhikṣus who violate the Pārājika precepts and then can no longer be bhikṣus. Whereas bhikṣus who violate the Pārājika precepts have to withdraw from the Saṅgha and cannot receive the Pārājika precepts again, the bodhisattva precepts can be received again properly. In other words, after making the resolution to attain bodhi and receiving the bodhisattva precepts, one will not withdraw and lose it no matter what. Violating a precept only temporarily causes it to lose its ability to function. One should thereafter take it again and recover the virtues of bodhi-mind precepts with new enthusiasm. Similarly, after one has resolved to attain bodhi and received the bodhisattva precepts, even if one withdraws into the Small Vehicle or regresses to the three evil destinies, one will ultimately return to the Great Vehicle way to perfect enlightenment by following the pure good roots of this bodhi-mind precept. In the Great Vehicle Dharma, evidently, nothing is more important than bodhi mind and the bodhisattva precepts.

THE PRACTICE OF THE BODHISATTVA WAY

123 Altogether, the bodhisattva way includes
The six transcendences and the four all-embracing virtues.
By entering the different grounds gradually,
One makes complete the virtues of a buddha.

A buddha's virtues, achieved through the practices of a bodhisattva, are ultimate and complete. Bodhisattvas should therefore vow to study infinite doctrines, not just a few. But in brief, the grades of the way to unsurpassed enlightenment consist of the six transcendences and the four all-embracing virtues. "Six transcendences" is a free translation of the six pāramitās. *Pāramitā* literally means to cross over or "reach the other shore." Giving, precepts, patience, diligence, dhyāna, and prajñā are doctrines to reach the other shore, so they are called pāramitās. The four all-embracing virtues, which can embrace and transform sentient beings, are giving, affectionate speech, conduct profitable to others, and identifying with others. The six transcendences are essential for accomplishing the Buddha Way, while the four all-embracing virtues are skillful means of benefiting sentient beings. The six transcendences can also be divided into the two ways of benefit to oneself and benefit to others. For example, giving, precepts, and patience belong to the way of virtue, which benefits others; meditation and wisdom belong to the way of wisdom, which benefits oneself; diligence is shared by both ways. But all six transcendences are beneficial both to oneself and to others.

It should be specifically mentioned here that buddhahood definitely cannot be attained by practicing only one deed or one doctrine. When the Buddha taught he sometimes emphasized certain things, such as the practice of a certain doctrine that would lead to supreme enlightenment quickly. But he sometimes taught in an inclusive way, teaching that by giving or by prajñā one will attain all six pāramitās. So if one holds to the erroneous view that one can become a buddha only by practicing a certain doctrine or deed without cultivating other virtues, then one is confused!

The doctrines should not be practiced partially or in small measure; nor can the grades of the way to become a buddha be completed in one day or one life. In the sūtras, the course of practice from the superficial to the profound level is divided into various stages of action—and among the important ones are the ten grounds. In the course of practice, bodhisattvas incessantly cultivate and initiate boundless virtues, which are like a ground from which myriad things can grow. Hence these stages are called grounds. When one completes the ten, one becomes a buddha.

The first ground is the ground of happiness. Before one enters it, one should practice the thirty minds. Thus, prior to the first ground, there are thirty stages—ten stages, ten practices, and ten transferences—that must be established. The first of the ten stages is called the purposive stage. This stage is the complete accomplishment of the practice of the ten minds such as faith and so on. When the practice of the mind of faith and so forth has not yet been achieved, these ten minds are listed as the ten locations of faith. The sequences and ranks of the practice of bodhisattvas unfold in this way.

There are, in sum, many stages from the superficial to the profound. Through the course of practice that gradually enters the different grounds, one can complete all the virtues of buddhahood and reach the ultimate goal of the bodhisattva's resolution to practice.

The Six Pāramitās

The Pāramitā of Giving

124 For the benefit of all sentient beings,
The body, all usable things,
And all good dharmas of the three periods,
Should not be saved but should be given away.

In the Dharma common to the Five Vehicles, giving is one of the items of the three blessed karmas. Giving does not appear, however, in the Dharma common to the Three Vehicles. For śrāvakas weary of the world and eager to seek enlightenment, giving does not have significant meaning. In the bodhi-way of the Great Vehicle, however, giving ranks as the first item of practice. Sacrificing oneself and being of benefit to others constitute the real meaning of giving, which coincides with the minds and acts of bodhisattvas. Giving in the Great Vehicle has a deeper and broader meaning than usual. It has to be practiced "in connection with bodhi mind, guided by great compassion, and take nonattainability as a skillful means." Giving is like this and although only it will be discussed below, all the other bodhisattva deeds also have to be practiced in connection with these three minds.

The giving in question entails sacrificing oneself for others. Not only does this giving eradicate stinginess and greed, it eliminates attachment to "I and mine." It becomes the great sacrifice that is without attachment to self and to things. Ordinary people find it hard to give because they hold on to what is theirs. Unaware of their mistake, they do not know the benefit of giving to sentient beings.

One has only to think of wealth and material things. For the sake of accumulating and gaining possession of things, people create boundless suffering in the world and endless international disputes, but eventually these things pass away due to impermanence. Although one can acquire many things by one's efforts, these possessions are really everyone's. Without society, one cannot obtain much wealth or a rich material life. A recluse living alone on a mountain may possess boundless territories, but he remains poor!

This is true not only for external things. One's body exists only through upbringing from parents, education from teachers, help from friends, public medical health care, and a country's legal order. If one acknowledges only oneself and considers only one's body as self, one not only increases one's afflictions, one also increases one's offenses. Even abundant knowledge, scientific inventions, and the practice of ethics and religions depend on the contributions of all of humankind. Thus, attachment to oneself is the root of all offenses and suffering, and giving to others can be the cause for all virtues and well-being. If one understands and practices this, the giving mind will grow tremendously.

This verse thus says three things. First, one's body (or body and mind as a whole) should be used to serve others; parts of one's body or even one's life should be sacrificed for the benefit of one's country and humankind. Second, all usable things, all one's usable wealth, should be properly given in the field of compassion and the field of respect. Third, good dharma, that is, all the good dharma that one has in the three periods—in one's past, present, and future lives—whether it be good worldly dharma, good world-transcending Dharma, or very best world-transcending Dharma of the Great Vehicle, should not be kept for oneself; instead one should be willing to give it to sentient beings.

Ordinary people think of these three categories of things—the body, wealth, and good dharma—as theirs and consider them meaningful only when they possess them. But bodhisattvas can practice giving without any reservations, giving to sentient beings to benefit them. Bodhisattvas practice, gather virtues, and transfer them to sentient beings in order to enable all sentient beings to become buddhas. Only then do bodhisattvas practice to become buddhas and gather virtues for themselves. The ability to forget oneself when one gives is the real giving of bodhisattvas.

125 Lower people give for the sake of themselves.
Middle people give for their own liberation.
Those who give all for the benefit of others
Are called great people.

Because of the different motives of almsgivers, the same act of giving will result in different virtues. Those who resolve to have better future lives and seek human and divine virtues are called the lower people. Although their giving may look virtuous, it actually comes from their utilitarian mind; they give for the sake of human and divine virtues. Although there are virtues to their giving, these are extremely limited. Those who have resolved to attain renunciation are called the middle people. These, weary of the suffering of births and deaths, give for the sake of their own liberation. Emphasizing liberation, they are not burdened by wealth and things, but nor do they value the positive meaning of giving for others' benefit. In the śrāvaka Dharma, there are people who would rather throw treasures into the ocean than use it to help the poor.

Those who resolve to attain bodhi are called the great people and are bodhisattvas. The giving of bodhisattvas is characterized by two aspects. First, giving for the benefit of others: one does not deny one's own virtues, but one does not pay attention to them; one gives for the benefit of others by bestowing happiness and alleviating suffering. Second, giving everything: bodhisattvas give their own body and mind, material wealth, all virtues and good Dharma. Having resolved to attain bodhi, bodhisattvas have already given all their own belongings unconditionally to sentient beings. Although they still own and use things, bodhisattvas think of them not as theirs but as belonging to all sentient beings. They are like employees or public servants who administer and manage belongings for others. When the owners are in need (when someone begs for alms) they respectfully return them without conditions. As for their own enjoyment, they are like the employees who legally earn their living. The great peoples' acts of bestowing all for others is most commendable.

126 The giving of wealth, dharma, and fearlessness
Is difficult but should be sympathetic and sincere.
The joy that comes from hearing of the need to give
Is superior to the happiness of Nirvāṇa.

As for the kinds of things to be given, there are three categories. The first is the giving of wealth, both external—things outside of one's body—and internal—one's body and life. The second is the giving of the dharma: either teaching and transforming sentient beings with one's own understanding and the practice of the Buddha Dharma or teaching them various kinds of beneficial knowledge and skills—medical, artistic, literary. The third is the giving of fearlessness: freedom from fear of being threatened or oppressed by rulers, thieves, gangsters; of being attacked by lions, tigers, wolves, snakes; of losing one's wealth or life due to floods, windstorms, earthquakes, plagues. The giving of bodhisattvas is thus not only philanthropic; it also includes active assistance—imparting one's knowledge, skills, and virtues, helping those in danger, relieving those in distress, eliminating violence, and protecting the good.

Two further points are worth mentioning with regard to the giving of bodhisattvas. First, even if something is not sufficient for the bodhisattva's own needs, or is a most beloved thing, or was obtained with great effort and sacrifice, the bodhisattva is willing to give it. Such giving is generally considered difficult. Second, bodhisattvas give sincerely. Ordinary people usually give reluctantly because other people come to ask, or they casually tell a subordinate to donate some money for them, or they give something only after making sarcastic and mocking comments. All this is improper giving. Bodhisattvas always give with a pure, respectful, and happy mind. They give in person and do not make people feel embarrassed.

Those who do not know the error of hoarding and the virtue of giving usually give reluctantly, particularly with regard to some major act of giving. Bodhisattvas, on the other hand, feel extremely joyful upon hearing of the arrival of people seeking alms no matter what the request. This joy, which is not only superior to the worldly happiness of the third dhyāna but also superior to the happiness of Nirvāṇa attained by the sages of the Two Vehicles, is a supreme happiness. Bodhisattvas then feel that virtues are being sent to them! Without those who seek alms, one cannot completely attain the virtues of giving. It is because people come to beg for alms that one's virtues can increase. Besides, if one's wealth, body, knowledge, and skills were not well used, and one were to lose them or die, would this not be a pity? Through giving in response to people's requests, one's impermanent belongings can be thrown into the ocean of the pāramitās and be transformed into the inexhaustible provisions necessary to become a buddha. So bodhisattvas feel happy upon hearing of a need to give, and in so doing realize the state of "being happiest in doing good."

127 Something should not be given
If you are unable, others are unreasonable, or requests are invalid.

Bodhisattvas should give everything, but in reality there are some things that should not be bestowed. Giving is for the benefit of others as well as for the benefit of one's cultivation. If giving something violates these principles, then one should not give. When something is given under these circumstances, it will increase one's own afflictions and offenses and those of others.

Situations in which things should not be bestowed are innumerable, but they fall into three areas. (1) Bodhisattvas should give their bodies, lives, and belongings without reservation, but this has to be practiced gradually until one's patience is strong and one's compassion is deep and without any reluctance; otherwise such giving will impede one's practice. For example, if one asks a weak person to carry a heavy load, it will only scare him into withdrawing. Also, if one has not yet thoroughly understood the profound scriptures, one should not give away these texts because doing so will hinder one's practice. For monks and nuns, the same is true of one's robe and bowl. (2) If those seeking alms are devils or non-Buddhists purposely coming to disrupt one, or if they are insane or childish, or if they have abnormal or unnecessary requests, bodhisattvas should not give to them. (3) What is really the purpose of the request for giving? If the request for one's life is for a trivial matter, one should not give it. "Do not abandon the important for the trivial," it is said. Or if people request help or supplies for acts of killing, stealing, and sexual misconduct, for harming sentient beings, or for gambling and fooling around, then one should not give. In sum, one should refuse if it is harmful to others and to one's cultivation.

128 The resolution to renounce is the superior aspect of bestowing,
So one should always practice this mental joy.

To practice the transcendence of giving, one of course actually has to give in order to benefit sentient beings. But in reality, no matter what one does, this kind of giving will not be able to satisfy everyone. In the course of bodhisattva practice, for instance, beginners sometimes encounter poverty and hardship and have nothing to give. One should know that in order to attain buddhahood on one's own, the transcendence of giving that relies on a mind of complete renunciation is supreme. The emphasis should be on the development of the aspiration to be able to give to all beings. Bodhisattvas should always cultivate a superior understanding of giving so that joy of giving can increase.

What is this superior understanding of giving with mental joy? It is the giving that is without actual substance. When a quiet meditative mind relies on the power of superior understanding, then vast, infinite, and varied wealth appears. Using this wealth, one makes offerings to all buddhas and gives to sentient beings. Having joy upon seeing others give is really virtuous, to say nothing of having much wealth appear in one's own mind and giving extensively in the fields of compassion and respect! This is skillful giving.

129 When attached to the three wheels,
Giving is described as worldly.
Giving that is not connected to the three wheels
Is called the world-transcending pāramitā.

"Exiting from the three realms and staying in the all-perfect wisdom" is the nature of pāramitā.[30] How can one reach the other shore by practicing giving? The commentaries say that the first five transcendences are like the blind, while prajñā is like the guide.[31] The reason that giving and other pāramitās enable one to enter the Buddha Way is entirely due to the embracing and guiding power of prajñā (wisdom). For giving to be a pāramitā, therefore, one must practice with the skillful means of nothing to be attained prajñā.

With regard to giving there are three wheels, or three aspects: (1) the giver, (2) the receiver, the beneficiary of the act of giving, and (3) the alms, the object given. Only when these three are present can giving take place. But if one does not have the illumination of the wisdom that comes from the nature of things being empty, then when one gives, one will be attached to these three areas as real. For example, one may think that there is a real self who gives, that there is an actual receiver of alms to whom one gives, and that there is a real object—big or small, good or bad—that is given. If one is thoroughly unable to understand emptiness—that all is without an inherent nature—one will be attached to phenomena everywhere. Grasping and attaching, one is bound to "I and mine" and is unable to leave the three realms to enter the Buddha Way. This kind of giving, which remains attached to phenomena, is called the worldly pāramitā of giving. Actually this kind of giving does not really become a pāramitā, but it is conventionally designated as such.

On the other hand, if in giving one can align oneself with either the nothing to be attained wisdom that comes from the realization of emptiness or the wisdom that does not differentiate with regard to the three wheels of giver, receiver, and object given, and if one can also understand profoundly the nature of things as empty by not clinging to the form of the self or the form of things, then this is giving with skillful means, unbound by afflictions. This giving, "able to act freely and depart from attachment," is called the world-transcending pāramitā of giving. The real world-transcending pāramitā is the giving done by the bodhisattvas of the great grounds, whose wisdom is nondifferentiating. Bodhisattvas above the purposive stage who align themselves with the wisdom that realizes emptiness are called "close to the pāramitā" bodhisattvas. Such bodhisattvas are able to approach the Buddha Way. The transcendence of giving should be empty of the substances of the three wheels. All practices and all pāramitās should be cultivated in such a manner.

The Pāramitā of Precepts

130 Keeping the precepts puts an end to the injury of others
And gives rise to universal fearlessness.

If one practices giving and yet is unable to keep one's body and mind proper, what one does often injures and disturbs sentient beings. This kind of help will not achieve the goal of benefiting sentient beings. Even children, if given candy with one hand and beaten with the other, will not have a good relationship with you. And if one is degenerate, one may lose one's enterprise of wealth. And then in a future birth one may lose one's human form, and then how can one be of benefit to others? In order to give, one needs to keep the precepts.

Although there are worldly precepts, world-transcending precepts, and supreme world-transcending precepts, the principle is the same—protecting lives. To protect lives means to be solicitous toward others and respect them. To respect and safeguard other people's rights and freedoms, one has to keep the precepts properly in one's mind and body and not injure others. The act of keeping the precepts is derived from the vow of not injuring others and is expressed in speech and in physical conduct. Keeping the precepts universally gives rise to fearlessness and creates harmony and freedom. Keeping the precept of not killing, for example, does not mean not killing only A or B or not killing just today and tomorrow; it means that one abandons forever the thought of killing any sentient being. Thus no one will ever be threatened by or fear being lulled by those who keep the precept of not killing. Not killing is explained based on the precepts of the rules and regulations and has the positive sense of benefitting sentient beings. When one is able to be like this, then one can speak of the embracing of the precept of the good Dharma and the precept of benefiting sentient beings.

131 Breaking the precepts is the root of all problems
Such as evil destinies and poverty.
Keeping the precepts is the root of threefold goodness:
A better future, decidedly superior fruit,
And—by keeping the pure precepts for the benefit of others—
Entrance to the Great Vehicle.

Why does one not accept and keep the pure precepts? Because one does not know about the mistake of breaking them and the virtue of keeping them. If one violates the serious precepts—the natural precepts—regardless of whether one has accepted them or not, one commits an offense. So it is strange that some who know that breaking the precepts is a serious matter are nevertheless afraid to keep them.

In reality, by relying on the blessings of the Three Treasures externally and the profound vow internally to receive the precepts one will be even more able to be pure and not violate the precepts. Breaking the precepts is the root of all problems, including falling into the three evil destinies and poverty. Ordinarily it is said that stinginess brings forth the retribution of poverty and breaking the precepts brings forth the retribution of falling into evil destinies. This understanding is based on a particular meaning. Birth as an animal or ghost is considered to be a regression, but some of these beings have blessed rewards; among humans, there are some who are utterly poor. Such are the different rewards and retributions of giving and keeping the precepts. If one violates the serious precepts and falls into hell, one will definitely be extremely poor, possessing nothing; if one keeps the highest pure precepts (of the world) one will be reborn in the heavens, rich and happy. So it is clear that violating the precepts is also the cause of poverty and keeping precepts is also the cause of being happy and wealthy. One should also know that if one concentrates only on one's conduct and on exercising self-control—without giving—one will be reborn as a human but have the retribution of poverty. If one keeps the precepts in connection with compassion, giving full expression to the positive meaning of benefiting others, one will definitely have riches, happiness, and glory when reborn in the heavens.

The virtue of keeping the precepts is the root of the threefold goodness. First, those who keep the precepts with the intention of having better future lives will be reborn as humans or divine beings with riches, happiness, and comfort. Second, those who keep the precepts by relying on the resolution to renounce will attain the holy fruit and the superior Dharma, and one will definitely not fall back into birth and death. Third, if one keeps the precepts by relying on bodhi mind to benefit others and keeps the pure śīla (precepts), one will enter the Great Vehicle. These precepts, called the Great Vehicle precepts, are the cause for becoming a buddha.

Therefore, when the specific liberating precepts of the seven classes of disciples—whether the upāsaka precepts, śrāmaṇera precepts, or bhikṣu precepts—are received and kept with bodhi mind as their origin, they become the specific regulations and rites for bodhisattvas. Some people think that the specific liberating precepts for the seven classes of disciples belong to the Small Vehicle and that because they are practitioners of the Great Vehicle, they do not need to accept and keep the specific liberating precepts of the śrāvakas. This deviant view causes confusion and leads to the decline of Buddhism.

132 Those who accept and keep the pure precepts
Should guard them as if they were a life preserver.
They should not look down on those who break them
Or be obsessed with keeping or breaking them.

Those who accept and keep the pure precepts and then break them do so because temptations of the environment or the impulse of afflictions are too strong. But, more important, this happens because one is too weak to keep the pure precepts. Otherwise one would be like a city with strong defenses that, despite being attacked by powerful enemies, holds fast and does not fall.

Guarding the pure precepts with strength is thus an important practice. Although ordinary people may not violate serious precepts, they often ignore minor mistakes because they do not know that small violations are the cause, however remote, for failure. This is like not fixing a minute leak that can lead to the bursting of a dam. Take, for example, not eating meat. If one is used to being a vegetarian, it is not easy for one to break this precept, for one is disgusted with the offensive smell of the meat. However, if one is not determined to avoid meat in the first place, or feels happy about eating meat even after being a vegetarian for a long time, one may break the precept because of one's weakness.

If one often commits small violations without repenting and purifying the precepts, then through the accumulation of small violations one risks violating the serious precepts. Here the Vinaya uses the metaphor of holding onto a floating bag. Floating bags were used by swimmers to keep them from drowning, just like modern life preservers. They should be particularly treasured and guarded. If one ignores even a minute leak, water will seep in and one risks drowning.

In the ocean of birth and death, before attaining the power of patience, bodhisattvas always vow to be born in the human world in order to see the Buddha, study the Dharma, and benefit sentient beings; the pure precepts are a life preserver that protects their human form and keeps them from failure and regression. Bodhisattvas who keep the pure precepts are therefore "equally protective of minor and the serious precepts." Compared to the way that śrāvakas keep the precepts, bodhisattvas are more rigorous.

The pure precepts of the bodhisattvas are practiced without ever departing from the three minds. So bodhisattvas do not look down on sentient beings who break the precepts. From the perspective of great compassion, precept breakers are to be pitied not despised. But although they have violated the precepts, it is still possible for them to return to purity and to become buddhas. Those who look down on others who break the precepts may think that they themselves are very pure and in accord with the Dharma. They are unaware that having already fallen into attachment to the concept of the self and the arrogance of the differentiating mind, they cannot accomplish the bodhisattvas' pāramitā of precepts.

If one looks down on those who break the precepts, then because of this mutual antagonism, one will find it difficult to teach them; one loses the bodhisattva's skillful means of benefiting others. So one should not scorn those who break the precepts but rather pity and comfort them, so as to influence them more easily. Bodhisattvas are also not obsessed with the appearance of keeping or breaking the precepts. The understanding that "both the keeping and the breaking of the precepts are unattainable" forms part of the pāramitā of precepts that are pure and empty of the substances of the three wheels.

The other aspects of the bodhisattva precepts are similar to the aforementioned "places of learning" for bodhisattvas.

The Pāramitā of Patience

133 To embrace and protect sentient beings,
Bodhisattvas practice the transcendence of patience,
Tolerating hateful insults, calmly accepting suffering,
And carefully observing the Dharma.

Bodhisattva deeds enable one to become a buddha. To become a buddha one must be mindful of sentient beings and keep the pure precepts in order to protect them. But sentient beings are ignorant; they may not be grateful for the alms given them or may respond with hatred and harmfulness. If one cannot firmly tolerate this, the virtues of giving and keeping the precepts will be destroyed. Even within worldly customs it is said that "people have to be patient for the sake of their countries" and that "lack of tolerance in small matters upsets great plans," to say nothing of the great event of saving sentient beings and becoming a buddha throughout infinite births and deaths! How can one not practice patience and still expect to succeed? Bodhisattvas have to practice the transcendence of patience. To be tolerant is one of the great bodhisattva deeds. Patience is tolerance, and tolerating insults is only one of the most important aspects of patience. Being patient means having firm determination, an ability to withstand attack and endure hardship. Regardless of the difficulty, one maintains oneself without being influenced by the external world and without changing one's objectives or making mistakes.

In the past, Śāriputra had practiced the bodhisattva deeds for sixty kalpas when someone went to beg him for his eye. Śāriputra told him that his eye would not be useful to the man, but the man insisted on his request. After Śāriputra gave him his eye, the man rejected it, saying it smelled foul. He threw it on the ground, and then left greatly dissatisfied. At this time, Śāriputra felt that sentient beings were indeed difficult to save, so his bodhi mind regressed. This is one example of failure due to impatience.

There are three categories of patience. First, tolerating hateful insults and harm: this includes harm from hateful enemies, injuries from knives and canes, false accusations made with malice, and malicious slander causing one to lose one's reputation and profit. These are the most difficult things for ordinary people to tolerate. Bodhisattvas should practice patience and pity those who attack them, knowing that they are driven by afflictions and influenced by evil forces. Second, calmly tolerating suffering of all kinds. Suffering is caused by external nonsentient things such as wind, rain, cold, heat; by external sentient beings such as snakes, scorpions, mosquitoes, lice; and by oneself—giving up lay life, begging for alms, traveling to teach, and doing one's practice can all bring suffering. All these situations have to be calmly tolerated through mental training and determination; if one cannot tolerate them, they will either trigger afflictions or crimes or will impede one's practice. Third, the patience to observe Buddha Dharma carefully, to awaken and enter the Buddha Dharma calmly. If one observes superficially, without calm and deep investigation, one cannot attain the profound and extensive benefits of the Dharma.

134 What benefit is there in being angry at others?
It increases the sorrow and suffering of oneself and others.
The fire of anger burns up the roots of goodness
While patience encompasses the five virtues.

It is most difficult for ordinary people to tolerate damage to their fame, wealth, career, and body. When they are injured they retaliate or seek revenge, and this is natural for ordinary people. In the development of human morality, however, particularly in the thorough understanding of the profound meaning of the Dharma, the discovery of and respect for patience naturally arises. If one becomes angry at others and seeks revenge, what benefit is there in the end? Such behavior is really unnecessary. One should know that one's own failings definitely cannot be entirely due to another's harm and destruction; primarily they are from one's own imperfection. In other words, one can only injure oneself.

The ancients said, "Virtuous people are concerned with life as a whole but not with daily adversity." Through one's practice of the Dharma, the damage and false accusations one receives at present will all be understood and reversed. The only thing to worry about is not moving upward and not achieving anything before death. According to the Buddha Dharma, an entire lifetime of injustice, insults, and sacrifice, let alone a single day, is insignificant in the endless course of births and deaths. What is lamentable is being unable to move toward the Buddha Way and remaining forever in the cycles of birth and death.

Therefore, one should not take revenge but should calmly tolerate all. Also, taking revenge on one's enemy will not undo the harm one has received; it only increases sorrow and suffering for oneself and others. One allows one's anger to flare up, and one becomes restless and distressed. Sometimes one may even recklessly cause greater damage. Returning hatred for hatred will not solve any problems. Thus, it is said, "Do not hate hatred, for eventually hatred will end. Patience can subdue hatred. This is called the Dharma of the Tathāgata."[32]

Practicing giving and keeping the precepts is not very easy. One thought of intolerance, one fit of anger, and all of one's accumulated virtue is destroyed. "Because of anger," it is said, "in an instant Buddhists can destroy hundred of kalpas of the good they have generated by giving and keeping the precepts."[33] Anger is therefore described as a fire that burns up the good roots of virtue. If one investigates and understands the anger's flaws and the virtues of patience, then one will be able to use reason to subdue anger and affliction.

The faults of being angry are several: (1) Disagreeable appearance: once anger has arisen, one becomes excited and one's countenance instantly becomes ugly. Cosmetologists say that if one gets angry frequently, one's face ages more quickly. (2) Tactless speech: once anger has replaced reason, a person may not understand what someone else is saying.

Being impulsive and nervous, one loses the ability to debate and to express oneself. (3) Abandonment by good people: the good friends of those who frequently are hot-tempered and angry will leave them because it is not worth becoming enemies. (4) Breaking of the precepts: when one is angry and bent on revenge, one has no regard for anything. One stops at nothing; one may kill, steal, lie, engage in sexual misconduct. (5) Regression: if the karma of anger accumulates, one will fall into the evil destinies when old age and death arrive.

Since one thought of intolerance can lead to such evil consequences, how can one not try to subdue it? Conversely, if one can tolerate hatred, one has all five virtues—an agreeable appearance, tactfulness, good friends, nonviolation of the precepts, and progress toward the Buddha Way. Although patience appears in the Dharma common to the Five Vehicles, the patience that "tolerates the intolerable" is found only in the bodhisattva deeds.

Comments on the First Three Pāramitās

135 The transcendences of giving, precepts, and patience,
Mostly taught to the laity,
Are the provisions for accumulating vast blessings
And the cause for a physical body like that of a buddha.

These pāramitās of giving, precepts, and patience need further discussion here to illustrate how all six pāramitās are practices required to become a buddha. This can be explained in three ways.

1. The focus of practice for monastics is concentration and wisdom. So although the first three transcendences should also be practiced by monastic people, the sūtras indicate that the Buddha taught them mostly to the laity. In particular, the bestowing of wealth and things is an important deed for lay devotees. Monastic people can give only according to the strictures within which they live. If, like the laity, they accumulate wealth and material things in order to give, this will lead to many impermissible faults.

2. The Buddha has perfect blessings and wisdom, so he is called the Honored One of Two Perfections. The Buddha's perfect blessings and wisdom come from his practicing the deeds that bring forth blessings and wisdom. This is like taking a journey to somewhere far away; one needs

to prepare enough provisions—traveling expenses, food, and so forth. Bodhisattvas practice for many kalpas to become buddhas; blessings and wisdom are their provisions for becoming buddhas. Of the two types of provisions, the first three transcendences are provisions for accumulating vast blessings and superior deeds, which are necessary to become a buddha.

3. With regard to the bodies of buddhas, the sūtras vary in differentiating the four bodies, the three bodies, and the two bodies. Basically they can be divided into the Dharma body and the physical body. The Dharma body is the great bodhi with the perfect enlightenment of the Dharma realm, which realizes the absolute truth and thereby becomes a buddha; the physical body is the solemn appearance of a buddha, which is adorned with boundless blessings. The first three transcendences are the causes and conditions for a physical body like that of a buddha. The last three, mostly taught to monastics, are provisions for wisdom and the Dharma body.

The Pāramitā of Diligence

136 The transcendence of diligence as taught by the Buddha is
The provision necessary for the attainment of blessings and wisdom.
One's mind should be insatiable, as vast as the ocean;
Even when one's strength is exhausted, one's mind should never stop.

Diligence can universally give rise to all good deeds and thereby to all virtues. Of the two kinds of provisions—blessings and wisdom—although diligence is said to belong to wisdom, the pāramitā of diligence as taught by the Buddha is actually common to both blessings and wisdom.

Although right diligence has already been explained when discussing the Dharma common to the Three Vehicles, the diligence of the Great Vehicle has a more profound meaning. To practice the bodhisattva deeds means to focus on the endless Dharma realm: approaching and paying homage to all buddhas, learning and practicing all dharmas, adorning all lands, saving all sentient beings, cutting off all afflictions, completing all virtues—everything is fully done "to the extremes of space and in the entire Dharma-realm." The mind is as vast as space and as deep as the ocean! Great vows, great deeds, and great results require limitless diligence. So bodhisattvas should have an boundless capacity to practice the transcendence of diligence. Seeking all the Buddha Dharmas and not being satisfied, attaining all virtues and not being content with just a few, bodhisattvas should be like the sea that receives the endless outflow of all the rivers. Only when one has such an insatiable mind can one attain the diligence of the Great Vehicle.

Two examples may illustrate this. In the first, two farmers work in the field. Farmer "A" works hard at harvesting but after gathering some of the harvest, goes home to rest and relax. Farmer "B" works hard without stopping until the harvesting is done. In terms of diligence, A may be more anxious, but in the end he is a lazy worker and B is the diligent one. Similarly, the śrāvakas' urgent pursuit of their own liberation, like that of one whose father and mother had just died, is not real diligence according to the Great Vehicle Dharma. Diligence must be distinguished from the rushing around that comes from having overestimated one's ability, as this next example shows. Two people are going up the hill. One runs quickly but does not get even halfway up when palpitations and sore legs force a retreat. The other person advances in great strides without rushing and, conserving energy, reaches the top without resting. In sum, only by insatiably and incessantly doing good deeds can this be considered the diligence of the Great Vehicle.

In the course of practice, some may break off or backslide due to exhaustion and the inability to keep moving. But mentally, the diligence of the bodhisattvas is unlimited and will never stop, even though their strength (physical, intellectual, or financial) may be exhaustible. The ancients said, "There is no grief as great as that of a person without any hope." To admit failure and quit trying is the real failure! There is a story about a traveler who, walking in the mountains, encounters a mountain ghost blocking his way. The traveler hits the ghost with his left hand, but the ghost seizes his hand. He then hits the ghost with his right hand, his left foot, his right foot, and finally his head, but the ghost seizes them all. The ghost says, "What a brave traveler! Now what can you do?" The traveler replies, "My mind will never be bound and wants to move on." The mountain ghost admires his courage and perseverance and lets him pass through. In the course of practicing the bodhisattva deeds, if one is unable to move on because of insufficient strength, one should be determined to advance like that traveler.

The Obstructions and the Ways to Overcome Them

137 The obstructions are procrastination, attachment to worldly pleasures,
Self-disparagement and timidity.

For those who are unable to practice the Great Vehicle Buddha Dharma diligently, there are only two categories of obstruction: not wanting to practice and not daring to practice.

The Buddha Way is so virtuous, why would some not want to practice it? Such behavior is due either to procrastination and laziness or to attachment to worldly pleasures. Some people are so habitually lazy that they cannot work hard on any good deed but always procrastinate; today's good deeds are delayed until tomorrow and this year's delayed until next year. But if such people remembered impermanence—that life only exists between breaths, that death does not discriminate between the old and the young, and that the human form is hard to attain—they might enliven their practice. Some people are greedy and attached to the pleasurable affairs of the world. Awfully busy, they live in sensual and monetary pleasures; so they do not want to practice the Buddha Way. But if they observed how worldly pleasures are not ultimate and often have bitter consequences—like honey on a blade—their attachments to worldly pleasures might decline and they might practice and attain the benefits of the Dharma.

Why do some not dare to practice? Because they disparage themselves, thinking that since these are the latter days of the Dharma and they are of dull capacity and have serious obstacles, they cannot really accomplish the profound, vast, and boundless Buddha Way. Being so intimidated, they dare not undertake Buddhist practice, so of course they will not be able to practice diligently! This type of timid sentient being will easily retreat to the Small Vehicle and follow that circuitous road.

Training the Mind Not to Retreat

138 Because of the difficulty of achieving buddhahood,
The long period of births and deaths,
And the vast provisions needed,
One must train the mind not to retreat or give up.

Those with timid minds who do not dare to practice the profound, vast, and perfect Buddha Way of the Great Vehicle usually become intimidated and regress upon hearing three things.

Upon hearing, first of all, that perfect buddhahood puts an end to all faults and completes all virtues, they consider themselves unfit and doubt that they can attain such perfect buddhahood. So they retreat. Instead they should think: "Countless bodhisattvas of the ten directions have practiced to the point of completion and become buddhas; why can't I?" Thus it is said, "They were zealous disciples and so am I; I should not retreat at this."[34] Those who fell onto evil destinies in the past have become buddhas, and those who are now on the evil destinies will become buddhas in the future. Since sentient beings on the evil destinies can become buddhas, why should those now living the precious lives of humans in the world, who are able to know the true Dharma and do good deeds, fear that they are unable to become buddhas?

Upon hearing, second, that bodhisattvas have to practice difficult and ascetic tasks such as giving up arms, legs, head, eyes, and so on, they feel it is too difficult and too miserable and that they cannot succeed, so they do not dare to practice and consequently retreat. This is also wrong. In innumerable past lives, we have fallen onto evil destinies and have gone through indescribable suffering; so why should one now be afraid of the suffering involved with practice directed toward the Buddha Way? If one has a chronic illness with unbearable pain that can be completely cured by undergoing surgery once, cannot one endure the pain of the operation? Furthermore, the difficult tasks of the bodhisattvas are different from the ascetic practices of non-Buddhists. Bodhisattvas cultivate right practices with skillful means and in their proper gradation. Achieving the power of patience with superior compassion, they give their bodies only when it is really beneficial to others and do not suffer for sake of cultivation.

Upon hearing, third, that the cultivation of bodhisattvas requires remaining in the sea of birth and death for a long time and accumulating such vast and boundless provisions requires much time, they feel they cannot do it, so they do not dare to start to practice. This perception is even more faulty. Bodhisattvas understand that birth and death are like illusions, so they can be in the midst of birth and death for a long time and do not suffer. Furthermore, boundless provisions bring forth boundless virtues; would anyone dislike so much virtue? Are there people who, having very much wealth, are bothered by the chore of counting it?

If one thinks of retreating, one should use these ideas to strengthen one's mind so that one can diligently carry on toward the Buddha Way.

On the other hand, there are people in the world who think that becoming a buddha is easy, convinced that by cultivating small virtues they can become buddhas. This may come from timidity and laziness or from their ignorance, just as "a newborn calf fears not the tiger." If one considers oneself to be infallible, it may be too late to acknowledge one's error when one discovers that this is not the case!

Taking the Easy Paths

> 139 Those who are timid and inferior,
> Wish to have an easy path to practice.

Although all sentient beings can eventually become buddhas, the truth is that they have different fundamental capacities. Some are suitable to practice bodhisattva deeds, some are not compatible with bodhisattva Dharma, and some want to follow the bodhisattvas but are afraid to practice. To those whose fundamental nature was suitable for bodhisattva deeds, the Buddha naturally taught the supreme way.

Those who are not suitable for the bodhisattva deeds have a poor and timid fundamental nature. Such people are described in a parable in the *Lotus Sūtra*: a poor man returns to his native country, and upon seeing an elder with incalculable wealth, he is seized with fear and runs away. Those with this type of fundamental capacity must be taught the skillful doctrine—the Śrāvaka Dharma and Pratyekabuddha Vehicles—in order to gradually embrace and transform them.

Other timid sentient beings—those who want to practice the bodhisattva deeds but lack self-faith and those who admire the ultimate perfection of buddhahood but lack the courage to get underway and diligently practice the vast bodhisattva deeds—lack faith and fear falling into the Small Vehicle or drowning in the sea of suffering. For these types the skillful means of the Two Vehicles is not suitable. So the Buddha has to use special methods to transform them. Those with a timid and inferior fundamental nature who want to become buddhas but do not want to practice the great deeds and difficult tasks of bodhisattvas wish to have a fast, easy, and simple path. This is not in tune with the vows or the bodhisattva deeds, however, because seeking to accomplish the Buddha Way definitely requires the practice of the great bodhisattva deeds.

This is similar to the discourse by Nāgārjuna Bodhisattva on the "Chapter on Easy Practice" in the *Daśabhūmivibhāṣā Śāstra*: "Some people queried Nāgārjuna, saying: 'As avivartins [nonretreaters], bodhisattvas can…through the practice of difficult deeds either eventually succeed or regress to the level of śrāvakas and pratyekabuddhas; if the latter occurs, this is a big decline!… If among the teachings of all buddhas, there is an easy path that leads to the skillful stage of avivartin, please tell us!' [Nāgārjuna] answered, 'What you said is timid, inferior, and small-minded; it is not something that a zealous disciple with determination to practice should say! Why? If one vows to attain the anuttara-samyak-saṃbodhi, then prior to attaining the stage of avivartin, one should not hesitate to sacrifice one's own body and life and should be diligent day and night, as if one's own head were on fire."[35]

140 The Buddha has special skillful means
To embrace and protect these beginners.

Although seeking a fast, easy path indicates that one is not a great zealous person—not, that is, a bodhisattva (see the *Treatise of the Great Zealous Disciple* by Deva Bodhisattva)—the Buddha with his infinite skill taught a special skillful means to embrace and protect timid and inferior neophytes, so that they would not lose faith and would enter the Great Vehicle. This is the doctrine of the easy path. In the *Daśabhūmivibhāṣā Śāstra*, after scolding his questioners, Nāgārjuna gave them their answer: "If you really want to hear about this skillful method, I should explain it now. The Buddha Dharma has infinite entrances; just like paths in the world, some are difficult and some are easy: walking on land is hard while riding a boat in a waterway is pleasant. The bodhisattva-way is the same: either one proceeds diligently with the difficult and ascetic deeds or one quickly attains the stage of avivartin by the skillfully easy deeds that rely on faith."[36] The easy path depends upon the faithful vow to enter into the stream of the Buddha Dharma.

The real meaning of the easy path is fivefold. First, the easy path entails being mindful not only of one buddha but of all buddhas of the ten directions. Moreover, "by single-mindedly chanting the name and being mindful of Amitābha Buddha and so forth (including all the great bodhisattvas), one can also attain the stage of not retreating."[37] Second, besides the chanting of the names of the buddhas and bodhisattvas, the easy path also includes "being mindful of them, prostrating to them, and praising them with verses."[38] Third, "those aiming toward the stage of avivartin not only have to be mindful, chant names, and prostrate, they should also repent, make requests, rejoice, and transfer their merit in all the lands of buddhas."[39] Thus the easy path is to practice the seven branches and Puxian (Samantabhadra) Bodhisattva's ten great vows. Fourth, the easy path was taught to the timid beginners with an emphasis on embracing and protecting their faith. We see this in the Śāstras of Nāgārjuna and Aśvaghoṣa: "Beginning to study this dharma, sentient beings wish to seek the right belief but their minds are weak.... They should know that the Tathāgata has special methods to embrace and protect their faith."[40] Fifth, the embracing and protecting of faith on the easy path is attained through either the faithful vow or the practice of mindfulness of the buddhas and so on, both of which lead to being reborn in a Pure Land. It is generally said that after reaching a Pure Land, people gradually practice and are determined not to retreat and to attain supreme bodhi.

Alternatively, at first the easy path can be relied on as a skillful means to stabilize their faith and then as a way to lead them into the difficult path. It is said, "Because bodhisattvas repent, make sincere requests, rejoice, and transfer their merit, their blessings and virtues increase and their hearts become gentle. Bodhisattvas believe and accept that all buddhas have infinite extremely pure virtues in which ordinary people do not believe. They also believe and accept that all great bodhisattvas carry out the pure and great deeds and the rare and difficult tasks such as taking pity on those who are injured, having incomparable virtues, and giving rise to the profound compassionate mind. Out of compassion, they want to spontaneously give others happiness at will; this is called kindness. Bodhisattvas are like this, relying on their kindness and compassion to cut off all greed and stinginess, and to be diligent in their giving."[41] Following this example will lead one from the bodhisattvas' easy and skillful path to the bodhisattvas' difficult and regular path!

141 Of these, one of the most special
Is to be reborn in the Most Blissful Land.
Blessed by the power of Amitābha Buddha,
They will not retreat from attaining enlightenment.

Relying on the faithful vow to enter the Buddha Way is a doctrine in which one depends on another's power. There are many such doctrines described in the sūtras and treatises of the Great Vehicle, but one of the very special ones, especially respected by Chinese Buddhists, entails chanting "Amitābha Buddha" to be reborn in the Most Blissful Pure Land. This land, beyond ten thousand million Buddha-lands, is where Amitābha Buddha is now expounding the Dharma and teaching. The way among buddhas is the same and their virtues and the power of their vows cannot be differentiated in superiority. What is so special about Amitābha's Pure Land? There is but one impartial Dharma realm in which all buddhas teach the same Way, so the differences among the various buddhas really do not matter. Although in the Great Vehicle sūtras the Pure Lands of the ten directions are extensively described with praise for the various easy paths, Amitābha's Pure Land is really the most commended and extolled. The unique features expressed by Amitābha Buddha were his having twenty-four great vows (or forty-eight vows) in the causal stage and having the Most Blissful World arise through the boundless virtues of his compassion and wisdom. It has been proclaimed that one only needs to have faith in the power of Amitābha's vows, to wish to be reborn in the Most Blissful World, and to chant "Amitābha Buddha"—whether for a day, two days, or even only ten times—with single-minded sincerity and respect in order to be blessed by the power of Amitābha Buddha and be reborn in the Most Blissful World after death.

In the Most Blissful World, material goods are extremely abundant, so there is no suffering from unfulfilled wishes. Associating only with exceptionally good people and working diligently on the Buddha Way, one does not suffer from being with people one hates or from parting with loved ones. Transformed and reborn from a lotus flower, one will definitely realize the Dharma that is without rebirth in this life, so there is also no suffering of old age, illness, and death. As the lotus flower opens, those having the superior grade and superior birth of being reborn in the Most Blissful Land will immediately see Amitābha Buddha and attain a state that is without rebirth. For the rest, who have the capacities of the middle and lower grades, birth and death have not yet ended; but because it is certain that they will end, it can be said that they have ended already. Although these latter people have not yet attained the stage of not retreating, they can be described as having done so. In sum, regardless of the length of time it takes, those practicing in the Most Blissful Pure Land will end birth and death and will not retreat from the unsurpassed bodhi.

If, therefore, one is timid and finds it difficult to practice the bodhisattva-way, fearing that one will fall into the Two Vehicles or that following the karmic forces will cause one to drift apart from the Buddha Way, then chanting Amitābha Buddha is most secure! It is a wonderfully skillful means that can best embrace and protect those sentient beings who are beginners so that they do not lose their faith.

The chanting of "Amitābha Buddha" should also be accompanied by prostrations, praise, repentance, the making of sincere requests, rejoicing, and the transference of merit. According to the five sequences in the *Jing tu lun* (The Pure Land Treatise), one should start with prostrations and praise and then move into practicing cessation, contemplation, and the transference of merit. That is, one should gradually accomplish wisdom, compassion, and skillful means. One can thereby quickly reach the stage of not retreating from the supreme bodhi. As Nāgārjuna's Śāstra puts it, "those aiming toward the stage of avivartin should not just be mindful, chant names, and prostrate."[42]

142 For those who cannot renounce worldly pleasures
But wish to attain enlightenment,
The Medicine Buddha vowed compassionately
To provide a Pure Land in the east.

As for the Pure Lands of the easy path, after proclaiming Amitābha Buddha's Most Blissful Pure Land, Śākyamuni Buddha also proclaimed the Medicine Buddha's Pure Crystal Pure Land in the eastern region to suit another type of fundamental nature. The doctrine of Amitābha Buddha's Most Blissful Pure Land rejects the reality of this present world. Because Lady Vaidehi experienced the suffering of this world deeply, she did not want to be reborn in this world, so the Buddha told her about the Most Blissful Pure Land. Those preaching the doctrine of the Amitābha's

Pure Land also say, "If one does not reject this world, one will not be reborn in the Most Blissful Land." This is a teaching that rejects the human world and emphasizes rebirth after death.

There are other kinds of people for whom a different way is more suitable. Those people who are presently in this world and who have healthy bodies and harmonious families, live in wealthy and powerful countries, and enjoy world peace are not inclined to reject such things. To embrace these types of beginners who cannot renounce worldly pleasures, and in order to enable them to direct themselves toward bodhi, Śākyamuni Buddha also proclaimed the Medicine Buddha's Pure Land.

The Medicine Buddha's Pure Land is in the east, which symbolizes growth, whereas Amitābha Buddha's Pure Land is in the west, which symbolizes retirement. To liberate the dead, Chinese Buddhists chant the name of Amitābha Buddha; to disperse calamity and prolong life, they chant the name of the Medicine Buddha. This amply reveals the difference between the pleasures of the future life and worldly pleasures of the present one.

The sūtras say that in the causal ground, the Crystal Light King Medicine Buddha made twelve great vows with great compassion. His aim was to develop knowledge, to promote enterprises, to save and heal those with bodily defects, poverty, illness, and helplessness, to enable people to enjoy abundant clothing and food, to keep people from believing in deviant teachers and non-Buddhists, to prevent people from breaking the law and being tortured for so doing, to bring equality between men and women, and to help all sentient beings become buddhas. Having such vows and deeds, the Pure Crystal Pure Land arose in the eastern world with purity and solemnity similar to that of the Most Blissful World. With this Pure Land doctrine the Medicine Buddha embraces and protects sentient beings' faith so that they might attain greater benefits as humans or divine beings, be reborn in this Pure Land, and eventually attain enlightenment.

In the past, when the national preceptor Yu Lin came across the *Medicine Buddha Sūtra*, he praised it as a supremely skillful teaching; he knew that few people are able to renounce the world and that most have little affinity with Amitābha's Pure Land. Through the Medicine Buddha's Pure Land doctrine, these people can be reborn in a Pure Land and become buddhas. So Yu Lin was full of praise: "In the world there are cranes that can carry one to Yangzhou; there is also the boat of the Tathāgata's virtue that can ferry one to the other shore."

The Four Powers

143 Superior understanding, strong will,
Joy and rest are the four powers.
If one cultivates them,
One can easily be diligent.

Timid and lazy sentient beings dare not directly enter the Great Vehicle with diligence, but they can enter it indirectly by means of the easy path of skillful means and the skillful method of the faithful vow. Actually, if one is skillful it is not difficult to attain diligence. One should cultivate the four powers:

First, the power of superior understanding. Superior understanding implies profound belief and understanding: of the principle of cause and effect, of the karmic results of good or evil, and of the virtues of the bodhisattva deeds and the consequences of violating them. Through deep belief and understanding, one generates a joyful desire to abandon all evil and achieve all virtues. This joyful desire gives rise to diligence and enables one to practice. Thus it is said, "Aspiration is based on belief, and diligence is based on aspiration." The more profound one's belief and understanding, the more diligent is one's practice.

Second, the power of a strong will. Some people casually practice this or that, without determination and perseverance, and eventually develop bad habits and accomplish nothing. So one must be cautious. Once one has started to practice, one should proceed from the beginning to the end without giving up. Only in this way can one develop firm will power. One should also respect and strengthen oneself when practicing. The great deed of becoming a buddha has to be done through one's own efforts, not through reliance on another. "Liberation can be only attained through self-cultivation."[43] (The root of the problem of Ānanda's failure in the Śūraṅgama Assembly was his reliance on others.) By affirming one's ability to practice and to subdue afflictions, one takes on the heavy responsibility of bodhisattva deeds until the goal is reached.

Third, the power of joy. In the course of practice, one is full of the joy of the Dharma. One tastes this delicious food but is not satiated: the more one practices, the more one is interested. Only by this diligent practice can one advance deeper and further.

Fourth, the power of rest. If one is physically and mentally tired, one should take a rest; otherwise one may become weary, which will impede one's cultivation. After having accomplished some virtue, one can take a short rest, but one should not be content.

If one cultivates these four powers, in time diligence will flow constantly like a stream.

General Comments on the Final Two Pāramitās

144 All the superior virtues of the Three Vehicles
Come from concentration and wisdom.

Dhyāna, or unperturbed abstraction, is sometimes equated with meditation, which is another name for concentration. Prajñā, or wisdom, is also called intelligence. In the successful practice of the śrāvakas and in the bodhisattva deeds, concentration and wisdom correspond with one another without any separation; this is called "the dual practice of cessation and contemplation" and "the equality of concentration and wisdom." The śrāvakas' and bodhisattvas' Dharma therefore usually equates the concentrations of dhyāna and samādhi with the concentrations connected with wisdom. For example, in the śrāvaka Dharma, there is the empty samādhi, the extraordinary dhyāna, and so on, while in the Great Vehicle there is the Śūraṅgama samādhi, the Tathāgata dhyāna, and so forth.

There are differences between concentration and wisdom with regard to the beginning of practice and their special functions, however. In the three superior studies of the śrāvaka Dharma, for example, there are the superior studies of both the mind (concentration) and wisdom; in the six pāramitās of the Great Vehicle there are the pāramitās of both dhyāna and prajñā. In terms of practice, concentration and wisdom are often called "cessation" and "contemplation" respectively, and these two are different. Practitioners of the Great Vehicle should be certain of the characteristics of concentration and wisdom; otherwise they will confuse dhyāna with wisdom, confuse attaining the fourth dhyāna with attaining the fourth fruition (arhatship), and attaining the virtues of concentration with attaining wisdom and becoming a buddha.

Concentration and wisdom are not just the essence of the Great Vehicle; they are also important for śrāvakas. Although the bodhisattva-way emphasizes the virtues of the vow to attain enlightenment, great compassion, the transference of merit, and so forth, without concentration and wisdom none of these can be accomplished. So the *Saṃdhinirmocana Sūtra* (Sūtra on the Explication of the Underlying Meaning) says: "One should know that all śrāvakas, bodhisattvas, Tathāgatas, all good worldly things, and all good world-transcending things are the results of this śamatha and vipaśyanā (cessation and contemplation)."[44] Cessation and contemplation are embraced by concentration and wisdom. Concentration and wisdom—cessation and contemplation—are important steps in practicing within the Great Vehicle, and all the superior virtues of the Three Vehicles come from them.

145 Those who practice cessation and contemplation
Should first practice putting the scattered mind to rest.
When cessation is achieved, contemplation is also achieved.
This rule of practice is the proper sequence.

But what are cessation and contemplation, and what are concentration and wisdom? Wisdom relies on "discernment to be its nature." *Vipaśyanā*, the Sanskrit term for contemplation, is described in the sūtra as "right thinking and discernment, the highest thinking and discernment, thorough reflection and thorough investigation."[45] Some people think that thorough understanding is the wisdom that comes from contemplation, but this is not in accord with the teachings in the sūtras. *Śamatha*, the Sanskrit term for cessation, is described in the sūtra as "the mind being focused in one state" and "the continuity of that mental state."[46] Cessation means "keeping the mind level" or in a state without scatteredness.

Cessation and contemplation are different. Those who practice both cessation and contemplation should practice cessation first. This does not mean that they must first accomplish concentration and only then cultivate the wisdom that arises from it, for the two complement each other. Before the practice of cessation is successful, there must already be wisdom derived from investigation. So why is it said that one should practice cessation first? This is because without concentration, wisdom cannot be attained. In the sūtras, when cessation and contemplation, concentration and wisdom, and dhyāna and wisdom are described, concentration is always explained first, then wisdom. This is the necessary sequence of practice. It must be followed, no matter how impressively someone explains otherwise.

DHYĀNA PĀRAMITĀ

> 146 Relyin[redacted]e abiding mind can produce the ability
> Both [redacted]ertake and to accomplish what needs to be done.

Why should one practice cessation and attain concentration? Because by doing so one can accomplish many beneficial undertakings. So it is said: "Regulating the mind and keeping it in a single place, one can accomplish anything."[47] Practicing cessation and attaining the abiding mind, the body and mind are at ease. When one's body and mind feel agile and comfortable, one has the power to do good and leave evil. Sentient beings' minds are always scattered. Their power to resist the temptation of desire, their power to subdue afflictions, and their power to practice good deeds are all very weak. They always feel that they have the intention but not the power to carry out good deeds, as if they were rowing a boat against the tide. It is the same with their bodies. Even those who are healthy sometimes feel troubled and exhausted; they feel dull, slow, weak, and powerless, as if chronically ill.

When one practices cessation and sustains right concentration, one is relying on the abiding mind and is able to undertake what needs to be done; mild physical bliss engenders physical diligence, and mild mental bliss engenders mental diligence; the terrible inabilities of the past are totally reversed. One practices courageously, and one accomplishes what needs to be done. What is it that needs to be done? Only by relying on concentration can śrāvakas attain the joy of the Dharma directly, superior knowledge and vision (the divine eye), wisdom that comes from differentiation, and liberation from all faults. Only by relying on concentration can practitioners of the Great Vehicle do all kinds of things to benefit sentient beings, understand profound meanings, and arouse physical and mental mild tranquillity, transcendental power, and so forth. In sum, without concentration, none of the superior virtues of the Buddha Dharma can be attained, so one should practice concentration with one's full attention.

The Five Faults and Eight Cutting Actions

147 Right concentration comes from extinguishing the five faults
By diligently practicing the eight cutting actions.

"Relying on compassion to abide in the pure precepts" is, aside from regulating the body and breathing and so on, the required provision for the cultivation of concentration, as was briefly explained in the Dharma common to the Five Vehicles. How can right concentration be initiated by diligent and attentive practice? Only by extinguishing the five faults: laziness, forgetting the holy words, stupor or restlessness, inaction, and action. To eliminate these five faults one needs to practice diligently the eight cutting actions: faith, aspiration, diligence, tranquillity, mindfulness, knowledge, thinking, and equanimity. If one does this, one naturally achieves concentration, just as one reaches one's destination after destroying obstacles on the way. The five faults and eight cutting actions are summed up in the accompanying table.

The Five Faults to Be Eliminated	The Eight Cutting Actions that Can Counteract the Faults
Laziness	Faith Diligence Aspiration Tranquillity
Forgetting the Holy Words	Right Mindfulness
Stupor or Restlessness	Right Knowledge
Inaction	Thinking
Action	Equanimity

148 Laziness, the barrier to concentration,
Can be counteracted with faith, diligence, aspiration, and
tranquillity.

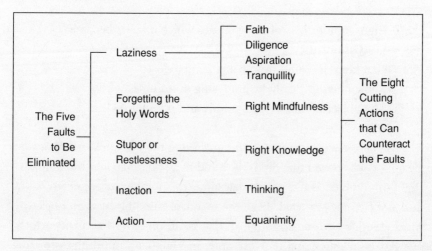

Concentration can be achieved only through faith, patience, and continuous practice. From the beginning until the completion of one's practice, laziness—lack of courage in doing good deeds, perfunctoriness and laxness—is the major barrier to the practice of concentration. It must be counteracted by faith, diligence, and so on. Since laziness is an affliction that impedes diligence, diligence must eliminate it.

Diligent practice of concentration must be based on aspiration, however. If one wholeheartedly is determined to achieve the concentration, one will practice with joy and not feel tired. But this determination must come from faith. If one deeply believes in the virtues of concentration, deeply believes that concentration can be achieved by practicing, one will succeed in one's practice. When "one's aspiration is based on belief and one's diligence is based on aspiration," of course one will diligently practice.

Faith in concentration requires one to believe, first of all, that the light bliss and the physical and mental sharpness that arise from concentration will enable one's body and mind to reach a new state. Firm belief in concentration's light bliss is an important step for arousing diligence. Practicing the four cutting actions of faith, aspiration, diligence, and tranquillity to extinguish laziness is absolutely necessary for the practice of concentration; they should receive special emphasis in the beginning of practice, however.

149 Right mindfulness of the object to which one has become
accustomed
Can keep the mind from being scattered.
Remembering clearly by not losing mindfulness,
The object of focus abides calmly and is revealed clearly.

Practicing cessation primarily means having the mind focused on a single object. The power that binds the mind to an object is right mindfulness. Right mindfulness is like a rope that binds the mind to its object so that it does not become scattered. Here the object of mindfulness is an object to which one has become accustomed, that is, an object of focus with which one has been practicing. For example, in practicing mindfulness of the Buddha, one has to first observe and investigate the appearance of the Buddha. Then during practice, one recalls the appearance of the Buddha, and it arises in one's mind. Those who are practicing the mindfulness of impurity observe the unclean appearance of bruises, pus, and decay.

Concentration can be achieved only by practicing mindfulness; it cannot be achieved through one's imagination. Having right mindfulness, one can counteract the fault of forgetting the holy words—the Dharma as taught by the sages. If one is constantly mindful of the holy words as one's object of focus, one can keep the mind from being scattered and have it gradually settle.

When sentient beings are alert, their minds are scattered; when their minds quiet down, they become stuporous and fall asleep. When stuporous and unclear, the mind is powerless. When the mind is clear but scattered, it is like a candle in the wind, wavering and unstable; this too is not very useful. The primary goal of practicing cessation and achieving concentration is to strengthen the power of the mind so that it can do the great things that ordinary people cannot do. So one has to cultivate one's mind, making it both clear and settled. This is accomplished by practicing right mindfulness assisted by right knowledge, which enables the mind to remember its object of focus. The loss of mindfulness obstructs right mindfulness and causes the mind to forget the object of focus.

When practicing, if one relies on the practice of right mindfulness and one's mind can settle on the object of focus and not be scattered, then one should let it continue to settle. But to settle and clear the mind, right knowledge is necessary. Right knowledge constantly looks after the mind, so that one knows for certain that it is settled on the object of focus. For example, those being mindful of the Buddha must not only stay with the appearance of the Buddha; they must also perceive this appearance clearly—that is, the Buddha's appearance should gradually be revealed with clarity. Such calm abiding and clear revelation—clarity and stillness—are important aspects of the process of practicing cessation. So one should not think that merely being attentive to one object is enough, for in doing this one may become stuporous and fall into a state of not remembering.

Some people think that if they practice both not clinging to appearances and being devoid of differentiation, then without ever holding the mind on one object, they will still be able to practice and have realizations. They are, of course, somewhat mistaken. Even if they do not cling to appearances or differentiate, they still need to understand this practice and rely on it attentively. Is this not keeping the mind in focus? If they do not think of anything (which is impossible for beginners), as if they were invisible spirits without any place to land, what will come of it? For example, Chinese Ch'an (Zen) practitioners raise such questions as "Who is mindful of the Buddha?" and "Who is towing the dead body?" Such questions are able to stir up feelings of doubt, which is slightly different from the method described above. Nevertheless, since this method can bring order to the mind and eradicate boundless erroneous thoughts, should this method not also be considered a practice of binding the mind to one thing?

150 The objects of mindfulness taught by the sages
Are able to purify the mind of illusions,
To correspond with the truth,
And to lead to renunciation.

Where should the mind be focusing before one has practiced to the point of attaining concentration? The sages say that there is no set object of focus. However, this does not mean that it can be just anything, but rather that among the various objects that can serve as an object of mindfulness, no single one is specified. The Yogācārins have said that there are four types of objects of focus: those that are universal, those that purify conduct, those that are skillful, and those that purify illusion. All the objects of focus taught in the scriptures accord with two major principles: they have the ability to purify the mind of illusions, and they correspond with the truth. All who focus on such objects to cultivate the abiding mind can gradually subdue afflictions or eliminate them. Only then can right concentration be initiated. Such concentration is attained through the practice of departing from desire (afflictions).

Objects of focus may be common to the world or world transcending, but only those that can lead toward the way of renunciation through the elimination of illusions and the realization of the truth are worthy objects. If one focuses on absurd or irrational objects, one will only increase one's afflictions; if one focuses on sexual desire, enemies, or meaningless things such as soil, wood, and rocks, one will be extremely lucky not to go insane, and one should forget about attaining concentration.

To counteract and subdue afflictions, there are contemplations of impurity to counteract greed, contemplations of kindness and compassion to counteract anger, contemplations of dependent origination to counteract ignorance, contemplations of the realms of the sense organs to counteract attachment to the concept of the self, and mindfulness of breathing to counteract mental scatteredness. In this way one can apply different methods to counteract increasingly strong afflictions.

There are also methods that correspond with the truth: focusing on the aggregates, on the realms of the sense organs, on sensations, on dependent origination, and on cause and effect—five skillful means to eliminate ignorance. Objects of focus that are world transcending and are able to eliminate illusion have a common characteristic: all are without an independently existing self and are by nature empty. All such objects of focus are common to both cessation and contemplation. Holding the mind on these objects, making it stay without being scattered and without any further investigation, is called either "not differentiating with respect to the image" or śamatha. This is the object of focus of cessation.

151 In the Great Vehicle, most people practice
Mindfulness of a buddha and mindfulness of breathing.

Although there are many objects of focus that one can use for the practice of cessation, the ones that are used the most in the śrāvaka Dharma are the contemplation of impurity and the mindfulness of breathing because they subdue greed and scatteredness and are easy ways to establish concentration. In the world of Great Vehicle Buddhism, however, most people practice mindfulness of a buddha and mindfulness of breathing. Mindfulness of breathing basically tends to emphasize the body. As the goal of the Great Vehicle is to become a buddha, mindfulness of a buddha is also an important doctrine of the Great Vehicle.

For example, if one can follow—single-mindedly and without scatteredness—the easy path method of chanting a buddha's name, one can attain the samādhi of mindfulness of a buddha. But the key point in this method is mindfulness of a buddha's physical appearance and virtues—or, as it was called in the past, mindfulness of a buddha's appearance and mindfulness of the contemplation of a buddha. Following this method can lead toward superior world-transcending dhyāna contemplation and thereby further leads to enlightenment. On a more superficial level, being mindful of a buddha acts as repentance for one's karmic obstructions and as a means to gather good roots. This method of being mindful of a buddha includes both superficial and profound levels. From early on some people have used mindfulness of a buddha instead of the differentiation of the realms of the sense organs within the schema of the five pure deeds of the Great Vehicle.

Besides being mindful of a buddha, one can be mindful of bodhisattvas such as Mañjuśrī, Guanyin, or Samantabhadra. Going a step further, since vajra beings and yaksas are manifestations of buddhas and bodhisattvas, one may also use them; but this changes one's practice into one that is oriented toward divine beings. This is because the appearences of such buddhas no longer look liberated and kind; they have been transformed to look angry and greedy. In this method, buddhas and divine beings have almost merged as one. The Great and the Divine Vehicles are distinct, however, and practicing cessation is not the same as practicing contemplation. Therefore, even though practices focusing on these manifestations are also called mindfulness of a buddha, whether in the end the emphasis is on concentration and leads to entrance into the Divine Vehicles or whether Divine-Vehicle deeds are transformed and lead to entrance into the Buddha Vehicle depends on whether the practitioners follow the distinctive feature of the Great Vehicle—correspondence with the three minds that guide one's practice.

152 Mindfulness of a buddha comes from focusing the mind
On a real buddha, not on a statue of a buddha.
To settle the mind by contemplating the form of a buddha
One should be familiar with various skillful means.

One should know that practice that takes mindfulness of a buddha as the object of focus is mental practice. Even the ordinary mindfulness of a buddha—inattentively chanting his name—emphasizes the mind, although not as much as focusing on the form of a buddha to practice cessation.

In the beginning of one's practice, one should observe and cling to the good form of a buddha. Even though it may be difficult to have this form arise in one's mind and keep it there firmly, one should nevertheless not practice by looking at an image of a buddha. Practicing cessation and achieving concentration is a function of the mind's consciousness being in a state of concentration, in which the mind does not associate with the five (sensory) consciousnesses. Practicing mindfulness by having the eye consciousness grasp the form of an external object has the effect of keeping the mind stuck on the outer gateway (that of the senses); one will definitely not enter concentration. One should know that when one's mind is collected inward, the form of the object upon which one's mind is being focused is an image that is established by consciousness.

This is so not just for the mindfulness of a buddha; all the practices related to cessation take the image of an object established by consciousness as a means to achieve calm abiding. When some of those who practice cessation experience some mild tranquillity—in which the five (sensory) consciousnesses are in a state of equality—without the differentiation of conjecture and thinking, they believe that they have attained the concentration that is without differentiation. But this is very wrong.

When one begins one's practice, one should have a clear image of the form of a buddha, for which one can use a stone or wooden statue or a portrait. One should focus on this image to collect the mind. During practice, however, one should think that the image one is focused on is a real buddha and not the statue of a buddha made from wood, stone, etc. Only in this way can one succeed. When one does so, a buddha will be visualized emitting light and expounding the Dharma. If one practices with the thought that this image is a statue of a buddha, these virtues will be lost.

One should be familiar with the many skillful methods that are used to contemplate the form of a buddha to keep the mind steadfast. "Be familiar with various skillful means," it is said. For example, when one takes mindfulness of the form of a buddha as one's initial practice, it is not necessary to have the image be too refined; having a general image of a particular buddha is good enough. When the form of that particular buddha arises and gradually becomes steady, if a certain part is particularly distinct, one may focus on that part in order to practice. This practice can be compared to cutting bamboo: once the initial node is cut, the rest will easily split open. Likewise, when contemplating the form of a buddha, if the general form is stable and distinct, one can then contemplate a refined form. When the power of one's mind gets stronger, even the contemplation of those forms of buddhas described in the *Avataṃsaka Sūtra* and elsewhere may be accomplished in one's practice.

One should be single-minded in the beginning, trying not to be mindful of many different things or eagerly wanting to have distinct, refined images—such efforts can become a barrier to concentration. In addition, since the form of a buddha is an image that arises from consciousness in dependence upon the power of one's mind, it must be in accord with cause and effect. If one focuses on the form of Amitābha Buddha but the image of Śākyamuni Buddha arises, or if one focuses on the form of a buddha but the image of a bodhisattva arises, or if one focuses on the form of a standing buddha but a sitting buddha arises, then what one focused on and what has arisen are not in accordance. So one should not focus on just any image that arises but rather on the image of the object that one initially chose for one's practice.

153 Mindfulness of breathing includes counting, following, and
stopping.
The breathing should not be blustery or gasping, nor should
one feel the breathing.

Mindfulness of breathing is a skillful and efficient method to practice cessation. Breathing is closely related to the coarse movements or the stillness of the body and mind. Thus the practice of concentration to calm the body and mind places great value on the breath. There are six steps to the practice of breathing: counting, following, stopping, contemplating, returning, and purifying. The last three are the methods of contemplation based on cessation. The first three are described as follows.

Counting the breaths: Taking the breath as one's focus, one uses the mind to lead the breath down below the navel when inhaling and to follow the breath up and out of the nose when exhaling. One exhalation and one inhalation is one breath. One should quietly count, breath by breath, up to ten and then start from one again. When one counts one's inhalations, one should not also count exhalations; when one counts one's exhalations, one should not also count inhalations. Counting one's breaths is like counting beads: holding the mind on the breath—centering on the object of focus—can keep one from forgetting. If, as a beginner, one does forget the count, then one should start counting from one again. One should keep this up until one can clearly and effortlessly count the breaths one by one.

Following the breaths: After some time, when the mind is calm, one no longer needs to count. One only needs to have the mind follow the breaths; the mind and the breath rely on each other. One follows the breaths up and down and feels them throughout the whole body. If one is able to do this, even inattentive counting will disappear.

Stopping the breaths: After a long time, when one's breathing practice is successful, the mind and the breath become as inseparable as the body and its shadow. Suddenly, the mind and the breaths become unmoving and the body and mind disappear as they enter into concentration. This is the successful accomplishment of the practice of cessation.

In this practice, it is better for one's breathing to be refined and long, but beginners should not try to force things, as this might be harmful to their health. Also, one's breaths should be even, not suddenly long and suddenly short. In the Buddha Dharma, the intention of regulating the breath has always been to collect the mind in order to enter into concentration, so one should not emphasize the body. After practicing for a long time, one may feel healthy and strong and have a sensation of warmth in the lower abdomen, or of the breath going all the way to one's heels and toes, or of the breath below the navel going downward to the coccyx and then upward along the spine. Alternatively, when one is breathing in this way, one may have hallucinations of light, forms, sounds, and so on. All of these experiences are natural physiological phenomena when one's breathing is smooth. Therefore, one should not be surprised or boastful; otherwise one will be like those practicing Qigong and Taoist alchemy!

As one practices, one's breaths should be subtle, closely connected, even, and long. One's breathing should not sound like the wind. Inhalations and exhalations that are too coarse are not acceptable. One's breathing should also not resemble gasping. Although breaths of this kind do not make noise, they are not smooth. Rough breathing can be compared to a knife scraping a piece of bamboo: the strokes leave marks. On the other hand, one's breathing should also not just be like regular breathing, which has become smooth and in which there is still an awareness of air going through the mouth and nose. Only breathing that does not resemble wind, gasping, or regular breathing and that is subtle, closely connected, even, and long (which the ancients described as "flowing gently" and "half existing") lives up to the standard for the practice of mindfulness of breathing.

154 Realizing the presence of stupor or restlessness,
With right knowledge, stop the mind from being scattered.

Having used right mindfulness to collect the mind and reach the stage of calmly abiding on the object of focus, one should use right knowledge to exterminate the faults of stupor or restlessness. Restlessness, a form of desire, is an attachment to certain enjoyable states. One's mind feels uncomfortable and this leads it to become scattered. Stupor, an aspect of ignorance, is physical and mental lethargy. Stupor leads to a subtle decrease in the strength of the mind's ability to concentrate on the object of focus.

When one is initially practicing, the major faults—scattered thoughts or stupor—are detected easily. These obvious faults are not what is being discussed here. What needs to be explained here is subtle stupor and restlessness, which one should realize after one's mind has calmly abided on the object of focus. If one is unable to recognize these or mistakes them for a stabilizing power of concentration, one's practice will stagnate; on the contrary, after some time, one may regress. So this is very important.

If, while practicing, one feels that the image is unstable and unclear, or that one's mental power is weak and unable to make noticeable progress, this is clear evidence of the presence of subtle stupor or restlessness. As long as right mindfulness is calmly in place and there is continuous mindfulness and close attention, right knowledge can arise. This enables one to realize that stupor or restlessness have arisen or are about to arise, and one can then stop the mind from being scattered.

155 To eliminate such problems and take action,
One should not follow or be influenced by them.

If, after one has realized the presence of subtle stupor or restlessness, one lets it go and takes no action to deal with it because this is too difficult, one makes the mistake of "not taking action." This mistake can be counteracted and eliminated only by thought. To think means to propel the mind and its attributes to do something, and in this case it means using thought to eliminate stupor and restlessness. If the problems are not too serious, then when stupor arises, one can make one's mind alert and strong or one can practice investigation. If restlessness arises, one slows down the mind or tries to focus calmly. Whether one is making one's mind alert or slowing it down in the course of one's practice of cessation or contemplation depends on the condition of the mind at a particular time. In this way one can reach the state of equilibrium and the Middle

Way. This can be compared to riding a horse: when the horse goes toward the left, one pulls it back toward the right and vice versa; the aim is to keep the horse in the middle.

When stupor or restlessness are serious and difficult, however, one should practice special methods. One can meditate on enjoyable and virtuous things such as brightness or bodhi mind. If restlessness is serious, one can meditate on offensive things such as impermanence. Then, after the stupor or restlessness is eliminated, one should follow one's original practice and abide calmly on the object of focus.

> 156 When these problems have been overcome, simply practice
> straightforwardly,
> And thus avoid the mistake of using too much effort.

When one practices to the point of eliminating stupor and restlessness, one's mind will be even and straightforward. Without exerting too much effort, one should then allow the mind to progress in equanimity. When in equanimity, one does not exert excessive effort but lets the mind move freely, evenly, and straightforwardly. This can be compared to someone riding a horse: if the horse does not pull toward the left or the right, one should loosen the reins and allow it to go straight. If one holds the reins too tightly, the horse will move back and forth from one side to the other because of the discomfort.

Practicing cessation works in the same way. If the mind has settled down and one continues to take action for the sake of preventing stupor and restlessness, one only makes the mind scattered. So one should practice equanimity to temper one's effort during this stage. This equanimity is the eighth cutting action. It can exterminate the fifth fault, that of action. Practicing in this way, one will soon attain concentration.

The Nine Abiding Minds

> 157 Inward abiding and continuous abiding,
> Calm abiding and abiding nearby,
> Harmonized abiding and quietude,
> Followed by supreme quietude,
> Single-pointed concentration,

And maintaining equanimity without action—
These methods of cessation, taught by the sages,
Are the nine stages of mental abiding.

From collecting the mind in the beginning stages of practice to attaining right concentration, there are nine abiding minds—nine stages in the practicing the abiding mind.

1. Inward abiding: The minds of ordinary people are always scattered—directed toward external things—a state that the Confucians call "the mind let loose." This state is analogous to chickens and dogs that will not return home after being let loose. Practicing cessation means to collect this dispersed mind and make it abide on an internal object of focus without letting it run toward external things.

2. Continuous abiding: When the mind initially becomes collected, it continues to buck like a horse unwilling to surrender. After one practices for a long time, the active mind slows down more or less and then abides continuously in an internal state without being scattered.

3. Calm abiding: At this stage, although the mind is said to abide continuously, it still momentarily forgets to be mindful and becomes scattered. However, the practices that have led to this stage have trained one to immediately detect the forgetfulness or scatteredness of the mind as soon as it begins to happen. Thus one can collect the mind in order to return to the object of focus. Only at this stage can the mind be described as calm and settled.

4. Abiding nearby: This stage marks the continued progress of one's efforts. Now one succeeds in not forgetting mindfulness and avoids being scattered. When such things are about to happen, one realizes it and can subdue the distraction before it occurs. Thus the mind calmly abides on the object of focus and does not become dispersed. That is why this stage is called abiding nearby.

5. Harmonized abiding: The five desires—for form, sound, odor, taste, tangible things; the three poisons—greed, anger, and ignorance; and the two types of person—males and females—are the ten objects that cause the mind to be scattered. When the mind is in equanimity and has definite knowledge of the virtues of concentration, one realizes the faults of desires. So, using stillness to subdue desires, the mind becomes gentle and harmonized and is no longer tempted by these ten objects.

6. Quietude: The ten objects are chiefly temptations of the external environment. There is also unwholesomeness coming from one's own mind: attachment to one's country, relatives, immortality, desire, anger, harm to others, and so forth. There are also the five hindrances—greed, anger, sleepiness, restlessness, and doubt. All these can be subdued by tranquil concentration. Such concentration cannot be disturbed and the mind becomes quiet. This quietness is like the silent serenity in the middle of the night, but it is not the extinction of Nirvāṇa.

7. Supreme quietude: The preceding quietude is achieved by subduing the various attachments that arise at times. At this more advanced stage, as soon as the attachments arise, one immediately dispels and eliminates them.

The first four abiding minds are the stages of abiding calmly on the object of focus. But one practices cessation and achieves concentration primarily for the purpose of departing from unwholesomeness such as desire. Once the power of concentration has become stronger—in the fifth to the seventh stages—one is at the point of subduing the afflictions. Only when the mind is quiet and pure can one proceed toward right concentration.

8. Single-pointed concentration: At this point, the mind is able to abide calmly and not be disturbed by internal and external bad elements. One has reached the stage of keeping the mind even and straightforward. From here one can diligently concentrate one's mind on a single object continuously.

9. Maintaining equanimity: This is a more advanced single-pointed concentration. With both skillful effort and without the need for more effort, one takes no action, lets the mind operate naturally, and continuously abides without scatteredness. Having practiced cessation up to this stage, one is close to attaining concentration.

The methods for practicing concentration vary, as does the time required to achieve it. Although the abiding mind is taught in various ways, the complete course of skillfully practicing cessation, from the initial step of collecting the mind to accomplishing right concentration, coincides with this doctrine of the nine abiding minds. Those who practice cessation should follow this skillful course and recognize their stages of progress. Doing so will keep them from arrogance, which could impede their progress.

158 If one attains wonderful light bliss in practice,
This can be called the achievement of cessation.

In the course of practicing cessation, one will already have had some physical and mental feelings of lightness and pleasantness, and one will certainly have had some experiences of heat, movement, etc. But one can operate effortlessly without differentiation only when one has reached the ninth abiding mind. But this mind, although it is close to concentration, has not yet achieved it.

The Achievement of Concentration

One must have attained mild physical and mental bliss, be comfortable, and have the ability to concentrate on the object of focus before one can be said to have achieved concentration of the first stage: peripheral concentration. At the commencement of concentration, the crown of one's head will first have a heavy but comfortable sensation. This is followed by a feeling of ease that is at first mental and then physical. This feeling is so strong that every part of the body is completely full of joy. This experience affects the mind forcefully, and one can be described as being "physically and mentally excited." After such impulses pass away, the body feels wonderfully comfortable, and the mind still abides firmly and calmly on the object of focus without making effort or differentiating. Only then can one be said to have attained concentration.

After coming out of this concentration, whether one is walking, resting, sitting, or lying down one feels light bliss and has the residual impact of concentration as if one were still in concentration. If one practices cessation and enters concentration again, then, having kept the mind from being scattered, one can enter concentration immediately and feel mild physical and mental bliss. This feeling can increase continuously.

159 In concentration clarity, nondifferentiation,
And a wonderful light bliss
Can be attained by Buddhists and non-Buddhists;
But concentration differs in terms of the wisdom that comes
from contemplation.

Those who achieve concentration can attain the superior virtues that arise from concentration. These virtues, present in all states of concentration, are clarity, nondifferentiation, and a wonderful light bliss. Clarity refers to the mind being extremely clear and pure. The image of one's object of focus is also extremely clear and pure, like the clear moon in a vast cloudless sky. Nondifferentiation refers to the mind abiding calmly and functioning naturally and clearly without any active effort. The mind at such times is as clear and pure as the peaceful ocean. In this state of concentration one is alert and quiet, and one feels wondrously blissful both physically and mentally. One is able to depart from evil and do good with great strength and spontaneity. This is very different from one's normal state, which can be compared to sailing a boat against the current. Of course one does not become attached to any objects of desire whatsoever. Even this lowest stage of concentration is profound and wonderful.

It is, nevertheless, common to all Buddhists—those following both the worldly and the world-transcending ways and those of the Great and the Small Vehicles. And it is common as well to non-Buddhist practitioners. It is common to all states of concentrations of the world, and ordinary people may practice and attain it.

Some people who especially favor Ch'an practice do not read or recite the scriptures of the Tripitaka, believing that to do so would only increase their knowledge and understanding but would not be very useful for their practice. Instead they practice single-mindedly, relying on some experience of their practice that they consider extraordinary. Because such a practice leaves desire far behind, such people do not feel the presence of the afflictions of the realm of desire. They therefore think they have cut off the afflictions and are no longer defiled by them. Because their minds function without effort or differentiation, such people think they have realized the wisdom that is without differentiation. They also believe that their actions and their stillness are one and that they are always in concentration.

Some think they are liberated; they say, for example, that they have achieved the fourth dhyāna or that they have attained the fourth fruition. Some think they have become buddhas. They do not know that this state is only the first step of concentration, a stage that is common to the worldly practices. Actually, there are not so many people who have had such experiences in their practice. But when some people who are practicing cessation have special physical or mental experiences, they become so wildly arrogant that they do not know who they really are! It is pitiable that those who practice meditation but not the wisdom that comes from contemplation, like those who think that dhyāna is prajñā, will never penetrate deeply into the world-transcending Dharma.

Since peripheral concentration is only the beginning stage of concentration, one needs the wisdom that comes from contemplation to differentiate between the worldly and the world transcending, between the Small Vehicle and the Great. If, after one has attained peripheral concentration, one practices the six contemplations, which extol the upper realms and despise the lower ones, then, progressing in sequence, one will achieve the worldly concentrations of form and formlessness. If one takes impermanence as the object of contemplation, one will gradually enter the contemplation of the nonexistence of "I and mine." This is the concentration of the Śrāvaka Vehicle. If, relying on this, one contemplates that the nature of things is emptiness—as neither created nor destroyed, in correspondence with the prajñā of the Great Vehicle—then one achieves the dhyāna of the Great Vehicle. If one practices only dhyāna but not the wisdom that comes from contemplation, one cannot be liberated from births and deaths, to say nothing of becoming a buddha! If, on the other hand, one practices concentration in accordance with the wisdom that comes from nonattainability, one will attain the dhyāna pāramitā that is empty of the essence of the three wheels.

Prajñāpāramitā

160 The prajñāpāramitā
Is nobly superior,
Because all liberation relies on it
And all buddhas come from it.

Of all the faultless virtues, prajñāpāramitā is considered to be the most noble. The sūtras praise it boundlessly. Why is it so worthy of respect? Among the boundless virtues of the Buddha Dharma, each one has its own distinctive superior qualities and values that are worthy of respect. But prajñā has a special significance: it is the foundation of the Buddha Dharma. The difference between ordinary people and sages, the worldly dharmas and the world-transcending Dharma, is the presence of prajñā.

Thus, all faultless virtues and all the sages of the Three Vehicles rely on prajñā. As is said in the sūtras, "Those who want to study at the level of the śrāvakas should learn the prajñāpāramitā.... Those who want to study at the level of the pratyekabuddhas should also learn the prajñāpāramitā.... Those who want to study at the level of the bodhisattvas should also learn the prajñāpāramitā."[48] In short, the one special quality of the Buddha Dharma that surpasses worldly dharma is prajñā, and no world-transcending sage or faultless virtue arises without it.

Prajñā is the foundation for the liberation of the practitioners of the Three Vehicles. All sages of the Three Vehicles rely on it to liberate themselves from birth and death, and all buddhas come from prajñā. In the *Prajñāpāramitā Sūtra* prajñā is the mother of buddhas: "Prajñāpāramitā can produce all buddhas,"[49] and "the transcendence of prajñā is the mother of bodhisattvas, and skillful means is their father."[50]

This being the case, one can ask whether prajñā is really the Dharma of the Small Vehicle or of the Great Vehicle? The broad meaning of prajñā is that it is that which has the ability to produce the holy Dharma. According to this definition, prajñā is a doctrine common to the Three Vehicles. As for the extent of their respective reliance on prajñā to realize emptiness, the śrāvaka's reliance can be compared to the breadth of a pore, while the bodhisattva's reliance is like the breadth of the universe;[51] but they are not different in substance. Of the three animals crossing the river, like the practitioners of the Three Vehicles, only the big elephant in the rut can reach the bottom—only buddhas can penetrate the truth of all Dharmas. Nevertheless, at different levels they all enter the stream of the nature of things. Hence, although the wisdom that comes from contemplating the Three Vehicles may differ in terms of skillful means and levels, the fundamental quality remains the same.

But according to a deeper understanding of prajñā, associating with prajñā can be compared to a woman uniting with a king and giving birth to a prince: the mother's status is elevated because of the son, because giving birth to a prince is different from giving birth to a common person. According to this understanding, prajñā is that which corresponds with bodhi mind and is guided by great compassion. It is adorned by the five transcendences, gathers all virtues, and goes toward the Buddha Way. From this perspective, "prajñā...belongs only to bodhisattvas" and can produce all buddhas.[52]

In the Great Vehicle, prajñā's direct realization of the emptiness of things is not only not an entrance into extinction, as it is in the Two Vehicles; it is instead a skillful means that embraces all virtues and becomes the collective form of all the pāramitās. Regardless of which understanding an explanation of prajñā is based on, prajñā is the special quality of the holy world-transcending Dharma, and cannot be matched by giving, dhyāna, etc. In addition, the practice of prajñā is a required method for attaining liberation from birth and death and becoming a buddha.

161 The direct realization of enlightenment comes from practice,
And practice comes from thinking and learning.
Virtuous friends and further learning
Are to be relied on for the development of wisdom.

Prajñā can also be categorized as extraordinary prajñā or worldly prajñā. The true prajñā is the prajñā that is directly and personally realized through practice. It is said, for example, that "prajñā, being very profound and solemn, affirms (absolutely accords with) the truth; superficial wisdom does not deserve to be called prajñā."[53]

One should know that prior to the advent of Buddhism the term *prajñā* was used to mean the faculty of the intellect that has the characteristic nature of differentiation. The prajñā that realizes the truth did not always exist in the world, however, so of course there was no previously existing term by which this realized truth might be designated. What then should it be called? The Buddha had the skill to enable sentient beings to follow this previously existing worldly wisdom in order to progress to higher and more profound levels and finally to realize directly the truth that surpasses worldly intellect. This process relies upon wisdom, which has the characteristic nature of differentiation. So although true prajñā differs from the wisdom that the world previously knew, it is still called prajñā. Actually, worldly intellect cannot be compared to true prajñā, which is attained through practice.

The direct realization of the Buddha Dharma does not come from one's imagination but from skillful means; its causes and conditions must be based on the threefold wisdom that comes from hearing, thinking, and practicing. The last of these, the wisdom that comes from practice, is the wisdom that comes from contemplation in accord with concentration.

Practicing means thinking deeply and discerning, with the wisdom that comes from thinking, the meaning of the Dharma. One does this so that the Dharma can be used as the object of focus for one's contemplation. The wisdom that comes from thinking has to originate in the wisdom that comes from hearing, that is "learning from the Buddha, or his disciples, or the scriptures."[54]

The detailed description of the threefold wisdom that comes from hearing, thinking, and practicing is known as the ten deeds associated with the Dharma: copying the scriptures, paying homage to the dharma, giving the scriptures to others, listening attentively to other's readings and recitations, reading the scriptures on one's own, receiving and maintaining the Dharma, explaining the scriptures to others, reciting the scriptures, pondering the Dharma, and practicing the Dharma.[55] The Buddha Dharma must be practiced in reliance upon the discourses of the buddhas and bodhisattvas, that is, the course of practice that relies upon the threefold wisdom. Especially for the practice of prajñā, one must start with hearing, thinking, and practicing.

The three kinds of prajñā ordinarily described together are as follows. The prajñā of truth, or extraordinary prajñā, is wisdom that comes from direct realization. The prajñā of contemplation is wisdom that comes from practicing and thinking. Wisdom that comes from thinking and hearing is prajñā that relies on words (thinking generally relies on words, but it need not do so). Worldly prajñā is wisdom that comes from hearing, thinking, and practicing. Since it can be the cause and condition for the extraordinary prajñā, it is given the conventional designation of prajñā—an instance of giving the cause a name based on the result. For those who practice prajñā, the scriptures of prajñā that are the objects of their hearing and thinking are also necessary provisions for their practice. The initial skillful means for practicing prajñā is hearing and thinking.

Being close to virtuous friends and learning from them is definitely necessary, and both of these should be relied on for the development of wisdom. Learning involves more than knowing many terms. According to the śrāvaka Dharma, learning about impermanence and the nonexistence of self is further learning. "If one is a hundred years old but does not understand the Dharma of existence and extinction, this long life is not worth as much as living for only one day and being able to understand such a Dharma."[56] In the Great Vehicle Dharma, learning entails understanding the emptiness that is neither created nor destroyed, as the *Laṅkāvatāra Sūtra* teaches. Only those who thoroughly understand these true meanings are good and knowledgeable people. Learning also involves—in the ten deeds associated with the Dharma—listening, reading, reciting, explaining. It also means understanding the meaning of the Dharma in reliance upon the scriptures.

Therefore, if one thinks that the wisdom that comes from hearing is useless for the practice of prajñā, one errs because this is not in accord with the Buddha Dharma. Although the wisdom that comes from hearing is only a beginning stage, one must rely on it to advance to the stages of thinking and practicing.

162 Prajñā is fundamentally nondual;
However, the practice varies because of people's different capacities.
The sūtras and treatises on prajñā
Are the closest guides for the practitioners of prajñā.

The study of prajñā as taught by the Buddha is a method that reveals the extraordinary nature of things based on dependent origination. Hearing, thinking, and practicing contemplation in reliance upon this method, one can attain direct realization. The content of prajñā—the content of realization—is fundamentally nondual and undifferentiated. That which is partially realized by all bodhisattvas and that which is completely realized by the buddhas of the ten directions is identical. Thus it is said that bodhisattvas "exhale through the same nostrils as the buddhas of the ten directions."

So in expounding the teachings and in practicing the wisdom that comes from contemplation, there should be no differences. Yet since sentient beings' fundamental capacities and preferences do differ, the Tathāgata had to use skillful methods to suit them. Even in a single sūtra, the understandings of the Dharma and its use as an object of focus for developing wisdom are not exactly the same. There are greater or lesser differences even in the sequences of practice. Through the transmissions from teachers to students and the formation of different schools, the differences between them have become more and more pronounced. In fact, due to the differences in fundamental natures, Buddhist teachings are different explications to accord with different capacities; there are different understandings to be had from hearing the same discourse, different treatises on the same sūtra, and so forth.

What then should be the basis for expounding the prajñāpāramitā? The founding teachers of Buddhism in China did have original understandings and practices, but overall they could not match the teachings of the Indian bodhisattvas, because the Indian scholars had fewer language differences between them and the Buddha Dharma. There were many schools for the study of the Great Vehicle in India. The Madhyamaka tradition, transmitted by the bodhisattvas Nāgārjuna and Āryadeva, and the Yogācāra tradition, transmitted by the bodhisattvas Asaṅga and Vasubandhu, are the two great schools. Among these, Nāgārjuna Bodhisattva expounded the contemplative wisdom of the nature of things being empty. Nāgārjuna's teaching is more direct and concise because his commentaries rely directly on the prajñā sūtras.

For example, Nāgārjuna's *Da zhi du lun* (Great Prajñāpāramitā Treatise) consists of extensive explanations of the *Prajñāpāramitā Sūtra.* Nāgārjuna's *Mūlamadhyamaka-kārikā* (Middle Treatise), *Śūnyatā-saptati-kārikā* (Commentaries on the Seventy Empty Natures), *Yuktiṣaṣṭikā* (The Sixty Verses on Reasoning), *Dvādaśamukha-Śāstra* (Treatise on the Twelve Entrances), *Vigraha-vyāvartanī* (The Treatise on Averting the Arguments), *Bao man lun* (Treatise on the Precious Garland), and so on, and Āryadeva's *Śata Śāstra* are generally acknowledged to be treatises that rely on the prajñā sūtras in order to elaborate on the doctrine of the empty nature of all things. With regard to both the understanding and the practice of the study of prajñā, the various sūtras of the prajñā lineage and the various treatises of the sect that studies Nāgārjuna can be said to the closest guidance one can find.

At this point, prajñā will be explained according to the guidance of these sūtras and commentaries. At the end of this explanation, the characteristics of the three systems of the Great Vehicle and the way to integrate them will be discussed in detail.

The Contemplation of the Two Truths

163 All buddhas, following the two truths,
Teach sentient beings the Dharma.
Following the conventional truth, one can attain the ultimate truth;
Following the ultimate truth, one can attain liberation.

The teachings of all buddhas rely on the two truths to teach sentient beings the Dharma. The two truths are ordinary worldly truth and extraordinary truth, also known as conventional truth and ultimate truth. This doctrine of two truths is an important entrance to the right contemplation of prajñā.

Sentient beings, their bodies and minds, along with everything that exists relative to sentient beings, are generally thought of as real things. In people's minds, matter is real matter, and spirit is real spirit. Every dharma has certain physical, biological, and mental relationships of cause and effect. As a result of the existence of these relationships one can discover the structure of matter, the functioning of the body and mind, and the organization of families and countries. These facts are generally acknowledged as real. This world of commonsense knowledge is called ordinary truth.

Ordinary truth includes simple and obvious things such as materials like wood and rocks that everyone can see. It also includes difficult and obscure things such as atoms and electrons, which can be detected only by scientific instruments. Likewise, everyone knows about this present life, but past lives and future lives can be seen only by the divine eye. Although dharmas vary from simple to difficult, they are all objects of knowledge. The three realms, the six transmigratory states, the five aggregates, the six sense organs, the afflictions, karma, suffering, and so on, that were taught by the Buddha, are all explanations of ordinary truth.

All along, sentient beings have been in the mental condition of ordinary truth. This condition is real, unquestionable, and unavoidable. It is real and generally acknowledged, but is it the ultimate truth? Not necessarily. Things believed to be true in the past have been found to not be true. For example, the atom was once thought to be indivisible and impenetrable, but it is now considered to be a cluster of electrons. Similarly, the colors green, yellow, etc., are now recognized as consisting of different wavelengths of light. In his perfect enlightenment, the Buddha knew that those realities of the world that are experienced by sentient beings are insubstantial and unreal, which is why they are called ordinary. They arise due to causes and conditions; none of them—no dharma—has real existence. Knowledge that everyone assumes to be real is unable to realize the truth of the world; on the contrary, the shortcomings of such knowledge reveal that everyone has barriers of ignorance. Only by eliminating this confused error—going beyond the views of commonsense knowledge—can one clearly see the truth of the world. This understanding is shared by all the Buddha Dharmas.

The practice of Buddha Dharma is therefore to discover, based on the right contemplation of the real world (conventional truth), the errors and unreality of commonsense knowledge, to eliminate that which is faulty and reveal that which is true, and thereby to advance further and realize the ultimate truth of the world. Ultimate truth is extraordinary truth, a state of special experience that is recognized by all the sages. The practice of prajñā reaches these conclusions: leaving behind illusions, one sees the truth; beginning with conventional truth, one attains ultimate truth; starting out as an ordinary person, one becomes a sage.

One should not by any means imagine that ultimate truth is something apart from the real world. The Buddha's teaching of the two truths points to the fact that beyond the reality recognized by the world lies a truth that all sages have realized. But this truth is reality; it does not exist apart from the real world. It follows that without relying on conventional truths, ultimate truth, which "reveals the nature of things through phenomena," cannot be attained.

One needs to practice in this way because we sentient beings—we humans—cannot thoroughly understand the true appearance of the world, we cannot be in harmony with ultimate truth. All our thoughts, actions, and speech, all our confusion and suffering—in individuals, families, societies, or countries—are irrational phenomena that do not accord with ultimate truth. The continual transmigration of individuals through birth and death—suffering continuing from the past life to the present and from the present life to the future—results from not being in accord with ultimate truth because of ignorance, erroneous views, confusion, and distortions. Thus, the Buddha expounded the two truths in order to teach people to practice reliance on conventional principles to attain the real prajñā. After attaining prajñā, one can rely on one's experience of ultimate truth to clear up ignorance and erroneous views. Then one can be liberated and advance toward buddhahood.

164 Everything that is conventionally established in the world
Can be recognized by "name and speech" consciousness.
Names, perceptions, and things are conventional,
But the conventionally true and false should be skillfully
differentiated.

Commonsense knowledge seems so real that it conceals the truth. If one understands that ordinary knowledge is established through conventions—that it is conventionally designated—one has the possibility of understanding reality. "Conventionally designated" does not mean that the knowledge is vacuous, nor does it refer to a simple confusion like calling a melon a gourd. It means that that it is formed in reliance on causes, conditions, and factors. What is recognized is not a real essence but a conventional one. Because it relies on causes and conditions to become this or that, it is said to be established.

The conventionally designated includes everything in our commonsense knowledge. The mind, specifically "name and speech" consciousness, perceives things. When an image or concept appears in our mind, we differentiate between this and that. Since this differentiation is similar to the way that language gives names to objects, it is called perception through name and speech. Ordinary cognition works this way. Adults, for example, are good with names and speech; they are able to recognize distinctions and speak clearly. Babies and animals also have cognition, as long as the six consciousnesses function; their cognition is not as clear as that of adult humans, but they can still sense what something is. Though they may be unable to say anything, they nevertheless can know what something is. Of course, what they know is limited and often mistaken.

The consciousnesses of our sense organs—eye, ear, nose, tongue, body, and mind consciousness—all cognize in this manner. All such cognition comes from habitual mental states: one accepts the way the world is, just as it is. On the basis of such worldly cognition, which does not seek the truth of fundamental knowledge, all the knowledge of the world is developed. If everything is analyzed according to ultimate truth, however, the customary knowledge of the world cannot be established.

That which is conventionally established may be easy to understand or not so easy, and it can be divided into three groups: conventional designation, conventional perception, and conventional things.

Conventional designation is easy to understand. For example, some people think that thinking or talking about a person is identical to the person in question, so that the name and the person (the word and its referent) are the same. They do not know that it is only through convention that a word corresponds with a meaning. If one does not think of someone as a person, that person remains what he or she is and does not disappear just for that. So it can be seen that the name and its meaning may not necessarily correspond. Knowing this, one can break up the stubbornness of thinking of the name as reality.

False perception was translated as "conventional grasping" by Master Xuanzang. For example, when people recognize a person, a house, or some other compounded thing, they always think of it as being real, although not necessarily with a definite name. They do not know that "person," "house," etc. are conventional establishments. For example, in ordinary language a person is formed by the aggregation of four limbs, a hundred bones, eleven internal organs, and so forth; a house is formed by the union of wood, stones, earth, metal, and labor. If these things are analyzed, then apart from their components, there are no real entities corresponding to them. They are only perceived as such. Why is this called conventional perception? It is because such a perception is a combined form established from a collection of various causes and conditions. Knowing this, one can eradicate the obstinate attachment that treats a compounded thing as if it were a monad. This is analogous to the previous understanding of the atom, which took it to be a real entity.

A conventional thing refers to the smallest entity which, after being analyzed, does not lose its inherent nature. Such a thing is the fundamental factor of life and the universe. For example, as far as is currently known, these things are electrons. But these are also conventionally established because they are still changeable.

In real time and space, that which can become a fundamental factor like the electron must be determined by relationships. Without causes and conditions, it cannot exist, so it too is conventionally established. This unreal existence of monads is the last stronghold of sentient beings' attachment to things as if they were real, and it is the most difficult unreal attachment to eradicate. The right contemplation of prajñā relies on prajñā "to first destroy the prajñāpti (conventional) designation, then the prajñāpti perception, and then the prajñāpti thing in order to reach reality."[57] These three conventional aspects should be skillfully studied. One should not think that just because they all are conventionally established that no differentiation is necessary.

That which is ordinary and conventionally established in the world can be divided into the two categories of the "true" and the "false," which should also be skillfully differentiated. For example, acts such as meeting people, talking, and working belong to the first category, but when these same activities happen in a dream they belong to the second. Personal activities during the day are facts in real time and space; they can be confirmed by others as real. This acknowledgment of them as real within the ordinary dharma of the world is called the "ordinary truth of the world."

On the other hand, dreams are only individual's psychic states, insubstantial and unreal aspects of the worldly dharma. The category of the "ordinary falseness of the world" includes such illusions. For example, when one places a pen in a glass of water, the pen looks as if it were crooked. If one's cornea is scarred and one sees unreal flowers falling disorderly upon the ground, this is an example of an illusion of the sensory organs. If one has false preconceptions, then one's erroneous understandings are illusions of consciousness. All of these types of illusions can be understood as insubstantial and unreal illusions of the ordinary perception through name and speech.

However, it is more difficult to understand that ordinary phenomena—"conventional things," whether mental, physiological, or physical—are also insubstantial and unreal illusions. Such an understanding requires the right contemplation of prajñā; only then can one recognize that these phenomena are ordinary conventional designations of the world. Because of these difficulties, the Buddha often used the ordinary falseness of the world, like the reflection of the moon in water, dreams, unreal flowers, and so on, to explain the illusions and unreality of ordinary truth. It is important to understand this difference and know about some of the illusions and unreality of the ordinary falseness of the world, and, as well, about emptiness when it is easy to understand (as in the case of unreal flowers, etc.). One must also be able to contemplate the emptiness that is more difficult to understand by using the ordinary truth of the world as one's object of focus. If one cannot do these things, one cannot thoroughly understand what is real in the world.

165 How does inherent nature exist?
This can be discovered by wisdom in accord with the ultimate truth.

The Buddha has revealed the wisdom that comes from contemplation and points toward the ultimate truth. Perception through name and speech is faulty and accords with what is commonly approved of in the world, but it can accord with the ultimate. But it is not the case that perception is based on the successful conclusion of an inquiry into what is ultimate. Although there is progress in the advancement of knowledge, such progress nevertheless relies on that which is generally acknowledged in the world—that is, "the self-explanatory," otherwise known as "that which obviously exists." Cognition is formed on this biased foundation, which does not seek the ultimate.

As an example of the ordinary conventions, take a ship that is in danger at a certain hour and minute of a certain day; it is located at such and such a degree and minute of longitude east. Hours and minutes do not exist within time itself, just as degrees and minutes of longitude cannot be found on the earth. By means of these conventionally acknowledged assumptions, however, people know the time and the location of the ship and can plan its rescue. In addition, modern scientists think the earth came from the sun, that living things came from nonliving matter, and that humans came from animals which in turn came from plants; thus they establish the order of evolution as an upward progression. But with regard to the reasons for the existence of these materials, the foundation upon which these materials are formed, their origins and their ultimate outcome, no one has investigated such questions to the very end. If one were to investigate these questions thoroughly, all knowledge would become untenable.

Also, philosophers hypothesize that the universe originated from substance, from production, from the mind, or from diverse origins. The hypothesized origin of the universe has been obtained not from seeking the ultimate but rather from designs and inferences based on the physical, biological, and mental phenomena. Ordinary worldly cognition and behavior work the same way. For example, when one says, "I planted the tree," one accepts the fact of planting the tree without any further investigation of what this "I" really is. Such knowledge is not ultimate and is characterized by relative contradiction. Such things may as well be accepted as ordinary worldly knowledge because sentient beings have always lived with this kind of mental state—thinking such things are real. Such thinking will never reach ultimate reality, however.

Extraordinary truth is the personal experience of ultimate reality. It relies on the investigation of ordinary phenomena to explore ultimate inherent nature. This kind of investigation is called the wisdom that comes from investigation which is in accord with extraordinary truth. In the continuum from the past to the future, it investigates what first existed and how it arose; it investigates the relationship between things, the absolute differences between them, and how they became individual entities.

With regard to conventional perception, this kind of investigation examines the smallest particles (not subdividable) that can cluster together to form something visible. It asks, "What in the end is this thing that cannot be subdivided? How did it arise and exist?" If one thinks that there is just one real essence of the universe, then investigate what this one essence is and how it exists. How can this single essence become differentiated? This is called searching for inherent nature. Inherent nature is self-essence. From its origin it has been as it is; it is as it is right now, and it will be so forever; it is the smallest or the largest, the very first or very last. Without any preconceptions and without imagining, one has to insist on getting to the bottom of the matter and find out what the ultimate is.

Although this is still within the realm of perception through name and speech, it departs from the usual path of ordinary worldly knowledge and enters into extraordinary truth. The characteristics of ordinary worldly phenomena are extensively described in the scriptures, as is the extraordinary wisdom that comes from contemplation—from hearing to thinking to practicing. This is especially true for the investigation of inherent nature and the profound penetration into the ultimate. Only through these can one thoroughly break down the fundamental ignorance of sentient beings and thoroughly understand the truth of the world.

166 Suffering comes from confusion and karma,
Which come from discrimination.
Discrimination evolves from meaningless elaboration:
Meaningless elaboration can be eliminated by the contemplation
of emptiness.

Extraordinary contemplation means seeking the inherent nature of all things and, in reliance upon that contemplation, realizing extraordinary truth. This investigation of the truth is the only door to liberation. That from which one is liberated is suffering. Suffering is the essence of sentient beings' bodies and minds, which arises from making contact with things.

Why do sentient beings suffer, and why do they transmigrate through cycles of birth and death? They do so because of confusion and karma. Karma arises from confusion. Confusion is ignorance, which primarily means having the affliction of the view of the "I and mine." A sūtra says, "Ignorance is caused by deviant thinking."[58] This ignorance comes from erroneous discriminations.

Sentient beings discriminate erroneously and do not know the truth because of meaningless elaboration. Erroneous discrimination arises in dependence upon phenomena. When it arises, one intuitively feels that the object is real, that it exists as an entity just as it appears, that it is unrelated to the mind's discrimination, and so forth. This is not only an illusion of erroneous discrimination; in ordinary people's minds, the object seems to be present as it appears. This is the source of fundamental error and is not in harmony with reality. If that which is recognized really existed as an entity the way it appears, then it would not be in accord with one's practical experiences or one's knowledge of principles, which means that no worldly and world-transcending things could be established. That which is not but appears to be is meaningless elaboration, and the mind's discrimination—perception through name and speech—cannot realize its own error.

If one investigates inherent nature correctly, analyzing it layer by layer to expose its ultimate existence, one will discover that there is no real inherent nature. That all things are without an inherent nature is the reality of all things.

By relying on the contemplation of emptiness, which does not posit an inherent nature, one can eliminate meaningless elaboration through continuous practice. After meaningless elaboration is eliminated, erroneous discrimination will not arise because it will have lost its object. When the mind's discrimination stops, prajñā will arise; then one will no longer have confusion or create more karma. Because of this, the body that suffers will no longer continue, and one is liberated. The liberation of sages is attained by relying on the contemplation of emptiness. Herein lies the reason that the Buddha speaks of the three gates of liberation as emptiness, formlessness, and desirelessness.

The Contemplations of Twofold Emptiness

167 All things arise from causes and conditions.
What arises conditionally is empty, without an inherent nature.
Being empty, all things are neither born nor extinct,
But are always in perfect stillness.

Whatever arises in the discriminating mind has the appearance of reality. How then can one know that what arises is meaningless elaboration not in harmony with reality? Because the reality of everything is not in harmony with one's actual experience; it is impossible to prove that each thing is real. Thus the Buddha proclaimed the Dharma of dependent origination to explain that all things—from the external world to the body and the mind, from the vast universe to the smallest dust particle—arise from causes and conditions. In other words, everything does not exist by itself but is determined by the relationship of causes and conditions. Everything follows the law of "when this exists, that exists; when this arises, that arises; when this expires, that expires; when this ceases, that ceases." If we depart from all these pragmatic experiences, then none of the principles of cause and effect can be discussed, never mind talking about the realization of the truth of everything.

All that arises from causes and conditions, whether from a prior, subsequent, or simultaneous relationship, illustrates that everything is without an independent nature. "Inherent" here means self-existent and self-created. Whatever is real should be independent and self-existent. If a phenomenon is dependent on and determined by causes and conditions, it cannot be said to exist as it is without relation to other phenomena. That which is real, self-existent, and independent would also have to exist permanently: if a phenomenon were truly independent from causes and conditions, then it would be impossible to account for changes originating from the entity itself.

Hypothetically, if a phenomenon is able to change, then it is not a unique self-entity. Changeability indicates that phenomena actually arise from causes and conditions and do not exist by virtue of their own inherent natures. Contemplating the interdependent existence of all things, one can see that they cannot be self-existent, independent, or permanently existing and also that they are not as real as they appear to the discriminating mind.

Anything that is without an inherent nature but that appears to be self-existent is an illusory meaningless elaboration. That which is without an inherent nature is called "empty" by the Buddha. "Emptiness" and "nothingness" have some similarities in the Chinese language, but they are different in Sanskrit. "Nothingness" means being without anything, while "emptiness" means that a nature inherent unto itself is unattainable—that is, there is no inherent nature.

All things that are without an attainable inherent nature can be established only in an ordinary and worldly sense—such existence is conventionally designated. Emptiness does not hinder the existence of the conventionally designated: being empty, a thing's existence is conventionally designated and arises from causes and conditions; having a conventionally designated existence arising from causes and conditions, a thing is empty without inherent nature. The contemplations of dependent origination, absence of inherent nature, emptiness, and conventional designation are different investigations of the same thing; in fact, they are all the same. So it is said, "All things that arise from causes and conditions I explain as emptiness, as conventional designation, and also as the meaning of the Middle Way."[59]

Relying on this kind of investigation, one can see that all conventionally established worldly things are like this—having existence and nonexistence, birth and extinction; they continue from the past to the future and indirectly relate to each other. These are all the things of reality. When one profoundly contemplates the basic principle of all things through emptiness, one knows that they exist conventionally without an independent nature. All existence and nonexistence, all births and deaths, are neither real existence nor real nonexistence, neither real births nor real deaths.

In spite of the fact that births and extinctions are infinitely variable and incessant, since they are empty without an independent nature of their own, all things are conventionally born and conventionally become extinct—they are neither really born nor really extinct. Originally all things are neither born nor extinct and are always abiding in absolute stillness. This explanation does not separate nonbirth and nonextinction from birth and extinction, but rather points directly to the essence of birth and extinction, whose true nature is neither born nor extinct.

Thus, even though all the things in the world appear to be born and become extinct continuously and with endless chaos, they are actually always in perfect stillness. The essence of chaos is stillness; one cannot talk about chaos as something separate from stillness. First, relying on the Dharma of dependent origination, one seeks that which is without an inherent nature. Then, through extraordinary contemplation, one gradually uncovers the real nature of all things. As one sūtra describes it, "All things are without an independent nature of their own; they are neither born nor extinct. Because they are neither born nor extinct, they are fundamentally still and quiet. Nirvāṇa is their inherent nature."[60]

168 A thing cannot arise by itself or through another;
It cannot arise from the two together or without cause.
Contemplating the empty nature of things
One can know that no thing has ever arisen.

Through their extraordinary contemplation in which all things are empty without an independent nature, bodhisattvas examine everything extensively. Relying on infinite skillful methods for their investigations, they thoroughly understand the absence of inherent nature. The broad explanation of these investigations includes two main methods: the contemplation of things being empty and the contemplation of the self being empty. "Things" mainly refers to conventional things and includes conventional perceptions and that which is conventionally designated. The self, which is one type of conventional perception, is the union of the body and mind taken as an individual sentient being.

The Contemplation of Things Being Empty

The most concise method for contemplating the emptiness of things is to contemplate the four kinds of nonarising. Things exist, but ordinary people cling to them by thinking that they either really exist or really do not exist. The Buddha expounded on the contemplation of the impermanence of arising and extinction: nonexistence leads to existence, and existence leads to nonexistence. Some people think that things really arise and pass, however. They cling to the inherent nature of arising and passing as real. This is the exact opposite of the neither-arising-nor-passing nature of the emptiness of things. This is why the Dharma of the Great Vehicle relies on the nonarising of causes and conditions as an important method to reveal the true meaning of the Buddha Dharma and to dispel the erroneous attachments of ordinary people, non-Buddhists, practitioners of the Small Vehicle who still have something to attain, and practitioners of the Great Vehicle.

If the dharma that is grasped by sentient beings as real does exist, it must also arise. How is it that it arises? How does it exist? There are only two categories of arising: with causes and conditions, and without them. Arising with causes and conditions has three subtypes: self-arising, arising from another, and mutual arising. So in total, there are four types. Self-arising means to arise and be constituted by itself. Arising from another means to arise in reliance upon others. It also means that whatever arises really exists. Mutual arising means that although the entity exists by itself, it needs other factors to enable it to arise. Although different schools supply their own explanations, all posit these four types.

Relying on the right principles of investigations, one can see that anything with real inherent nature could not possibly arise in any of the following four ways.

1. It cannot be self-arising, cannot produce itself. Since the self-entity already exists, it is already produced. To speak of a self-entity and then to speak of production is contradictory. Let us pose this question: Is there any difference between the self-entity that has not yet arisen and the self-entity that has already arisen? If there is a difference, then that which has arisen is existing and that which has not yet arisen does not exist. If the self-entity that has not arisen does not exist, then how can the self-entity be produced by a self that does not exist? If the self-entity that has not arisen exists, then with respect to that which has already arisen it is no longer the "self-entity," because they are different. If one posits that there is no difference between the self-entity that has not yet arisen and the self-entity that has arisen, then there should be no difference between arising and not arising. Moreover, if the self-identity that produces and the self-identity that is produced are the same "self-entity," then it should be able to produce still more "self-entities." This is the error of endless production.

2. A thing with a real inherent nature also cannot arise from another. If, prior to its arising, a thing has no "self-entity," then there is no

"self" that can be relative to some other thing; without the self, there is no other. If the meanings of both "self" and "other" cannot be established, how can something arise? If the other really is other, a differentiated other with its own nature, then it cannot produce itself, just as a cow cannot produce a horse. Some think that the Buddha's teachings of "arising from causes and conditions" and "arising in reliance upon others" are the same as arising from another. Insistence that something produced by another inherently exists and has its own nature should be refuted.

Although the Buddha spoke of the arising from causes and conditions, this conditioned arising is without an inherent nature and cannot be said to inherently exist. Causes and conditions and all things that arise do not have a specific inherent nature; although they are "other" in a conventional sense, they are definitely not other "self-entities."

3. Anything with real inherent nature cannot arise mutually. Mutual arising is a combination of self-arising and arising from another. If these factors are separated, neither self-arising nor arising from another can be established. Since both self-arising and arising from another are not possible, how can mutual arising be possible? For example, A is blind and unable to see things, and so is B; if these two blind people work together, can they now see?

4. Anything with real inherent nature also cannot arise without cause. Everything that is seen in the world has a relationship of cause and effect. Without a cause or condition, nothing can be established. That which is good or evil, erroneous or correct, also cannot be established. If things were to arise without cause, then those who commit the ten evils and five serious offenses might be born in the heavens or become buddhas, which is definitely impossible.

In sum, all things believed to have a real inherent nature belong to these four kinds. Things do not exist independently. Because independent nature and independent production cannot be established, reality arises conditionally and is conventionally established. Relying both on conditioned arising and on conventional designation to contemplate emptiness, one comes to understand that all things are fundamentally not produced. As is said in the sūtras, "That which arises from conditions is nonarising because it does not have inherent nature that is capable of arising,"[61] and "All things are always in the form of perfect stillness."[62]

The Contemplation of the Self Being Empty

169 The self is neither identical to the five aggregates
Nor is it separate from the aggregates.
They do not belong to or coexist with each other.
For these reasons it is known that there is no self.

There are two kinds of self, called in Sanskrit *pudgala* and *satkāya*. *Pudgala*, translated as "taking on numerous transmigratory states," means to be reborn incessantly amid birth and death. Humans and animals all have an individual entity—the union of body and mind—that can be said to be the conventional self. But sentient beings, unable to understand this, always think that sentient beings transmigrate with real bodies. They thus form an attachment to the concept of the pudgala self. *Satkāya* means to accumulate. In the union of one's body and mind, one has the feeling of a self, which corresponds to the characteristics of self-love and arrogance and which is in opposition to a conventionally designated other. This—the satkāya view—is an erroneous attachment to that which fundamentally does not exist. With regard to other people, one is attached to the concept of the pudgala self; with regard to oneself, one is both attached to the pudgala self and, even more so, to the satkāya view.

The ordinary mental state of sentient beings in the world is an attachment to self. But this sense of self comes from intuition, and most people have not really asked themselves what the self actually is. Although religious scholars and philosophers infer different kinds of self according to their different perspectives, they consider the self to be the primary entity of life and the entity that transmigrates; they believe that it is self-created and that it transmigrates with its selfhood unchanged.

Real existence, self-existence, and permanent existence are characteristics included in the concept of the self. This definition is exactly the same as the definition of inherent nature discussed above. The nonexistence of inherent nature with regard to things and the nonexistence of the self with regard to sentient beings are therefore interchangeable. Things are empty without inherent nature, and the self is empty without inherent nature. Furthermore, things are without a self, and persons are without a self.

People are attached to the satkāya self, however. Because of their erroneous attachment to it as real, unitary, and permanent, they go on to talk about being happy. They think their own body is independent, so they feel free and comfortable. From this perspective on the fundamental nature of the self (to which they are erroneously attached), the self should be happy; from this perspective on the functions expressed by the self, the self should make decisions, and power and volition should be controlled by the self (mastery is the definition of the self). Thus, the desire to have mastery is characteristic of the satkāya self. If one thoroughly understands the nonexistence of inherent nature and thoroughly understands that a real, unitary, and permanent self cannot be attained, however, the misconception of a comfortable self that has mastery will lose its foundation and be eliminated.

There are only two categories of the self to which ordinary people are attached: that which is identical with the aggregates and that which is separate.

If one investigates correctly, relying on right principles, one will find that the self that exists independently cannot be said to be identical with the five aggregates. What is actually the self? Common phrases such as "I walk," "I imagine," or "I act" do not indicate a separation between the body and mind. The general attachment to the self is a clinging to the aggregates as the self. But the five aggregates are many, miserable, and they arise and become extinct without permanence. They do not conform to the definition of the self: being unitary, happy, and permanent. If the five aggregates are really the self, then the self cannot be established.

After some consideration, religious scholars generally tend to advocate that the self is separate from the aggregates, thinking that there is a mystical self that is permanent, happy, and wonderful, which is separate from the five aggregates of body and mind. However, if one analyzes this rightly, one will find that there is definitely no self outside of the aggregates. This is because without the five aggregates it is impossible to describe the self, prove its existence, or express its function. Some religious scholars, holding that the five aggregates are subordinate to the self and are the tools of the self, say that they belong to each other: the self uses the legs to walk, uses the eyes to see, uses consciousness to understand and cognize. Some say that the self and the aggregates coexist with each other: if the self is greater than the five aggregates, then the five aggregates are in the self; if the five aggregates are greater than the self, then the self is inside the five aggregates. But since all these explain the self as existing apart from the aggregates, naturally they cannot be established.

The self and the aggregates do not belong to or coexist with each other. Both belonging and coexistence imply a simultaneous presence of two things that can be clearly differentiated. Yet, apart from the five aggregates, the concepts to which people are attached—the self as subordinate or the self as coexistent—are impossible. It is impossible to prove that there is a separate entity of a self, so neither of these concepts can be established.

After investigating in this way, it becomes clear that there is no entity of the self like that to which sentient beings are erroneously attached. The concept of the self is based upon the conventionally designated and conventionally established unitary nature of the continuous union of the body and mind. Originally, the self to which people are attached was limited to these two categories. Later, however, the Vātsīputrīyas and others insisted upon an "indescribable self" that is "neither identical with the aggregates nor separate from the aggregates." This viewpoint misunderstands the conventionally established self as independently existent; it results from "clinging to the conventional as real."

170 If there is no self, no "I,"
How can there be a "mine"?
The nature of all things is empty,
So of course the self is too!

In the prajñā scriptures, the teachings of the emptiness of the self and the emptiness of things generally substantiate each other. The self is empty, therefore things are also empty; things are empty, therefore the self is also empty. If one understands that sentient beings have no self, no "I," then how can there be "mine"? That which is "mine" includes the things of the self and the things upon which the self relies. For example, my body, my wealth, my fame and position, my country, etc., all relate to me and belong to me; they are things of the self.

The self is also the conventional perception that is formed by the body and mind. Thus, things such as the five aggregates, the six sense organs, the six elements, the six consciousnesses, and so on are all conventional things upon which the self relies. All that I own and upon which I rely are things. Without a self, there is no "mine." So, since the self is empty, the Dharma is also empty. Conversely, the inherent nature of all things seems to be real yet is empty, to say nothing of the self that is established in reliance upon these things! Needless to say, this self is also empty.

This verse contains extraordinarily profound meanings that only the great Mādhyamikans can understand thoroughly and reveal according to reality. In the śrāvaka Dharma, the Buddha mostly speaks of the nonexistence of the self, while explicit discourses on things being empty are rare. In the transmission of the Buddha Dharma, therefore, the teachings on emptiness were divided into two schools. The Sarvāstivādins (such as the scholars of Abhidharma) of northwestern India thought that the Buddha spoke only of the nonexistence of the self, so they thought that things were not empty. In the Mahāsāṃghika of mid-southern India, some said that the Buddha had spoken of the emptiness of the self and also the emptiness of things, in, for example, the *Satyasiddhi-Śāstra* (Treatise on Realizing Reality). Needless to say, the Mahāyāna Buddhist sūtras say that the nature of all things is empty. With regard to the emptiness of the self and things, the Yogācāra system (derived from the Sarvāstivādin) believes that the Hīnayāna speaks of only the self being empty while the Mahāyāna speaks of both the self and things being empty. The Madhyamaka system is closer to the school of mid-southern India, so it considers the Hīnayāna to have had the teaching of the emptiness of both the self and things, just as the Mahāyāna does.

Synthesizing the Emptiness of Things and the Emptiness of the Self

These teachings can be synthesized drawing on selected passages from Nāgārjuna: "Because the Hīnayāna disciples were of dull capacity, they were taught that sentient beings were empty.... Because the Mahāyāna disciples were sharp, they were taught that things were empty";[63] "sentient beings with dull capacities were taught the nonexistence of the self; sentient beings with sharp capacities and profound wisdom were taught that all things are fundamentally empty."[64] All Mahāyāna and Hīnayāna sūtras are clear about this.

One cannot say that the śrāvaka disciples were not taught that things are empty, however: "If whole truth is expounded, then it will be taught that all things are empty; if the teaching is skillful, then it will speak of the nonexistence of the self. Both of these ways of teaching are in accord with the characteristics of prajñāpāramitā. Thus, the Buddhist sūtra says that those progressing toward Nirvāṇa are going in the same direction—there is no other way."[65] This clearly reveals that although the explanations of the emptiness of both the self and things may be either explicit or implicit, both are right contemplations of prajñā and the way of liberation through One Vehicle and one flavor.

Thus it is said, "One should not even be attached to the self (the 'I') and 'mine,' let alone other things! The emptiness of sentient beings and the emptiness of things are ultimately identical."[66] That is, those who can realize the nonexistence of the self and "mine" will definitely be able to understand the emptiness of things. This is because the meaning of the emptiness that one contemplates is in all cases without inherent nature. Contemplating that the self is without inherent nature, one understands the emptiness of the self; if one relies on this to contemplate all things, of course one will realize that they are also empty.

However, "śrāvakas only destroy all the afflictions (from the arising of the self and from causes and conditions) and depart from all love for things. Being fearful of the suffering from old age, illness, death, and evil destinies, they do not want to thoroughly investigate the whole truth and penetrate all things but instead only focus on liberation."[67] They urgently seek enlightenment by directly contemplating the nonexistence of the self and "mine" but do not go on to the more profound contemplation of the emptiness of things. But this is just a case of not going deeper (the Buddha also did not explain the emptiness of things to them), which is definitely not the same as attaching to things as real—as these two passages illustrate: "Without sentient beings, there is no basis for things";[68] and "Without the self and 'mine,' naturally the emptiness of things can be realized."[69] In this way, the teaching of the nonexistence of the self by the śrāvakas can be connected with the emptiness of things without contradiction.

Although the "Contemplating the Dharma" chapter in the *Mūlamadhyamaka-kārikā* teaches the extensive contemplation that all things are empty and are neither produced nor destroyed, nevertheless, right contemplation, from the extensive to the concise, still begins with the realization of the nonexistence of the self and "mine." On this critical point concerning birth and death, the world-transcending way of liberation is definitely without any discrepancy. This may be explained either explicitly or implicitly, extensively or concisely, however, according to people's different capacities.

In this way, all those who thoroughly understand that the self is empty will definitely be able to understand that things are empty. They may not contemplate that things are empty in depth or teach that things are empty, but they will positively not be attached to the existence of inherent nature. If one clings to things being real, one not only does not understand that things are empty, one also does not understand that the self is empty; one not only does not eliminate one's attachment to things, one also does not eliminate one's attachment to the self. Thus it is said, "Clinging to the form of things is the same as being attached to the self, others, sentient beings, and life; clinging to the form of that which is not a thing, it is the same as being attached to the self, others, sentient beings, and life."[70] Nāgārjuna's treatise also says, "If one realizes that the aggregates are not real, the view that there is a self will not arise. Having eliminated the view that there is a self, none of the aggregates will again arise.... As long as the attachment to aggregates is present, the view that there is a self will continue to exist."[71] Who says that śrāvaka sages know that the self is empty yet believe that all things really exist? Without understanding that things are empty and without leaving behind attachment to things, how could one depart from attachment to the self?

Thus, it can be inferred that the Buddha's teaching was originally of one flavor. Those who are superficial see only the superficial, and those who are profound see the profound. The superficial and the profound have always been consistent, but they have been interpreted and practiced differently in the hands of people who are extremely biased.

Skillful Means to Attain Direct Realization

171 Karma and confusion stem from discrimination.
Discrimination comes from the mind,
And the mind depends on the body.
Therefore, contemplate the body first.

Contemplating emptiness means investigating the empty nature of all sentient beings and things. Nāgārjuna, following the spirit of the Buddha's teaching, thought that beginners should start by contemplating the body first. What does this mean? Birth and death come from karma and confusion, which in turn stem from discrimination. This illusory and erroneous discrimination comes from the mind. The minds of humans and sentient beings who are able to make the resolution to study Buddhism also depend on the body. Since confusion and karma are derived from the mind, the Buddha Dharma is clearly a philosophy of life that has purity of the mind as its goal.

Contemplating the Body to Attain Direct Realization

Although the Buddha Dharma's focus is on the mind, the mind relies on the body, and the body is really where sentient beings' firm attachment is localized. Because of the ālaya ("storehouse consciousness") of desire, happiness, joy, and bliss, one cannot put an end to birth and death. The reason that ālaya consciousness is so desirous is that "this consciousness is hidden in and embraced by the body, and they share tranquillity and disturbance together."[72]

Almost all of the daily activities of human beings are done for the sake of the body. Since the body is stable for a certain period, it is easy for one to cling to it as eternal. Clinging to it as eternal will lead one to be attached to happiness and purity. But since the mind is changing from instant to instant, clinging to it as eternal and attaching to happiness and purity are contrary to common sense. Such attachment arises from the discriminating reasoning and teachings of religious scholars and philosophers. In Nāgārjuna's treatise these are called "the teachings of the Brahman King" in reference to the ancient ideas of Brahmanism.[73] If sentient beings concentrate on clinging to this body, this will be a great obstacle that will prevent them from making resolutions and being liberated. Therefore one should contemplate the body.

The grades of the way as taught by the Buddha give the highest ranking to the fourfold mindfulness, which is also called the Way of the One Vehicle. The fourfold mindfulness also relies on the contemplation of the body first. Contemplating the body as impure, suffering, impermanent, and without a self, one can realize the emptiness of the body. Once one is able to subdue the erroneous attachment to the body, one should further contemplate that all worldly things of the body and mind are empty. Contemplating the nonexistence of the self and "mine," one moves toward liberation.

In the Buddha Dharma, some teachings straightforwardly take the mind as their principal focus. Practice means to contemplate the mind directly. This may not be suitable for sentient beings with ordinary capacities who are attached to their bodies. For them, it would be like trying to capture robbers and their leader (i.e., the untamed mind) without first encircling them tightly and breaking into their fortress (i.e., the body). Contemplating the mind may be easy to talk about, but it is difficult to do. Some people, because of their incessant attachment to their bodies, want to become buddhas by cultivating the body!

Contemplating the Nonexistence of "I and Mine" to Attain Direct Realization

172 Knowing there is no "I" or "mine,"
Dissociating from everything, internal and external,
Extinguishing all discrimination,
One is in accord with reality.

Relying on the right contemplation of the nonexistence of "I and mine," Mahāyāna practitioners investigate the internal—the body and the mind—and the external—the world—and know that everything only *seems* to be reality and that there is no inherent nature. Contemplating that the self has no inherent nature is called the contemplation of the emptiness of the self; contemplating that things have no inherent nature is called the contemplation of the emptiness of things. With success in one's practice of the contemplation of emptiness, one can dissociate from the meaningless elaboration of all things and no longer have the "I and mine" attachment to things.

When all discrimination is extinguished, the faultless prajñā will appear. Thus it is said, "When all things do not arise, prajñāpāramitā should arise."[74] It is also said, "All speech comes to an end, mental activities also stop; neither arising nor perishing, all things are like Nirvāṇa."[75] When the directly realized prajñā appears, it is in accord with the reality of all things. It is called the nature of emptiness, the nature of things (*dharmatā*), the realm of things (*dharmadhātu*), true suchness (*bhūtatathatā*), and so on. All these names are conventionally established linguistic designations. This directly realized prajñā really is the right Dharma which, surpassing all discriminating erroneous attachment, time and space, and quality and quantity, realizes the absolute.

Since the realizations of followers of the Two Vehicles and of buddhas and bodhisattvas are the same in terms of the nonexistence of the self and the nonexistence of things, what is the difference between the Two Vehicles and buddhas and bodhisattvas? Both of the Two Vehicles realize the "nature of nondiscrimination,"[76] as described in the "Chapter on the Ten Grounds" in the *Avataṃsaka Sūtra*. The *Prajñāpāramitā Treatise* also says, "The severing of defilements and the wisdom that comes from the Two Vehicles are similar to the bodhisattvas' realization of nonarising (of things)."[77] However, bodhisattvas have bodhi mind and great compassion, transfer their virtues to benefit others, and extensively save sentient beings through the power of their own vows; how can this not differ from the Two Vehicles! Thus the Mahāyāna and the Hīnayāna differ in terms of vows and practices but not in terms of wisdom.

Although followers of the Human and Divine Vehicles are said to have realized the same nondiscriminating nature of things, there are still some differences. Śrāvakas do not relate to anything as "I" or "mine," and they have eliminated the barrier of afflictions. Through the wisdom of the emptiness of the self and things, bodhisattvas not only realize the nondiscriminating nature of things and eliminate afflictions, they are also able to practice profoundly and realize the emptiness of things, depart from all meaningless elaboration, and eradicate all residual habits. Practicing the purely formless deeds, bodhisattvas completely and perfectly realize the purest realm of things and become buddhas. Can the Two Vehicles match this?

Correctly Understanding Nondiscrimination to Attain Direct Realization

173 Real nondiscrimination
Should not lead to erroneous schemes.
The meditation on the mean
Is to be done without the discrimination of inherent nature.

Directly realized prajñā is called nondiscriminating wisdom, and the nature of things that is realized is called the nondiscriminating nature of things. The sūtras often say that during the cultivation of prajñā, one should not reflect on it, should not grasp, and should not discriminate. How is it that anyone, aside from those who are already enlightened, can practice contemplation (discrimination, selection, and reflection) in order to cultivate prajñā without being reflective, grasping, and discriminating? No wonder some Buddhist practitioners persuade others not to think of anything and to experience directly! No wonder some people assume that nondiscriminating concentration without investigation is the realization of profound nondiscriminating wisdom! Thus, whether the realization of nondiscriminating wisdom or the nondiscriminating contemplative wisdom is the subject at hand, the real meaning of nondiscrimination should be skillfully and correctly understood. One should not mistakenly fall into the erroneous schemes of non-Buddhists who are confused about the right contemplation taught by the Buddha.

Nondiscrimination has many different meanings. For example, wood and rock do not discriminate, but of course this is not the type of nondiscrimination taught in the Buddha Dharma. "Thoughtless concentration"—having neither the activities of the mind nor its attributes—is also nondiscriminating but is non-Buddhist. Naturally occurring inattention is also called nondiscrimination, but this also cannot be said to be nondiscriminating wisdom, for it is achieved without effort and without attention. The same goes for the five faulty consciousnesses, stupor, unconsciousness, and so forth.

In addition, in the second dhyāna and above there is neither reflection nor investigation. This kind of nondiscrimination, without reflection or investigation, is common to the second dhyāna and above, but it is different from nondiscriminating wisdom. If, then, the wisdom of nondiscrimination is achieved not through inattentiveness, not through reflecting, and not through differentiating between thoughts, how is it achieved? To practice nondiscriminating meditation on the mean, one must have right contemplation and be without "discrimination of inherent nature." Knowing that the discrimination of inherent nature is unattainable, one directly realizes the nondiscriminating nature of things.

Discrimination of inherent nature is attachment to meaningless elaborations that are unreal but seem to possess an inherent nature. As was stated above, the existence of inherent nature is the locus for the attachment to "I and mine." If the discrimination of inherent nature arises, one is unable to understand the emptiness of the self and things or dissociate from the attachment to "I and mine." So one must discriminate, investigate, and come to the decision that the existence of inherent nature is unattainable. Only when there is no trace of such existence can one dissociate completely from it. Doing so is the contemplation of emptiness—the discrimination of that which is without inherent nature.

Discrimination is not necessarily the discrimination of inherent nature; and the discernment that the discrimination of inherent nature is unattainable (the contemplation of emptiness) is not only nonattachment but is also a tremendously skillful means leading to the realization of indescribable nondiscriminating wisdom. That one should not be reflective, should not grasp, and should not discriminate—as the sūtras teach—really means that one should not be reflective of the existence of inherent nature, should not grasp it, and should not discriminate it. It does not mean one should cultivate prajñā by not remembering, not thinking, and not discriminating. If all discriminations are attachments, then would the wisdom that comes from listening, thinking, and practicing as taught by the Buddha not be distorted? If nondiscriminating wisdom could arise without the requisite awakening of wisdom from listening, thinking, and practicing, then it would arise without a cause.

When one contemplates nondiscrimination—by contemplating that the discrimination of inherent nature is unattainable—and is close to attaining nondiscriminating wisdom, however, exerting effort to discriminate and be selective becomes an obstacle, which is why the sūtra says not to be reflective and so forth. This is called "being attached to the Dharma which accords with the way," which is like eating raw or unripened food that gives one indigestion and causes one to become sick.[78] It can also be compared to shooting an arrow: if one is too nervous and tense, one may not hit the target. Here is another analogy: A long time ago, there was a person who wrote a letter to a person of high status, but, fearful of having made a mistake, he sealed and reopened it many times; finally, out of confusion, he mailed an empty envelope. His blunder became the butt of jokes. Likewise, when one has successfully reached the state of having the contemplative mind, one should not again deliberately discriminate.

174 Relying on the right understanding of emptiness,
Investigate and dwell in tranquillity.
With cessation and contemplation complementing each other,
One can skillfully enter calmness and extinction.

In order to cultivate prajñā and to be in accord with reality, one must first profoundly and carefully come to the decision that everything exists through conventional designation and is without inherent nature. Then one can attain the firm right understanding that sees no conflict between nonexistence and existence. Both the existence of conventional designation and emptiness and the nonexistence of an inherent nature are complementary and do not contradict each other. Thus it is said, "The appearance of existence is fundamentally empty; fundamental emptiness is the appearance of existence." To cultivate the wisdom that comes from listening and thinking means to have a profound understanding that there is no inherent nature; it does not mean annihilating all that exists through mundane dependent origination.

Following the Sequence of Cessation and Contemplation to Attain Direct Realization

If one has not yet attained a meditative mind, one's inattentive mind still investigates with discrimination. If, when practicing cessation, one has attained light bliss and achieved right concentration, then one can use the right understanding of empty nature (which does not contradict conventional existence) to practice contemplation. This contemplation relies on concentration to enter the stage of cultivating wisdom.

One then takes emptiness, the nonexistence of an inherent nature, as one's object of focus and investigation. This is called "differentiating with respect to the image." After investigating the image for a long time, one then practices calm abiding with emptiness as one's object of focus. Such concentration is called "not differentiating with respect to the image." This is nondiscrimination without additional investigation. Having abided calmly, one can then practice investigation again. This practice of mixing cessation and contemplation consistently takes emptiness, the nonexistence of an inherent nature, as its object of focus.

When the contemplative mind is skillful, it abides calmly, clearly, and purely like the clear sky without any hazy clouds. At that time, "all things are directed toward emptiness." Contemplating all the appearances of things, one sees nothing for the emotions to dwell on; everything is just like wisps of smoke. When the practice of contemplation is nearly accomplished, one should lessen one's effort; only when light bliss arises again from the power of contemplation can it be said that one has accomplished the practice of contemplation. Thereafter, cessation and contemplation complement each other, and this is called "the cooperation of cessation and contemplation."

With the wisdom that comes from contemplation of nondiscrimination, the abiding mind of nondiscrimination can arise. This abiding mind in turn brings forth the wisdom of nondiscrimination. When cessation and contemplation are in equilibrium, the power of contemplation is profound and thorough. In the end, even the form of emptiness disintegrates and disappears, and one can skillfully enter the calmness and extinction of the nonarising nature of things. Then, prajñā—nondiscriminating wisdom—comes forth: "prajñāpāramitā can extinguish all deviant views, afflictions, and meaningless elaborations and can lead to fundamental emptiness."[79] It is also said, "The eye of wisdom sees nothing at all."[80] The doctrine of mere consciousness also says that the true realization of the way is separate from all forms. The wisdom that comes from fundamental emptiness—the wisdom that enables a common person to become a sage—was also known to the Indian Mahāyāna scholars. It is so superior that it cannot be compared with the skillful means that have been proposed in the latter days of the Dharma for the purpose of integrating everything, for such proposals do not emphasize the important points.

175 Excellent is the true prajñā!
Excellent is the true liberation!
Following this unparalleled and holy wisdom,
One can perfectly complete all virtues.

The skillful practice of prajñāpāramitā is the only one that enables ordinary people to enter the level of sages. Thus it is especially praised. Excellent it is! This is the true prajñā that was realized and expounded by the Buddha! It is not just the intellectual understanding of ordinary people and non-Buddhists. It is also not the seeming wisdom that comes from the Hīnayāna and Mahāyāna practitioners who think there is something that can be attained. It points out the root of the basic problem of birth and death among sentient beings and provides fundamental breakthroughs on the important points.

So profound and difficult is the meaning of "emptiness is the nature of things" that worldly scholars cannot dream of it. Excellent indeed! Only through it can one attain true liberation, which is very different from the liberation imagined by non-Buddhists and ignorant people, for whom this means being reborn in the heavens or in a state of deep concentration.

The sūtra says, "Relying on prajñāpāramitā, bodhisattvas have no hindrances in their minds; because there are no hindrances, they have no fear. Staying far away from distorted imagination, they reach the ultimate Nirvāṇa. Because all buddhas of the three periods rely on prajñāpāramitā, they attain the anuttara-samyak-saṃbodhi."[81] Both the virtue of Nirvāṇa, which is shared in common with the śrāvakas, and the virtue of great bodhi, which is not, rely on this unparalleled holy wisdom for the complete perfection of all virtues. Thus, it is said that prajñāpāramitā is the very profound Dharma treasury of all the buddhas. Studying Buddhism without practicing this doctrine would be like coming across a mountain of treasures and returning empty-handed!

The Three Different Systems of Thought

176 The nature of the Dharma has never been dual
But is presented differently under different conditions.
Whether a system of thought reveals the whole truth or not,
Wise people should skillfully make their own decision.

To attain liberation from birth and death and become a buddha, one must rely on the direct realization of the nature of things. The nature of things—the reality of all things—has never been dual or differentiated. "It is characterized by being universal and one." All the sages of the Two Vehicles, bodhisattvas, and buddhas have realized this same nature of things. Sages, a sūtra says, "are differentiated by the unconditioned nature of things."[82] In reality, there is no difference in the unconditioned nature of things; the levels of its realization differ, however. For example, empty space is fundamentally without differentiation, but because there are square or round containers, space is said to be square or round.

Relying on dependent origination, the Buddha realized the nature of things. This is why he also expounded the nature of things based on dependent origination. This nature is fundamentally without differentiation, but it must be presented skillfully as different teachings under different conditions. The nature of things is very profound: when it is taught, some people will not understand or accept it and indeed may even slander it.

The Mahāyāna Dharma can be divided into three different great systems. Venerable Master Taixu called them the Wisdom of the Empty Nature of Things system, the Mere Consciousness of the Forms of Things system, and the Complete Enlightenment of the Realm of Things system. I call them the Empty Nature Mere Name system (Madhyamaka), the False Imagination Mere Consciousness system (Yogācāra), and the Truly Eternal Mere Mind system (Tathāgatagarbha). Though the names are different, the contents are basically similar. The ancient Huayan tradition, which understands the development of these systems differently, divided the Mahāyāna into the Form of Things tradition, the Refuting Form tradition, and the Nature of Things tradition; these are also the three systems of the Mahāyāna.

Sometimes, these three systems may confuse people. Adherents of the three may be at odds with one another, each group believing that its own system reveals the whole truth and the others do not. For example, the Hua Yen tradition is based on the third system, so it depicts the first two as temporal teachings and its own tradition as the real one. The Yogācāra tradition, based on the second system, proclaims itself "the tradition corresponding to the truth" and calls the first system a teaching of unwholesome emptiness and the third system the particular philosophy of "this land"—that is, *Chinese* Buddhism. The Three Treatises tradition (Madhyamaka) is based on the first system and calls itself the "Great Vehicle that realizes that there is nothing attainable" and unavoidably overcriticizes scholars of other systems.

Since each of these traditions offers sūtras as proof and claims to possess treatises that reveal the whole truth, the disputes have been difficult to resolve. Since these issues are concerned with the nature of things and the practice directed toward the realization of prajñā, one cannot carelessly generalize about them. What does it really mean to reveal the whole truth or not? Who is really revealing the whole truth? Wise people should skillfully come to their own decisions. Only then can they thoroughly understand the real aims of the Buddha Dharma and also the great function of skillful means as taught by the Buddha.

Although the prajñā nature of things was briefly explained above according to scriptures, this explanation may not be read sympathetically by scholars of other systems. So it is essential to explain the three schools. To do so briefly, the different opinions of the scholars of later periods will be put aside; information will be sought directly from the fundamental scriptures. Although this information may not entirely suit the taste of all readers, it is less likely to merely reflect my own biases.

The Empty Nature Mere Name System

177 All things arise from conditions.
Dependent origination has no inherent nature and is empty.
Because it is empty, it has to arise in accordance with conditions.
Thus are all things established.
The meaning of the Middle Way in both existence and emptiness
Has been discussed above.

The Mahāyāna Empty Nature Mere Name system is based on, among others, the prajñā and Mādhyamika scriptures. One thing needs to be clarified at the outset: the first priority of the Indian teaching of Mahāyāna (like Hīnayāna) was to establish how all things are related and how the karmic results of good or evil and the confusing transmigration of births and deaths come into existence. These are the extremely essential teachings upon which the discourses of the good Dharmas of human and divine beings rely.

On the other hand, how to thoroughly understand the nature of things, eliminate illusions, and realize the truth is the basis for the holy Dharma of the Three Vehicles. Thus, it was necessary to establish what course of practice could lead to Nirvāṇa and the completion of bodhi. These are actually the two great doctrines of the accumulation of suffering and the way to extinction. Although these doctrines cannot be completely understood by ordinary people, those who truly teach Mahāyāna Buddhism will never forget them. Judging from the teachings and realizations of the scriptures, the main difference between the three systems of the Mahāyāna Buddha Dharma lies in the different views of how all things are established, karmic results in particular.

According to the *Wu jin yi jing* (Sūtra [Taught by] Akṣayamaṭi), those sūtras that demonstrate the worldly and the ordinary reveal only the partial truth, while those that demonstrate the extraordinary are sūtras that reveal the whole truth. Those that are manifested in conventional designations, sentences, and establishments reveal the partial truth, while those manifested as profound and abstruse reveal the whole truth. Those that reveal the existence of the self reveal the partial truth, while those that reveal the nonexistence of the self, emptiness, and birthlessness reveal the whole truth.[83] This is similar to the teachings of the *Sanmodi wang jing* (Samādhi-rāja [Moon Lamp] Sūtra), and other sūtras.[84]

The *Prajñāpāramitā Sūtra*, the *Mūlamadhyamaka-kārikā*, and other scriptures likewise extensively proclaim that the nonexistence of inherent nature, emptiness, and neither production nor extinction are the ultimate teachings and that they reveal the whole truth with well-defined principles. According to this position, the self and all things are worldly and conventional establishments. From the karmic results of birth and death to the attainment of the accomplishment of the Three Vehicles, and even Nirvāṇa, all things are established upon conditioned existence; all things exist "only in name, only conventionally." All things in ordinary worldly existence are established by perception through name and speech; but, based on extraordinary investigation, they have no inherent nature and cannot be established. This is the "establishment of all things based on fundamental impermanence,"[85] as opposed to the establishment of everything based on real characteristics. As the *Prajñāpāramitā Sūtra* explains, "The world has names, such as śrotāpanna, and even arhat, pratyekabuddha, and buddha; but in the supreme reality, there is no knowledge, no attainment, no śrotāpanna, and no buddha.... In the world's terminology the six transmigratory states are different, but according to the supreme reality they are not.... In supreme reality, there is no karma or result."[86] Also: "The self is like an illusion or a dream.... The Buddha Way is like an illusion or a dream.... I say Nirvāṇa is also like an illusion or a dream. If there is something surpassing Nirvāṇa, I say it is also like an illusion or a dream."[87] This is the real proof that everything is like an illusion or a dream and is only conventionally designated and mundanely established.

The Mādhyamikans, who thoroughly understand the profound view of the Empty Nature Mere Name system, say that matter and mind, defilement and purity, worldly and world-transcending things are conventional establishments ("conventional designations") and arise from conditions. This is actually the fundamental position that was taught by the Buddha in the *Sheng yi kong jing* (Sūtra on the Emptiness of Ultimate Truth). Everything that arises from conditions exists as conventional designations. Extraordinary investigation reveals that everything is empty without inherent nature and that not a single dharma can be established.

This does not mean that emptiness, the nonexistence of an inherent nature, annihilates everything and denies the establishment of all things, however. On the contrary, if things were not empty and without an inherent nature but instead had an inherent nature, then they would be things with a fixed existence. A thing that really existed and had an inherent nature would not need to arise from conditions. In such a case, that which had not arisen could not arise, that which had not become extinct could not become extinct, and ordinary people would remain ordinary people and could not become buddhas! Fortunately, because of emptiness everything has to arise from conditions; relying on causes and conditions, all things can be established. Those doing good will get good rewards, while those doing evil will get evil retributions. Those who are confused will transmigrate through the cycle of birth and death, while those who are enlightened will be liberated.

Moreover, relying on the dependent origination of empty nature, one will neither be attached to birth and death nor abide in Nirvāṇa but will instead extensively practice the bodhisattva deeds to become a buddha. If there is no emptiness, nothing can be established; with emptiness, everything can be established. This is explained in the chapter "Contemplating the Four Truths" in the *Mūlamadhyamaka-kārikā* and is firmly evidenced in the *Vigraha-vyāvartanī* (Treatise on Ending Disputes) through such quotations as "Relying on the existence of emptiness, all things can be established"[88] and "Whoever has attained this emptiness has attained the whole truth."[89] All things are established according to dependent origination in accord with emptiness.

Thus, from the perspective of the conventional establishment of the world, everything is like an illusion; from the perspective of the nonexistence of an inherent nature, everything is empty. Illusory existence does not contradict empty nature, and empty nature does not contradict illusory existence. The Middle Way, in which emptiness and conventional existence as well as the two truths simultaneously exist without contradiction, is the teaching of the whole truth according to the Empty Nature tradition. This presentation is identical to the earlier discussions on the prajñāpāramitā.

The False Imagination Mere Consciousness System

178 All things are without an inherent nature.
Those who skillfully understand will be able to understand this.
But for those who have not accomplished the five deeds,
The Buddha repeatedly explained the *Saṃdhinirmocana Sūtra.*

The system of False Imagination Mere Consciousness is based on the *Saṃdhinirmocana Sūtra* (Sūtra on the Explication of the Underlying Meaning), the *Yogācāra-bhūmi* (Yoga Treatises), and other texts. The teaching as transmitted by Master Xuanzang that the forms of things are mere consciousness best expresses the gist of this system. The *Prajñāpāramitā Sūtra* has been described as a teaching of the Second Period (in this periodization, Hīnayāna teachings are those of the First Period) and the *Saṃdhinirmocana Sūtra* as of the Third Period. In addition, Asaṅga transmitted the *Yogācāra-bhūmi* after Nāgārjuna. Thus, the scriptures of this system appeared later than did the scriptures of prajñā.

Indescribableness is the ultimate nature of all things, which nothing surpasses; this indescribable nature is the whole truth. This is the view established by the Mādhyamikans in reliance upon the *Prajñāpāramitā Sūtra* and the *Wu jin yi jing.* In the *Saṃdhinirmocana Sūtra*'s view, however, the whole truth and esoteric (partial) truth are relative; that which is explained clearly and is easily understandable reveals the whole truth, while that which is explained in a concealed and secret manner reveals the partial truth. In extraordinary truth, therefore, that which is esoteric and that which is whole are differentiated. When relying on the Buddha's teaching in the *Saṃdhinirmocana Sūtra* to understand the extraordinary (empty) nature of things, one should realize that the reason why both esoteric truth and the whole truth exist is the different fundamental capacities of sentient beings.

The sūtra says, "All things have no inherent nature, there is neither birth nor extinction. Being fundamentally calm and quiet, inherent nature is Nirvāṇa. After listening to the Dharma of this sūtra, those sentient beings who have already planted the good roots of the superior grade and cleared various afflictions and who continue to mature, to practice the Mahāyāna teachings, and to accumulate the superior provisions of blessings and wisdom will understand the very esoteric meanings of my (the

Buddha's) teaching in accordance with the truth. They will have deep faith regarding such Dharma and will thoroughly understand such principle as the truth through their right wisdom. Because they rely on this wisdom to understand thoroughly and practice skillfully, they can swiftly realize the ultimate."[90] From this it is clear that those with a mature fundamental capacity, having the ability to skillfully understand the profound nature of things, can realize and align themselves with the teaching that all things have no inherent nature. They can do this through the right wisdom that comes from practice and do not require the Buddha's teachings from the *Saṃdhinirmocana Sūtra.*

However, those who have not accomplished all of the five deeds have problems with the teaching that all things are without an inherent nature. The sūtra says that there are sentient beings who have planted good roots of the superior grade, cleared various afflictions, continued to mature, and frequently practiced the Mahāyāna teachings but who have not yet accumulated the superior provisions of blessings and wisdom. Some, after listening to this teaching, feel that it is extremely difficult. They cannot understand it but are able to believe in it (interpreting it according to their own opinions). They think that "all things being empty and without inherent nature" is synonymous with total nonexistence (Nāgārjuna called them "non-Buddhist followers of Mahāyāna"). They receive no eventual benefit for themselves, and on the contrary their wisdom regresses. As for those who listen to these people when they teach, some follow their teachers and become attached to the view of nonexistence, while some object to the teaching that all things have an empty nature.

In addition, after listening to the teaching that all things have no inherent nature, those who have not accomplished all of the five deeds without belief or understanding say, "These were not the Buddha's words, they were spoken by Māra."[91] This is similar to what Nāgārjuna relates: "The five hundred sects of śrāvakas…heard the teaching that everything is fundamentally empty as is taught in the prajñā sūtras and felt as if a knife had been thrust in their hearts."[92] For those with dull capacities who believe but do not understand or misunderstand, or who neither believe nor understand, the Buddha repeatedly taught the *Saṃdhinirmocana Sūtra*: "Relying on the three types of nature that have no inherent nature, with secret intention I declare that all things are without inherent nature."[93] Actually, things that originate dependently—are of dependent nature—and things that are calm and extinct—are of ultimately real nature—do inherently exist. It is not that everything is nonexistent; some things are nonexistent and others really exist. Only this teaching quells the objections of those who neither believe nor understand. Those who mistakenly believe that everything is nonexistent will also no longer misunderstand. Those who believe but do not understand can rely on this to practice as well.

According to the sūtra, this is the teaching of the whole truth for those who have accomplished all five deeds and are able to realize that all things are empty without inherent nature and that everything can be established. However, there are those with weak ability, who have not accomplished the five deeds and who are unable to establish all things or who annihilate all things in light of the teaching that "all things are empty without inherent nature." For them, this teaching is so esoteric and abstruse that they need Buddha's simple explanation. The meaning of Nāgārjuna's treatise is also like this. This is analogous to people thinking of the ocean as extremely deep, but since King Rāhu-asura can stand in it with the water only coming up to his navel, how deep can it be? Similarly, people who lived in the mountains heard that salt was a taste-enhancer, so they put a handful of salt in their mouths; it was intolerable. Ordinary people clearly understand that salt can enhance taste, but in the mind of these ignorant people living in the mountains, this fact is esoteric and abstruse. Therefore, whether something is abstruse or not, esoteric or not, is not dependent on the Dharma itself but on the fundamental capacities of the listener.

179 Either there is no inherent nature
Or there is inherent existence.

The doctrine of the Yogācāra transmitted by Asaṅga is based on the *Saṃdhinirmocana Sūtra*'s explanation of the whole truth, which is expounded for those who have not accomplished the five deeds. Such people hold that "all things are without inherent nature and exist conventionally" is equivalent to "nothing exists," and in which case nothing could be established. Thus they reason that it is only correct to have two categories—conventional existence without inherent nature and real existence with inherent nature—and that "based on the real, the conventional is established." A quote from the scriptures illustrates this point: "The various aggregates such as form and so forth must exist prior to the conventional establishment of the pudgala; there has to be something real in order for the conventional establishment of the pudgala to exist. For this to be the case, something real—various things such as form, etc.—must exist before the conventional descriptions of various things such as form, etc., are able to become manifest; without something real the conventional descriptions of various things such as form, etc., cannot become manifest. If there is only conventional existence—without something real and without any foundation—then even conventional existence cannot exist; thus, such a position is called annihilating all things."[94]

In the *Saṃdhinirmocana Sūtra* the conventional is divided into two types: the imaginary and the dependent. "What is the imaginary character of all things? Through conventional designation, all things, including verbal expressions that arise from this process, are established as having different inherent natures. What is the dependent character of all things? That the inherent natures of all things arise from conditions."[95] The imaginary character "comes from the establishment of conventional designation, not from the establishment of individual existence; this is why it is called the character with a nature that is without inherent nature." The arising of a thing in dependence upon another (the dependent character) "exists by virtue of dependence on other conditions and not by itself; this is why it is called arising with a nature that is without inherent nature."[96] Therefore, the fundamental position of this system is limited to two options. Either there is a conventional existence that is without inherent nature that, in conventional discourse, is said to have inherent nature; this is the imaginary character. Or there is really something that has inherent existence that is called the indescribable inherent nature; this is the dependent nature.

Things that arise from causes and conditions have inherent existence. This means that inherent nature is engendered from the conditions of all things. Alternatively, the indescribable self-nature is called the nature of the eighteen realms (which are the six sense organs with their corresponding objects and consciousnesses), in which "realm" has the sense of "not losing its inherent nature." It is not that these things are grasped as having real existence; when they are engendered from causes and conditions, they already inherently exist. This is fundamentally different from the view of Mādhyamikans, who perceive this as the characteristic feature of meaningless elaboration—that which is seemingly real but is actually unreal. With regard to everything that is grasped as having real existence, however, both systems generally acknowledge that there is no inherent nature.

From the perspective of the Buddha's teaching there should not be any dispute. Those who have accomplished all of the five deeds understand that "all things are without inherent nature and are only conventionally designated," that emptiness does not contradict existence, and that by relying on emptiness all things can be established and can exist. Thus they can believe and understand reality with penetrating thoroughness. On the other hand, those who have not accomplished the five deeds are bound to misunderstand—holding, for example, that "all things are empty" means that everything does not exist and that since emptiness is nonexistence, of course nothing can be established. But if such persons rely on the simple and explicit explanation that says that there is really something with inherent existence, then they can believe and understand that all things are empty, and gradually enter the Buddha Way.

However, the Yogācārins of later years—not knowing that the teachings of Maitreya and Asaṅga were for those of a certain fundamental nature, those who have not accomplished the five deeds—are unable to understand the intent of the Tathāgata's teaching. On the contrary, they think that without regard for a person's fundamental capacity, they must rely on the *Saṃdhinirmocana Sūtra*'s explanation of the whole truth.

This, however, raises some problems. First, they think that although the Prajñā sūtras teaching—that all things are empty—was of course thoroughly understood by the Buddha, it is not explained clearly and is easily misunderstood, so they must follow the new explanation in the *Saṃdhinirmocana Sūtra*. Second, although they dare not refute Nāgārjuna, they instead say that Nāgārjuna's meaning is the same as theirs (as was explained in the *Saṃdhinirmocana Sūtra*). They also firmly oppose the Mādhyamikans as well as the teaching of the whole truth that all things are of empty nature and are only conventionally designated. They even say, "Do not talk with them. Do not live with them,"[97] thereby stirring up discord between sects.

If only they recalled that there are still those have been able to accomplish all of the five deeds and who have the profound understanding that "because of the existence of emptiness, all things can be established," then the different sects could suit different capacities and preach their own ways without dispute!

> 180 Dependent origination that has inherent existence
> Is baseless discrimination.
> Based on consciousness, dependent origination can be established
> And then cause and effect can be well founded.

That which arises from conditions and has inherent existence is identical with dependent nature. Being dependent on others is the law of all dependent origination. But the Mahāyāna Mere Consciousness system takes mere consciousness as its main doctrine, so being dependent on others is, by nature, baseless discrimination. That is, it is the faulty consciousness (sentient beings' manifest activities have never been faultless).

There are eight types of consciousnesses, but the "fundamental discrimination" is the so-called "basis of all knowledge"—ālaya consciousness—which is the foundation of all things. Relying on the fundamental ālaya consciousness, all things that are produced by dependent origination are established. Ālaya consciousness, which is also translated as "storehouse consciousness," contains infinite "seeds." These seeds engender manifest activities—the seven consciousnesses along with the associated mental activities, sense organs, objects, and the world as receptacle. When all these things are engendered, they in turn are "perfumed" to become seeds stored in ālaya consciousness. In this way, the nature of the ālaya consciousness is that of seeds, and all cause and effect can be well founded.

Students of the Mere Consciousness tradition rely on inherent existence to establish all things, so cause and effect also inherently exist. Ālaya consciousness, which is by nature seedlike, is called "the dependent origination of discriminating inherent nature." For example, the seed of eye consciousness engenders eye consciousness, the seed of the ear engenders the ear, the seed of greed engenders greed, the seed of the color green engenders the color green, the seed of the faulty engenders the faulty, the seed of the faultless engenders the faultless. Whatever seed engenders a particular manifest activity is in turn "perfumed" to become a particular seed. This seedlike nature is called "the differentiated function of direct production of the seed's own fruit"; this is the view of cause and effect in which inherent nature is understood to produce inherent nature. In addition to the seed, other factors still need to be present before the fruit is produced, however; this is called dependence or "relying on another to arise."

As can be seen, this mere consciousness view of cause and effect—that the seed of inherent existence engenders the manifest activity of inherent existence—and the emptiness view of cause and effect—that there is no inherent nature—differ significantly.

181 Things outside the mind are nonexistent,
And the mind's consciousness is not, in principle, nonexistent.
Realizing that false external objects are manifested through
mere consciousness,
One can enter reality.

Based on the view of cause and effect in which consciousness faultily discriminates, seeds engender manifest activities, and manifest activities perfume seeds, it can be said that things outside the mind are nonexistent. Sentient beings intuitively think that external objects are real and are objectively existing forms—that is, matter. Upon introspection, the mind also seems to be a perceived object. Sentient beings have held this distorted and erroneous view from the beginning, and all their attachments to the self and things come from it. This is the imaginary character that is empty, without inherent nature. But the conventional must be based on the real; the mind's consciousness, which inherently exists and is the basis for all of conventional existence, is not, in principle, nonexistent. If the mind's consciousness were also to be without inherent nature, then nothing could be established.

Because, since beginningless time, the mind and the objects have been connected to one another and "perfumed" to become "seeds," consciousness is baseless but has individuality. When consciousness is engendered from its own seed, then that seed, that phenomenon, which has consciousness as its nature, therefore also engenders manifest activity. That which has become manifest has two characteristic features: that which can discriminate and that which is the object of discrimination. It seems that the mind and the object are independent, but actually the object is not separate from the mind and has mental consciousness as its nature.

Although the form of the object outside the mind does not exist, the form of the object that is not separate from the mind's consciousness does exist and is engendered from the seed of the object itself (this is called the natural object; it is nonexistent only if it is formed from the erroneous attachment of the mind's consciousness). Thus, all the causes and effects that have a dependent nature can be established; nevertheless, the nature of all things is consciousness! They all also exist inherently, so they cannot be said to be empty without inherent nature.

Just as mere consciousness is relied upon to establish cause and effect, mere consciousness is also relied upon to establish confusion and enlightenment. Sentient beings—not understanding that the external, the phenomenal, is mere consciousness—are utterly confused and mixed up, and take these as the source for their attachment to the self and to things. From this erroneous attachment the afflictions arise and create karmic results, which are then "perfumed" in ālaya consciousness. When the seed of karma matures, reward or retribution is received. Ālaya consciousness is therefore called consciousness with fruits that mature at varying times—such is the essence of the transmigrations through the cycles of birth and death. On the other hand, if one relies on contemplation to thoroughly understand that external objects are really nonexistent, that they lack inherent nature, and that they manifest and become established only through consciousness, then, based on their dependent nature, one can know that their imaginary nature is empty.

If phenomena are empty and cannot be attained, then baseless discriminating consciousness will not arise. Realizing that objects are not attainable and that consciousness is in turn not attainable, one can enter the reality of mere consciousness—emptiness, the truth. The truly real nature is that which relies for its manifestation on nonattaching dependent nature; thus it also cannot be said to be empty. For example: "It is said, the reason for mere imaginary nature is the object; the reason for dependent nature is discrimination; the reason for ultimately real nature is the twofold emptiness"; and "Based on consciousness that is attainable, objects that cannot be attained are engendered. Based on objects that cannot be attained, consciousness that cannot be attained is engendered. Because by nature consciousness can be attained, it also becomes that which cannot be attained. Thus, it is known that both that which is attained and that which is not attained are equal."[98]

Consciousness is attainable and exists inherently; and based on this, cause and effect and confusion and enlightenment can be established.

Such is the main doctrine of the False Imagination Mere Consciousness system. For those who have not accomplished all of the five deeds, this doctrine is truly ingenious. Moreover, establishing the conventional based on the real was originally the basic position of the Hīnayāna Sarvāstivādin (a realist school). Embracing and transforming the teachings of the Hīnayāna Sarvāstivādins into the Mahāyāna teaching that the nature of all things is empty—through explaining the true nature of all things and the eighteen realms through the doctrine of mere consciousness—demonstrates the inconceivably skillful means of the Buddha and the bodhisattvas.

The Truly Eternal Mere Mind System

182 Some may think that the law of arising and extinction
Cannot be the foundation of being bound and being liberated
Because they are afraid of the phrase "the nonexistence of the self."
Therefore, the Buddha again embraced them with skillful means.

This system is based on *Tathāgatagarbha*—that is, the realm of the Tathāgatas, the realm of sentient beings, the original inherent purity of the mind—as described in the sūtras *Ru lai zang* (Tathāgatagarbha), *Śrīmālādevī*, *Laṅkāvatāra*, and so on and in treatises such as *Ratnagotravibhāga* (Treatise on the Discrimination of the Precious Nature), *Dasheng qi xin lun* (Awakening of Faith), and so forth. In India and China, the broad transmission of this system was subsequent to that of the prajñā scriptures.

The Mādhyamikans, following the ultimate teaching that neither the self nor things have inherent nature, say that dependent origination arises and perishes like an illusion, which is in accord with the Dharma seals of impermanence and the nonexistence of the self. The Yogācārins' position on inherent existence is that all things arise and perish impermanently. They also say that of the six characteristics of seeds, the first one is momentariness. With regard to the nonexistence of the pudgala self, they are also penetratingly thorough (the Hīnayāna Sarvāstivādin and Sautrāntika systems are also close to the Yogācāra system in this respect). For theists and those non-Buddhists who are connected to the Buddha Dharma, however, such a concept is extremely difficult to believe and understand. How can there be transmigration without an entity of the self? If birth and extinction are momentary, how can the previous life and the future life be connected? In the Buddha Dharma these questions have been asked since ancient times. For example: "If the self is really nonexistent, who is it that goes from one state of existence to another in the cycles of birth and death?"[99]

The *Laṅkāvatāra Sūtra* says, "If the birth and extinction of aggregates, the elements, and the sense organs are without a self, then who is born? Who perishes? Ignorant people follow birth and death without realizing that suffering can be ended, and without knowing Nirvāṇa."[100] The above passage, spoken by Great Wisdom Bodhisattva, represents the questions of the typical ignorant person who thinks that without permanence and a self neither transmigration nor liberation can be established. In the minds of ignorant people, everything is born and becomes extinct. Such impermanent birth and extinction is suffering, and thus they cannot imagine the ending of suffering and attainment of happiness! It seems to them that there has to be an eternal and immutable self.

This type of sentient being is found both inside and outside Buddhist teachings, for there are those who think that it is difficult for the law of birth and extinction to be the foundation both for birth and death and for Nirvāṇa. These sentient beings—described by the Buddha as being afraid of the phrase "nonexistence of the self"—are those who, upon hearing of the nonexistence of the self, become frightened that there is no foundation for being bound to birth and death and being liberated and therefore fear annihilation after death. The Buddha had to adapt to these people and embrace them with the skillful means of the doctrine of Tathāgatagarbha.

There are many sūtras on the Buddha's teaching of Tathāgatagarbha. These may create the impression that among sentient beings in the cycle of birth and death, or in the minds of sentient beings, there exists an entity like the Tathāgata that has the appearance of complete wisdom and virtue or of the splendid marks and signs. Such would be very close to the Indian teaching of the atman. Thus, based on ten Mahāyāna sūtras—the Tathāgatagarbha scriptures—the Tibetan Jonangpa school established the Mahāyāna Buddhist system of the ātman. The Chinese also have this type of doctrine, which holds the realization of the "real" self as supreme. Fortunately the Buddha knew of sentient beings' ignorance and defined in advance the real meaning of Tathāgatagarbha in the *Laṅkāvatāra Sūtra.*

Thus, although this teaching embraces and transforms the non-Buddhists who advocate the reality of the self, it is actually linked to the Mahāyāna teachings of emptiness.

183 The profound Tathāgatagarbha
Is the basis of good and evil.

Sentient beings, represented by Great Wisdom Bodhisattva, requested that the primary entity of transmigration in birth and death have a buddha's Nirvāṇa essence. For such persons the Buddha taught the Tathāgatagarbha doctrine. It is said, for example, "Tathāgatagarbha is the source of good and evil. It can create all the sentient beings of all the transmigratory states, like a magician who can transform himself into various characters.... Inherent nature is without defilement and is ultimately pure."[101] That which is transformed into various characters like a magician can be said to be the primary entity of transmigration. That inherent nature is without defilement and is ultimately pure reveals the original existence of the buddha's Nirvāṇa essence, taught widely in the Tathāgatagarbha sūtras.

The very profound Tathāgatagarbha, which the Tathāgata thoroughly realized with complete clarity, can be only partially realized by the great bodhisattvas with sharp capacity and profound wisdom. Why is it called Tathāgatagarbha? In the causal ground of sentient beings, perfect and ultimate buddhahood can be described as "already accomplished." For example: "The pure inherent nature of Tathāgatagarbha transforms into the thirty-two characteristic features and enters the bodies of all sentient beings like a priceless treasure that is covered by dirty clothes. The storehouse of the Tathāgata, being eternal and immutable, is also like this. It is covered by the dirty clothes of the aggregates, the elements, and the senses and is defiled by the afflictions of greed, anger, and unreal and erroneous thoughts."[102] Therefore, Tathāgatagarbha can be explained as that which contains all the Tathāgata's virtues and which, more important, is mainly covered by defiled things. Thus, when dissociated from the covering afflictions, Tathāgatagarbha is also called Dharma body.

As for Tathāgatagarbha being the primary entity of transmigration and liberation, it is said that "this Dharma body, which has passed through the bonds of boundless afflictions since the beginning of time, following the ups and downs of the world in the cycle of birth and death, is called sentient beings." (This refers to that which "transforms into various characters like an actor," as described in the *Laṅkāvatāra Sūtra.*) It is also said that "The realm of sentient beings is the Dharma body, and the Dharma body is the realm of sentient beings."[103] Sentient beings and buddhas are equal; there is no difference between them. Thus where sentient beings exist, this is called the realm of sentient beings; where bodhisattvas exist is the realm of bodhisattvas, and where Tathāgatas exist is the realm of Tathāgatas. On the surface, this doctrine appears to be very similar to that of the great Brahman (which is analogous to the Dharma body) and the atman (which is analogous to the realm of sentient beings) in the Vedānta philosophy of India.

Through Tathāgatagarbha, birth, death, and Nirvāṇa as well as sentient beings and buddhas are established, so Tathāgatagarbha is called "the source of good and evil." In other words, it is the cause for the defilement of birth and death and also for the purity of buddhahood. There are said to be many different kinds of causes, however. For example, there are ten causes in the Yogācāra and six causes in the Sarvāstivādin. What kind of causes are these actually? Some scholars are influenced by the metaphysics of myriad things coming from one origin—the production of wonderful existence from eternal nothingness—and think that good and evil have always existed within Tathāgatagarbha, that they have Tathāgatagarbha as their substance, and that they are engendered from Tathāgatagarbha. This cannot be explained in detail here.

In short, Tathāgatagarbha was regarded in India as the cause, and this understanding certainly had its own meaning there and then. For example, as said in the *Śrīmālādevī Sūtra*, "Tathāgatagarbha, separate from the conditioned form, is eternal and immutable. So Tathāgatagarbha is that which is depended upon, it is that which supports, and it is that which establishes. The World-Honored One! It is not separate, not cut off, not dissociated, and not different from the inconceivable Buddha Dharma. The World-Honored One! That upon which the annihilating, dissociating, differing, and non-Buddhist conditioned things depend, and that by which they are supported and established, is Tathāgatagarbha."[104] This passage, and those resembling it in the *Wu shang yi jing* (Sūtra on the Unsurpassed Basis) and the *Ratnagotravibhāga,* all say much the same: that Tathāgatagarbha is depended upon, that it supports, that it establishes, and that these contributory conditions serve as causes.

For example, to say that the four elements can give form to matter definitely does not mean that the four elements are the substance that produces matter. Matter is said to be formed according to the five causes: production, dependence, establishment, support, and nurturing. All this means is that apart from the four elements, things that are formed cannot exist. (The phrase "It can form all the sentient beings of all transmigratory states" in the *Laṅkāvatāra Sūtra* also refers to the same process of formation.) Three of the five causes—dependence, support, and establishment—are the same as the sūtra's "that which is depended upon, that which supports, and that which establishes." Therefore, the existence of good and evil is based on Tathāgatagarbha, but their existence does not have Tathāgatagarbha as their substance, nor are they produced from the Tathāgatagarbha.

Tathāgatagarbha can be the cause that is depended upon, supports, and establishes because it is eternal and immutable. Even though sentient beings of various states of existence transmigrate or are liberated in Nirvāṇa, Tathāgatagarbha is eternally and immutably the basis of dependence for everything. Because it has such an eternal and immutable existence, those who hear of impermanence and the nonexistence of the self and become worried about the whereabouts of transmigration and liberation can feel relieved.

Tathāgatagarbha as the basis of dependence can be illustrated by the following analogy. The sun and the dark clouds depend on the empty sky to exist and are not separate from it. However, the sun and the dark clouds do not have the empty sky as their substance, and they are definitely not produced by it. In like manner, Tathāgatagarbha is the cause of birth, death, and Nirvāṇa.

How is Tathāgatagarbha the cause of evil? Since the beginning of time, there have been conditioned things not in accord with and separate from Tathāgatagarbha, although they depend on Tathāgatagarbha to exist: the aggregates, the elements, the sense organs, the afflictions of desire, anger, ignorance. These can be compared to the dust covering a clear mirror. Because of them, the transmigrations of defiled births and deaths continue. So it is said, "Based on Tathāgatagarbha there is birth and death."

How is it the cause of good? Again since the beginning there have been inconceivable Buddha Dharmas that are in accord with and not different or separate from Tathāgatagarbha, and that also depend on Tathāgatagarbha to exist—such is Buddha nature. Since these Buddha Dharmas are in accord with and not different from Tathāgatagarbha, why is there no talk of production but only of dependence? First, they are unconditioned Dharmas, which cannot be said to be produced. Second, if, for example, in ālaya consciousness there are faulty "seeds," they cannot be said to be different from ālaya consciousness. It can only be said that the faulty manifest activities are produced from the faulty seeds in ālaya consciousness. It cannot be said that they are produced from ālaya consciousness itself. To say that everything is produced from ālaya consciousness is to make the error of having one cause engender many effects. Therefore, to say that things are neither different nor separate does not mean that they are one. In the same way, that which sentient beings already have—that which can be the cause of the faultless and pure virtuous nature undifferentiated from Tathāgatagarbha—can only be said to "depend on Tathāgatagarbha"—that is, to rely on, to be supported by, and to be established by Tathāgatagarbha.

184 Being permeated by residual habits from beginningless time,
Tathāgatagarbha is called ālaya.
From it there is birth and death
And the realization of Nirvāṇa.

The most important thing about the Buddha's Tathāgatagarbha doctrine is that its eternal immutability and its Dharma body with pure inherent nature serve as the basis for birth and death and Nirvāṇa. Tathāgatagarbha is found in the aggregates, the elements, and the senses. Thus the teachings on Tathāgatagarbha are not necessarily integrated with ālaya consciousness as it is understood by the Mere Consciousness system. In the case of sentient beings, however, everything comes from the mind, and ālaya consciousness is the fundamental consciousness on which knowledge is based. So naturally this Tathāgatagarbha system of thinking is transformed: based on Tathāgatagarbha, ālaya consciousness exists, and based on ālaya consciousness everything exists.

Tathāgatagarbha with pure inherent nature exists deep in ālaya consciousness. Thus, in the *Śrīmālādevī Sūtra*, Tathāgatagarbha is also called the "the heart (mind) of pure inherent nature," a teaching that one's nature and mind is originally pure. From this, the True Mind system of thinking is developed. But this refers to the real heart (mind)—its core and essence—and should not be mistaken for the mind in general.

The *Abhidharma Mahāyāna Sūtra* says, "From beginningless time, all things have relied on the realm from which the existence of various transmigratory states and the realization of Nirvāṇa arise."[105] This realm is Tathāgatagarbha and is also ālaya consciousness. The connection between these two is as follows. Although the inherent nature of Tathāgatagarbha is pure, from beginningless time it has been permeated by the false and defiled residual habits of meaningless elaboration, which are then called ālaya consciousness—just as the vast sky, when covered by floating clouds, becomes neither bright nor clear. The content of the ālaya consciousness has a true form (Tathāgatagarbha) and a karmic form (permeated by meaningless elaboration); the union of these two is ālaya.

In Asaṅga's and Vasubandhu's teaching of Mere Consciousness, such an explanation would be difficult to believe or understand, but in this system the ālaya consciousness exists on the basis of Tathāgatagarbha! Originating from the defiled seeds of this ālaya consciousness—in which the karmic form is not separate from the true form of Tathāgatagarbha—are various states of existence within the transmigrations of birth and death. Since the Tathāgatagarbha is eternal, immutable, and inseparable from birth and death, it can be said to transmigrate through various states of existence. This can be compared to empty space being square in a square vessel and round in a round vessel.

Moreover, because the true form of ālaya consciousness—Tathāgatagarbha—has an inseparable and undifferentiated pure nature, this form is not embraced by ālaya consciousness but by the Dharma realm. (The Yogācāra teaching of the faultless seed is similar. Although this teaching is in accord with the scriptures, saying that the faultless seed is the same as conditioned arising and extinction does contradict them.)

Thus, one can be disgusted with birth and death and be delighted by Nirvāṇa; one is able to make the resolution to practice, to destroy afflictions, and to realize Nirvāṇa. If one can completely depart from all falseness and defilement and accomplish all pure virtues, then Tathāgatagarbha will be freed from its bonds. At this point, it is called the Dharma body and is no longer called ālaya consciousness.

The two systems of False Imagination Mere Consciousness and Truly Eternal Mere Mind expounded different teachings to suit different fundamental natures. But historically they occurred close together. Both take the dharma of real existence as the basis for the establishment of all things and the mind's consciousness as the center, and they seem to have influenced each other considerably.

185 The Buddha taught that the empty nature of things
Is Tathāgatagarbha.
True suchness is undifferentiated,
And should not be mixed with non-Buddhist views.

In order to reach non-Buddhists and some Hīnayāna practitioners attached to the self, the Tathāgata spoke of Tathāgatagarbha as eternal and immutable as well as transmigrating through the cycles of birth and death. He also said that the Tathāgata's wisdom, virtues, and splendid marks and signs are realized in the bodies of sentient beings. But what *is* this Tathāgatagarbha? Does it actually exist, with its boundless marks and signs, in miniature inside the bodies of sentient beings? Is it really the same as the non-Buddhists' notion of Self, the essence of which is the eternal and pure Brahman? The Tathāgata, being compassionate and skillful, specifically and clearly defined this term in the *Laṅkāvatāra Sūtra*: the empty nature of all things is called Tathāgatagarbha. In this sūtra he says, "The Tathāgatagarbha that I teach differs from the Self taught by non-Buddhists. Great Wisdom Bodhisattva! Sometimes, terms such as emptiness, formlessness, wishlessness, suchness, reality, the nature of things, the Dharma body, Nirvāṇa, being without an inherent nature, neither production nor extinction, fundamental stillness, the inherent nature of Nirvāṇa, and so forth, are used to describe Tathāgatagarbha. In order to put an end to ignorant people's fear of the nonexistence of the self, the Tathāgata, worthy of worship and perfectly enlightened, expounds the doctrine of Tathāgatagarbha which is separate from the state of erroneous imagination of nothingness.... For example, with the help of labor, water, wood, a wheel, and a rope, a potter can make various vessels out of clay. The Tathāgata is also like this. With regard to the Dharma, which is without inherent nature and which is separate from all features of false erroneous imagination, I spoke of either Tathāgatagarbha or the nonexistence of the self with various wise and skillful means."[106]

Tathāgatagarbha, then, is the profound empty nature of things, which points directly to the present body and mind of sentient beings—the fundamental nature that is empty and still. The reason fundamental nature was given a new guise and called "Tathāgatagarbha," as if it were the atman, was simply to teach non-Buddhists who were frightened of the phrase "the nonexistence of the self" and who, upon hearing that the self and things are empty and that the self does not exist, would refuse to accept this teaching and even slander it. Herein lies the Tathāgata's skillfulness: this teaching sounds like that of the atman, so people believed and accepted it. Later, through gradually deepening their understanding, they realized that their previous understanding was mistaken. What they had originally heard was the very thing that they were frightened of—emptiness and the nonexistence of the self.

According to the *Ratnagotravibhāga* the emptiness of things—true suchness—is undifferentiated: "The Dharma body is undifferentiated with respect to everything. True suchness is undifferentiated. They both have real Buddha nature. Thus it is said that sentient beings always have Tathāgatagarbha."[107] With respect to the undifferentiated nature of things, where there are sentient beings true suchness is called "the realm of sentient beings," and where there are buddhas it is called "the realm of the Tathāgatas." The undifferentiated nature of things is eternally pure, calm, and immutable. The Buddha took this undifferentiated nature of things to be his nature and body, so it is called Buddha nature and the Dharma body.

The *Ratnagotravibhāga* also says that Buddha nature was expounded in order to keep sentient beings far from the five kinds of faults—the fifth of which is "the conception that the body has an atman."[108] Believers and practitioners of the teaching of Tathāgatagarbha should pay particular attention to this point. They should not think that they have penetrated the ultimate truth when they are actually mixed up with non-Buddhist views.

The Integration of the Different Systems of Thought

186 With every transformation, these skillful means become more
admirable
While the empty nature of things remains nondual.
The wise should skillfully integrate them
As one pure Way.

Having explained prajñāpāramitā and glanced at some arguments about the Dharma, I shall offer some conclusions to this portion of the text.

Looking at the three Mahāyāna systems, one has to praise the Tathāgata's ingenuity—with each transformation, his skillful means become more admirable. But investigations into Tathāgatagarbha will always find a direct realization of the nondual and undifferentiated emptiness of things. For instance, the Empty Nature Mere Name system takes the direct contemplation of the empty nature of things as its primary purpose.

The False Imagination Mere Consciousness system expounds extensively upon the character of things. With regard to practices directed toward realization, this system first uses the existence of consciousness to prove the nonexistence of objects and then uses the nonexistence of objects to prove that consciousness will not arise, thereby arriving at the nonattainability of both the mind and objects. Because this system teaches inherent existence through dependence, there must also be reality even in the manifested emptiness that is without attachment. Nevertheless, this system can still eliminate boundless afflictions and put an end to various erroneous attachments. Thus, if one can progress up to the point of accomplishing all the five deeds, how can one not enter the direct contemplation of the real nonexistence of inherent nature? It was therefore unnecessary for Bhāvaviveka to take the empty nature of real existence as "true suchness in the semblance of the self"![109]

Although the Truly Eternal Mere Mind system established the teaching of Tathāgatagarbha, which resembles the atman, nevertheless the Buddha had long before revealed that "Tathāgatagarbha is without a self." The sequence of practice is, first, to contemplate the nonreal nature of external objects, which is called "meditation investigating the meaning." Then one proceeds to an understanding of the twofold nonexistence of the self and to the nonarising of erroneous imagination (consciousness), which is called "meditation focusing on suchness." Finally, when prajñā arises, one has achieved "Tathāgata meditation," which is "without any erroneous imagination and without a self with respect to things."[110] This sequence is similar to the sequence of direct contemplation practiced by adherents to the False Imagination Mere Consciousness system. The three systems are therefore different in their adaptation to sentient beings but are identical in that they eventually turn toward the direct realization of the empty nature of things.

With regard to the skillful means, the Empty Nature Mere Name system established all things in fundamental emptiness; for those who are unable to understand such a teaching, the skillful means of "relying on the real to establish the conventional" has to be used to teach inherent existence through dependence. This method is best adapted to the fundamental nature of Hīnayānists and can guide them to the Mahāyāna practice. In general, however, ordinary people and non-Buddhists do not believe in impermanence and the nonexistence of the self (emptiness). So the Buddha, using skillful means, said that Tathāgatagarbha resides in all sentient beings. This is extraordinarily effective in embracing and guiding those worried about the emptiness of the self and those non-Buddhists attached to the self.

Embracing and transforming the different fundamental natures of sentient beings—from those who have accomplished the five deeds to Hīnayānists to ordinary people and non-Buddhists—the scope of Tathāgatagarbha becomes ever broader. The skillfulness of this teaching is indeed superb, which is why it is so popular. Recently, the Christian journal *Jing Feng* said that Buddha nature (Tathāgatagarbha) is similar to the notions of God and the soul. Of course, non-Buddhists will use this similarity to lure Buddhist disciples, and against this we should be vigilant; nevertheless, this is a result of the similarity of such forms.

Moreover, establishing everything upon the emptiness of things is really a great action—like carrying bundles of straws through flames without their catching fire—which cannot actually be performed by the ordinary. But in reality there is nothing else on which all things can be based. So to transform those non-Buddhists who are attached to the self, the Buddha esoterically explained the emptiness of things as Tathāgatagarbha. This teaching seems to take the self as its basis of support, but it actually teaches the emptiness of things.

With regard to those who have not accomplished all of the five deeds and whose fundamental nature is similar to the Hīnayānists, the sūtra says, "The Buddha said that Tathāgatagarbha is ālaya. Ignorant people cannot understand that the storehouse is the ālaya consciousness."[111] Thus ālaya is indeed Tathāgatagarbha; that which is based on Tathāgatagarbha and is permeated by the false and unreal from beginningless time is called ālaya consciousness. It is a pity that some practitioners do not know that ālaya consciousness is actually based on the empty nature of things—Tathāgatagarbha—and therefore cannot realize this for themselves.

As for the faulty ālaya consciousness, it can only be said to be the center of birth and death and of defiled things. The ālaya consciousness is also based on and permeated by the transformation consciousness. The relationship between these consciousnesses is that they serve as cause and effect for each other. Therefore, the ālaya consciousness is only a relative basis of support.

The systems discussed above can be compared to different modes of selling medicine—a pill of immortality. (The *Laṅkāvatāra Sūtra* uses the parables of a doctor giving prescriptions and a potter making vessels.) The Empty Nature Mere Name system is like an old shop without elaborate decor that sells its medicine honestly. Only those who really know the goods will come to buy; some people dislike the medicine sold here because it looks unpleasant and has a strong odor, so they are unwilling to buy it. So a new storefront is installed and methods to promote sales are studied. The medicine is then made into capsules that are coated with sugar and packaged in exquisite bottles and boxes. The sale of the medicine increases, and more lives are saved. This is like the False Imagination Mere Consciousness system's teaching during the three periods of teaching. Ignorant children still do not want to take it, however, so another method is used: the medicine is mixed with large amounts of sugar and made into airplanes and dolls—resembling toys that are sold in the streets. In this way, more people buy the medicine and, theoretically, still more lives are saved. This is like the Truly Eternal Mind Only system.

Actually, all the medicines, if they are taken, can save lives just as well. That which save one's life is not the bottle, box, sugar coating, or capsule, to say nothing of sugary airplanes and dolls; it is the pill of immortality. The packaging is skillful means. Skillful means can lead to the ultimate, but only as a method and not the goal. The erroneous translation "skillful means are the ultimate" is harmful. If one buys a box or bottle because it is exquisite but does not want to take the medicine, this is wrong. If, after buying the airplane or doll, one fondly looks at it or plays with it as if it were a toy, this is a real shame. If the medicine is mixed with too much sugar, moreover, it may become too weak or its properties may change, such that taking it cannot save one's life. Selling the medicine honestly has its advantages.

The three systems are fundamentally identical. The wise should skillfully integrate them into the doctrine of one pure Way with one flavor of liberation in order to avoid further disputes. The most important thing is not to become so attached to the skillful means that one forgets reality.

What, after all, was the Tathāgata's great intention when he appeared in the world and preached the Dharma?

THE FOUR ALL-EMBRACING VIRTUES

187 The way to ripen all sentient beings
Is through the four all-embracing virtues taught by the
Buddha:
Giving, affectionate speech,
Beneficial conduct, and working together.

In the bodhi-way, the six pāramitās that enable one to accomplish the Buddha Way have been explained. The four all-embracing virtues to embrace and transform sentient beings that the Buddha taught are the way that is beneficial to others and ripens all sentient beings. The four all-embracing virtues are four methods to embrace sentient beings. Whenever people gather to form a collective relationship, then in order for one to be able to function as a leader with the trust of the masses and to have them be willing to accept one's teachings and put them into practice one definitely cannot depart from these four all-embracing virtues. This holds true whether one is a lay person or a monastic person, whether the group is a family, a society, or a country, and either within the Saṅgha or among lay disciples.

The four all-embracing virtues are fundamentally common to the world; worldly leaders also should not depart from the principles of these four virtues. Since bodhisattvas have the primary goal of being of benefit to others, naturally they need these four Mahāyāna virtues all the more. Mahāyāna's benefit to others requires that there be "people with similar vows and similar practices" and that bodhisattvas have a position of leadership.

The first of the four all-embracing virtues is giving. (Of the six transcendences of bodhisattvas, giving is also ranked first.) Giving material benefits is the key to embracing sentient beings. Regardless of how ferocious an animal is, if you feed it everyday, it will obey you. Non-Buddhists provide relief in the form of assistance, medicines, and the like to attract others; the result is that they increase the number of their disciples—which accords with the principle of giving.

The second of the virtues is affectionate speech. The proper bearing for conversation is to have a pleasant appearance and a sincere attitude. People who are being addressed should know that the words being spoken, whether they are good worldly dharmas or world-transcending Dharma, are for their benefit. Even if the words are a reprimand, they will be accepted willingly.

Conduct beneficial to others is the third virtue. That which is said to or requested of people should be feasible, so people can reap the benefits and increase the virtues of the Buddha Dharma. That which is not necessary, not wished for, or impossible, even if it is a good thing or good deed, will often drive them away.

The fourth virtue is working together. A senior officer sharing weal and woe with his soldiers will have their support and fullest effort. In the past, abbots and everyone within monasteries lived the same life—eating meals in the refectory, meditating in the hall, working in the fields—with no discrimination. Thus, there were few obstacles to the abbots' management of people. The youth Sudhana made fifty-three visits to various good and knowledgeable people who taught him the doctrines that they themselves practiced. If what one practices and what one teaches are not identical, will others follow?

In summary, bodhisattvas rely on these four all embracing virtues to practice, so they are the leaders of sentient beings and are beneficial to them.

THE RESULTS OF PRACTICING THE BODHISATTVA WAY

188 One should initially cultivate bodhi mind
And then practice the ten good deeds.
When bodhi mind is firmly set,
One can enter the way of the Great Vehicle.

The six transcendences and the four all-embracing virtues are methods practiced by bodhisattvas, based on bodhi mind and corresponding with the three minds. These methods range from the superficial to the profound, which is why the scriptures establish the sequential stages of practices. As described in an earlier verse, one can practice "by gradually entering the different grounds."

The Stages of the Bodhisattva Way

Those who resolve to practice the Mahāyāna bodhi way should initially resolve to attain bodhi and cultivate the bodhi mind. Because they are able to be constantly mindful of seeking the Buddha Way and transforming sentient beings, they do not retreat from mindfulness even when in a hurry or in an unfavorable situation. To cultivate bodhi mind means to accept the bodhisattva precepts and practice the ten good deeds. Using the deeds of the Human Vehicle to enter the Great Vehicle in the style of bodhisattvas who have superior compassion—such is the Mahāyāna way.

The Ten Minds

According to the sūtras, when one begins to practice, one is called a ten-fold-faith bodhisattva or a ten-good-deeds bodhisattva. Practicing the ten minds—the faithful mind, the diligent mind, the recollecting mind, the concentrated mind, the mind of wisdom, the giving mind, the ethical mind, the protective mind, the able mind, and the reflecting mind—primarily means practicing the Mahāyāna mind of faith. But in the beginning, one may "practice the ten good deeds for ten thousand kalpas, regressing and progressing, like a feather blown east or west by the winds."[112] If one practices continuously without regression, then after ten thousand kalpas, one can attain a bodhi mind that does not regress and never retreats. One can then enter the first stage of the Great Vehicle way—that of making the resolution.

To successfully cultivate the mind of faith, one must rely on the ten good deeds, the six transcendences, and so forth. Successful cultivation is described in the scriptures: "Having pure superior strength and increased determination, one is called a bodhisattva beginning to practice for three countless great kalpas."[113] Successfully cultivating the mind of faith is not easy, however. To strengthen the faith of beginners with timid and weak minds, the Buddha taught the easy path as a skillful means. There is no harm in being reborn in a Pure Land; when the power of patience is achieved, then one can practice the extensive difficult deeds of transforming sentient beings. Alternatively, the Buddha persuaded beginners to cultivate the divine body in order to first become yogis who possess the illuminating dhāraṇī. Some people, unable to endure the long path of birth and death and the varied natures of sentient beings, and unable to conceive of the Buddha's virtues, lost the bodhi mind. So the Buddha spoke of the "magical city" to allow them to practice on a limited basis and then return to the Great Vehicle after a little rest. All these are special skillful means for those beginners of the Great Vehicle who are not yet accomplished.

The Thirty Stages

189 Relying on various superior understanding and practices,
And richly accumulating the two provisions,
After one countless kalpa
One can enter the level of sages.

Having successfully cultivated the mind of faith, one enters the first of the ten stages—the stage of making the resolution. Having arrived at this stage, the bodhisattva-way will be accomplished in a specified time—one is already at the beginning of the three countless great kalpas. Within this specified time, the sūtra says there are thirty levels in three divisions, as follows.

First, the division of the ten stages: the stages of (1) making the resolution, (2) control, (3) cultivation, (4) noble birth, (5) skillful means, (6) having the right mind, (7) no regression, (8) youth in buddhahood, (9) being a Dharma prince, and (10) consecration.

Second, the division of the ten activities: (1) joyful activity, (2) beneficial activity, (3) activity without resentment, (4) limitless activity, (5) activity without ignorance, (6) well-manifested activity, (7) unimpeded activity, (8) exalting activity, (9) perfecting the dharma activity, and (10) truly real activity.

Third, the division of the ten transferences of merit: (1) transference for the purpose of helping all sentient beings part from the form of sentient beings, (2) transference of indestructible faith, (3) transference for the purpose of attaining the impartiality of all buddhas, (4) transference that reaches to all, (5) transference of the store of endless virtues, (6) transference of good roots to all without discrimination, (7) transference of the impartial contemplation of all sentient beings, (8) transference of the form of reality, (9) transference of liberation without attachment or bonds, and (10) transference of infinite dharma realms.

These thirty levels of the three ranks are collectively called the "ground of superior understanding and practices"; they are not yet the ground of the direct realization of the nature of things. Within these thirty stages, bodhisattvas practice the six transcendences and the four all-embracing virtues, accumulating richly the two kinds of provisions—blessings and wisdom that are vast without limits. Hence these stages are also called the "level of the provisions." One must go through these thirty stages for the long period of one countless kalpa before one can advance to enter the level of sages—the ground of extreme joy—with faultless manifested activities.

According to the *Pu sa ying luo ben ye jing* (Sūtra of the Original Karma of Bodhisattvas as a Necklace of Precious Stones), the division of the ten stages emphasizes the accomplishment of, and the calm abiding in, the extraordinary understanding of emptiness; the division of the ten activities emphasizes both the contemplation of the emptiness of that which exists through conventional designation and the great compassion that benefits sentient beings; and the division of the ten transferences emphasizes the wisdom that comes from contemplation that is impartial with regard to the empty and the conventional. According to the practitioners of the Sarvāstivādin and Yogācāra schools, when the ten transferences are complete the sequence of direct contemplations—of "warmth, summit, patience, and the supreme Dharma of the world"—is established. This sequence is called the four additional actions; it is also separately classified as "the level of additional actions."

Bodhisattvas who practice the bodhisattva deeds benefit others first. Thus, it is possible for most bodhisattvas of the thirty levels to become political leaders in the world, capable of administering benevolent policies to benefit the masses. The size of the kingdom is differentiated based on the extent of a bodhisattva's virtues. The bodhisattvas of ten good deeds are usually kings of smaller countries, iron chakra kings who use military force for unification and then rule with benevolent policies. The bodhisattvas of the ten stages are usually copper chakra kings who rule two continents. The bodhisattvas of the ten activities are usually silver chakra kings who rule three continents. The bodhisattvas of the ten transferences are usually gold chakra kings who rule four continents without having to rely on military force.

Those who practice the tenfold faith but fail are defeated bodhisattvas. They mostly have the karmic result of becoming kings who rule through good government for the benefit of the people. Beginners in the practice of the Mahāyāna bodhisattva-way therefore live mostly in the human world without abandoning true worldly dharmas. Not until they have realized and entered the level of sages can they be present everywhere in the human and divine worlds with responsive destinies!

The Ten Grounds

190 Upon entering the first ground, that of extreme joy,
A bodhisattva is born into the Tathāgata's family.
Having cut the three bonds,
Such a bodhisattva has the supreme virtue of giving.

Those within the causal ground of bodhisattvas who directly realize the nature of things are the bodhisattvas of the ten grounds—also called the ten abiding grounds. The first ground is that of joy or extreme joy. "Ground" has the sense of "that which is able to produce virtues." Those who directly realize the nature of things can produce various faultless virtues based on it, just as the earth can produce grass, trees, and precious metals and jewels. The first ground is the level of bodhisattvas who understand the way and directly realize the nature of things. The bodhi mind that corresponds to the nature of things is called extraordinary bodhi mind.

Having partially realized the supreme bodhi, such bodhisattvas can also be called partially realized buddhas. Upon the initial realization of the holy nature, a bodhisattva attains the world-transcending mind and tastes the joy of liberation as never before. Through investigating all of the Tathāgata's virtues, each of which one also has a portion, and through being able to become accomplished, one attains incomparable joy. Because one thoroughly understands the emptiness of things, one no longer has "fear of having no means of livelihood, fear of sacrificing one's reputation, fear of dying, fear of falling into the evil destinies, or fear of addressing an assembly."[114]

Upon entering the first ground, one is said to be "born into the Tathāgata's family," which means all buddhas. Such a bodhisattva, having the transcendence of wisdom as "mother" and skillful means as "father," partially realizes the Dharma body of a buddha. From then on, as the

Buddha's true child, one can carry the buddhas' "family undertaking" on one's shoulders and continue to make the "buddha-seed" prosper; thus one is said to be born in the Tathāgata's family.

All those who realize the nature of things can eliminate the afflictions. The bodhisattvas of the first ground eliminate all the barriers of the afflictions by understanding the Way. In short, they have cut off the three bonds—the view of the self, attachment to inappropriate precepts, and doubt. Mādhyamikans say that the attachment to the self and to things is the barrier of the afflictions and that this attachment can be cut by both the Mahāyāna and Hīnayāna. The difference is that the śrāvakas eliminate confusion and realize the truth through directly contemplating the nonexistence of the "I and mine." They do not necessarily contemplate emptiness deeply, however, so they are unable to eliminate residual habits—that is, barriers to their understanding. On the other hand, bodhisattvas can, with profound discernment, reach an extraordinary understanding of the empty nature of things even as beginners. Afterward they contemplate the nonexistence of the "I and mine" and fully realize that things are empty. They thereby cut the three bonds and are able to gradually eliminate the residual habits. When the residual habits are completely purified, they then become buddhas.

As for the bodhisattva deeds, one has to practice extensively the six transcendences, the four all-embracing virtues, and boundless methods for the benefit of oneself and others. According to the extraordinary meaning of the sūtra, however, giving—the virtue perfected by bodhisattvas of the first ground—is supreme; this is also called the completion of the pāramitā of giving. There is nothing that bodhisattvas of the first ground cannot give. The virtues of each ground are extraordinarily extensive, as is thoroughly described in the *Daśabhūmika Sūtra.* Nāgārjuna Bodhisattva has briefly summarized the virtues of the first ground in the following description: "The initial ground is called 'joy,' because attaining it is such a rare happiness; having completely eliminated the three bonds, one is born into the family of buddhas. Because of the rewards of this ground, one now practices the transcendence of giving. One will attain unperturbed comfort in the worlds of hundred of buddhas. One will also be a great wheel-turning king of Jambudvīpa and other continents, continuously turning the precious wheel, the wheel of the Dharma, in the world."[115]

191 The bodhisattva, by keeping the precepts complete and pure,
Enters the undefiled ground.

Bodhisattvas of the second ground are more inclined toward the pāramitā of precepts; they possess the virtue of keeping the precepts completely and purely. The precepts are the ten good deeds as described in the *Daśabhūmika Sūtra.* Bodhisattvas of the second ground practice the ten good deeds themselves and also teach others to practice them. Extensively practicing the ten good deeds with the Mahāyāna mind, they attain the complete purity of physical, verbal, and mental karmas.[116] They are no longer like the bodhisattvas of the first ground, who still make unintentional or trifling mistakes, thus "defiling" the precepts. This is why they are said to have entered the undefiled ground.

192 At the radiant ground, a bodhisattva with superior patience
Attains the wisdom that eliminates all darkness.

In the descriptions of the virtues of practice in the various grounds, two courses of practice are combined. In the first—in which the practice of the ten grounds corresponds to that of the ten pāramitās—the first six grounds are the ground for giving, for precept keeping, for patience, for diligence, for concentration, and for wisdom.

In the second course, the first three grounds are the ground for giving, for precept keeping, and for concentration. These rely on the mental activity of the Great Vehicle to practice the worldly good dharmas that are shared with the Five Vehicles. The fourth, fifth, and sixth grounds are the ground for practicing the thirty-seven grades of the way, for the Four Truths, and for dependent origination. These rely on the mental activity of the Great Vehicle to practice the worldly good dharmas that are shared in common with the Three Vehicles. Because of these different courses, there are minor differences of the items of practice in the third, fourth, and fifth grounds. These are only skillful explanations for the sake of establishing the levels of the ten grounds; actually, bodhisattvas of every ground have to practice all doctrines completely. The minor differences between the two courses do not affect the objective. The six grounds and their respective virtues and practices may be summarized as follows:

First ground: superior giving—practice giving
Second ground: superior keeping of the precepts—practice the ten good deeds
Third ground: superior patience—practice meditation
Fourth ground: superior diligence—practice the grades of the Way
Fifth ground: superior concentration—practice the Four Truths
Sixth ground: superior prajñā—practice dependent origination

Of the ten transcendences, the third ground, the "radiant" ground, emphasizes the superiority and completion of the pāramitā of patience. This ground is called radiant because bodhisattvas of this third ground, diligently seeking the Buddha Dharma, are able to learn and retain the dhāraṇī and to accept and maintain all the Buddha Dharmas. In addition, they diligently practice meditation—the four dhyānas, the four formless concentrations, and the four infinite concentrations. Through their learning of the Dharma and their practice of meditation, their wisdom grows bright like a fire and dispels darkness. In deep concentration, the darkness of desire, anger, and ignorance dissipate, and one's mind is bright and clear.

193 Completely diligent in cultivating the branches of enlightenment,
The bodhisattva enters the ground of blazing wisdom,
In which the view of the self completely disappears.

With regard to the practice of the ten pāramitās, bodhisattvas of the fourth ground have completely perfected the pāramitā of diligence. With regard to the practice of the Dharma common to the Three Vehicles, the bodhisattvas of the fourth, fifth, and sixth grounds cultivate the thirty-seven branches of enlightenment. Because they diligently practice these, the light of wisdom shines even more brightly. All attachments to the self and to things based on selfhood become permanently extinct without any residue, like wood consumed by a fire. Thus it is called the ground of blazing wisdom.

194 Upon entering the ground that is difficult to overcome, with superior concentration
The bodhisattva can skillfully understand all the principles of the truth.

The fifth ground, called the ground that is difficult to overcome, emphasizes the superiority and completion of the pāramitā of concentration. With regard to the practice of the Dharma common to the Three Vehicles, these bodhisattvas can skillfully and penetratingly understand all the principles of truth—the Four Truths, the two truths, and so forth. This ground is difficult to overcome because one reaches it only after undergoing the utmost difficulties. What is that which is reached? Upon having directly realized the empty nature of things earlier during the first ground, all the forms of meaningless elaboration were completely eliminated—as it is said, "prajñāpāramitā can extinguish all deviant views and meaningless elaborations, which leads to fundamental emptiness."[117] However, when these bodhisattvas depart from the realization of real concentration, the form of existence also arises. At this time there is either undifferentiated wisdom, which is attained subsequently, or wisdom that comes from skillful differentiation. Thus it is said "skillful means is about to depart from fundamental emptiness,"[118] which describes the time when these bodhisattvas purify the Buddha-world and transform sentient beings.

At such a time, although these bodhisattvas can understand that everything is illusional, they do so relying on the power of the meditative mind and do not realize things as they really are. This is because the perceived objects seem to be real—the form of meaningless elaboration—and still arise in the same way. Until they have directly realized emptiness through prajñā, by relying on the residual power of the wisdom that comes from emptiness, they cannot understand that things are without nature and illusional. This can be illustrated by an example: looking up at the sky and observing the "clouds speeding past and the moon moving," we know that only the clouds are moving and not the bright moon. The immediate sensory experience, however, is that the moon is moving; only after one's mental consciousness has passed judgment does one know that only the clouds are moving.

The mental states of the bodhisattvas prior to the fifth ground are analogous to this example. When seeing empty nature free from all forms, they see nothing. When they see the form of a thing, they are unable to simultaneously realize its empty nature. All along they have been in this state of separating emptiness and existence: each appears only without the other. Due to the continuous cultivation and realization of the wisdom that comes from empty nature, their power of prajñā becomes stronger. So when seeing all existing things, they are able to be free from the real form (of meaningless elaboration). Thus they can illuminate both illusory existence and emptiness, that is, the nonexistence of an illusional inherent nature. Only in this way is there really no obstruction between the ultimate and the conventional, and no dualism between emptiness and existence. After going through practices without limit, this ground is reached; thus it is called difficult to overcome.

The previous direct realization of emptiness (in the first ground) marked a first barrier between the ordinary person and the sage. At this point, the second barrier, which can be said to be the barrier between the Mahāyāna and the Hīnayāna, is crossed. Only by directly realizing that emptiness and existence are not dualistic will one have neither disgust about birth and death nor happiness about Nirvāṇa. When one is free from both abiding in birth and death and abiding in Nirvāṇa, one surpasses the mental state of the Hīnayāna sages.

195 The sixth is the ground of manifestation.
The bodhisattva with superior wisdom
And in the concentration of complete extinction
Will see, with clarity, all Buddha Dharmas
And the true nature of dependent origination.
Such constant stillness and compassionate mindfulness
Surpasses that of the Two Vehicles.

Practice in the sixth ground (that of manifestation) emphasizes the superiority and completion of the pāramitā of prajñā or wisdom. Having reached this point, bodhisattvas dwell in the concentration of complete extinction, in which faulty mental consciousness no longer arises. If the sages of the Two Vehicles enter the concentration of complete extinction, they think they have realized reality and have given rise to the thought of entering Nirvāṇa—this is the Hīnayānist's being "drunk with the wine of samādhi" as described in the *Laṅkāvatāra Sūtra*, which is also identical with the entrance into the concentration of complete extinction. In the *Prajñāpāramitā Sūtra*, therefore, the Buddha advises the bodhisattvas that to avoid falling into the Small Vehicle they should not enter the concentration of complete extinction if the strength of their compassionate vow is inadequate. However, bodhisattvas of the sixth ground can enter this concentration, supported by prajñā and the great compassionate vow. In so doing, they intimately realize the nature of things and all the Buddha Dharmas manifest clearly; thus this ground is called the ground of manifestation.

In this very profound wisdom of emptiness, the bodhisattvas perceive clearly and profoundly the true nature of dependent origination, which is the nonduality of illusory existence and emptiness. Although it is possible for bodhisattvas of the fifth ground to achieve simultaneous contemplation of the ultimate and the conventional, this is extremely rare. When they reach the sixth ground, needing only to "practice more formless thinking," they can directly realize the Middle Way of dependent origination, which is without any obstruction between emptiness and existence. Thus, bodhisattvas of the sixth ground are always in stillness and yet are always compassionately mindful of sentient beings. Perpetual stillness is the direct realization of prajñā. This is the nonduality of great compassion and prajñā—the distinctive and extraordinary Mahāyāna Dharma—a nonduality that surpasses the realizations of the Two Vehicles. Most of the bodhisattvas of the sixth ground practice the contemplation of dependent origination, which corresponds to emptiness. These bodhisattvas also reach the state in which all Buddha Dharmas manifest; this is the Middle Way.

The Hīnayāna Sarvāstivādin school says that there are four kinds of dependent origination, of which one is called "dependent origination in a single thought." This school thinks that the twelve links of dependent origination are not necessarily based on the three periods but rather can be established even in a single thought. In explaining the sixth ground, the "Chapter on the Ten Grounds" of the *Avataṃsaka Sūtra* extensively explains dependent origination and also mentions this teaching of "dependent origination in a single thought." For example, it says, "The falseness and unreality of the three worlds arise from the mind. The twelve links of dependent origination are all based on the mind."[119] This explanation is basically similar to that of the Sarvāstivādin school. This school's interpretation of the Dharma had an extraordinary influence on the Great Vehicle's Mere Mind philosophy in terms of both the adaptations to the capacity and style of this philosophy and its expansion. The Buddha Dharma is really inconceivable!

196 At the ground that goes far, in the concentration of
complete extinction,
Each thought can alternate between being in and out of
concentration;
The transcendence of skillful means is like a strong fire
That ends the second countless kalpa.

The seventh ground, that which goes far, is even more profound and wonderful. While in the concentration of complete extinction, these bodhisattvas can move into or out of concentration with each thought. The ordinary movement into and out of concentration requires skillful means even at levels that are beyond thinking, but now these bodhisattvas can accomplish this with each thought. Not only are they able to move in or out whenever they want, their moving into concentration is identical with their moving out of concentration. This is described in the *Vimalakīrtinirdeśa Sūtra*: "Without arising from the concentration of extinction, they can manifest various dignified demeanors."[120]

Because this concentration is profound and wonderful, the prajñā based on this concentration also reaches the state of "formless activity that requires effort but is without form." As was mentioned earlier, ever since the first ground the wisdom that realizes emptiness is formless; when one moves out of deep contemplation, however, there is a subsequently attained wisdom that still has form. (One should not confuse "having form" with being attached.) In the fifth ground, bodhisattvas can rarely attain formless activity without any obstruction between emptiness and existence. The sixth ground is more advanced in that these bodhisattvas need only to practice more formless thinking in order to manifest formless activity. Nevertheless, most of the time this activity is interrupted. Only when they attain the seventh ground can these bodhisattvas uninterruptedly manifest formless activity.

With regard to the ten pāramitās, the sixth, prajñāpāramitā, emphasizes the knowledge of reality. In addition there are four pāramitās that are functions of prajñā: skillfulness, aspiration, power, and transcendental wisdom. (When only six pāramitās are taught, these four pāramitās are included within prajñā.) With regard to the ten transcendences, the transcendence of skillful means in the seventh ground is superior to the preceding ones, like a fire that is even more scorching. With regard to the duration of practice, at the end of the seventh ground the second countless kalpa is finished.

The differences between the three great countless kalpas also have special significance. The first countless kalpa spans the time between one's initial resolution and one's direct realization of emptiness. After that, one becomes a sage and enters the second countless kalpa. Upon the completion of the seventh ground, on the verge of reaching the completely pure formless activities, the second countless kalpa is finished and one enters the third. Therefore, the sūtra says that the seventh ground is like the borderline between two countries. Prior to this ground there are activities that have form, those that are a combination of form and formlessness, and those that require effort but are formless. After they attain this ground, bodhisattvas' activities are purely formless and effortless, and therefore this ground is called the ground that goes far.

197 Entering the motionless ground,
Without form and without effort,
The bodhisattva cuts off all confusion of the three realms.
Such a bodhisattva's great vows are extremely pure.
Through illusory samādhi
The bodhisattva appears in different forms throughout the three realms.

From the seventh ground one enters the eighth, the motionless ground. Whereas the formless activities of the seventh ground still involve effort, the eighth is without form and without effort. At this point, wisdom and virtue increase spontaneously, and the afflictions no longer have manifested activities. Bodhisattvas of this ground are not moved by afflictions or efforts; hence this ground is called motionless. It is like using much strenuous effort to cross a river in a dream; when one suddenly wakes up, all the effort stops.

The afflictions of the three realms have not yet been totally eliminated, but they will no longer give rise to any danger. This is because bodhisattvas are not anxious to eliminate all the afflictions as long as they are in control of them. Sometimes bodhisattvas can use them as a skillful means to benefit themselves and others.

Upon entering the eighth ground, however, bodhisattvas spontaneously and completely break through the barrier of afflictions. Of all bodhisattvas, only those who enter the eighth ground realize the birthlessness that cuts off all the confusions of the three realms, just as arhats do. The formless activities of the bodhisattvas in the eighth ground, their realization of the undifferentiated nature of things, and their attainment of the realization of birthlessness are, indeed, identical to the arhats' realization of Nirvāṇa. Their complete elimination of the afflictions of the three realms is also the same as that of arhats.

Thus the *Daśabhūmika Sūtra* says that bodhisattvas are to enter Nirvāṇa upon entering the eighth ground. Because of the power of a buddha's support and the power of bodhisattvas' original vows, naturally they will not enter Nirvāṇa in the same way as the Hīnayānists. From this point on they enter the way of bodhisattvas, which is truly distinct from that of the Two Vehicles. From now on, the profound state of the Mahāyāna (that is, formless activity), which was extremely difficult for bodhisattvas of the fifth ground to enter, is fully attained.

With regard to the ten transcendences, the great vows of bodhisattvas of the eighth ground are the most pure. As for their formless and effortless activities, they can give rise to the illusory samādhi universally appearing in all forms and preaching all Dharmas in the three realms. This is like the great being Universal Gateway (Guanshiyin Bodhisattva), who "instantly appears in whatever form corresponds to the need of the one who requires deliverance and preaches the Dharma." Such is the profound state of all bodhisattvas in and above the eighth ground. Not only do they know that existence is illusory, but their formless activities also appear as illusions (and without meaningless elaborations), and these illusions are identical with and equal to emptiness. Because their activities are purely formless, it is said that bodhisattvas of the eighth ground give rise to illusory samādhi.

198 At the ground of good wisdom, with unhindered understanding,
The bodhisattva completes and purifies all powers.

The formless and effortless activities are even greater at the ninth ground, that of good wisdom. These bodhisattvas' realizations, needless to say, are effortless; even preaching the Dharma to others is effortless.

Bodhisattvas of the ninth ground can attain the fourfold wisdom that comes from unobstructed understanding—of the Dharma and its meanings. Protecting the Buddha's Dharma treasury, they are the highest and most eloquent masters among all who preach the Dharma. They are able to preach all Dharmas with a single voice, simultaneously expounding every corresponding doctrine for infinite beings with different fundamental natures; they do this spontaneously, without exerting effort. Of the ten pāramitās, the bodhisattvas of the ninth ground completely perfect and purify the pāramitā of all powers.

199 At the tenth ground, that of the Dharma cloud,
All buddhas shower light upon the bodhisattva's head.
With increased wisdom, and pouring the rain of the Dharma,
Like a great cloud the bodhisattva helps the good grow.

The tenth ground is called the ground of the Dharma cloud. Attaining this ground can be compared to receiving the title of crown prince and ascending the throne. In India a crown prince had to be ritually baptized before he ascended the throne: water taken from the four oceans was poured over his head. The bodhisattva who reaches the tenth ground is a Dharma prince, one who has reached "the stage of being next in line for a high position" and is about to become a perfectly complete buddha. When this happens all buddhas of the ten directions give off a great radiance, which showers upon the bodhisattva's head. This means that the light of bodhi wisdom from all buddhas has entered the mind of the bodhisattva, whose wisdom has become identical with that of all buddhas and whose treasury of bodhi mind is just as full and pure. It symbolizes becoming a buddha.

This ground is called that of the Dharma cloud because the tenth ground excels the nine others in the pāramitā of wisdom. Only the wisdom of a buddha can match that of bodhisattvas of the tenth ground. Not only can these bodhisattvas preach the Dharma comfortably, they can also manifest supernatural powers and appear throughout the realm of things. They pour down the great rain of the Dharma like a torrential rain, so that all the vegetation on the earth, great and small, receives moisture and grows stronger.

Bodhisattvas of the tenth ground "have engendered great compassion from the power of their vows. Their blessings and wisdom are like dense clouds of varied colors, and they are completely illumined without fear, like flashes of lightning. Like the roll of thunder, they preach the Dharma in order to subdue Māra. In a single thought they omnisciently and omnipresently appear in the numberless worlds, raining good Dharma, raining ambrosial Dharma."[121] Thus these bodhisattvas, preaching the Dharma with supernatural power, are able to nurture all the good roots of sentient beings like a great cloud pouring down a timely torrential rain.

The Duration of the Bodhisattva Way

200 The way cultivated by the bodhisattva
Passes through three countless kalpas and ten grounds.
Whether bodhisattvas become buddhas suddenly or gradually
Depends on their different capacities.

The way that the bodhisattva cultivates is as follows: resolving to attain bodhi, receiving the bodhisattva precepts, and practicing the six transcendences and four all-embracing virtues. The duration of the bodhisattva's practice is three great countless kalpas. As for the levels that a bodhisattva must pass through and the nature of the realm of things a bodhisattva must realize, they are included in the ten grounds. All these have been explained. However, there is one question that still needs to be answered.

That bodhisattvas have to practice for three great countless kalpas is the final conclusion of śrāvaka Buddhism, but this does not necessarily hold true for the Mahāyāna sūtras. The *Dasheng qi xin lun* sūtra concludes that the sūtras' indefinite explanation is a skillful explanation that from the point of successful achievement of the mind of faith to the point of becoming a buddha, one does definitely need to pass through three great countless kalpas.[122] Nāgārjuna's treatise has a different view, however: the process of becoming a buddha can be either quick or slow, and one may have to go through countless kalpas! But can the practice of becoming a buddha really be differentiated as sudden and fast or gradual and slow?

Originally, there were two kinds of explanation regarding the three great countless kalpas. The first was in terms of kalpas of time. If a certain amount of time is one small kalpa, then eighty small kalpas equal one great kalpa. Ten times ten such kalpas make a hundred great kalpas, and ten of these make a thousand. Great kalpas then become "countless" (literally "numberless," but actually they are quantifiable), and with further computation they increase to three great countless kalpas. The sūtras say that only after such long period of practice can one completely become a buddha.

The second explanation was in terms of kalpas of virtuous deeds. Depending on one's virtuous deeds, the length of time necessary to become a buddha varies. This is like counting a person's manual production per workday. For example, the output of a person who operates a number of machines may be equivalent to thirty or a hundred workdays of manual labor. Something similar happens when one calculates the time needed to become a buddha. Three countless great kalpas are still required, but since the kalpas are measured in terms of the bodhisattva's virtues, the actual length of time may vary greatly.

According to Nāgārjuna's discourse, bodhisattvas (such as Śākyamuni Buddha) generally have to pass through three great countless kalpas. Some may require even more time, but those of especially sharp capacity do not need this long. Maybe the bodhisattvas Aśvaghoṣa and Asaṅga did not mention this because it is very rare to have such a sharp capacity. In any case, whether bodhisattvas become buddhas suddenly or gradually depends on their different capacities, as is described in the sūtras.

What follows will briefly explain the duration of the bodhisattva way according to the teaching in Nāgārjuna Bodhisattva's "Chapter on Rebirth." (Nāgārjuna coordinated this text with the sequence in the *Ru ding bu ding yin jing* [Sūtra on the Mudra(s) for Descent into the Fixed and the Unfixed (Realms)].)

1. Those with scarce blessings, dull capacity, and a weak mind		after resolving to practice they may or may not attain buddhahood after infinite countless kalpas	
2. Those with a few blessings but sharp capacity		after resolving to practice gradually the six transcendences they may take three great countless kalpas to become a buddha	
3. Those with abundant blessings, sharp capacity, and a strong mind	A.	after resolving to enter the level of a bodhisattva attained	(the summit level)
		after resolving to abide a little while and then enter the level of a bodhisattva attained	(the summit level)
	B.	after resolving to become buddhas and to turn the wheel of the Dharma attained	(the first ground)
	C.	after resolving to transform living beings and to adorn buddha lands in accord with prajñā attained	(above the first ground)

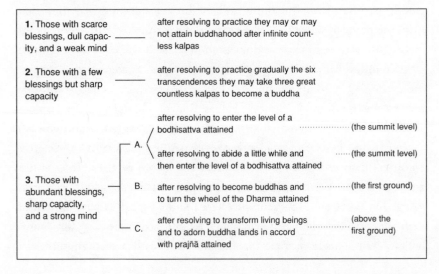

1. There are those who proceed as if they were riding a goat. Having resolved to advance and move on for a long time, some are still unable to arrive. It is said, for example, "Bodhisattvas who have made the initial resolution, fish eggs, and amra flowers—these three things are similar in that there are many at the initial stage but very few can come to fruition."[123] This may well be the most common fundamental nature.

2. There are those who proceed as if they were riding a horse (or in the sūtras an elephant). They may need to practice for three great countless kalpas or one hundred great countless kalpas before they can attain anuttara-samyak-saṃbodhi.

3. There are those who proceed as if they were riding on a supernatural power. This includes three categories: (a) Those who proceed as if they were riding on the supernatural power of the sun and moon. Nāgārjuna subdivided this category into two groups. Some ascend to the level of a bodhisattva as soon as they make the initial resolution; some ascend after practicing for a little while. There are many explanations of the bodhisattva level (based on the *Prajñāpāramitā Sūtra*), but the culminating stage, in short, is the one from which one does not fall into the evil destinies, low families, or the domain of the Two Vehicles. (According to the stages of practice in the *Avataṃsaka Sūtra*, the stage of making the resolution is the stage from which one will not fall.) (b) Those who proceed as if they were riding on the supernatural power of the śrāvakas. After making the initial resolution, they accomplish great bodhi and the Way in eight aspects (having partial realization of the first ground, they can appear in a hundred buddha worlds and accomplish the Way in eight aspects). (c) Those who proceed as if they were riding on the supernatural power of the Tathāgata. After making the initial resolution, they are in accord with prajñā, transform sentient beings, and adorn the buddha lands. These are the bodhisattvas of the skillful way who are between the first ground and the ninth ground.

Although it is definitely impossible to become a buddha as soon as one makes the initial resolution, there are those who realize anuttara-samyak-saṃbodhi just after they have made the resolution and entered the first ground. There are also those who do even better: just after they have made the resolution, they completely perfect themselves and are able to save sentient beings by relying on the skillful way. Those of the second type, who practice for three great countless kalpas to accomplish bodhi, are of gradual capacity; Śākyamuni Buddha was one. Those of categories (a) to (c) are of a sharp capacity that is suddenly enlightened; such bodhisattvas are rare and precious!

Why are some capacities gradual and some sudden? Why is it that the process of becoming a buddha is slow or fast? The answers lie in the preparations prior to making the resolution. First, there are "those whose blessings and causal factors were scarce in previous lives. They are also of dull capacity, and their mind is not firm."[124] Is it any wonder that they have still not reached their goal, even though it has been such a long, long time since they made the resolution? They are like those who resolve to take an examination but never study. Second, there are those who "had a few blessings in previous lives and have sharp capacities."[125] They resemble those who have a poor academic record but work for a long time with rich experience: if they study continuously and take the examination every year, they will have a chance to enroll. Third, there are those who "for all their past lives have always preferred the truth and disliked deceit. These bodhisattvas also have sharp capacities and a firm mind, and they accumulate infinite blessings and wisdom."[126] Because of this they can ascend to a high level just after they make their resolution. They are like those who have a brilliant academic record and study in depth; when they take the examination, they will succeed.

Those who study Buddhism therefore ought not to go on about "sudden" or "gradual" enlightenment, for this is all empty talk! It is better to examine one's own state of preparedness! Modern Chinese Buddhist thinking is very eccentric: it gives no consideration to people's particular blessings or causes and conditions. What are their capacities? How are they provisioned in terms of blessings and wisdom? After making the resolution to study Buddhism, they want to be enlightened suddenly and want to become buddhas immediately. Without examining themselves and their own resolve, they think that such and such is the great teaching that will enable them to become a buddha easily. This can be compared to wanting to become a leader and deciding to run for president without first pausing to examine one's academic record and experience.

Some people are even more ludicrous. They admit that they are of dull capacities and face strong karmic barriers and shallow wisdom, but they think that they can practice an easy doctrine and become a buddha. Such thoughts do not accord with the true Dharma. Those who truly resolve to study Buddhism should practice diligently. One should accumulate spiritual provisions, build sharp capacities, and have a firm mind. Without asking about sudden or gradual enlightenment or about when one will become a buddha, one should just keep on cultivating. This is the normal way for bodhisattvas.

The Attainment of Buddhahood

201 When three countless kalpas are completed,
The bodhisattva ascends to the ground of wonderful
enlightenment.

From the ground of bodhisattva one ascends to the ground of wonderful enlightenment—the buddha ground. A buddha's great bodhi is called "unsurpassed right omniscience and enlightenment." "Right" is also translated as "wonderful." Thus buddhahood is both omniscience and wonderful enlightenment.

From the first ground to the eighth, bodhisattvas completely eliminate the barriers of the afflictions of the three realms; their residual habits—the barriers to their understanding—have been eliminated bit by bit since the first ground. These residual habits are due to the manifestation of the forms of meaningless elaboration. That is, these bodhisattvas cannot attain an unobstructed knowledge and understanding of the Dharma, for they still have some ignorance. Because of habitual afflictions from beginningless time, moreover, residues of the afflictions remain even though the barriers of the afflictions have been eliminated. Śrāvakas call these residual habits "undefiled ignorance," and Mahāyānists call them the "defiled abode of ignorance." Through the cultivation of formless wisdom, these residual habits are brought to a state of nonarising; they become more and more diminished, while the emptiness of things becomes clearer and clearer.

When all is clear and pure, one's wisdom endures longer and grows vaster, and one understands everything more profoundly. In the end, one is ultimately perfect and able to become a buddha only when "all the infinitesimal ignorance of the known states" and the "infinitesimal barriers of ignorance" are purified.[127] "No forms of the eternal barriers will arise and the purest truth will appear."[128] This is the manifestation of "the purest realm of things." The *Prajñāpāramitā Sūtra* says that having "one thought that is in accord with the wonderful wisdom" and eliminating all afflictions and residual habits, one becomes a buddha.[129] Having made the resolution and practiced up to this level, one at last truly has perfect virtues.

The Three Bodies of a Buddha

202 The body of a buddha is of utmost stillness and extinction,
Impartial and without discrimination.
Like a maṇi pearl,
It has wonderful effects that benefit all sentient beings.

What follows describes the virtues of the buddha ground based on the three bodies.

The first of the three is the *Dharma body*, the inherent body of a buddha. The Dharma body is in accord with all Buddha Dharmas and is their basis of support. It is a pure manifestation of the nature of the emptiness of things, which is dissociated from the storehouse of afflictions. It is complete, brilliant, independent, ultimate, and supreme. Having practiced from the bodhisattva grounds up to the attainment of the state of having "activities without the manifestation of any form that is perpetually dissociated from all barriers," a buddha is of utmost stillness and extinction. As for comparing one buddha with another, all are equal. From a buddha's perspective, everything—the dependent environment and the direct consequence, sentient beings and buddhas, people and the Dharma, wisdom and suchness—all are equal. There is discrimination in neither the nature of the emptiness of things nor in the bodhi. Thus it is said, "The absolute is like the wisdom of suchness, this is called the Dharma body."

Undifferentiated suchness and the wisdom of the Dharma body may be compared to a pearl and a pearl's brightness—it is impossible to differentiate these two; a pearl and its brightness are one and the same. All the phrases and sentences describing and praising the body of the buddha in the scriptures are only metaphors. As for the virtues that are of benefit to others, they are like the precious maṇi pearl that has the wonderful supernatural function of being of benefit to all sentient beings. The maṇi pearl is the wish-fulfilling pearl. It is capable of responding to sentient beings' needs, producing various treasures to satisfy their hearts' desires. The precious pearl functions without thought or intensified effort; it is just naturally the way it is. Buddhahood's benefits to sentient beings are also like this.

203 In the body that flows out of the nature of things,
Everything appears moment after moment:
The phenomena of buddhas, of bodhisattvas,
Of the Two Vehicles, of all sentient beings,
Of the three periods of time, and of all the ten directions.
The dependent and the direct consequences coexist without conflict.
From one, everything appears
And everything enters into one.

The second of the three bodies is the *reward body*, otherwise known as the body engendered by the nature of things—the buddha's body that flows out of the nature of all things. In many of the Mahāyāna sūtras, this body and the Dharma body are not strictly differentiated (this is according to the conception of the two bodies that are taken as the first body and the transformation body). Only the great bodhisattvas perceive this body manifested in its form adorned with boundless virtues. Thus the reward body is differentiated from the Dharma body (which is the body of virtues arising from the relation of the nature of things). "Flowing" means "of the same order of outflow" or "like produces like": all the boundless virtues and adornments as well as the nature of things belong to the same order, just as light and heat are of the same order as the sun.

This body is that in which everything appears moment after moment: the phenomena of buddhas, of bodhisattvas, of the Two Vehicles, of sentient beings, and of the three periods and ten directions. Phenomena of buddhas include their virtues, the signs and marks of a buddha's body, the purity and adornment of buddha lands, the completion of a buddha's Dharma assembly, the omnipresent extension of a buddha's voice, the infinite life span of a buddha, a buddha's wisdom, supernatural powers, benefits to sentient beings, the accomplishment of the way in eight aspects, and so forth. Phenomena of bodhisattvas include the initial resolution, the acceptance of the bodhisattva precepts, the practice of the six transcendences and the four all-embracing virtues, travels throughout the worlds of the ten directions, homage paid closely to all buddhas of the ten directions, listening to and upholding the preaching of the Dharma by the buddhas of the ten directions, the deliverance of all sentient beings, various difficult and ascetic deeds, various previous destinies, and so forth. Phenomena of the Two Vehicles include the initial aspirations of śrāvakas and pratyekabuddhas, cultivation, abiding in aranya, the practice of the deeds of dhūta, travels and teachings among people, entrance into Nirvāṇa and so on. Phenomena of sentient beings include the sentient beings of the six transmigratory states with various abiding places, various names, various forms, various styles of living, various kinds of suffering, and so on. The four categories above are the phenomena of both ordinary people and sages in the ten realms of things. Finally, phenomena of the three periods include previous lives, present lives, future lives, a moment, infinite kalpas, and so on; and phenomena of the ten directions include the infinite, countless, and indefinable worlds of the ten directions, whether big or small, upright or tilted, suffering or happy, as well as mountains, rivers, earth, grass, trees, and forests.

All these are simply dependent consequences—the world as receptacle and direct consequences of this—sentient beings and buddhas. They exist for all lengths of duration and as all kinds of phenomena—from a moment to infinite, countless, and indefinable kalpas, and from a molecule to infinite, countless, indefinable worlds in the ten directions. All the limitless dependent phenomena and direct phenomena in limitless time and space, arising moment after moment, coexist without conflict. Because the body that flows out of the nature of things exists everywhere and because there is nowhere that it does not exist, everything exists within it.

This body is undifferentiated throughout the entire universe and the realm of things. It is true suchness. Everything that is connected to it is without conflict or difference: a single point chosen at random reveals all, and all enters into the one as well. In this way the ancient founders of the Tiantai and the Huayan schools have mapped out the manifold endless realms as described in the extensive explanations of the *Avataṃsaka Sūtra* (Flower Adornment Sūtra).

204 The ten powers, the fourfold fearlessness,
The eighteen distinctive characteristics,
Great compassion, the threefold karma that needs no guarding,
And wonderful wisdom are the virtues of buddhas.

The pure and perfect Dharma body is in accord with the totality of all the virtues. But a buddha's virtues are embraced by the body that flows out of the nature of things. Although the virtues of buddhahood are inconceivable, one hundred and forty distinctive virtues are described. A few commonly known ones are noteworthy:

First, a buddha has the virtue of the ten powers. These are established in order to subdue the extraordinary abilities of Māra. These ten powers are the power to know what is right and wrong in every condition; to know the varied consequences of karma; to know of all the stages of meditation, liberation, samādhi, and concentration; to know the different capacities and faculties of all beings; to know what sentient beings understand; to know the actual condition of every individual; to know the causes and effects of sentient beings in all worlds; to know the results of karma in previous lives; to know of the death and birth of all beings; and to be free from all faults.

Second, a buddha also has the virtue of the fourfold fearlessness, which expresses his absolute faith in benefiting himself and others: fearlessness in proclaiming his omniscience, in proclaiming his freedom from all faults, in proclaiming the Way to end all sufferings, and in exposing the barriers to the way.

Third, a buddha also has the virtue of the eighteen distinctive characteristics that are not established in common with ordinary people or the Hīnayāna. These eighteen characteristics are faultlessness of body, faultlessness of speech, faultlessness of thought, impartiality, perfect steadiness of mind, perfect self-sacrifice, the undiminishing aspiration to save sentient beings, unflagging zeal, unfailing mindfulness, unfailing wisdom, unfailing liberation, unfailing knowledge and understanding of transcendence, unobstructed knowledge of the past, unobstructed knowledge of the future, unobstructed knowledge of the present, accordance of all deeds with wisdom, accordance of all speech with wisdom, and accordance of all thought with wisdom.

Fourth, a buddha also has the virtue of great compassion. Fifth, a buddha has the threefold karma that needs no guarding. "Needs no guarding" refers to the threefold karma of the Tathāgata, purely manifested and faultless. Thus there is no need to cover and guard it for fear that others may know about it. Sixth, a buddha has the virtue of the Tathāgata's wonderful wisdom: wisdom without a teacher, natural wisdom, omniscient wisdom, the seed of all wisdom. All these virtues of buddhas are pure and most perfect.

205 A buddha, abiding in a Pure Land,
Has eighteen perfections, and,
Together with all bodhisattvas,
Enjoys the bliss of the Dharma.

The buddha of the body that flows out of the nature of things dwells in a Pure Land. This Pure Land is universally present and manifests in eighteen perfections; it cannot be said to exist in the east or the west, however big or small. Such a perfect Pure Land is described in the *Fo di jing* (Sūtra on the Buddha Stage) and the preface of the *Saṃdhinirmocana Sūtra*: "The Bhagavān dwells in a palace most brilliantly adorned with the seven treasures, which emit a great brightness that universally illuminates all the boundless worlds. There are wonderful ornaments interspersed in infinite places that are boundless and unfathomable, surpassing places attainable in the three realms and superior to that which arises from the world-transcending good roots. With the appearance of the most independent and pure consciousness, the capital in which the Tathāgata abides is the place where all great bodhisattvas gather and where infinite divine beings, dragons, humans, and nonhumans are at service. This palace—maintained by the extensive taste of the Dharma and bliss; being of benefit to all sentient beings; eliminating all the confinement and defilement of afflictions and disasters; completely free of all devils; surpassing all adornments and being the basis of support for the adornment of the Tathāgata; with great thinking, wisdom, and action as its paths; with great cessation and wonderful contemplation as its vehicles; with great emptiness, formlessness, and wishlessness as the entrances to its liberation; with infinite virtues as its adornments—this palace is established by the Great Precious Flower King."[130]

This passage describes a Pure Land's eighteen perfections: perfect manifested color, perfect form, perfect area, perfect measure, perfect causes, perfect effects, perfect ruler, perfect assistants, perfect subordinates, perfect steadfastness, perfect enterprises, perfect embracing and being of benefit, perfect fearlessness, perfect abodes, perfect paths, perfect vehicles, perfect entrances, and perfect bases of support.

A buddha of a Pure Land with eighteen perfections has the body that flows from the nature of things. This body can be divided into two: that which is received for the buddha's own use and that which is received for the use of others. The first is "received for use" because just like the previously described body of perfect steadfastness, this body "is maintained by the extensive taste of the Dharma and bliss." A buddha abides in a Pure Land, enjoying the bliss of the Dharma and expounding the Dharma to great bodhisattvas, who also enjoy the bliss of the Dharma. Such a perfect Pure Land is full of the joy of the Dharma. Thus, it is said that the buddhas and bodhisattvas enjoy the wonderful bliss of the Mahāyāna Dharma in the Pure Lands.

206 The true meaning of all the Dharma
And the wisdom that realizes the truth
Are unchanging and undifferentiated.
Therefore, there is no other Vehicle.

Abiding in a perfect Pure Land, the body that flows out of the nature of things teaches the Dharma to the great bodhisattvas. Is this teaching the Dharma of the Five Vehicles, the Dharma of the Three Vehicles, or the Dharma of the One Vehicle? It is of course the Dharma of the One Vehicle. A buddha is an enlightened one who has great bodhi as his essential nature; all benefits to oneself and others are based on enlightenment. The cause and condition for the great event of the Buddha's appearance in the world was to preach the Dharma to enable people to enter a buddha's knowledge and understanding—great bodhi.

Realization comprises the object of realization—the true meaning of all things—and that which does the realizing. The true meaning of all things is emptiness, which is free of erroneous imagination. All things that sentient beings think are real are conceptions of inherent nature and are merely meaningless elaborations. Only the emptiness of things without any nature is reality. Thus it is said in the sūtras, "That the nature of all things cannot be attained is the inherent nature of all things."[131] This true meaning is undifferentiated. The emptiness of the self and the emptiness of things are like a grass fire and a charcoal fire: although these fires burn different substances, they are of the same nature.

That which realizes the true meaning of the Dharma is wisdom that, once attained, is never lost. This unconditioned prajñā is expressed through faultless residual habits. This is not the Dharma of momentary birth and death. Therefore, this true suchness that is realized and the true wisdom that realizes it do not change. Whether true suchness is bound or is pure and free from defilements, it stays the same; there is no change. True wisdom is an unconditioned virtue that corresponds with the nature of things; it too does not change.

Suchness and wisdom are also undifferentiated. Although they are established in dependence on the ordinary world, they do not conflict with the suchness and the wisdom within enlightenment. The reality of the Buddha Dharma is unchanging and undifferentiated. There are therefore neither Five Vehicles nor Three Vehicles. The great Dharma expounded to the great bodhisattvas by a buddha is none other than the One Vehicle—one Way and one purity. Since bodhisattvas should know both the temporary and the real, infinite vehicles are described within the One Vehicle; however, everything in the bodhisattva Dharma returns to one.

207 The buddha, having attained the motionless body
And having compassionately vowed to save the beings of the three realms,
Appears in pure or defiled lands
To enable all to enter Nirvāṇa.

The third of the three bodies of a buddha is the *transformation body.* This is a buddha's body that manifests for bodhisattvas below the level of the ten grounds, sages of the Two Vehicles, and ordinary people. Whereas the arising of the body that flows out of the nature of things is analogous to the sun's light and heat, which extend everywhere but cannot be dissociated from the sun, the transformation body is different: it is like the reflection of the moon in water. A buddha's Dharma body always abides, without coming or going, without appearing or disappearing; thus, buddhas attain a motionless body. But because of the "perfuming" and the initiation of the compassionate vow to save sentient beings of the three realms, the transformation body is able to arise without any effort, coming and going, being born and dying, like the elder who entered the burning house in the *Lotus Sūtra* parable. The transformation body, which transforms sentient beings through teaching and guidance, may manifest as a great buddha body—sixteen, a thousand, or ten thousand feet tall. The life span manifested may be a thousand kalpas, a hundred kalpas, or eighty years.

A buddha may manifest in a Pure Land or a defiled land. Although the perfect reward land is universally everywhere, only when sentient beings' wisdom increases do they perceive that anyplace can be a perfect Pure Land in an instant. For example, this saha world is a defiled land, but from the perspective of the Brahmā king it is a preciously adorned Pure Land, and the Most Blissful Pure Land added is a transformation land. But according to the *Jing tu lun*, if one can completely practice the five doctrines—accomplishing wisdom, compassion, skillfulness, virtues, and the transference of merit—one can also enter the perfect transformation land. For the purpose of adapting to the arising and maturing of some sentient beings' good roots, however,. any Pure Land can be said to reside in the east, west, south, or north, and the life span of a buddha and the height of a buddha's body can be said to be limited—all such are transformation lands and transformation bodies.

Why does the transformation body of a buddha manifest such differences? Because the fundamental natures of sentient beings are different. Some persons should be addressed with stern, earnest words, words that describe the three evil destinies and the suffering of sentient beings, so they will resolve to practice—this is the doctrine of subduing. Some should be treated with affectionate speech that is pure and comforting so they will resolve to practice—this is the doctrine of embracing. A buddha with a transformation body uses these two doctrines to transform sentient beings.

Adaptations to capacities are like different medicines. They are all wonderful: thoughts about which are superior should not arise. Śākyamuni Buddha appeared in a defiled land and Maitreya Buddha will appear in a Pure Land, but there is no difference in their Buddha Dharma. Also, because it is difficult to practice in a defiled land, the Buddha persuaded people to be reborn in the Pure Land where it is easy to be successful. Both the *Vimalakīrti Sūtra* and the *Sukhāvatīvyūha Sūtra* (Buddha of Infinite Longevity Sūtra, sometimes known as The Pure Land Treatise) say, however, that practicing in a defiled land for a day is superior to practicing in a Pure Land for a kalpa, and that practicing in a defiled land is easier than doing so in a Pure Land.[132] It is also said that Śākyamuni Buddha praised the Pure Lands, making people admire them. Furthermore, when bodhisattvas from the Pure Land came here to participate in the Dharma assembly of Śākyamuni Buddha, the buddhas of their respective Pure Lands always admonished them not to be disdainful.

Thus, a buddha's compassionate vow takes the form of two skillful means to transform sentient beings of the three realms, enabling them to enter Nirvāṇa, leave birth and death, and turn to the way of buddhas.

208 In order to relieve people's exhaustion,
A lovely city is magically created.
Eventually the true form is revealed.
Therefore, there is only one Buddha Vehicle.

The preaching of the Dharma by buddhas with transformation bodies are not all identical. In some buddha lands their preaching is mixed with the Dharmas of the Five Vehicles and the Three Vehicles, and there are both laity and monks and nuns. Some buddhas expound only the Dharma of the One Vehicle, and there are no monks or nuns. Some buddhas do not even appear in monastic form. (It is said that the heavenly King Buddha was like this.) Some expound the Three Vehicles and eventually return to the Dharma of One Vehicle. Some expound the Dharma of the Three Vehicles because the capacities of the listeners are immature. Such buddhas enter Nirvāṇa without ever expounding the One Vehicle. Legend says that Prabhūtaratna Buddha was like this. When Śākyamuni Buddha transformed this saha world and preached the Dharma, he initially expounded the Dharma of Three Vehicles and then eventually returned to One Vehicle. In the *Lotus Sūtra*, the Buddha discloses the proper course of the teachings: "applying the partial teaching to the whole truth and exposing the partial teaching to reveal the whole truth."

Some have resolved to attain bodhi, but on the long path of birth and death they have forgotten their way or retreated. For those of this type, the more they are told of the profundity and greatness of the Buddha Way, the more they fear to practice. So the Buddha designed skillful means, explaining that the vehicles of the śrāvakas and pratyekabuddhas are easy to practice, that they are a fast and good way to end birth and death, and that they lead to ultimate liberation. Only through this encouragement could such people resolve to practice. This can be compared to a caravan with travelers who are becoming exhausted from their long journey; some are reluctant to move on. To relieve and encourage them, the leader magically creates a lovely city just ahead. The travelers pluck up their courage and reach the city, where all their needs are satisfied:

clothing, food, and other necessities. When they are rested, the leader tells them that this is a magical city and that the real destination—the city of treasures—lies before them. Now full of vigor, the company again advances toward their destination. In like manner, the Buddha waits for his disciples to rely on the Dharma and realize arhatship; then he explains that the Two Vehicles are only a skillful means, and he reveals the truth that enables sentient beings to apprehend a buddha's knowledge and understanding. So although the Buddha spoke of the Three Vehicles, there is only the one. Only the Buddha has attained the great Nirvāṇa; the Nirvāṇa of the Two Vehicles is not real. Although the One Vehicle taught by the Buddha has various meanings according to the scriptures, the Way is neither dual nor differentiated. It eventually returns to one.

The Ultimate One Vehicle: Universal Buddhahood

209 All good Dharmas
Lead toward the Buddha Way.
Therefore, all sentient beings
Can ultimately become buddhas.

From the standpoint of the One Vehicle, all good Dharmas lead toward the Buddha Way. Not only does the good world-transcending Dharma of the Three Vehicles lead there, so do the good dharmas of the Human and the Divine Vehicle. Everything in the world—every iota of kind thought or good deed—leads toward the Buddha Way. The Buddha Dharma is another name for good dharmas.

What are good dharmas, after all? That which goes toward the Dharma, follows the Dharma, and corresponds with the Dharma is good. All that which accords with dependent origination with emptiness as its nature—in thinking, in dealing with people, in handling affairs—is definitely good. That which is good is the Dharma, and that which is not is non-Dharma.

Some Buddhist philosophers who believe that the Dharma has inherent nature say, "This is faulty good Dharma, that is faultless good Dharma; this is the good Dharma of the Two Vehicles and that is the good Dharma of a buddha." When differentiated according to sentient beings' emotional attachments, good Dharma is divided into different categories. Although the real and present world of sentient beings seems to actually exist in this way, from the perspective of the truth, it is not so. Good Dharma is good Dharma; whether it is faulty or faultless depends on whether it is associated with fault or not. The "faulty good" is good that is mixed with the afflictions; when dissociated from the afflictions, it is faultlessly good.

In the past there was a famous discussion about "the good not receiving their reward." Sentient beings' transmigrations through the cycles of birth and death are due to their afflictions and karma. Being reborn as a human or divine being is due not to good Dharma but to the afflictions that are mixed with the good Dharma. All sentient beings are "unlike wood or stone, born to have good and evil (seeds) from the very first conscious thought."[133] All are born with some good, thus all have the inclination toward loftiness, happiness, and brightness. However, when they do not take the Buddha Way as their main doctrine but instead follow deviant paths, they are reborn as humans or divine beings. When they eventually discover the ultimate objective and turn toward the Buddha Vehicle, they will realize that all these good dharmas are just the skillful means to become a buddha. Hence, bringing the palms together and bowing toward a buddha and "reciting but once 'Namo Buddha' can accomplish the Buddha Way."[134]

On the other hand, this turning away from the Buddha Way is analogous to a nation without a benevolent and brilliant leader or proper national policies. Although its people seek progress, the nation usually ends up taking deviant paths; fiscal administration and the quality of life become unsatisfactory. If people have a benevolent and brilliant leader administering a perfect policy toward which all work together at the same pace, they will enter an ideal era.

So it is not the case that all sentient beings are without good Dharma; it is just that they have not yet carried it out thoroughly. If, however, they have good Dharma and aim toward loftiness and brightness, they will eventually turn toward the Buddha Way, stride forward, and ultimately become buddhas. All sentient beings can become buddhas; this is the ultimate truth. Those practicing the Buddha Dharma should embrace all good Dharmas and abandon none; such is the real purpose of the Buddha Dharma.

May all sentient beings become buddhas!

Notes

Works cited have been identified by the following abbreviations:

DV	*Daśabhūmika-vibhāṣā*
DZ	*Da zhi du lun*
GT	*The Great Treatise on the Sequence of Attaining Enlightenment*
L	*Laṅkāvatāra Sūtra*
MP	*Mahāprajñāpāramitā Sūtra*
PS	*Pañcaviṃśati-sāhasrikā-prajñāpāramitā Sūtra*
SA	*Saṃyuktāgama* — self
SN	*Saṃdhinirmocana Sūtra*
SS	*Saddharmapuṇḍarīka Sūtra*
T	*Taishō shinshū daizōkyō* (Edition of the Chinese canon, Tokyo: Takakusu and Watanabe, 1922–33.)
V	*Vimalakīrtinirdeśa Sūtra*

Chapter 1. Taking Refuge in the Three Treasures

1. SS 1 (abridged quotation), T 9, p. 7a.
2. SA 3, T 3, p. 17b.
3. DZ 11, T 25, p. 142b.
4. *The Book of Changes*, "Xi ci" (section A). "Wandering souls" are souls with no one to worship them.
5. *The Analects of Confucius*, "Yong Ye Chapter."
6. *Mahāyānasaṃgraha* 1, T 31, p. 136c.
7. *Avataṃsaka Sūtra* 43, T 9, p. 670c.
8. SA 36, T 2, p. 263c.
9. *Sukhāvatīvyūha*, T 12, p. 348a.
10. *Dīrghāgama* 2, extracted from the *Mahāparinirvāṇa Sūtra*, which says, "The Tathāgata does not say that 'I control people or I gather people.'" T 1, p. 15a.
11. *Si fen lu* (*Dharmaguptaka-vinaya*) 43, T 22, p. 883b.
12. *Da ming jing* (Great Name Sūtra). According to the *Abhidharma-nyāyānusāra* 37, the Buddha told Great Name, "Those male laymen who have reached manhood and want to take refuge in the Buddha, Dharma, and Saṅgha should have a sincere mind and earnestly proclaim: 'I, being an Upāsaka, wish for the Honored One to keep me in mind and protect me with compassion. From now to the end of my life I will protect living beings.'" T 29, pp. 552c–553a.
13. DZ 2, T 25, p. 66c.
14. *Śūraṅgama Sūtra* 1, T 19, p. 109a.

Chapter 2. Attending to the Dharma to Enter the Path

1. *Śūraṅgama Sūtra* 1, T 19, p. 106c.
2. GT 1, p. 19a, from the "Gatha on Listening."
3. DZ 18, T 25, p. 196a.
4. *Śūraṅgama Sūtra* 6, T 19, p. 130c.
5. "Aging, sickness, death," see T 2, p. 339c, and "desire, anger, ignorance," as seen in T 2, p. 95c.
6. GT 1, quotation of sūtra, p. 11a.
7. GT 1, p. 11c.
8. *Abhidharma-skandha-pāda Śāstra* 2, T 26, p. 458b.
9. GT 1, quotation from the *Sūtra of Miao Bi's Inquiry*, p. 15c.
10. *Mahāparinirvāṇa Sūtra* 6, T 12, p. 639b.
11. *The Analects of Confucius*, "Shu Er" chapter.
12. GT 2, quotation of sūtra, p. 22a.
13. SA 27, T 2, p. 195b.
14. *Abhidharma-mahāvibhāṣā Śāstra* 172, quotation of sūtra, T 27, p. 867c.
15. *Si shi er zhang jing* (Sūtra in Forty-two Sections), T 17, p. 724a.
16. V 1, T 14, p. 528a.
17. *Yogācāra-bhūmi* 61, T 30, p. 643c.
18. GT 3, p. 40c.
19. Ibid.
20. Ibid.
21. SS 3, T 9, p. 20b.
22. DZ 71, T 25, p. 555a.
23. SS 1, T 9, p. 9a.

Chapter 3. The Dharma Common to the Five Vehicles

1. SA 28, T 2, p. 204c.
2. *The Biography of Fan Pang*, in *The History of Later Han Dynasty*.
3. *Dharmapada* 1, T 4, p. 565a.
4. *Madhyamāgama* 3, "The Parable of Salt, T 1, p. 433a–b.
5. The original passage is to be checked. *Dharmapada* 3: "Evil-doers who seem to have fortune now will receive retribution for their offenses when the evil matures. That those who do good seem to be receiving disaster happens only because their good has not yet matured. When it matures, they will get their blessings." T 4, p. 564c.
6. SA 33, T 2, p. 237b–c
7. *Zhuangzi*, "Keeping in Good Health" chapter.
8. GT 3, Introduction, p. 50c.
9. SA 10, T 2, p. 69c.
10. *Madhyamāgama* 3, T 1, p. 440a.
11. *Madhyamāgama* 6, T 1, p. 460b.
12. *Ru zhong lun* (*Madhyamakāvatāra*) 1, p. 12c.
13. *Saṃyutta-nikāya* 55, Pāli Tripiṭaka 16c, p. 236.
14. GT 4, quotation of sūtra, pp. 66c–67a.
15. Ibid., p. 67a.

CHAPTER 4. THE DHARMA COMMON TO THE THREE VEHICLES

1. SA 17, T 2, p. 121a.
2. *Abhidharma-mahāvibhāṣā Śāstra* 6, T 27, p. 26c.
3. *Śrīmālādevīsiṃhanāda Sūtra,* T 12, p. 221b.
4. *Mahāparinirvāṇa Sūtra* 27, T 12, p. 524b.
5. *Mahāparinirvāṇa Sūtra* 7, T 12, p. 406 b-c.
6. *Fo chiu banniepan lueshuo jiaojie jing* (Sūtra of the Teachings and Regulations Expounded Briefly by the Buddha as He Neared His Parinirvāṇa), T 12, p. 1112a.
7. *Abhidharma-mahāvibhāṣā Śāstra* 34, quotation from "Chapter on meaning," T 27, p. 176b.
8. *Satyasiddhi Śāstra* 2, T 32, p. 251a.
9. *Abhidharma-skandha-pāda Śāstra* 12, T 26, p. 513a.
10. *Xiu xing dao di jing* (Sūtra on Practicing the Stages of the Way) 2, T 15, p. 192b.
11. *Abhidharma-prakaraṇa-pāda Śāstra* 1, T 26, p. 693a.
12. SA 12, T 2, p. 80c.
13. SA 12, T 2, p. 83c.
14. *Mahāyānasaṃgraha* 1, T 31, p. 134a.
15. SA 13, T 2, p. 88b.
16. SA 26, T 2, p. 190b.
17. SA 44, T 2, p. 322b.
18. *Dīrghāgama* 4, extracted from *Mahāparinirvāṇa Sūtra,* T 1, p. 25a-b.
19. *Laṅkāvatāra Sūtra* 5, T 6, p. 617b.
20. *Cheng wei shi lun* (*Vijñaptimātratāsiddhi Śāstra*) 6, T 31, p. 29c.
21. *Si fen lu* (*Dharmaguptaka-vinaya*) 33, T 22, p. 799b.
22. *Shi song lu* (The Monastic Code in Ten Recitations) 45, T 23, p. 327a-c.
23. *Si fen lu* (*Dharmaguptaka-vinaya*) 48, T 22, p. 924b-c.
24. *Gen ben shuo yi qie you bu bi chu ni pi nai ye* (*Mūlasarvāstivāda-bhikṣunī-vinaya*) 19, T 22, p. 14b.
25. *Mo hesengqi lu* (*Mahāsāṃghika-vinaya*) 38, T 22, p. 535a.
26. *Fo chiu banniepan lueshuo jiaojie jing,* T 12, p. 1111a.
27. *Fo shuo da ji fa men jing* (Sūtra on the Dharma Entrances to the Great Collection [as Taught by the Buddha]), T 1, p. 227c.
28. *Fo chiu banniepan lueshuo jiaojie jing,* T 12, p. 1111a.
29. *Yogācāra-bhūmi* 25, T 30, p. 420a.
30. *Yogācāra-bhūmi* 22, T 30, p. 405c.
31. Ibid., p. 406a.
32. *Fo shuo da sheng yi jing* (Sūtra on the Great Meaning of Life [as Taught by the Buddha]), T 1, p. 844b.
33. *Abhidharma-skandha-pāda Śāstra* 11, quotation of sūtra, T 26, p. 305a.
34. SA 1, T 2, p. 2a.
35. Ibid.
37. Ibid.
38. SA 10, T 2, p. 72b.
39. Ibid., p. 71a.
40. SA 12, T 2, p. 83c.
41. SA 47, T 2, p. 345b.
42. SA 34, T 2, p. 246a.
43. SA 9, T 2, p. 60a.

44. SA 12, T 2, p. 84c.
45. Ibid., p. 85c.
46. SA 34, T 2, p. 245b.
47. SA 10, T 2, pp. 66c–67a.
48. SA 14, T 2, p. 99c.
49. SA 15, T 2, p. 103c–104a.
50. SA 14, T 2, p. 97b.
51. *Mahāparinirvāṇa Sūtra* 2, T 1, p. 204c.
52. *Fo chiu banniepan lueshuo jiaojie jing*, T 12, pp. 1110c–1111a.
53. DZ 2, T 25, p. 72a.
54. *Abhidharma-mahāvibhāṣā Śāstra* 143, T 27, p. 735b.
55. *Zhao lun* (Treatises of Seng Zhao), T 45, p. 160a.
56. SA 30, T 2, p. 217b.
57. *Dīrghāgama* 8 (The Long Discourses), T 1, p. 51b.
58. SA 26, T 2, p. 190b.
59. SA 13, T 2, p. 93a.
60. SA 9, T 2, p. 63a.
61. SA 9, T 2, p. 63b.

Chapter 5. The Distinctive Dharma of the Great Vehicle

1. PS 5, T 8, pp. 250a–256b.
2. SA 11, T 2, p. 72c.
3. SS 2, T 9, p. 10c.
4. Ibid., p. 16b.
5. Source as yet unknown.
6. GT 8, quotation of treatise, p. 47c.
7. DZ 40, T 25, p. 350a.
8. DZ 58, T 25, p. 472c.
9. DZ 39, T 25, p. 345a–b.
10. DZ 38, T 25, p. 342b.
11. Ibid.
12. SS 4, T 9, p. 28a.
13. *Mahāvairocanābhisaṃbodhi-vikurvitādhisthāna-vaipulya-sūtrendrarāja-nāma-dharmaparyaya* 7, T 18, p. 54c.
14. SS 1, T 9, p. 8c; and *Dasheng qi xin lun* (*Mahāyānaśraddhotpāda Śāstra*), T 33, p. 583a
15. V. T 14, p. 530b.
16. DZ 32, T 25, p. 298b.
17. SS 1, T 9, p. 9b.
18. *Mahāprajñāpāramitā Sūtra* 348, T 6, p. 727b.
19. SS 4, T 9, p. 29a.
20. DZ 36, T 25, p. 333c.
21. Ibid.
22. *Tan jing* (Platform Sūtra), T 48, p. 339b.
23. *Mahāprajñāpāramitā Sūtra*, 412, T 7, p. 67b.
24. *Madhyamakāvatāra* 1, quotation from the treatise, p. 3c.
25. *Mahāvairocanābhisaṃbodhivikurvitādhisthāna-vaipulyasūtrendrarāja-nāma-dharma-paryaya* 1, T 18, p. 1b–c.

26. *Śrīmālādevīsiṃhanāda Sūtra* T 12, p. 217b.
27. SS 3, T 9, p. 19b.
28. GT 9, quotation of sūtra and treatise, p. 67a.
29. *Ren wang bo re bo luo mi jing* (*Kāruṇikarāja-prajñāpāramitā Sūtra*) 1, T 8, p. 827b.
30. *Mahāprajñāpāramitā Sūtra* 416, T 7, p. 88c.
31. DZ 29, T 25, p. 273a.
32. *Avadānas* 16, T 4, p. 697a.
33. *Madhyamakāvatāra* 1, p. 26a.
34. *Commentary of Mahāyānasaṃgraha* 6, T 31, p. 414b.
35. DV 5, T 26, pp. 40c–41a.
36. Ibid., p. 41b.
37. Ibid., p. 42c.
38. Ibid., p. 43c.
39. Ibid., p. 45c.
40. *Dasheng qi xin lun* (*Mahāyānaśraddhotpāda Śāstra*), T 32, p. 583a.
41. DV 6, T 26, p. 49b–c.
42. DV 5, T 26, p. 45a.
43. GT 12, T 26, p. 37.
44. GT 14, quotation of sūtra, p. 49a.
45. SN 3, T 16, p. 698a.
46. Ibid., p. 698b–c.
47. *Fo chiu banniepan lueshuo jiaojie jing*, T 12, p. 1111a.
48. PS 3, T 8, p. 234a.
49. PS 14, T 8, p. 323b.
50. V 2, T 14, p. 549c.
51. DZ 79, T 25, p. 618c.
52. DZ 43, T 25, p. 371a.
53. DZ 70, T 25, p. 552a.
54. DZ 18, T 25, p. 196a.
55. *Madhyāntavibhāga* 2, T 31, p. 474b.
56. *Fu fa zang yinyuan zhuan* (The Transmission of the Causes and Conditions Concerning the Bequeathing of the Dharma Treasury), 2, T 50, p. 302c.
57. DZ 41, T 25, p. 358c.
58. SA 13, T 2, p. 92c.
59. *Mūlamadhyamaka-kārikā* 4, T 30, p. 33b.
60. SN 2, T 16, p. 693c.
61. GT 19, quotation of sūtra, p. 49c.
62. SS 1, T 9, p. 8b.
63. DZ 31, T 25, p. 287b.
64. DZ 26, T 25, p. 254a.
65. Ibid.
66. DZ 31, T 25, p. 292b.
67. Ibid., p. 287b–c.
68. Ibid., p. 288b.
69. Ibid., p. 292b.
70. *Vajracchedika-prajñāpāramitā Sūtra*, T 8, p. 749b.
71. *Ratnāvalī*, T 32, p. 494a.
72. SN 1, T 16, p. 692b.
73. DZ 31, T 25, p. 289a.

74. DZ 40, T 25, p. 496c.
75. DZ 1, T 25, p. 61b.
76. *Avataṃsaka Sūtra* 26, T 9, p. 564c.
77. DZ 71, T 25, p. 555a.
78. PS 3, T 8, p. 233b.
79. DZ 71, T 25, p. 556b.
80. *Dasheng zhang zhen lun* (The Treatise of Mahāyāna Logic) 2, T 30, p. 274c.
81. *Prajñāpāramitāhṛdaya Sūtra*, T 8, p. 848c.
82. *Vajracchedika-prajñāpāramitā Sūtra*, T 8, p. 749b.
83. *Bian liao bu liao yi shan shuo zang lun* (The Treatise of the Treasury of Skillful Explanations on Differentiating Between the Final and Non-Final Truth), 3, quotation of sūtra, p. 1a–c.
84. Ibid. p. 2c.
85. V 2, T 14, p. 547c.
86. PS 7, T 8, p. 271c.
87. PS 8, T 8, p. 276a-b.
88. *Madhyamaka Śāstra* 4, T 30, p. 33a.
89. GT 17, quotation of the treatise, p. 32a.
90. SN 2, T 16, p. 695b.
91. SN 2, T 16, p. 696a.
92. DZ 63, T 25, p. 503c.
93. SN 2, T 16, p. 694a.
94. *Yogācāra-bhūmi* 36, T 30, p. 488b.
95. SN 2, T 16, p. 693a.
96. SN 2, T 16, p. 694a.
97. *Yogācāra-bhūmi* 36, T 30, p. 488c.
98. *Madhyāntavibhāga* 1, T 31, pp. 464c–465a.
99. *Cheng wei shi lun* (*Vijñaptimātratāsiddhi Śāstra*) 1, T 31, p. 2b.
100. L 4, T 16, p. 570b.
101. Ibid.
102. L 2, T 16, p. 489a.
103. *Bu zeng bu mie jing* (*Anunatvapurṇatva-nirdeśa-parivartra*), T 16, p. 467b.
104. *Śrīmālādevīsiṃhanāda Sūtra*, T 12, p. 222b.
105. *Mahāyānasaṃgraha* 1, quotation of sūtra, T 31, p. 133b.
106. L 2, T 16, p. 489b.
107. *Ratnagotravibhāga* 3, T 31, p. 828a.
108. *Ratnagotravibhāga* 4, T 31, p. 840c.
109. *Dasheng zhang zhen lun* (The Treatise on the Hand-Held Jewel of the Mahāyāna) 2, T 30, p. 275a.
110. L 2, T 16, p. 492a.
111. *Ghana-vyūha Sūtra* 1, T 16, p. 747a.
112. *Ren wang hu guo bo re bo luo mi jing* (*Kāruṇikarāja-prajñāpāramitā Sūtra*) 2, T 8, p. 841b.
113. *Mahāyānasaṃgraha* 2, T 31, p. 146b.
114. *Avataṃsaka Sūtra* 23, T 9, p. 545a.
115. *Ratnāvalī*, T 32, p. 503c.
116. *Avataṃsaka Sūtra* 24, T 9, p. 549a.
117. DZ 71, T 25, p. 556b.
118. Ibid.

119. *Avataṃsaka Sūtra* 25, T 9, p. 558c.
120. V 1, T 14, p. 539c.
121. *Avataṃsaka Sūtra* 27, T 9, p. 573b.
122. *Dasheng qi xin lun* (*Mahāyānaśraddhotpāda Śāstra*), T 32, p. 581b.
123. DZ 4, T 25, p. 88a.
124. DZ 35, T 25, p. 342c.
125. Ibid.
126. Ibid.
127. SN 4, T 16, p. 704b–c.
128. *Mahāyānasaṃgraha* 2, T 31, p. 148c.
129. *Mahāprajñāpāramitā Sūtra* 372, T 6, p. 919b.
130. *Fo shuo fo di jing* (*Buddhabhūmi Sūtra*), T 16, p. 720b–c; and SN 1, T 16, p. 688b.
131. PS 10, T 8, p. 292b.
132. *Aparimitāyuḥ Sūtra* 2, T 12, p. 338b; and V 2, T 14, p. 552b.
133. *Ren wang hu guo bo re bo luo mi jing* (*Kāruṇikarāja-prajñāpāramitā Sūtra*), T 8, p. 828c.
134. SS 1, T 9, p. 9a.

Selected Bibliography

Sanskrit Titles—As Primarily Referred to in the Text

Abhidharma Mahāyāna Sūtra
Lost sūtra quoted in the *Mahāyāsaṁgraha.*

Abhidharma-mahāvibhāṣā Śāstra = *Mahāvibhāṣā Śāstra*
Apidamo da piposha lun.

Abhidharma-nyāyānusāra [*Śāstra*]
Apidamo shun zhengli lun, T.1562, *Treatise on Conforming to Correct Reasoning in the Abhidharma,* by Saṅghabhadra. Often referred to simply as the *Nyāyānusāra.*

Abhidharma-prakaraṇa-pāda Śāstra
Apidamo pinlei zu lun, T.1542.

Abhidharma-skandha-pāda Śāstra
Apidamo fa yun zu lun, T.1537.

Āgama[*-sūtra*]*s*
Ahan jing. The *sūtra* division of the early Buddhist Canons. Different versions of these may be organized in four or five collections.

Aparimitāyuḥ Sūtra = The Large *Sukhāvatīvyūha Sūtra.*

Avataṃsaka Sūtra
Huayan jing, T.278. *The Flower Ornament Sūtra.*

Daśabhūmika Sūtra
Shi di jing, T.286-287, *The Ten Stages Sūtra.*

Dharmaguptaka-vinaya
Si fen lu, T.1428, *The Monastic Code of the Dharmaguptakas.*

Dharmapada
Fa ju jing, T.210, *Verses on the Dharma.* Translated from the Pāli by Max Müller as *Sacred Books of the East,* Vol. 10, Part 1, (Oxford, 1881).
Chu yao jing, T.212. Also referred to as the *Udānavarga.*

Dīrghāgama
Chang ahan jing, T.1, *Long Discourses.* One of the collections comprising the *Āgamas*; cf. the *Dīgha-nikāya*, the first section of the *sutta* division of the Pāli Canon.

Dvādaśamukha Śāstra
Shi'er men lun, T.1568, *The Treatise on the Twelve Entrances*, attributed to Nāgārjuna.

Ghana-vyūha Sūtra
Dasheng miyan jing, T.681, *The Sūtra on the Invisible Splendor of the Mahāyāna.*

Laṅkāvatāra Sūtra
Ru lengjie jing, T.671. Referred to variously as *Dasheng ru lengjie jing*, T.672, and *Lengjie abaduoluo bao jing*, T.670; all references are, however, to T.671.

The Large *Sukhāvatīvyūha Sūtra*
Da amita jing, T.364, translated by Wang Rixiu.

Madhyamāgama
Zhong ahan jing, T.26, *Middle Length Discourses.* One of the collections comprising the *Āgamas*; cf. the *Majjhima-nikāya*, the second section of the *sutta* division of the Pāli Canon.

Madhyāntavibhāga
Bian zhong bian lun, T.1600, *The Treatise on Discriminating the Middle and the Extremes.*

Mahāparinirvāṇa Sūtra
Da ban niepan jing, T.374, *The Great Parinirvāṇa Sūtra* (Mahāyāna version).

Mahāprajñāpāramitā Sūtra
Da bore boluomiduo jing, T.220, *The Perfection of Wisdom Sūtra in 100,000 Lines.*

Mahāyānasaṃgraha
She dacheng lun, T.1594, *Summary of the Mahāyāna*, translated into Chinese by Xuanzang.

Mahāvairocana-[*abhisaṃbodhi-vikurvitādhisthāna-vaipulya-*]*sūtra*
Da piluzhena [*chengfo shenbian jiachi*] *jing*, T.848, *The Great Sun Buddha Sūtra.*

Mahāvibhāṣā Śāstra
Da piposha lun, T.1545, *The Great Extended Discourse.* Often referred to as the *Mahāvibhāṣā.*

Mūlamadhyamaka-kārikā
Zhong lun, T.1564, *The Middle Treatise*, attributed to Nāgārjuna.

Nirvāṇa Sūtra = *Mahāparinirvāṇa Sūtra*
Da ban niepan jing.

Pañcaviṃśati-sāhasrikā-prajñāpāramitā Sūtra
Mohe bore boluomi jing, T.223, *The Perfection of Wisdom in 25,000 Lines.* This work also forms the second section of the *Mahāprajñāpāramitā Sūtra.*

Prajñāpāramitā-hṛdaya Sūtra
Bore boluomiduo xin jing, T.251, *The Heart Sūtra,* translated by Xuanzang.

Prajñāpāramitā Sūtra
Bore boluomi jing. A general title for the *Perfection of Wisdom Sūtras.*

Ratnagotravibhāga-[*mahāyāna-uttaratantra*] *Śāstra*
Jiujing yicheng paoxing lun, T.1611, *The Treatise on the Discrimination of the Precious Nature,* translated into Chinese by Ratnamati.

Ratnāvalī
Bao xing wang zheng lun, T.1656, attributed to Nāgārjuna.

Saṃdhinirmocana Sūtra
Jie shenmi jing, T.676, *The Sūtra on the Explication of the Underlying Meaning.*

Saṃyuktāgama
Za ahan jing, T.99, *Connected Discourses.* One of the collections comprising the *Āgamas*; cf. the *Saṃyutta-nikāya,* the third section of the *sutta* division of the Pāli Canon.

Śata Śāstra
Bai lun, T.1569, *The Hundred Question Treatise,* attributed to Āryadeva.

Satyasiddhi Śāstra
Cheng shi lun, T.1646, *The Treatise on Accomplishing the Real,* attributed to Harivarman.

Śrīmālādevīsiṃhanāda Sūtra
Shengman [*shizihou yicheng da fangbian fangguang*] *jing,* T.353, *The Sūtra* [*on the Lion's Roar*] *of Queen Śrīmālā,* translated by Guṇabhadra.

Subāhu-paripṛcchā Sūtra
Miaobei pusa suowen jing, T.896, *The Sūtra on the Inquiries of Subāhu Bodhisattva.*

Śūnyatā-saptati-kārikā
Qishi kongxing lun, Commentaries on the Seventy Empty Natures, attributed to Nāgārjuna. Only eighth century and later Tibetan translations exist; there are modern translations into Japanese and English.

Śūraṅgama Sūtra
Dafoding rulai miyin xiuzheng liaoyi zhu pusa wanxing shoulengyan jing, T.945.

Upāsaka-śīla Sūtra
Youposai jie jing, T.1488. *The Sūtra on the Moral Behavior of the Laity,* translated by Dharmakṣema.

Vairocana Sūtra = Mahāvairocana Sūtra
Da ri jing.

Vajracchedika-prajñāpāramitā Sūtra
Jin'gang bore boluomi jing, T.235, *The Diamond Sūtra,* translated into Chinese by Kumārajīva.

Vigraha-vyāvartanī
Hui zheng lun, T.1631, *The Treatise on Averting the Arguments*, attributed to Nāgārjuna.

Vimalakīrti-[nirdeśa] Sūtra
Weimojie [suoshuo] jing, T.475, *The Sūtra Taught by Vimalakīrti.*

Yogācāra-bhūmi
Yujia shidi lun, T.1579, *The Treatise on the Stages of Practice of Meditation.*

Yuktiṣaṣṭikā
Liushi song ru li lun, T.1575, *The Sixty Verses on Reasoning*, attributed to Nāgārjuna.

Chinese & English Titles — As Primarily Referred to in the Text

Bao man lun (*Ratnamālā*) = *Bao xing wang zheng lun* (*Ratnāvalī*)
The Ratnāvalī. Rājaparikathā-ratnamālā is the Sanskrit title referred to in the Tibetan translations; *pao xing wang* of the Chinese title may translate Sātavāhana. See above.

The Bodhisattva Rule
Yujia pusa jie = *Pu sa jie ben* (*Bodhisattvaprātimokṣa*), T.1501, translated by Xuanzang.

The Brahmā Net Sūtra
Fan wang jing (*Brahmajāla Sūtra*), T.1484. A Chinese indigenous sūtra.

"Chapter on Contemplating the Dharma"
Guan fa pin (*Ātma-parīkṣā*). Chapter 18 of the *Mūlamadhyamaka-kārikā*, T.1564, *The Middle Treatise.*

"Chapter on Contemplating the Four Truths"
Guan si di pin (*Āryasatya-parīkṣā*). Chapter 24 of the *Mūlamadhyamaka-kārikā* , T.1564, *The Middle Treatise.*

"Chapter on Easy Practice"
Yi xing pin (unknown). Chapter 9 of the *Daśabhūmivibhāṣā* (*Shi zhu piposha lun*), T.1521, *The Extended Discourse on the Ten Stages Sūtra*, attributed to Nāgārjuna.

"Chapter on Rebirth (in the Pure Land)"
Wang sheng pin (unknown). Chapter 4 of the *Da zhi du lun*, T.1509, *The Treatise on the Perfection of Wisdom*, attributed to Nāgārjuna.

"Chapter on the Ten Stages"
Shi di pin (*Daśabhūmi-parīkṣā*). Chapter 22 of the *Avataṃsaka-sūtra*, T.278. This chapter also circulated as an independent text in Sanskrit and Chinese. See *The Ten Stages Sūtra.*

The Commentary on the Summary of the Mahāyāna
She dasheng lun shi (*Mahāyānasaṃgrahabhāṣā*), T.1598, attributed to Vasubandhu.

The Extended Discourse on the Ten Stages Sūtra
Shi zhu piposha lun (*Daśabhūmika-vibhāṣā*), T.1521.

The Great Collection Sūtra
Da ji jing (*Mahāsaṃnipāta Sūtra*), T.397.

The Great Name Sūtra
Da ming jing (*Mahānāma Sūtra*). Referred to in Sanghabhadra's *Nyāyānusāra*, T.1562, in response to Vasubandhu's citation in his *Abhidharmakośa-bhāṣya* IV.30a-31c, T.1558.

The Great Treatise on the Sequence of Attaining Enlightenment
Puti dao cidi guang lun. A Chinese translation of Tsongkhapa's *Great Stages of the Path* (Tibetan: *Byang chub lam rim chen mo*), composed originally in Tibetan, by Fazun prior to 1949.

The Kṣitigarbha Sūtra
Xukongzang jing (*Kṣitigarbha Sūtra*). This title is an abbreviation of *Sheng Xukongzang pusa tuoluoni jing*, T.1147, *The Sūtra on the Dhāraṇī of Ārya Kṣitigarbha Bodhisattva.*

The Lotus Sūtra of the Wonderful Law
Miao fa lianhua jing (*Saddharmapuṇḍarīka Sūtra*), T.262, translated by Kumārajīva.

The Monastic Code in Ten Recitations
Shi song lüṛ (*Daśabhāṇa-vāra-vinaya*), T.1435. The monastic code of the Sarvāstivāda.

The Monastic Code of the Mahāsāṃghikas
Mohe sengzhi lü (*Mahāsāṃghika-vinaya*), T.1425.

The Monastic Code of the Mūlasarvāstivāda for Nuns
Genben shuo yiqie youbu bichuni binaiye (*Mūlasarvāstivāda-bhikṣunī-vinayavibhaṅga*), T.1443.

The Perfection of Wisdom Sūtra on [*the Protection of the State by*] *Benevolent Kings Ren wang* [*hu guo*] *bore boluomiduo jing* (unknown), T.245. A Chinese indigenous sūtra.

The Platform Sūtra [*of the Sixth Patriarch*]
[*Liu zu*] *Tan jing*, T.2007.

The Pure Land Treatise
Jing tu lun = *Wuliangshou jing youpotishe yuan sheng jie* (*Sukhāvatīvyūhopadeśa*), T.1524, attributed to Vasubandhu.

The Samādhi-rāja [*Moon Lamp*] *Sūtra*
Sanmodi wang jing = ? *Yue deng sanmei jing* (*Samādhi-rāja-*[*candrapradīpa*] *Sūtra*), T.639-641.

The Smaller *Sukhāvatīvyūha Sūtra*
[*Foshuo*] *Amita jing* (*Amitābha/Amitāyus Sūtra*), T.360.

The Sūtra in Forty Two Sections
Sishi'er zhang jing (unknown), T.784.
Sūtra of the Original Karma of Bodhisattvas as a Necklace of Precious Stones Pu sa ying luo ben ye jing, T.1485. A Chinese indigenous sūtra.

The Sūtra of the Original Vows of Bhaiṣajyaguru Tathāgata
Yao shi jing = *Yao shi rulai ben yuan jing* (*Bhaiṣajyaguru-praṇidhāna-viśeṣa-vistara*), T.449.

The Sūtra of the Teachings and Regulations Expounded Briefly by the Buddha as He Neared His Parinirvāṇa
Fo chui ban niepan lue shuo jiaojie jing (unknown), T.389.

The Sūtra on Neither Increase Nor Elimination
Bu zeng bu mie jing (*Anunatvapurṇatva-nirdeśa-parivarta*), T.668.

The Sūtra on Practicing the Stages of the Way
Xiuxing dao di jing (*Yogācāra-bhūmi*), T.606. A Sarvāstivāda text.

The Sūtra on the Buddha Stage [*as Taught by the Buddha*]
[*Foshuo*] *fo di jing* (*Buddhabhūmi Sūtra*), T.690

The Sūtra on the Contemplation of Amitāyus Buddha
Guan wu liang shou jing (*Amitāyurdhyāna Sūtra*), T.365.

The Sūtra on the Dharma Entrances to the Great Collection [*as Taught by the Buddha*]
[*Fo shuo*] *da ji famen jing* (*Saṃgīti Sūtra*), T.12.

The Sūtra on the Emptiness of Ultimate Truth
Sheng yi kong jing (unknown), T.655.

The Sūtra on the Great Meaning of Life [*as Taught by the Buddha*]
[*Fo shuo*] *da sheng yi jing* (*Mahānidāna Sūtra*), T.52.

The Sūtra on the Mudra(s) for Descent into the Fixed and the Unfixed [*Realms*]
Ru ding bu ding yin jing (*Niyatāniyatāvatāramudrā Sūtra*), T.646.

The Sūtra on the Salt Analogy
Yan yu jing (*Loṇūpama Sūtra*). This is the eleventh section of the Chinese translation of a *Madhyamāgama* (*Zhong ahan jing*), T.26; it corresponds to the Pāli *sutta* found in the *Anguttara-nikāya*, III.99.

The Sūtra on the Seventy-Seven Types of Wisdom
Qi shi qi zhong zhi jing (Pāli: *Ñānassa vatthūn*). The sixteenth section of the fourteenth chapter of a Chinese translation of the *Saṃyuktāgama* (*Za ahan jing*), T.99. See *Saṃyutta-nikāya*, XII.34.

The Sūtra on the Unsurpassed Basis
Wu shang yi jing (*Anuttarāśraya Sūtra*), T.669.

The Sūtra [*Taught by*] *Akṣayamaṭi*
Wu jin yi jing (*Akṣayamaṭi*-[*nirdeśa-*] *Sūtra*), T.403.

The Transmission of the Causes and Conditions Concerning the Bequeathing of the Dharma Treasury
Fu fa zang yin yuan zhuan (unknown), T.2058.

The Treatises of [Seng] Zhao
Zhao lun, T.1858, by Seng Zhao.

The Treatise of the Treasury of Skillful Explanations on Differentiating Between the Final and the Non-Final Truth
Bian liao bu liao yi shan shuo zang lun.

Treatise on Entering the Middle Way
Ru zhong lun (*Madhyamakāvatāra*).

The Treatise on the Accomplishment of Consciousness-Only
Cheng wei shi lun (*Vijñaptimātratāsiddhi Śāstra*), T.1585.

The Treatise on the Awakening of Faith in the Mahāyāna
Dasheng qi xin lun (*Mahāyānaśraddhotpāda Śāstra*), T.1666. Probably a Chinese indigenous sūtra.

The Treatise on the Great Man
Da zhangfu lun (*Mahāpuruṣa Śāstra*), T.1577, attributed to Āryadeva.

The Treatise on the Hand-Held Jewel of the Mahayana
Dasheng zhang zhen lun (*Mahāyāna-hastamaṇi Śāstra*), T.1578.

The Treatise on the Perfection of Wisdom
Da zhi du lun (*Mahāprajñāpāramitopadeśa Śāstra*), T.1509, attributed to Nāgārjuna and translated into Chinese by Kumārajīva. This text is frequently known by its Chinese and sometimes by its reconstructed Sanskrit title.

Yi jiao jing = *Fo yi jiao jing*, an alternate Chinese title for *Fo chui ban niepan lue shuo jiao jie jing*, T.389, *The Sūtra of the Teachings and Regulations Expounded Briefly by the Buddha as He Neared His Parinirvāṇa.*

Non-Buddhist Sources

The Analects of Confucius
Lun yu.

"The Biography of Fan Pang"
Fan Pang zhuan, Chapter 67 of the *History of the Later Han Dynasty* (*Hou Han shu*).

Dao de jing
Laozi.

The Book of Changes
Yi jing.

Zhuangzi

AGAMA SUTRA

↳ EXTRAORDINARY EMPTYNESS SUTRA

Index

Wisdom Publications

WISDOM PUBLICATIONS, a not-for-profit publisher, is dedicated to making available authentic Buddhist works for the benefit of all. We publish translations of the sutras and tantras, commentaries and teachings of past and contemporary Buddhist masters, and original works by the world's leading Buddhist scholars. We publish our titles with the appreciation of Buddhism as a living philosophy and with the special commitment to preserve and transmit important works from all the major Buddhist traditions.

If you would like more information or a copy of our mail-order catalogue, please contact us at:

WISDOM PUBLICATIONS
199 Elm Street
Somerville, Massachusetts 02144 USA
Telephone: (617) 776-7416
Fax: (617) 776-7841
E-mail: info@wisdompubs.org
Web Site: http://www.wisdompubs.org

THE WISDOM TRUST

As a not-for-profit publisher, Wisdom Publications is dedicated to the publication of fine Dharma books for the benefit of all sentient beings and is dependent upon the kindness and generosity of sponsors in order to do so. If you would like to make a donation to Wisdom, please contact our Somerville office.

Thank you.

Wisdom Publications is a non-profit, charitable 501(c)(3) organization and a part of the Foundation for the Preservation of the Mahayana Tradition (FPMT).